Applications of Large Language Models (LLM) in Healthcare Systems

This book offers a comprehensive exploration into the role of large language models (LLMs) in modern healthcare. It focuses specifically on the lifecycle of LLM deployment in healthcare settings, including transparency, accountability, data privacy, and regulatory compliance to ensure safe and effective use.

By bridging the gap between technical artificial intelligence (AI) development and clinical application, this book highlights the critical collaboration between clinicians and data scientists to create representative datasets and fine-tune models for clinical accuracy and interpretability. Real-world challenges such as mitigating bias, managing AI hallucinations, and safeguarding patient confidentiality are explored, alongside strategies for continuous improvement and long-term impact assessment.

Key features include:

- Case studies illustrating LLM applications in clinical decision support, medical imaging, patient communication, and administrative automation.
- In-depth discussion of data privacy, regulatory compliance, and ethical considerations in AI healthcare applications.
- Insights into overcoming challenges like bias, hallucinations, and interoperability with existing health information systems.
- How LLMs could revolutionize patient care in future, including operational efficiency and personalized medicine.

This book is an essential resource for clinicians, healthcare executives, technologists, data scientists, and students seeking to harness the power of LLMs to improve patient outcomes and streamline healthcare delivery.

Applications of Large Language Models (LLM) in Healthcare Systems

Opportunities, Challenges, and Ethical Considerations

Edited by
Azadeh Zamanifar, Miad Faezipour, Farhad Soleimanian Gharehchopogh, and Amirfarhad Farhadi

CRC Press
Taylor & Francis Group
Boca Raton London New York

CRC Press is an imprint of the
Taylor & Francis Group, an **informa** business
A CHAPMAN & HALL BOOK

First edition published 2026
by CRC Press
2385 NW Executive Center Drive, Suite 320, Boca Raton FL 33431

and by CRC Press
4 Park Square, Milton Park, Abingdon, Oxon, OX14 4RN

CRC Press is an imprint of Taylor & Francis Group, LLC

ISBN: 9781041124917 (hbk)
ISBN: 9781041124948 (pbk)
ISBN: 9781003665083 (ebk)

DOI: 10.1201/9781003665083

Typeset in Sabon
by Deanta Global Publishing Services, Chennai, India

Contents

Preface

The integration of artificial intelligence (AI) into healthcare represents one of the most profound shifts in modern medicine, and large language models (LLMs) stand at the forefront of this transformation. As these models evolve from research to clinical tools, their potential to improve diagnostics, facilitate administrative workflows, and personalize patient care are undeniable. Yet, there are complex challenges—ethical dilemmas, data privacy risks, and the urgent need for robust governance frameworks. The rapid adoption of LLMs in healthcare has sparked both enthusiasm and caution. Recent studies highlight their use in medical education, clinical decision support, and patient communication, yet also reveal persistent concerns about algorithmic bias, dataset transparency, and regulatory gaps. These are the main content of this book. Our aim is to provide a comprehensive, interdisciplinary resource that equips healthcare professionals, AI developers, and policymakers with the knowledge to navigate this landscape.

What distinguishes this work is its focus on the entire lifecycle of LLM integration. Rather than treating technical development and clinical application as separate domains, we emphasize collaboration between data scientists, clinicians, and ethicists. For instance, chapters addressing bias mitigation draw on real-world cases where unrepresentative training data led to disparities in diagnosis accuracy. Similarly, sections on regulatory compliance analyze evolving global standards, offering actionable strategies for aligning AI systems with legal and ethical norms.

This book is designed for different audience: clinicians seeking to use AI responsibly, technologists building healthcare-specific tools, data scientist, and policymakers thinking about the future of medical AI regulation. By combining technical information with ethical rigor, we hope to improve a future where LLMs augment—rather than replace—human expertise. The road ahead is complex, but with thoughtful collaboration, LLMs can become good resource in the pursuit of equitable, efficient, and patient-centered care.

List of Contributors

Sina Abbaskhani
Department of Computer Engineering
Science and Research Branch, Islamic Azad University
Tehran, Iran

Khalil Alipour
Department of Mechatronics Engineering
University of Tehran
Tehran, Iran

Farshid Babapour
Department of Medical Radiation Engineering
SR.C., Islamic Azad University
Tehran, Iran

Martin Cunneen
Kemmy Business School
University of Limerick
Castletroy, Limerick, Ireland

Miad Faezipour
School of Engineering Technology
Prudue University
West Lafayette, IN

Amir Fallahzadeh
Department of Computer Engineering
Science and Research Branch, Islamic Azad University
Tehran, Iran

Amirfarhad Farhadi
School of Computer Engineering
Iran university of Science and Technology
Tehran, Iran

Amirmohamad Mataji
Department of Computer Engineering
Science and Research Branch, Islamic Azad University
Tehran, Iran

György Molnár
Faculty of Electrical Engineering
Óbuda University
Budapest, Hungary

Nasser Mozayeni
Department of Computer Engineering
Iran university of Science and Technology
Tehran, Iran

Arezou Naghib
Department of Computer Engineering
Ur. C., Islamic Azad University
Urmia, Iran

Enikő Nagy
Faculty of Informatics
Óbuda University
Budapest, Hungary

Deniz Noor mohammadzadehmaleki
Department of Computer Engineering
Tabriz Banch, Islamic Azad University
Tehran, Iran

Kiana Pilevar Abrisham
Department of Mechatronics Engineering
University of Tehran
Tehran, Iran

Homayoun Safarpour
Department of Software Engineering
University of Szeged
Szeged, Hungary

Mohammad Saleh
Department of Computer Engineering
University of Science and Culture
Tehran, Iran

Farhad Soleimanian Gharehchopogh
Department of Computer Engineering
Ur. C., Islamic Azad University
Urmia, Iran

Azadeh Tabatabaei
Department of Computer Engineering
University of Science and Culture
Tehran, Iran

Alireza Taheri
Department of Computer Engineering
Science and Research Branch, Islamic Azad University
Tehran, Iran

Parisa Tavana
Department of Computer Engineering
Science and Research Branch, Islamic Azad University
Tehran, Iran

Midya Yousefzamani
Department of Medical Radiation Engineering
SR.C., Islamic Azad University
Tehran, Iran

Azadeh Zamanifar
Department of Computer Engineering
SR.C, Islamic Azad University
Tehran, Iran

Editor bios

Azadeh Zamanifar is currently head of computer engineering department at Islamic Azad University, Science and Research Branch. She received her B.Sc. degree in Computer Engineering (Hardware) from Tehran University in 2002. She went on to complete her M.Sc. degree in Computer Engineering (Software) at the University of Science and Technology in 2008, before obtaining her Ph.D. in Software Engineering from Shahid Beheshti University in Tehran, Iran. Currently, she serves as the Head of the Software and AI Department at Islamic Azad University, Science and Research Branch. Her research interests include health care systems, Machine Learning and distributed systems.

Miad Faezipour is an associate professor of electrical and computer engineering technology at the School of Engineering Technology, Purdue University. She is also a full member of the Regenstrief Center for Healthcare Engineering (RCHE) and a core faculty member of the Applied AI Research Center (AARC) at Purdue University. She is the founder and director of the Digital/Biomedical Embedded Systems and Technology (D-BEST) research laboratory. She received M.Sc. and Ph.D. degrees in electrical engineering from the University of Texas at Dallas. Prior to joining Purdue University in August 2021, she had served the Computer Science & Engineering and Biomedical Engineering programs of the University of Bridgeport, CT, as a faculty member for ten years. Her research interests primarily include healthcare technology, digital/biomedical embedded hardware/software co-designs, biomedical signal/image processing, computer vision, healthcare/biomedical informatics, artificial intelligence and AI-based bio-data augmentation. She is a Senior Member of IEEE, EMBS, and the IEEE Women in Engineering.

Farhad Soleimanian Gharehchopogh: Farhad Soleimanian Gharehchopogh is an associate professor in the Department of Computer Engineering at Urmia Branch, Islamic Azad University, since 2015, and brings a wealth of experience to his role. He received a B.S. from the Shabestar Branch, Islamic Azad University in 2002, and an M.S. from Cukurova University in Adana, Turkey. He earned his Ph.D. in Computer Engineering from Hacettepe University in 2015. Dr Farhad has published over 200 journal articles, many in high-impact journals, with over 9,000 citations. His research interests span Data Mining and Machine Learning. Much of his work has been on improving the understanding, design, and performance of algorithms, mainly through the application of engineering.

Amirfarhad Farhadi holds a Ph.D. in Artificial Intelligence and is currently a Postdoctoral Fellow at Iran University of Science and Technology. He also serves as an adjunct professor in the Department of Computer Engineering at the Science and Research Branch of Islamic Azad University. His research expertise spans Artificial Intelligence (AI), machine learning, deep learning, transfer learning, reinforcement learning, natural language processing (NLP), and healthcare systems. Dr Farhadi serves as a reviewer for esteemed journals, including IEEE Transactions on Pattern Analysis and Machine Intelligence (TPAMI) and IEEE Transactions on Neural Networks and Learning Systems, among others. In addition to his academic contributions, he holds patents in robotics and actively participates in the AI industry, focusing on innovative applications and technological advancements.

Chapter 1

Large language models in clinical applications

Homayoun Safarpour, Amirfarhad Farhadi, Martin Cunneen, György Molnár, and Enikő Nagy

1.1 INTRODUCTION

Could a context-specific, clinically trained large language model (LLM)* system be the clinician's most knowledgeable assistant? Such a model could become an intelligence support tool, always ready to help inform more accurate and informed diagnoses. The model could facilitate broader treatment of ailments, generate medical documents, and help address and answer complex queries on demand in a clinical setting. Recent innovations have not transformed science fiction into scientific reality, but progress is unmistakable. As the need to prioritize patients based on clinical urgency and deliver timely, accurate treatment grows, LLMs present a high-value opportunity to support more efficient and scalable approaches to medical and healthcare delivery.

There are several branches to the use of clinical LLMs, each offering distinct benefits in practice: most notably, knowledge retrieval with embedded intelligence, real-time diagnostic support, medical documentation, and improved patient communication. Such approaches could positively transform the way doctors access biomedical literature, interact with electronic health records (EHRs), and automate both administrative and diagnostic workflows.

These clinically focused, context-specific models are already available, and their accuracy and sophistication are increasing at a striking pace. Models such as GPT-4, ClinicalBERT, and Med-PaLM are making their mark on clinical practice, offering real-time insights that sharpen diagnoses, improve how clinicians communicate with patients, and take on the heavy lifting of documentation tasks [1–3]. In daily work, systems like ChatCAD allow a clinician to talk through cases, get guidance on differential diagnoses, or discuss diagnostic tests, adding a valuable new layer to medical education and everyday clinical reasoning [1].

* Throughout this chapter, "LLM" refers specifically to clinically trained large language models designed for use in healthcare and biomedicine.

DOI: 10.1201/9781003665083-1

If you step back and look at the past decade, it's almost dizzying how many LLM-driven innovations have arrived. Every few weeks brings something new: tools that help support and empower patient conversations, models that explain conditions and treatments in simple language, and software that generates individualized documents such as outpatient clinic letters [1, 3, 4]. These developments are not just incremental—they have begun to make LLMs into true partners for practicing clinicians. Still, this story is not only about progress. LLMs are powerful, but they also come with a set of challenges and unresolved questions. One key area is understanding patient language in its real-world context. Although LLMs have shown strong potential for grasping patient concerns expressed in everyday terms [5], issues of fairness and demographic bias remain a concern. As technology spreads, the field is learning that continuous evaluation is needed to spot disparities and keep them in check.

Meanwhile, the pace of research and clinical testing is picking up. By late 2023, at least 27 clinical trials were underway, putting LLM-based tools to the test for documentation, decision support, and research in real healthcare environments [6]. The push to adopt these models also calls for a clear-eyed appreciation of older approaches. Symbolic and rule-based systems, once the backbone of medical artificial intelligence (AI), still matter. In fact, today's neuro-symbolic frameworks blend statistical learning with explicit rules, extending the line from classic expert systems all the way to modern generative AI [7].

A quick look back reminds us that this is a long story. Early artificial intelligence in healthcare was all about expert systems and basic machine learning—think of Mycin, a rule-based system for infectious diseases that, while powerful, had a narrow focus and limited adaptability [8]. The 2010s brought neural network models, especially recurrent networks, that could learn more from data but often struggled with complex, sequential clinical records [9, 10]. Everything changed with the introduction of Transformers in 2017: suddenly, models could process large-scale datasets in parallel, unlocking the power and flexibility that make today's LLMs possible [11, 12].

Now, in this current wave, LLMs built on advanced Transformer architectures—and often further tailored for biomedical contexts—show remarkable abilities. They predict clinical outcomes, support intricate decision-making, and synthesize vast clinical knowledge with impressive fluency [12]. Already, more than 80 clinical language models have been built from EHR data and related sources, each one designed for a different clinical need or challenge [13]. Their presence in real-world workflows is unmistakable. You see LLMs in telehealth chat platforms, within EHR systems, and even as "scribes" that help doctors and nurses manage documentation, streamline care, and facilitate clearer communication between healthcare teams and patients [3].

As we move forward, this chapter will dig into the most significant domains where LLMs are already reshaping clinical work: diagnostics and decision support, patient communication and clinical chatbots, education and training, and the integration of LLMs into everyday healthcare and telemedicine workflows. Each section highlights real case studies and recent research, shares benchmark results, and reflects on the practical considerations that matter most for clinical implementation.

Through this examination, our aim is not only to showcase the promise of LLMs in medicine, but also to keep a close eye on the practical challenges that remain, especially those involving bias, equity, and oversight [13]. Only with careful integration, ongoing review, and open discussion can LLMs truly become partners in delivering smarter, more efficient, and more responsive healthcare [14].

To guide you through this landscape, the rest of this chapter is organized as follows: Section 1.2 examines diagnostics and clinical decision-support systems (CDSS); Section 1.3 explores patient-facing chatbots; Section 1.4 discusses AI-driven education and training; Section 1.5 reviews literature and knowledge management; and Sections 1.6–1.8 present performance evaluation, workflow integration, and conclude with key takeaways.

1.2 DIAGNOSTICS AND CLINICAL DECISION SUPPORT SYSTEM (CDSS)

The complex cognitive processes of clinical reasoning and decision-making that doctors must undertake are both time-consuming and demanding, requiring accuracy and the synthesis of vast and heterogeneous clinical data. Modern medical practice is no longer based solely on theoretical knowledge; rather, it depends on clinicians' ability to integrate large volumes of information, recall rare disease presentations, and stay up to date with evolving recommendations [15]. The growing complexity of medical knowledge has made diagnostic support tools increasingly valuable, helping clinicians avoid missed diagnoses and reduce cognitive overload [15, 16].

One of the most promising applications of large language models (LLMs) in healthcare is their potential to augment these very reasoning processes. When suitably prompted with patient-specific data, LLMs can provide differential diagnoses that mirror expert clinical thinking [17, 18]. In practice, this rapid reasoning and data integration may significantly improve point-of-care decision-making.

In early research and experimental investigations, LLMs have shown the capacity to provide differential diagnoses as a second pair of eyes that substantially coincide with those of real human specialists, personalize learning experiences for medical professionals by adapting to individual learning styles and addressing specific knowledge gaps in clinical practice, and generate assessment notes that are closely aligned with expert opinions across a broad spectrum of cases [4, 19].

Beyond direct diagnostic reasoning, LLMs may enhance the features of traditional clinical decision-support systems (CDSS). Conventional CDSS integrated into electronic health records (EHRs) are mainly rule-based and limited in their capabilities. For instance, these systems may initiate alerts when a patient is prescribed contraindicated medication or if their target monitored level falls alarmingly low. Although these alerts can be lifesaving, they often fail to provide the rationale behind their recommendations, frequently generate high false alarm rates in complex clinical settings, and rely predominantly on static, manually constructed policies [20].

A notable example is Google's Med-PaLM, designed to answer medical questions and benchmarked against physician performance on exam-style queries. Med-PaLM and similar models have shown that well-trained LLMs can recall facts from guidelines and literature with high accuracy and reason through multistep clinical scenarios [21]. When extended to patient-specific inquiries, these models employ techniques such as prompt chaining or tool augmentation, where the LLM retrieves details from a patient's chart to generate tailored, evidence-based answers.

1.3 WORKFLOW OVERVIEW

To orient the reader before we dive into individual use cases, Figure 1.1 condenses the entire LLM-enabled clinical decision support loop into six ordered stages. Each thick arrow represents *both* a data transfer and a transfer of accountability:

1. **Multimodal Patient Inputs:** Laboratory panels, imaging metadata, free-text notes, physiologic waveforms, and patient-reported outcomes—are pooled into a single ingestion stream.

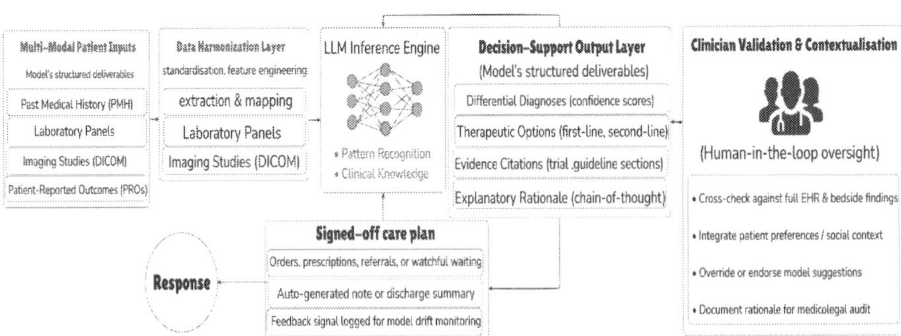

Figure 1.1 LLM-assisted clinical decision support pipeline.

2. **Data Harmonization Layer** standardizes those heterogeneous signals (Fast Healthcare Interoperability Resources [FHIR] mapping, time-stamp alignment, PHI redaction) so the downstream model consumes a clean, self-consistent *context bundle.*
3. **LLM Inference Engine** performs probabilistic pattern-matching across that bundle, fusing biomedical priors with patient-specific cues to build a ranked differential and surface therapeutic targets.
4. **Decision support Output Layer:** Diagnostic hypotheses, treatment options, supporting citations, and calibrated confidence scores—are emitted in a structured form.
5. **Clinician Validation and Contextualization** supplies indispensable human context: the attending cross-checks model suggestions against real-time findings and modulates them considering patient preferences, resource constraints, and medicolegal norms.
6. **Final Therapeutic Action:** (orders, prescriptions, referrals, or watchful waiting) is executed and documented; the interaction is logged to feed a drift-monitoring loop.

In short, the pipeline braids machine-scale knowledge retrieval with human clinical acumen, turning raw data into an evidence-anchored care plan in seconds rather than minutes. Each stage makes explicit *who, or what, is accountable* for the transformation it performs, thereby providing a practical contract between software engineers and frontline clinicians.

Despite these promising developments, the use of LLMs in diagnostics and decision-support remains experimental and requires careful oversight. Clinicians must remain the ultimate decision-makers, validating AI-generated recommendations through their expertise. Studies highlight the need for robust safeguards: LLMs can occasionally display inconsistent reasoning or unwarranted confidence, and recommendations could shift with irrelevant information or subtle rewording of questions [22]. These findings emphasize the need for ongoing scrutiny of AI reasoning.

To address these concerns, developers are exploring multilevel checks and balances. One strategy uses secondary verification models or algorithms to double-check critical recommendations, ensuring suggested medication doses remain within safe bounds. Another restricts LLM usage to thoroughly validated, well-defined clinical scenarios. Advanced prototypes increasingly utilize ensembles of AI agents: one generates a recommendation, another checks for safety and guideline compliance, and a third confirms correct interpretation of patient-specific data. Multi-agent architectures enhance reasoning and factual accuracy, promote divergent thinking, and leverage the complementary strengths of multiple LLMs [23]. This approach emphasizes the potential benefits of using several LLMs to improve task performance while also suggesting the need for strategies that minimize computational demands.

LLMs offer significant potential as versatile assistants in clinical diagnostics and decision support. They can integrate information across diverse sources, apply broad medical knowledge, and generate transparent, explanatory outputs. As advisory tools, LLMs act as ever-available junior consultants, complementing human expertise and broadening access to specialized knowledge. This collaborative framework empowers an AI-human scientific collaboration via a series of meetings between a human researcher and a team of interdisciplinary LLM agents [24], which can be pivotal for addressing intricate, multistep tasks [25]. The Search Tree, Analyze and Repair, and Selection (STARS) strategy enable multiple LLMs to generate a large array of responses, which could lead to both improved outcomes and increased computational requirements [26]. Thus, it becomes critical to implement cost-effective solutions that manage the energy output of such systems effectively.

Furthermore, these models allow for reduced energy use while maintaining or enhancing performance levels, demonstrating a direct route toward more sustainable model deployments, like dynamic tensor reconfiguration (DTR), which achieves significant reductions in computational latency and energy consumption [27]. As pilot studies and real-world implementations progress, continuous validation and careful monitoring will be crucial for realizing benefits and managing risks.

1.4 PATIENT COMMUNICATION AND CLINICAL CHATBOTS

Clear and responsive communication is the foundation of effective healthcare delivery. In daily clinical practice, patients often grapple with questions about their symptoms, new medications, follow-up plans, or even test results that arrive outside office hours. Traditionally, such queries are relieved by in-person consultations, phone calls, or patient portals, but these methods rarely provide the real-time, interactive support that patients seek, especially outside standard clinic hours. Large language models (LLMs) have begun to bridge this gap, acting as conversational partners that extend the reach of healthcare providers who can converse with patients, answer common medical questions, clarify instructions, and offer tailored health education at any hour [2, 4], enhancing the flexibility and context of responses [28].

LLM-driven agents can interpret patient queries, triage symptoms, and provide targeted education by leveraging retrieval-augmented generation (RAG) methods. These systems not only personalize advice and handle symptom triage but also detect bias and deliver patient-facing responses through chatbots [29]. For instance, a patient might type, "I've had a persistent cough and mild fever for three days; should I be worried?" Rather than merely listing possible causes, an LLM chatbot can engage conversationally, probe for alarming signs (such as shortness of breath, chest pain, or travel history), and provide advice tailored to the patient's context [5, 30]. This flexible interaction mimics the questioning style of skilled healthcare professionals, assisting in appropriately triaging cases. Research shows that conversational agents leveraging LLMs improve patient engagement and understanding by offering personalized responses based on the nuances of the conversation, similar to interactions with skilled nurses or physicians [30].

Research demonstrates both the promise and pitfalls of these systems. LLM-powered triage assistants in urgent care show a high degree of alignment between the AI's recommendations and those of clinical staff. However, studies also highlight persistent demographic biases—some symptom descriptions or patient profiles led to subtle variations in advice, underscoring the need for careful oversight and ongoing bias mitigation [5]. In practice, healthcare organizations often deploy these tools with "human-in-the-loop" monitoring so clinicians can review or intervene when necessary.

LLMs are also revolutionizing the creation of patient education materials to deal with the challenge that patients often receive generic or overly technical summaries that can be challenging and hard to comprehend. LLMs can produce tailored summaries, which empowers patients to engage more actively in their own healthcare and receive related information [31]. For accuracy of generated information, experts, in this case physicians, can quickly review and edit these drafts before sharing them, ensuring accuracy and appropriateness. Initial findings suggest that personalized, simplified summaries significantly improve patient comprehension and satisfaction, fostering increased engagement and adherence to care recommendations [32].

Furthermore, LLMs have shown promise in refining educational materials by generating content that retains essential clinical information while translating it into patient-friendly language [32]. Modern chat agents are now embedded in chronic disease dashboards and remote monitoring workflows; when a worrisome pattern emerges, the system escalates to a human clinician [4].

To keep responses current and verifiable, these agents increasingly rely on a retrieval-augmented generation (RAG) pipeline, a two-stage process that first pulls evidence snippets from a medical index and then weaves them into the LLM's answer. Figure 1.2 grounds this idea in the context of bedside question-answering, demonstrating how the user's query is embedded, matched against a vector index of medical documents, and the retrieved passages are concatenated into an *augmented prompt*. The clinical LLM then produces an answer that is both conversational and evidence-linked.

Once this evidence-grounded reply is drafted, routine questions, such as drug–drug compatibility or lab-result explanations, can be answered

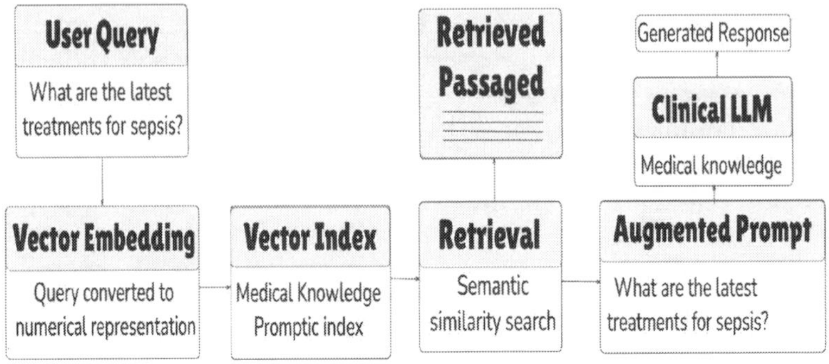

Figure 1.2 Retrieval-augmented generation pipeline.

automatically, while higher-risk or ambiguous cases are routed to staff for review [4].

Despite these advances, several challenges persist. Primarily, safety remains a critical concern, as patients may place undue reliance on AI-generated advice without fully grasping its limitations. Consequently, such systems are often designed conservatively, advising users to consult their healthcare provider for any ambiguous or critical issues. For example, LLM-driven systems can automatically detect potential emergencies and issue alerts like, "Your symptoms sound serious; please seek immediate medical attention" [33].

The requirement for rigorous training on diverse patient narratives is essential to mitigate bias, while maintaining strict privacy safeguards is vital for guaranteeing that patient data remains confidential. This involves running models within secure, hospital-managed environments that protect sensitive information [34]. Additionally, addressing potential biases inherent in AI models ensures they perform equitably across varied demographics, thereby improving the overall effectiveness of healthcare delivery systems [35]. By breaking down barriers of jargon and accessibility, these AI-powered tools help ensure that patients are truly partners in their health journeys.

LLM-powered chatbots and communication aids represent a paradigm shift in patient engagement. They promise more accessible, timely, and tailored information, helping patients understand and manage their conditions more effectively. As technology matures, ongoing evaluation, human oversight, and an unwavering focus on equity and trust will be essential to realizing these benefits without unintended harm.

Figure 1.3 highlights the strict separation of a hand-curated *knowledge base*, an *inference engine* that applies IF–THEN rules, and the dual interfaces that mediate between end-users and developers. External databases/programs were typically bolted on as afterthoughts, making continuous learning all but impossible.

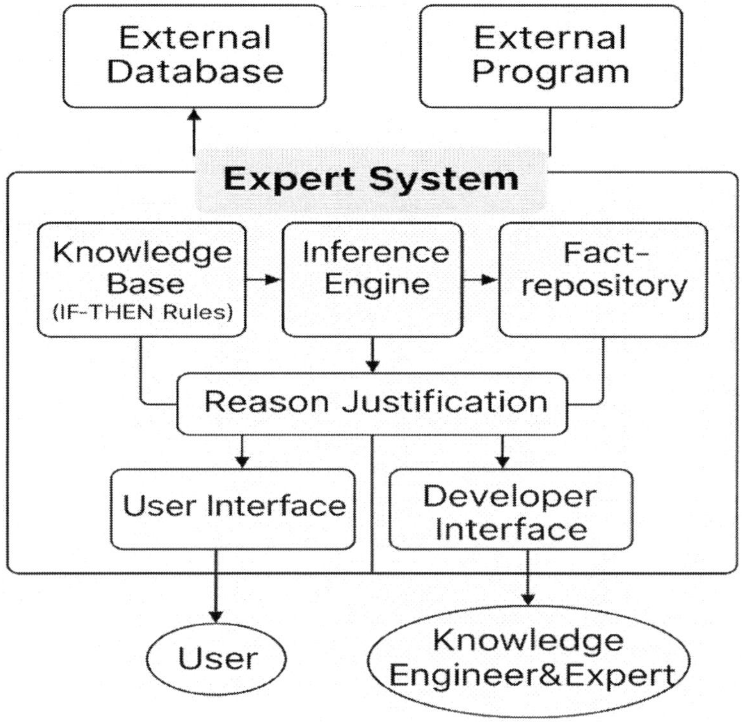

Figure 1.3 Classical rule-based expert-system architecture.

From static rule bases to self-evolving agent collectives: While classic expert-system shells (cf. Figure 1.3) relied on handcrafted IF–THEN production rules and a single inference loop, recent work shows that we can now model an *entire* hospital as a constellation of LLM-powered agents that learn like a sandbox in which resident, nurse, and doctor agents—each backed by an LLM—cycle autonomously through triage, registration, diagnostics, and follow-up care, with every interaction stored as a synthetic but medically plausible EHR entry. Over successive simulated days, the doctor agents accumulate thousands of such cases and refine their practice without any human-labeled data [33, 36].

MedAgent-Zero: learning by doing (and by failing): The key innovation is a parameter-free training loop called *MedAgent-Zero*. Correct decisions are archived as few-shot exemplars, whereas mistakes trigger a reflection step that distills reusable "never-again" principles before the case is rerun [36]. This dual cache, *record library + experience base*, acts as a fast, retrieval-augmented memory that sharpens diagnostic accuracy with every patient seen [36]. After only ~10 000 virtual encounters (the workload of a junior physician over two years), the evolved agent reaches 96% accuracy on in-simulation cases and 93% on an external subset of MedQA, outperforming fine-tuned GPT-4 baselines [36].

Why this is relevant for clinical AI: By embedding learning inside a closed, end-to-end workflow—rather than bolting rules onto a static knowledge base—Agent Hospital demonstrates three qualities that traditional expert systems lacked: (i) *scalability*, because agents can treat limitless synthetic patients for pennies; (ii) *continual adaptation*, as new experience immediately updates future reasoning; and (iii) *ecosystem evaluation*, enabling rigorous A/B testing of safety, bias, and drift before real-world deployment. In short, the field is moving from brittle logic boxes toward living, data-generating micro-worlds that let LLM clinicians practice, make errors, and improve—long before they ever meet a human patient [36].

1.5 MEDICAL EDUCATION AND TRAINING

The influence of large language models (LLMs) is not limited to clinical practice; it also extends to medical education and the training of healthcare professionals. Medical training is a lengthy and information-dense journey, requiring students and residents to master vast amounts of knowledge while honing critical-thinking skills. LLMs offer novel opportunities to enhance learning, assess knowledge, and practice clinical reasoning in a low-stakes environment. LLMs have shown promise in transforming traditional learning methodologies by generating contextually relevant information, thus enabling students to explore complex subjects at their pace [37].

Additionally, the potential of LLMs to improve the usability and credibility of educational resources in healthcare allows these models to facilitate personalized learning experiences and foster deeper engagement with medical content, which is essential for developing critical-thinking and problem-solving skills among medical students [38]. Furthermore, the adaptability of LLMs allows them to serve as valuable cognitive tools in the education of healthcare professionals, effectively responding to diverse learning needs [39].

The application of LLMs in educational settings not only enriches the learning experience but also prepares future healthcare providers for the complexities of clinical practice. Enhanced access to personalized, AI-driven resources promotes a more inclusive educational environment, helping bridge knowledge gaps and support students from various backgrounds in mastering medical concepts. As AI technology advances, its integration into medical education can significantly improve students' knowledge, skills, and competencies, thereby enhancing healthcare delivery [37]. Recent surveys show that learners already turn to ChatGPT-style tools as supplemental resources because the model explanations often go beyond what a static search engine returns [40].

Researchers have also documented how LLMs adapt explanations to match individual cognitive styles, thereby fostering more profound engagement and self-paced learning [41]. Such adaptability signals a shift from one-size-fits-all pedagogy to a more personalized, dialogue-centered approach—one that could fundamentally reshape how future clinicians acquire and reinforce knowledge [42].

1.5.1 Interactive virtual tutors

LLMs now serve as on-demand instructors: a student can type *"Explain, in plain language, how β-blockers help heart failure."* and receive a stepwise answer—slowing heart rate, lowering afterload, and blunting neuro-hormonal stress—followed by clarifying Q&A. Classroom pilots report higher satisfaction than static e-texts because the explanation adapts to follow-up queries and even offers short quizzes [40, 41]. These improvements in engagement reflect the evolving role of LLMs in supporting educational practices. LLMs assist in generating practice scenarios, facilitating differential diagnosis brainstorming, and enhancing multiple-choice question reviews, thereby enriching the educational experience for medical students [43]. This capacity for customization not only promotes interactive learning but also enables educators to integrate LLM outputs into structured curricula, thereby enhancing the overall learning process [44]. However, accuracy remains paramount; many educational institutions restrict models to domain-tuned checkpoints that cite sources or explicitly express uncertainty. Such measures are essential to maintain the integrity of educational content and ensure that students receive reliable, evidence-based information [45].

1.5.2 Automated question generation

The automation of multiple-choice questions through AI can significantly alleviate the time and expense associated with question development, thus transforming medical education [1]. Moreover, LLMs have shown proficiency in generating high-quality examination items across various medical domains, reinforcing their role as valuable tools in educational settings [46]. LLMs, including GPT-4, can achieve impressive results on medical score assessments like the USMLE, indicating their efficacy in supporting medical training through reliable question generation [47]. However, while the potential for personalized learning exists, the practical implementation and effectiveness in real-world settings require further research to be substantiated [48]. By harnessing the generative power of LLMs, educators can enhance the overall learning experience while ensuring that assessment materials are relevant and challenging, thereby preparing students more effectively for real-world medical practice [49].

1.5.3 Low-stakes clinical simulations

Modern LLMs can now act as synthetic "standardized patients," opening new possibilities for clinical education. When trainees conduct free-text medical interviews, these models respond as if they were real patients, staying in character even as the scenario unfolds and the questioning changes. This allows residents to rehearse uncommon conditions, for example, pheochromocytoma, whenever they need, and to receive instant feedback compared to expert clinician approaches [42]. By repeating these virtual simulations, students can build confidence with rare or challenging presentations, something that would be difficult to experience in real clinics. It is not only about practicing questions; the ability to reply and reflect on the conversation provides a unique space for guided self-improvement.

1.5.4 Benchmarking knowledge

In terms of raw knowledge, there have been striking advances as well. In one widely discussed experiment, Kung et al. showed that even an early version of ChatGPT performed at or above the pass mark on all three USMLE medical licensing steps, despite no special medical fine-tuning [50]. While just "passing" does not put a language model on par with experienced doctors, this result is a strong signal that modern models capture much of the information found in the medical curriculum. This makes them useful not just for fast fact-checking, but also for identifying weak spots in a student's learning. Recent systematic reviews confirm that, although there are still gaps and blind spots, LLMs can help spotlight areas for further study or revision [45, 51].

1.5.5 Curriculum codesign and continual learning

Educators are now bringing LLMs directly into the curriculum, whether by using them to help draft lecture outlines or by generating fresh clinical vignettes that human faculty can then adapt or annotate. In practice, physicians and teachers also find it handy to use these models for quick updates, asking about changes in guidelines or recent drug approvals, effectively turning LLMs into a kind of customizable medical news feed. The value here is not just in speed, but also in the capacity to keep course content up to date. When models are linked to real-time retrieval tools, their answers can be cross-checked with the most recent literature before being shown to students or clinicians [52]. This approach helps avoid outdated material and ensures everyone is learning from the latest available research [51].

Incorporating LLMs into teaching not only speeds up content creation, but also encourages students to engage more deeply, questioning, comparing, and building on what the models provide [45]. In workshops, feedback sessions, or even informal discussions, students often express that these tools make them more active participants in their education rather than passive recipients.

1.5.6 Caveats and future literacy

Of course, for all the progress, there are important caveats. Even the best language models sometimes produce answers that sound convincing but turn out to be incorrect or misleading. In some cases, they may oversimplify complex situations or unknowingly reinforce the biases present in their training data. This means that, in all educational and clinical use, language models should be viewed as helpful assistants, not as substitutes for peer-reviewed guidelines, authoritative sources, or expert judgment. They are best as an aid for gathering information, sparking discussion, or prompting further investigation, not as the last word in important clinical decisions.

It's one thing to acknowledge the promise of LLMs in the classroom and clinic, but quite another to teach people how to use them wisely. That's why many teachers and researchers are now pushing for "AI literacy" to become a fundamental skill set, not just for students, but for faculty and practicing clinicians as well. The days when it was enough to simply read the latest review or guideline are over. Now, students are asked to make judgment calls: when do you trust what the model suggests? When should you look elsewhere or ask for a second opinion from a human or a database? [53, 54].

Building this kind of discernment isn't something you pick up in a single afternoon. It takes time and deliberate practice: comparing model answers to gold-standard resources, pulling up old exam questions and seeing how the AI handles them, even setting up debates between students and the model itself to hash out what's reliable and what's suspect [45, 51]. It's not about blind faith or total mistrust; it's about asking good questions and not being afraid to push back.

Of course, the burden of adaptation isn't only on the students. Teachers, too, are having to rethink what it means to mentor in an AI-rich world. Professional development must be ongoing. Many schools now hold regular workshops, journal clubs, or even peer-led sessions focused on new digital tools, giving everyone a chance to share what works, talk through ethical dilemmas, and admit what's confusing or still uncertain [52]. These conversations aren't just technical; they're about building a new culture, where it's normal to question what AI produces and to discuss its limitations as a group.

In the end, what matters is not just using the latest tool, but cultivating a mindset that values skepticism, discussion, and a willingness to say, "I don't know, let's check." That's the kind of environment where critical thinking grows, and where tomorrow's clinicians will learn to balance the breadth of AI with the depth of human experience [45, 53]. As the curriculum shifts, and as technology becomes even more embedded in practice, it will take more than added content to keep up. It will take a community, built around honest reflection and a shared commitment to patient safety and scientific rigor.

1.6 LITERATURE AND KNOWLEDGE MANAGEMENT

Large language models (LLMs) are increasingly being employed as knowledge management assistants—helping users retrieve, summarize, and interpret medical knowledge more efficiently than ever before [55]. Traditionally, if a doctor wanted to know the latest evidence regarding a therapy, they would perform a PubMed search and manually read through the results. However, using an LLM-based system can automate much of this work. For example, a physician could ask, "What do recent studies say about the efficacy of Drug X for treating lupus in pediatric patients?" The system could access a database of medical literature, extract pertinent excerpts and results from clinical trials or meta-analyses, and enable the LLM to produce a succinct summary of the findings, potentially including references [56].

Retrieval-augmented generation (RAG) is a technique often used in the application of LLMs. By combining generative models with retrieval systems, this method improves the quality of information retrieval and enables more precise and contextually appropriate replies [57, 58]. The ability of retrieval-augmented generation (RAG) helps users make well-informed choices based on the most recent research and close gaps between a wealth of medical literature and real-world clinical knowledge [59]. By grounding the LLM's response in the retrieved text, the system can provide specific, up-to-date information and reduce the chance of hallucination. Connecting the model to real-time literature feeds, physicians get up-to-date guideline changes and medication approvals in summary form, reducing content staleness [52]. Figure 1.4 illustrates such a pipeline, where an embedding model finds relevant text snippets (e.g., paragraphs from journal articles or guidelines) that an LLM then weaves into a final answer. This approach enables clinicians to obtain quick, evidence-based answers to complex questions, complete with the context from original sources.

In advanced perspectives, an LLM can be fine-tuned on an organization's internal knowledge base and queried in natural language. A clinician might ask, "Do we have any active clinical trials for patients with stage III lung cancer with EGFR mutations?" Instead of manually checking multiple protocol documents or contacting the research office, they could receive an immediate answer if the information is stored in the system's corpus

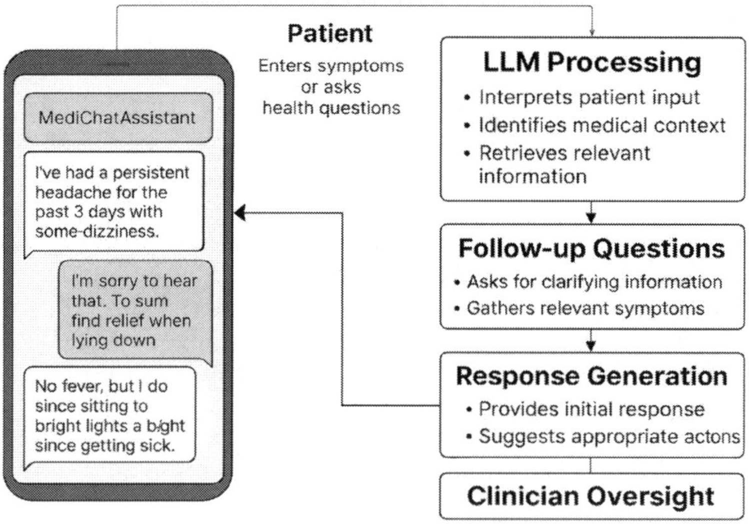

Figure 1.4 Patient-facing symptom-checker chat flow.

[60]. Similarly, hospital administrators can query an LLM about policies, such as "What is the procedure for reporting a medication error?" and get direct responses drawn from policy manuals. The integration of LLMs into healthcare practices is increasingly being explored by major electronic health record vendors, indicating that these LLM-driven tools are transitioning from prototypes to real-world pilot tests within clinical workflows [61].

To scale effectively, LLMs need to understand two sets of text: the trial eligibility criteria, which can be long lists of required patient characteristics, and the patient's record, which includes diagnoses, lab values, treatments, and other important information [62] to make things more efficient and accurate [63]. This capacity shows how powerful LLMs are at making the research process better and making it easier for healthcare professionals and clinical trial sponsors to work together [64].

Researchers have successfully trained LLMs to perform this as a classification task, using an LLM to categorize each eligibility criterion for a given patient as "met," "not met," or "uncertain," effectively simulating the checklist a human coordinator would use [65]. Notably, one recent study reported that a fine-tuned LLM achieved about 93% accuracy (with a similarly high F1-score) in classifying trial eligibility criteria, matching the performance of prior machine learning approaches [65].

In parallel, LLMs can function as semantic search engines over extensive trial databases: Given a patient profile, the model can retrieve a shortlist of trials that are likely to be relevant, on which it subsequently performs detailed criteria checks. The advantages are substantial activities that previously took hours of reviewing trial descriptions can now be completed in seconds, unveiling opportunities that might otherwise remain hidden. Actual implementations of AI-driven trial matching are already being observed; for instance, several cancer centers have begun integrating these tools into their EHR systems. When an oncologist looks at a patient's data, a sidebar may show trials that the patient is eligible for based on an analysis done by the LLM [66]. This proactive approach makes sure that patients know about relevant research projects, which gives them more options for getting the latest medicines. Moreover, it assists researchers by accelerating enrollment, a widely recognized bottleneck in the clinical trial process. Institutions utilizing LLM-based matching have reported that the automated filtering process significantly reduces the array of potential trials, leaving a more manageable number for human reviewers to confirm. In practice, an AI may condense hundreds of available trials into just a few that fit the patient, which a clinician or research coordinator can then validate. This enhancement of the human workflow represents a transformative shift in how patients are connected with studies, potentially increasing both the speed and diversity of trial enrollment [66].

On the other hand, the employment of LLMs in knowledge management is not without its challenges. A primary concern involves ensuring that the information retrieved or generated is accurate and current. Given that medical knowledge evolves quickly, where new studies can change previous understandings and guidelines are updated periodically, having an LLM that relies on outdated training data can lead to unanticipated gaps in knowledge [67]. A successful mitigating method is retrieval-augmented generation (RAG), which includes new data from live databases or document indices [68].

To avoid personal data from being exposed outside secure settings, trial matching patient records must be protected by strong privacy controls. Implementing on-premises models behind a hospital's firewall and using de-identification or encryption technologies helps ensure compliance with privacy rules like Health Insurance Portability and Accountability Act (HIPAA) in the United States [69]. Another issue is the LLM's interpretation limits with sophisticated logical constructions. Trial matching eligibility requirements might be complex, such as "(A and B) or (C and D), and not E, unless F." LLMs may struggle with layered logic without guidance. Researchers have tried dividing jobs into smaller parts or asking the model to explain its reasoning process. For example, the AI may evaluate criteria sequentially or explain its rationale, such as announcing, "Criterion 5 indicates no heart failure; the patient record shows no history of heart failure, therefore meets this criterion" [70]. Stepwise reasoning may improve transparency and accuracy.

In fact, it is investigated that an active inference prompting strategy—iteratively asking the model to verify and refine its answers—elicits more reliable responses from LLMs in medical practice [44]. Such methods have the AI double-check its own work or provide a rationale, which can help humans follow the logic and catch errors. LLMs are becoming invaluable tools for managing the immense volume of biomedical knowledge. They assist clinicians and researchers in quickly locating relevant papers, clinical trials, or crucial details in patient records and presenting this information in an understandable form. By doing so, LLMs can accelerate evidence-based practice and research. As these systems evolve, we expect them to serve not just as search engines but as intelligent research partners, able to justify their answers with sources, suggest related information ("Have you considered this other study on a similar question?"), and even identify knowledge gaps where no useful information exists (prompting further investigation or research to fill the void).

1.7 PERFORMANCE EVALUATION AND BENCHMARKS

As large language models (LLMs) are becoming part of daily clinical work, a simple but important question remains: Are these systems truly safe and effective? In the past, hospitals only had to worry about simple rules or expert systems, software that did what you expected. But LLMs are different. They sometimes give amazing answers, but other times they surprise you, and not always in an effective way. Some responses are spot on; others are incomplete or even dangerously wrong. Because of that, checking how well they work is not a one-time step; it is something we have to do all the time, both before and after the models are in use [71].

Recently, there has been a real shift in how we test these models. It's no longer enough to throw some medical school test questions at them and see how they score. We need more depth, more realism, and more attention to the details that matter to doctors and patients. That is where evaluation frameworks come in. Researchers are now using not just lists of facts, but clinical vignettes—short, realistic cases that capture the messiness of real medical practice [72, 73]. Imagine a case with overlapping symptoms, conflicting lab results, or an unclear patient history [74]. These are the moments that trip up not only AIs, but sometimes humans too.

The point is not only to see if the model "knows" the answer, but to watch how it reasons. Does it follow the right steps? Does it explain its thinking in a way a doctor would trust? Often, researchers compare the LLM's answers directly with those of real clinicians, and sometimes the AI does very well. But other times, especially with tricky or ambiguous cases, the cracks begin to show [75].

We have already seen some headline results: LLMs like Med-PaLM and GPT-4 can now pass standardized tests that were once the sole domain of board-certified doctors [21, 47]. That's a big milestone, but it is only a small piece of the puzzle. Medical exams focus heavily on recall and "textbook" reasoning. In the real world, patients rarely fit the mold. There is always an extra detail, an unusual lab result, or a social factor that changes the answer. As impressive as passing an exam is, it doesn't guarantee safety or reliability at the bedside.

If you dig deeper into the literature, you find that even minor tweaks in how a question is asked can throw these models off [22, 76]. Change a single word in the prompt, "main" diagnosis versus "primary" diagnosis, and you can see accuracy shift dramatically. Human doctors notice these subtleties; models, so far, often do not. These are not just academic points, but significant issues that could matter in patient care.

Another area that often gets less attention is natural language processing for tasks like summarizing clinical notes or extracting key data. Shared datasets from the i2b2/UTHealth challenges let us see how well models do at identifying problems, medications, or symptoms buried in long, messy records [77]. The usual metrics—recall, precision, F1—tell one story, but even a high score does not mean every critical point is captured. More than once, models have missed a medication allergy or a crucial lab abnormality [4, 78]. This is why numbers alone can be misleading.

As testing has gotten more sophisticated, adversarial examples have entered the picture. Researchers deliberately try to "trick" LLMs with edge cases, hidden contraindications, or conflicting data, to see where they stumble. Sometimes these are subtle, like a drug that should be avoided because of an allergy mentioned only once in a long record. The point is not to embarrass the model, but to surface weaknesses before real patients are put at risk. There is even work now using one AI model to grade another, although this approach still needs caution; just because one model flags a mistake does not mean it is always right either [23].

Another theme that has come up repeatedly is fairness. It's an uncomfortable fact that LLMs trained on real-world medical data can inherit all the biases and gaps that exist in literature. Studies show that responses can shift based on the patient's name, gender, or race, even when everything else is the same [79]. Testing for these disparities is becoming routine, and it sometimes means just swapping out a detail in a case vignette and checking if the advice changes. If it does, the model needs more work, either in how it is trained or in how it is filtered before clinical use [80].

Transparency is another piece of the puzzle. Doctors and patients alike want to know not just what the model recommends, but why. Can the AI show its reasoning? Can it point to the data or the guidelines that led it to an answer? Some models do better when prompted to "show your work," and this practice is spreading [21, 78]. The more the model can explain, the easier it is for people to trust—or, just as importantly, to catch and correct a mistake.

Once an LLM is in use, the work does not stop. Real-world monitoring is crucial. If clinicians keep ignoring or correcting the AI's recommendations, that's a sign that the model might be off, or the clinical context has changed. Some hospitals now review AI logs and outcomes routinely, not just to find errors but to see where models can improve.

One of the more promising trends is the growth of evaluations outside the "standard" use case. LLMs are now being tested in languages other than English and in specialties like neurology or psychiatry, where the challenges can be very different from general medicine [39, 49]. Sometimes, the results are impressive. Other times, the models reveal important gaps, especially when cultural context or local knowledge is required.

In the end, the direction is clear: simple tests are not enough. Comprehensive, ongoing, and context-aware evaluation is needed. Modern frameworks now include everything from exam scores and simulated patient vignettes to adversarial challenges, fairness checks, and transparency audits. Only by combining all these approaches can we hope to really understand what LLMs are good at, where they are safe, and where human oversight remains essential.

The goal is not to "prove" that an AI is perfect, but to build trust, identify failure points, and improve both the models and the systems around them. That way, as LLMs become an everyday tool in clinics and hospitals, they will support, not undermine, the clinical judgment and patient safety that medicine demands.

1.7.1 Just-in-time inference at the point of need

Whether the encounter occurs in a busy clinic or via a web browser, clinicians expect an LLM's answer in half a second or less. In practice, internal latency budgets at some large health systems are about 150–200 MS for triage chatbots and 400–600 MS for more complex decision support queries (e.g., checking an order set) [81]. Two complementary strategies help keep round-trip times within these targets:

1. **Sharding and caching:** A slim, optimized inference microservice co-located with the EHR database handles short prompts (e.g., a quick question about a single lab result), while longer summarization or analytical jobs are offloaded to a separate GPU server pool. This prevents minor queries from getting stuck behind big jobs. Additionally, the system caches results for common retrieval sub-queries—for instance, if multiple prompts ask for "latest creatinine level," the vector database lookup for that piece of data can be reused rather than repeated each time. By caching frequently needed facts and partial results, the

pipeline removes redundant computation and database hits, thereby shaving off precious milliseconds [81, 82].

2. **Token streaming:** There's a big difference between waiting for a whole answer and watching it appear, word by word, in real time. With token streaming, as soon as the large language model begins to generate its response, those words are immediately sent to the user interface. The clinician doesn't have to wait for a full paragraph to appear before they can start reading, instead, the answer starts coming through almost instantly, even as it's still forming in the background. This simple shift makes the experience feel more responsive, often cutting the perceived delay in half, which is especially important when the answer is complex or lengthy. For example, if a doctor is checking for possible drug-drug interactions, even a short lag of a second or two can seem long under pressure. But when the system streams the output, "No known interaction between Drug A and ..." as the rest loads—the clinician sees the process in motion and knows that progress is being made [82].

   This kind of prompt feedback does more than save time. It also gives the practitioner confidence in using the system, especially during fast-paced, high-stakes decision-making. When time is of the essence, as it often is in busy clinical environments, the ability to see partial answers in real time can support momentum and reduce frustration [83]. Behind the scenes, this responsiveness depends on smart system architecture: distributing workloads efficiently, minimizing bottlenecks, and making sure that the technical infrastructure keeps up with the demands of healthcare data processing [84]. If an AI tool makes the workflow even a little slower or more complicated, most providers will set it aside, regardless of its sophistication [85]. Mental workload and stress are especially prevalent in emergency rooms and critical care [86]. Automatic systems that detect medication interactions and recommend essential measures might enhance patient safety and results [87].

1.7.2 Workflow hooks for telemedicine

Remote visits introduce additional integration points that can harness LLMs to streamline care before, during, and after the virtual encounter:

- **Pre-visit triage chatbots:** In today's telemedicine workflows, pre-visit triage chatbots are changing how clinicians interact with patients before a live consult. These automated agents can handle patient-reported symptoms, prioritize cases by urgency, and ensure that essential information is collected before a visit begins. Studies have shown that chatbots powered by LLMs can accurately map patient free-text inputs to standard medical codes, improving both efficiency and triage accuracy [5, 88]. Such tools not only free up clinical staff for more complex tasks, but also streamline the intake process, making telehealth more accessible for both patients and providers.

- **Asynchronous follow-up and data monitoring:** Asynchronous follow-up—where data and messages are reviewed after a virtual visit—has become central to remote care. LLMs automate much of this work by continuously watching for incoming patient data, such as new lab results, home-monitored vitals, or updates in symptom diaries. For example, an LLM integrated with the EHR can spot abnormal test values, summarize what's clinically significant, and generate a draft notification for either the patient or the care team [2, 6]. With large numbers of patients submitting data outside of regular visits, this automation helps clinicians stay ahead without missing important changes.
- **Patient-reported data synthesis:** Another area where LLMs excel is in digesting patient-reported outcomes—whether daily blood sugar logs, blood pressure records, or symptom diaries. Rather than just collecting raw numbers, these models can pick up on trends over time and flag early warning signs. For example, if a diabetic patient's glucose levels slowly increase over two weeks, the system might summarize, "Your average fasting glucose has risen from 110 to 135 mg/dL," and prompt a review by the care team [4, 83]. This ability to synthesize and contextualize patient data is key for proactive care, especially when combined with alerting mechanisms for urgent findings.
- **Drafting clinician responses and education:** Drafting responses to patient messages can be repetitive and time-consuming for providers. LLMs can now generate initial drafts for clinicians to edit, saving valuable time while ensuring consistency and thoroughness. For example, when a patient writes in asking, "Should I continue my blood thinner after the surgery?" the model can prepare a suggested response, including citations from up-to-date guidelines or referencing the patient's latest lab values [1, 45]. In parallel, LLMs can create personalized educational materials or health reminders—tailored to each patient's current status—further extending the reach and personalization of care [51, 52].
- **Lab-result alerts and urgent notifications:** Timely notification of abnormal results is a perennial challenge in digital medicine. LLM-enabled agents can automatically review incoming lab values and flag those that need follow-up. For instance, if a potassium result is elevated, the model might draft a note advising a repeat test or notify the provider directly, reducing the risk of critical findings being overlooked [86, 89]. By integrating these alerts into daily workflow, LLMs

help close gaps in asynchronous data review and keep care teams responsive to urgent needs.

1.7.3 Patient-reported data synthesis

Patient-reported data synthesis. LLMs can digest longitudinal inputs (daily blood sugars, blood pressure logs, pain diaries, etc.) submitted by the patient and generate trends or risk assessments. For example, if a diabetic patient's glucose readings gradually climb, the system might produce a summary ("Your average fasting glucose has increased from 110 to 135 mg/dL over two weeks") for clinician review.

1.7.4 Drafting clinician responses

Drafting clinician responses. After receiving a patient portal question or update, an LLM can draft an appropriate follow-up message. For instance, if a patient asks, "Should I continue my blood thinner after the surgery?" the model could produce a clinician-vetted draft response citing recent guidelines or lab values. This can drastically reduce repetitive writing for providers.

1.7.5 Generating follow-up questions

LLMs can even pre-generate follow-up questions when a patient reports new symptoms. In asynchronous contexts, clinicians often ask multiple clarifying questions at once to avoid repeated messaging. An LLM agent might pull from the patient's history and EHR to suggest these questions automatically, covering a broad differential diagnosis [90].

Early studies indicate that such LLM applications can save clinician effort and improve information quality. For example, the Talk2Care system used a voice-assistant interface to collect older adults' health updates and an LLM dashboard to summarize the information for providers; the investigators found that this enriched the clinical data and "considerably save[d] providers' efforts and time" [91]. Likewise, asynchronous messages often assume the physician already knows the patient's history, requiring the system to integrate fragmented EHR data for context [91]. By automatically generating context-aware follow-up items, LLMs can reduce the back-and-forth messaging load that contributes to provider burnout [91]. In short, automating post-visit follow-up tasks with LLMs can streamline care coordination: the model tracks lab flows and patient inputs, flags issues, drafts communications, and alerts the care team as needed, all subject to human oversight.

1.7.6 Telemedicine gateway overlay

Telemedicine systems often use a "gateway" or middleware layer to ingest and manage data from remote patients. This telemedicine gateway sits at the boundary between patient devices (wearables, home monitoring kits, patient apps) and the clinical EHR/platform. Its core role is to collect heterogeneous inputs, adapt formats, and securely forward data into the telehealth infrastructure. The gateway can be divided into modules for data parsing, local storage, and integration/upload [92]. In practice, the gateway may pull medical examination reports via File Transfer Protocol (FTP) and collect wearable device streams via RESTful Application Programming Interface (API) or socket connection. It then standardizes and caches the raw data (to prevent losses under high concurrency) before uploading them over encrypted channels to a unified backend database [92]. In a smart-home telemedicine study, the gateway ensured that all incoming sensor data (heart rate, glucose readings, imaging reports, etc.) were parsed and reformatted into a common structure before entering the platform [92].

Security and privacy are paramount in this gateway overlay. All ingress and egress must be encrypted (e.g., using Transport Layer Security (TLS) / HTTPS) and authenticated, with strict identity and access controls. Indeed, experts emphasize that telehealth data flows, including vital signs from devices, patient-reported outcomes, and video consultation interactions, require robust encryption and auditability to protect patient confidentiality [90]. Compliance with regulations (HIPAA in the United States, General Data Protection Regulation (GDPR) elsewhere) is mandatory: data in transit and at rest should be protected with strong cryptography and only accessible to authorized users [93]. For example, a telehealth video call may be encrypted end-to-end, and any notes or transcripts sent to the provider's EHR must travel over a secure FHIR (Fast Healthcare Interoperability Resources) API. In fact, modern APIs (HL7 FHIR with OAuth2/OpenID Connect) are designed to interoperate with gateways while enforcing audit logs and encryption [93]. In some designs, the gateway also handles pseudonymization or tokenization of PHI before sending it to third-party analytics (including LLM services), ensuring no raw identifying data leaks out of the protected network.

In this architecture, LLM integration occurs either within the gateway layer or on secure backend services. For example, patient-entered data and video transcripts can be fed (with consent) to an LLM engine via the gateway, and the LLM outputs (e.g., summaries or recommendations) are then written back into the patient's record. Patient-facing LLM tools may use the same gateway pathway: one demonstration ("LLM on FHIR") built a conversational interface that uses GPT-4 to query a patient's FHIR record and provide understandable health information. It showed that an LLM could translate complex lab results and notes into patient-friendly language, which could be delivered through the telehealth portal (while filtering sensitive details). Such applications highlight the need for strict data filtering and on-device inference where possible to protect privacy [93].

In the context of live video visits, AI "scribes" and digital assistants (e.g., ScribeMD) are emerging: they listen to the clinician-patient conversation, run speech-to-text and then LLM summarization, and generate visit notes or checklists. These outputs must traverse the gateway with appropriate encryption and have clinician review before finalizing in the chart. Overall, the telemedicine gateway overlay ensures secure data ingress and egress for all telehealth interactions. It enforces privacy by encrypting all telemetry, using authenticated APIs, and employing data integration standards (e.g., FHIR) to connect LLMs with EHR data. Any video or chat-based integration of LLMs must comply with institutional cybersecurity policies. For instance, token-based access and audit trails can track every LLM query on patient data. By designing the gateway with security-first principles [14], and by following recommended telehealth practices (encryption, multifactor authentication, regular audits [93]), healthcare organizations can overlay LLM capabilities onto existing workflows without compromising data integrity or confidentiality.

It's vital to remember that integrating LLMs into workflows isn't solely a technological task; human factors are equally important. Patients and clinicians need to trust and feel comfortable with AI involvement. Much depends on how the AI's suggestions or drafts are presented in the EHR or telehealth app—this might make a physician find it useful or bothersome. Training and changing management are also crucial. Healthcare workers need to develop AI literacy, understanding the system's strengths and weaknesses so they know when to trust it and when to be cautious. Surveys of medical students show that they are generally receptive to AI technologies, but they also want guidance and training on how to use them appropriately [54].

Deployment should come with clear institutional policies and ethical guidelines that address questions such as: "Who is responsible if the AI makes a mistake?" "How can patients know that AI-generated content is from AI?" These considerations ensure that LLM integration truly improves care and doesn't accidentally undermine patient trust or clinician autonomy.

Integrating LLMs into healthcare workflows, including telemedicine, requires a thoughtful combination of engineering and design. When implemented correctly, LLMs act like invisible assistants in the background—triaging patients, retrieving important data, documenting interactions, and following up—all while human clinicians remain in control and focus on the aspects of care that require their expertise. Early pilots in this area show promising improvements in efficiency and patient satisfaction, but scaling successfully will require robust infrastructure and ongoing oversight. As LLM technology continues to advance, we can expect even deeper integration into routine care. The goal is to have an "AI copilot" present in every consultation, whether in person or on screen, working alongside healthcare providers to deliver safe, effective, and compassionate care.

1.8 CONCLUSION

Large language models are no longer speculative curiosities; they are already reshaping how we read the clinical record, converse with patients, and design decision support tools. In earlier sections, we traced that evolution from single-task chatbots to multi-agent ecosystems that can ingest charts, guidelines, and sensor streams in real time. What, then, should the reader carry forward?

First, we need a broadened view of evidence. The best deployments combine the statistical power of LLMs with the nuanced judgment that clinicians bring from real-world experience. A model that can instantly retrieve every trial of a rare therapy is most valuable when a clinician can weigh that information against the subtle clinical signs present at the bedside. Successful projects focus not only on building bigger models, but also on creating better feedback loops where physicians can correct, annotate, and ultimately help teach the system.

Second, there is a duty to remain vigilant. These models can still hallucinate, inherit hidden biases, and fail at the edge cases that matter most. Establishing guardrails, maintaining audit trails, and assigning sunset dates for outdated model checkpoints must become as routine as hand hygiene. Hospitals that treat AI as a living medical device—version-controlled, monitored, and recalled when necessary—will better protect patients and support responsible innovation.

Third, we are invited to design for trust. Transparency is not just an ethical slogan; it is an essential interface requirement. Clinicians need to understand why a differential diagnosis was ranked first, and patients deserve clear, accessible explanations for every automated note they receive. When a model reveals its reasoning and cites the evidence behind a recommendation, skepticism can turn into informed partnership.

Finally, the future research agenda must treat healthcare as an ongoing dialogue. The next wave of progress will test multimodal models that can reason across images and waveforms, evaluate outcomes over time rather than at a single point, and help reduce disparities in care between resource-rich and resource-poor settings. Such progress will not come from algorithms alone, but from interdisciplinary teams who are willing to share data responsibly, publish failures openly, and keep patients at the center of every conversation.

Medicine remains a human art. The promise of large language models is not to replace that art, but to make it more precise, more equitable, and more humane. If we succeed, the next time a clinician searches for guidance, the answer will arrive in seconds: transparent, evidence-based, and ready for human wisdom to make the final decision.

REFERENCES

1. H. C. Lucas, J. S. Upperman, and J. R. Robinson, "A Systematic Review of Large Language Models and Their Implications in Medical Education," *Medical Education*, 58, 1276-1285, 2024. doi: 10.1111/medu.15402.
2. S. Aydın, M. Karabacak, V. Vlachos, and K. Margetis, "Large Language Models in Patient Education: A Scoping Review of Applications in Medicine," *Frontiers in Medicine*, 11, 1477898, 2024. doi: 10.3389/fmed.2024.1477898.
3. J. B. Longwell *et al.*, "Performance of Large Language Models on Medical Oncology Examination Questions," *JAMA Network Open*, 7, e2417641 2024. doi: 10.1001/jamanetworkopen.2024.17641.
4. D. Van Veen, C. Van Uden, L. Blankemeier, J.-B. Delbrouck *et al.*, "Adapted Large Language Models Can Outperform Medical Experts in Clinical Text Summarization," *Nature Medicine*, 30(4), 1134–1142, 2024.
5. J. Lee, T. Shang, J. Baik *et al.*, "Investigating LLMs in Clinical Triage: Promising Capabilities, Persistent Intersectional Biases," *arXi/v preprint arXiv:2311.16079*, 2023.
6. M. Omar, G. N. Nadkarni, E. Klang, and B. S. Glicksberg, "Large Language Models in Medicine: A Review of Current Clinical Trials Across Healthcare Applications," *PLoS Digital Health*, 3(11), e0000662, 2024.
7. J. Talukdar, T. P. Singh, and B. Barman, "Robotic Process Automation: A Path to Intelligent Healthcare," in *Artificial Intelligence in Healthcare Industry*, Springer, 2023, pp. 159–168. doi: 10.1007/978-981-99-3157-6_9.
8. C. A. Kulikowski, "An Opening Chapter of the First Generation of Artificial Intelligence in Medicine: The First Rutgers AIM Workshop, June 1975," *Yearbook of Medical Informatics*, 24, 188–190, 2015. doi: 10.15265/iy-2015-016.
9. I. Kolyshkina and S. Simoff, "Interpretability of Machine Learning Solutions in Public Healthcare: The CRISP-ML Approach," *Frontiers in Big Data*, 4, 660206, 2021. doi: 10.3389/fdata.2021.660206.
10. G. Štiglic, P. Kocbek, N. Fijačko, M. Žitnik, K. Verbert, and L. Cilar, "Interpretability of Machine Learning-based Prediction Models in Healthcare," *Wiley Interdisciplinary Reviews: Data Mining and Knowledge Discovery*,10, e1379, 2020. doi: 10.1002/widm.1379.
11. O. Agafonov, A. Babić, S. Sousa, and S. Alagaratnam, "Editorial: Trustworthy AI for Healthcare," *Frontiers in Digital Health*, 5, 1427233, 2024. doi: 10.3389/fdgth.2024.1427233.
12. S. A. Alowais *et al.*, "Revolutionizing Healthcare: The Role of Artificial Intelligence in Clinical Practice," *BMC Medical Education*, 23, 524, 2023. doi: 10.1186/s12909-023-04698-z.
13. N. Naik *et al.*, "Legal and Ethical Consideration in Artificial Intelligence in Healthcare: Who Takes Responsibility?" *Frontiers in Surgery*, 9, 862322, 2022. doi: 10.3389/fsurg.2022.862322.

14. S. Xie *et al.*, "Towards Generalist Biomedical AI," *arXiv preprint arXiv:2307.14334*, 2023. Available at: https://arxiv.org/abs/2307.14334
15. B. Dercksen, M. Struys, F. Cnossen, and W. Paans, "Qualitative Development and Content Validation of the 'SPART' Model; A Focused Ethnography Study of Observable Diagnostic and Therapeutic Activities in the Emergency Medical Services Care Process," *BMC Emergency Medicine*, 21, 126, 2021. doi: 10.1186/s12873-021-00526-z.
16. E. McBee *et al.*, "Context and Clinical Reasoning: Understanding the Medical Student Perspective," *Perspectives on Medical Education*, 7, 5, 318–324, 2018. doi: 10.1007/s40037-018-0417-x.
17. M. K. Alam, D. S. A. Alanazi, S. R. F. Alruwaili, and R. A. I. Alderaan, "Assessment of AI Models in Predicting Treatment Outcomes in Orthodontics," *Journal of Pharmacy and Bioallied Sciences*, 16, S852_S858, 2024. doi: 10.4103/jpbs.jpbs_852_23.
18. D. Restrepo *et al.*, "Analyzing Diversity in Healthcare LLM Research: A Scientometric Perspective," 2024. doi: 10.1101/2024.06.18.24309113.
19. Y. Xie, I. Seth, D. J. Hunter-Smith, W. M. Rozen, and M. A. Seifman, "Investigating the Impact of Innovative AI Chatbot on Post-pandemic Medical Education and Clinical Assistance: A Comprehensive Analysis," *Australian and New Zealand Journal of Surgery*, 93, 3365–3371, 2023. doi: 10.1111/ans.18666.
20. R. T. Sutton, D. Pincock, D. C. Baumgart, D. Sadowski, R. N. Fedorak, and K. I. Kroeker, "An Overview of Clinical Decision Support Systems: Benefits, Risks, and Strategies for Success," *NPJ Digital Medicine*, 3, 17, 2020. doi: 10.1038/s41746-020-0221-y.
21. S. Azizi, A. Karthikesalingam *et al.*, "Toward Expert-Level Medical Question Answering With Large Language Models," *Nature Medicine*, 31(3), 943–950, 2025.
22. P. Hager, F. Jungmann, R. Holland et al., "Evaluation and mitigation of the limitations of large language models in clinical decision-making," *Nature Medicine*, 30(9), 2613–2622, 2024.
23. E. Croxford *et al.*, "Automating Evaluation of AI Text Generation in Healthcare With a Large Language Model (LLM)-as-a-Judge," *medRxiv*, 2025. doi: 10.1101/2025.04.22.25326219.
24. K. Swanson, W. Wu, N. L. Bulaong, J. E. Pak, and J. Zou, "The Virtual Lab: AI Agents Design New SARS-CoV-2 Nanobodies with Experimental Validation," *bioRxiv*, 2024. doi: 10.1101/2024.11.11.623004.
25. M. Elgabry and S. D. Johnson, "Cyber-Biological Convergence: A Systematic Review and Future Outlook," *Frontiers in Bioengineering and Biotechnology*, 12, 1456354, 2024. doi: 10.3389/fbioe.2024.1456354.
26. J. R. Kirk, R. E. Wray, P. Lindes, and J. E. Laird, "Improving Knowledge Extraction From LLMs for Task Learning Through Agent Analysis," *Proceedings of the AAAI Conference on Artificial Intelligence*, 38, 17643–17651, 2024. doi: 10.1609/aaai.v38i16.29799.
27. S. Aturd, J. E. Roberts, C. White, and S. Walker, "Dynamic Tensor Reconfiguration in Large Language Models Using Adaptive Contextual Folding," *OSF Preprints*, 2024. doi: 10.31219/osf.io/93srw.

28. B. Bonnechère, "Unlocking the Black Box? A Comprehensive Exploration of Large Language Models in Rehabilitation," *American Journal of Physical Medicine & Rehabilitation*, 103, 563–569, 2024. doi: 10.1097/phm.0000000000002440.
29. A. Lastrucci, E. Giarnieri, E. Carico, and D. Giansanti, "Revolutionizing Cytology and Cytopathology with Natural Language Processing and Chatbot Technologies: A Narrative Review on Current Trends and Future Directions," *Bioengineering*, 11, 1134, 2024. doi: 10.3390/bioengineering11111134.
30. L. Laranjo *et al.*, "Conversational Agents in Healthcare: A Systematic Review," *Journal of the American Medical Informatics Association*, 25(9), 1248–1258, 2018. doi: 10.1093/jamia/ocy072.
31. J. Will, M. Gupta, J. Zaretsky, A. Dowlath, P. Testa, and J. Feldman, "Leveraging Large Language Models to Improve Readability of Online Patient Education Materials: Cross-Sectional Study," *JMIR Preprints*, 2024. doi: 10.2196/preprints.69955.
32. C. Preiksaitis *et al.*, "The Role of Large Language Models in Transforming Emergency Medicine: Scoping Review," *JMIR Medical Informatics*, 12, e53787, 2024. doi: 10.2196/53787.
33. N. Kalischek, R. C. Daudt, T. Peters, R. Furrer, J. D. Wegner, and K. Schindler, "BiasBed - Rigorous Texture Bias Evaluation," *Proceedings of the IEEE/CVF Conference on Computer Vision and Pattern Recognition (CVPR)*, 20630–20640, 2023. doi: 10.1109/cvpr52729.2023.02128.
34. M. Ayaz and M. Numan, "Unveiling Cultural Narratives: A Qualitative Inquiry Into Cultural Representation in Language Education Under Pakistan's Single National Curriculum," *International Journal of Research and Innovation in Social Science*, 8, 67–74, 2024. doi: 10.47772/ijriss.2024.804011.
35. E. Rama, S. Ekhtiari, G. Thevendran, J. Green, K. Weber, and V. Khanduja, "Overcoming the Barriers to Diversity in Orthopaedic Surgery," *The Journal of Bone and Joint Surgery (American)*, 105, 2093–2100, 2023. doi: 10.2106/jbjs.23.00238.
36. X. Li *et al.*, "Agent Hospital: A Large Language Model-Driven Agent Environment for Medical Problem Solving," *arXiv preprint arXiv:2405.02957*, 2024. Available at: https://arxiv.org/abs/2405.02957
37. A. K. D. Dhanvijay, M. J. Pinjar, N. Dhokane, S. R. Sorte, A. Kumari, and H. Mondal, "Performance of Large Language Models (ChatGPT, Bing Search, and Google Bard) in Solving Case Vignettes in Physiology," *Cureus*, 15, e42972, 2023. doi: 10.7759/cureus.42972.
38. M. A. Quttainah, V. Mishra, S. Madakam, Y. Lurie, and S. Mark, "Cost, Usability, Credibility, Fairness, Accountability, Transparency, and Explainability Framework for Safe and Effective Large Language Models in Medical Education: Narrative Review and Qualitative Study," *JMIR AI*, 2, e51834, 2024. doi: 10.2196/51834.
39. P. Saowaprut, R. S. Wabina, J. Yang, and L. Siriwat, "Evaluation of Large Language Models in Thailand's National Medical Licensing Examination," *medRxiv*, 2024. doi: 10.1101/2024.12.20.24319441.

40. S. K. Biri, S. Kumar, M. Panigrahi, S. Mondal, J. K. Behera, and H. Mondal, "Assessing the Utilization of Large Language Models in Medical Education: Insights From Undergraduate Medical Students," *Cureus*, 15, e47468, 2023. doi: 10.7759/cureus.47468.
41. A. M. Alkalbani *et al.*, "A Systematic Review of Large Language Models in Medical Specialties: Applications, Challenges and Future Directions," *Research Square*, 2024. doi: 10.21203/rs.3.rs-5128451/v1.
42. F. Aljindan *et al.*, "ChatGPT Conquers the Saudi Medical Licensing Exam: Exploring the Accuracy of Artificial Intelligence in Medical Knowledge Assessment and Implications for Modern Medical Education," *Cureus*, 15, e45043, 2023. doi: 10.7759/cureus.45043.
43. C. W. Safranek, A. E. Sidamon-Eristoff, A. Gilson, and D. Chartash, "The Role of Large Language Models in Medical Education: Applications and Implications," *JMIR Preprints*, 2023. doi: 10.2196/preprints.50945.
44. R. Shusterman, A. C. Waters, S. O'Neill, P. Luu, and D. M. Tucker, "An Active Inference Strategy for Prompting Reliable Responses From Large Language Models in Medical Practice," *Research Square*, 2024. doi: 10.21203/rs.3.rs-5079480/v1.
45. M. Sallam, "ChatGPT Utility in Healthcare Education, Research, and Practice: Systematic Review on the Promising Perspectives and Valid Concerns," *Healthcare*, 11, 887, 2023. doi: 10.3390/healthcare11060887.
46. N. Oh, G. Choi, and W. Y. Lee, "ChatGPT Goes to the Operating Room: Evaluating GPT-4 Performance and Its Potential in Surgical Education and Training in the Era of Large Language Models," *Annals of Surgical Treatment and Research*, 104, 269-276, 2023. doi: 10.4174/astr.2023.104.5.269.
47. D. Brin *et al.*, "Comparing ChatGPT and GPT-4 Performance in USMLE Soft Skill Assessments," *Scientific Reports*, 13, 20123, 2023. doi: 10.1038/s41598-023-43436-9.
48. Y. Artsi, V. Sorin, E. Konen, B. S. Glicksberg, G. N. Nadkarni, and E. Klang, "Large Language Models for Generating Medical Examinations: Systematic Review," *medRxiv*, 2024. doi: 10.1101/2024.01.06.24300920.
49. M. C. Schubert, W. Wick, and V. Venkataramani, "Performance of Large Language Models on a Neurology Board–Style Examination," *JAMA Network Open*, 6, e2346721, 2023. doi: 10.1001/jamanetworkopen.2023.46721.
50. T. H. Kung *et al.*, "Performance of ChatGPT on USMLE: Potential for AI-assisted medical education using large language models," *PLOS Digital Health*, 2(2), e0000198, 2023.
51. S. Zeng *et al.*, "Artificial Intelligence-Generated Patient Education Materials for *Helicobacter pylori* Infection: A Comparative Analysis," *Helicobacter*, 29, e13115, 2024. doi: 10.1111/hel.13115.
52. C. Boscardin, B. C. Gin, P. B. Golde, and K. E. Hauer, "ChatGPT and Generative Artificial Intelligence for Medical Education: Potential Impact and Opportunity," *Academic Medicine*, 98, 840–844, 2023. doi: 10.1097/acm.0000000000005439.
53. L. M. Amugongo, P. Mascheroni, S. G. Brooks, S. Doering, and J. Seidel, "Retrieval Augmented Generation for Large Language Models in Healthcare: A Systematic Review," *Preprints*, 2024. doi: 10.20944/preprints202407.0876.v1.

54. M. Teng *et al.*, "Health Care Students' Perspectives on Artificial Intelligence: Countrywide Survey in Canada," *JMIR Medical Education*, 8, e33390, 2022. doi: 10.2196/33390.
55. N. Luckner, P. Purgathofer, and G. Fitzpatrick, "Involving Students in the Co-Creation of a Complex, Evolving Learning Environment," *Interaction Design and Architecture(s)*, 42, 42–63, 2019. doi: 10.55612/s-5002-042-004.
56. E. T. Johnson, J. K. Bande, and J. Thomas, "Retrieval Augmented Medical Diagnosis System," *Biology Methods and Protocols*, 10, bpaf017, 2025. doi: 10.1093/biomethods/bpaf017.
57. H. Scott, "Theoretically Rich Design Thinking: Blended Approaches for Educational Technology Workshops," *International Journal of Management and Applied Research*, 10, 174–187, 2023. doi: 10.18646/2056.102.23-023.
58. H. S. Mahalegi, A. Farhadi, G. Balogh, and E. Nagy, "Application of Generative AI in Resource Optimization in Healthcare Systems," in *Application of Generative AI in Healthcare Systems*, Springer Nature Switzerland, 2025, pp. 175–200. doi: 10.1007/978-3-031-82963-5_7.
59. H. Murad and I. K. Ajlan, "Implementation of Problem Based Learning (PBL) in Digital Era in Higher Education of Iraq," *International Journal of Information Technology and Computer Engineering*, 3, 12–17, 2023. doi: 10.55529/ijitc.35.1.12.
60. P. Deeksheetha, S. Sakthi, and N. Kareem, "Knowledge, Attitude and Practice of Biomedical Waste Management Among Undergraduate Dental Students of a Private Dental Institution in Chennai," *International Journal of Research in Pharmaceutical Sciences*, 11, 3007–3011, 2020. doi: 10.26452/ijrps.v11ispl3.3007.
61. M. T. Story, "One Needle Is Better Than Two: The Philosophy Surrounding Use of Local Anesthesia in Northern India," *Journal of Pain & Palliative Care Pharmacotherapy*, 31, 137–139, 2017. doi: 10.1080/15360288.2017.1298687.
62. M. Muzzammil, M. S. Minhas, S. A. A. R. Ali, R. Jooma, M. O. Minhas, and S. Jabbar, "Primary Trauma Care Course: Alternative Basic Trauma Course in Developing Countries. 'The Need of the Hour,'" *International Journal of Clinical Practice*, 75, e14327, 2021. doi: 10.1111/ijcp.14327.
63. A. Bibye, "Untitled," *European Journal of Biology and Medical Science Research*, 10, 22-26, 2022. doi: 10.37745/ejbmsr.2013/vol10n4.
64. A. Olaifa, R. D. Govender, and A. Ross, "Knowledge, Attitudes and Practices of Healthcare Workers About Healthcare Waste Management at a District Hospital in KwaZulu-Natal," *South African Family Practice*, 60, 137-143, 2018. doi: 10.1080/20786190.2018.1432137.
65. S. Ray, A. N. Sarker, N. Chatterjee, K. Bhowmik, and S. Dey, "Leveraging Large Language Models for Clinical Trial Eligibility Criteria Classification," *Digital*, 5(12), 2025.
66. J. Beattie *et al.*, "Utilizing Large Language Models for Enhanced Clinical Trial Matching: A Study on Automation in Patient Screening," *Cureus*, 16, e60044, 2024. doi: 10.7759/cureus.60044.
67. T. Kojima, S. Gu, M. Reid, Y. Matsuo, and Y. Iwasawa, "Large Language Models Are Zero-Shot Reasoners," *arXiv preprint arXiv:2205.11916*, 2022. doi: 10.48550/arxiv.2205.11916.

68. T. Yan *et al.*, "Evaluating the Performance of GPT-assisted Identification and Classification of Eating Disorders with Text-Based Chinese Social Media Data." *JMIR Preprints*, 2024. doi: 10.2196/preprints.58054.
69. C. Weng, S. W. Tu, I. Sim, and R. Richesson, "Formal Representation of Eligibility Criteria: A Literature Review," *Journal of Biomedical Informatics*, 43, 825-838, 2010. doi: 10.1016/j.jbi.2009.12.004.
70. A. Chowdhery *et al.*, "PaLM: Scaling Language Modeling With Pathways," *arXiv preprint arXiv:2204.02311*, 2022. doi: 10.48550/arXiv.2204.02311.
71. J. Eckrich *et al.*, "Urology Consultants Versus Large Language Models: Potentials and Hazards for Medical Advice in Urology," *BJU International Compass*, 5, 162-168, 2024. doi: 10.1002/bco2.359.
72. M. Omar *et al.*, "LLM-Guided Pain Management: Examining Socio-Demographic Gaps in Cancer vs Non-Cancer Cases," *medRxiv*, 2025. doi: 10.1101/2025.03.04.25323396.
73. V. Sorin, B. S. Glicksberg, Y. Barash, E. Konen, G. N. Nadkarni, and E. Klang, "Diagnostic Accuracy of GPT Multimodal Analysis on USMLE Questions Including Text and Visuals," *medRxiv*, 2023. doi: 10.1101/2023.10.29.23297733.
74. A. Farhadi and A. Taheri, "Application of GenAI in Synthetic Data Generation in the Healthcare System," in A. Zamanifar and M. Faezipour (Eds.), *Application of Generative AI in Healthcare Systems*, Springer Nature Switzerland, 2025. doi: 10.1007/978-3-031-82963-5_3.
75. R. J. Davis *et al.*, "Evaluating the Effectiveness of Artificial Intelligence–powered Large Language Models Application in Disseminating Appropriate and Readable Health Information in Urology," *The Journal of Urology*, 210, 1154-1160, 2023. doi: 10.1097/ju.0000000000003615.
76. F. Busch, L. Hoffmann, C. Rueger et al., "Current Applications and Challenges in Large Language Models for Patient Care: A Systematic Review," *Communications Medicine*, 4(1), 21, 2024.
77. J. Lee *et al.*, "BioBERT: A Pre-Trained Biomedical Language Representation Model for Biomedical Text Mining," *Bioinformatics*, 36, 1234-1240, 2019. doi: 10.1093/bioinformatics/btz682.
78. S. Chen *et al.*, "Natural Language Processing to Automatically Extract the Presence and Severity of Esophagitis in Notes of Patients Undergoing Radiotherapy," *JCO Clinical Cancer Informatics*, 7, e2300048, 2023. doi: 10.1200/cci.23.00048.
79. T. Zack *et al.*, "Coding Inequity: Assessing GPT-4's Potential for Perpetuating Racial and Gender Biases in Healthcare," *medRxiv*, 2023. doi: 10.1101/2023.07.13.23292577.
80. L. Salmi *et al.*, "A Proof-of-Concept Study for Patient Use of Open Notes With Large Language Models," *JAMIA Open*, 8, ooaf021, 2025. doi: 10.1093/jamiaopen/ooaf021.
81. D. Rubins, A. Wright, T. Alkasab, M. S. Ledbetter, A. Miller, R. Patel, N. Wei, G. Zuccotti, and A. Landman, "Importance of clinical decision support system response time monitoring: a case report," Journal of the American Medical Informatics Association, vol. 26, no. 11, pp. 1375–1378, 2019. doi: 10.1093/jamia/ocz133.

82. S. Reddy *et al.*, "Evaluation Framework to Guide Implementation of AI Systems Into Healthcare Settings," *BMJ Health & Care Informatics*, 28, e100444, 2021. doi: 10.1136/bmjhci-2021-100444.
83. V. Gilvaz, G. P. Abraham, S. Radhakrishnan, and Z. Hasmath, "From Admission to Discharge, How Artificial Intelligence Could Optimize Patient Care: A Brief Review," *American Journal of Hospital Medicine*, 3, 2019. doi: 10.24150/ajhm/2019.016.
84. A. Väänänen, K. Haataja, and P. Toivanen, "Survey to Healthcare Professionals on the Practicality of AI Services for Healthcare," *F1000Research*, 9, Article 23883, 2020. doi: 10.12688/f1000research.23883.1.
85. M. Hoseini, "Patient Experiences With AI in Healthcare Settings," *AI-Tech Journal*, 1, 12-18, 2023. doi: 10.61838/kman.aitech.1.3.3.
86. T.-G. Kennedy-Dixon, M. Gossell-Williams, J. St. E. Hall, and B. Anglin-Brown, "The Prevalence of Major Potential Drug-Drug Interactions at a University Health Centre Pharmacy in Jamaica," *Pharmacy Practice*, 13, 601, 2015. doi: 10.18549/pharmpract.2015.04.601.
87. M. C. N. Setiawati, C. Mutiarawati, U. Chasanah, and L. F. Fauziyyah, "Statins Drug Use and Drug-Drug Interactions," *JIFFK Jurnal Ilmu Farmasi Dan Farmasi Klinik*, 17,51-59, 2021. doi: 10.31942/jiffk.v17i2.4068.
88. R. Vavekanand, P. Karttunen, X. Yue, S. Milani, and H. Li, "Large Language Models in Healthcare Decision Support: A Review," *Preprints.org. Preprint posted online on July 18, 2024*, 2024. doi: 10.20944/preprints202407.1842.v1.
89. A. Abatal and A. Korchi, "Transforming Healthcare Systems With Artificial Intelligence: Revolutionizing Efficiency, Quality, and Patient Care." 2023. doi: 10.21203/rs.3.rs-3175341/v1.
90. Z. Yang *et al.*, "Talk2Care: Facilitating Asynchronous Patient-Provider Communication with Large-Language-Model," *arXiv preprint arXiv:2309.09357*, 2023.
91. J. Gatto, P. Seegmiller, T. Burdick, I. S. Khayal, S. DeLozier, and S. M. Preum, "FollowupQ: Follow-Up Question Generation for Enhanced Patient-Provider Conversations," *arXiv preprint arXiv:2503.17509*, 2025.
92. Y. Bai *et al.*, "Med-Gemini: Towards Multimodal Biomedical Generative Foundation Models." 2024. Available at: https://arxiv.org/abs/2503.17509
93. K. Wang *et al.*, "Evaluation of Large Language Models for Trustworthy and Safe Healthcare." 2024. Available at: https://arxiv.org/abs/2402.01711

Chapter 2

Administrative efficiency: Providing healthcare operations

Alireza Taheri, Amirfarhad Farhadi, Azadeh Zamanifar, and Amirmohammad Mataji

2.1 INTRODUCTION

Exceptional abilities of LLMs in understanding natural language and generating text, hardly distinguishable from human-generated text, present an excellent opportunity to automate tasks traditionally done by the human workforce. Healthcare services are paramount to the well-being and development of every nation. Medical and technological advancements consistently contribute to the progressive enhancement of healthcare outcomes. The advent of computers and electronic devices made monitoring patients, treatment, and care processes easier and more accessible. This increased accessibility to healthcare services globally, simultaneously elevating the demand for quality care. As healthcare access expanded, the complexity of healthcare systems consequently escalated. Moreover, progress in scientific understanding broadens the range of available medical services, including diagnostic capabilities, which contributes to the growing administrative and operational burden within healthcare systems. Tests are more comprehensive, clinicians monitor patients throughout their medical background, and treatments are increasingly personalized. Patients expect to receive quality care by spending more time with physicians who can accurately analyze their medical history, interview them, and diagnose their diseases. This cannot be easily achieved as the number of patients arises faster than the healthcare system can provide adequate resources and personnel to effectively manage them. Based on the study done using the data from the National Center for Health Statistics in the United States, between 1975 and 2010, there has been a growth of 150% in the number of physicians, while the number of administrators has grown by over 3200% [1]. The drastic rise in administrators can be attributed to new regulations such as the Health Information Technology for Economic and Clinical Health Act (HITECH), which strengthens the privacy and security of electronic health record (EHR). A primary set of goals for the HITECH Act included efforts to improve quality, safety, and efficiency in healthcare delivery, engage patients in their care, increase coordination of care among providers, and ultimately improve the health status of the population, all while ensuring

DOI: 10.1201/9781003665083-2

the crucial aspects of privacy and security of health information [2]. The increased volumes of data also led to the utilization of more personnel to process and record them. Although there have been debates regarding the benefits of physicians who are also involved in administrative operations, it is not the best and maybe not feasible as the administrative work pressure can lead to physician burnout and occupy most of their time, which can be allocated for patient care [1]. According to the College of Healthcare Professions, medical administrators are nonclinical healthcare professionals who handle office and clerical duties in medical settings. Unlike clinical medical assistants, who mostly work directly with patients, their responsibilities primarily involve a wider range of administrative tasks [3]. The widespread adoption of EHRs has led to a substantial increase in the time demands placed on clinicians. Healthcare providers are mostly overwhelmed by the volume of administrative tasks, which can lead to burnout and a decrease in patient care quality [4].

The increasing adoption of artificial intelligence (AI) tools and services is transforming various industries, including LLMs for domain adaptation, sentiment analysis, summarization, fraud detection, mobility management, etc. [5–8]. Their utilization by clinicians marks a significant shift in the healthcare industry. McKinsey's 2024 global survey reveals that 31% of healthcare professionals are now regular AI users, almost twice as much as the previous year [9]. This underscores the growing acknowledgment that transformation is necessary for this field to boost productivity. Recent LLMs, like ChatGPT, can understand complex language and generate human-like responses due to training on massive datasets [10]. These models show promise in assisting clinicians with documentation, claim processing, patient education, scheduling appointments, and so much more [4]. Such generative AI technologies are expected to revolutionize various aspects of healthcare [11]. LLMs can significantly assist with various administrative tasks. For example, GPT-4 offers a transformative way to enhance doctor–patient communication, leading to a better understanding of patient needs. It can streamline the documentation of medical histories by asking relevant questions, interpreting responses, and presenting this information to physicians in a structured, concise format.

Additionally, studies have assessed GPT-3.5 and GPT-4's ability to generate accurate International Classification of Diseases (ICD) billing codes from text descriptions, demonstrating their potential to improve the efficient use of billing codes in healthcare [12]. Using LLMs can directly address the significant healthcare worker shortage across the world. The sources highlighted that physicians could spend up to 49% of their time on EHRs and desk work, indicating a substantial administrative burden that AI could potentially alleviate [13]. Traditional approaches to healthcare administrative tasks have utilized medical natural language processing (NLP) through rule-based systems or machine learning. However, a major drawback has been the need for task-specific annotations and lengthy model training. Creating these algorithms is time-consuming and requires significant effort from medical professionals, who often spend weeks or months on detailed manual annotation. Moreover, these human-annotated datasets' scarcity and small scale can result in models that cannot generalize well to new, unseen data [14].

A key area where LLMs boost administrative efficiency is generating clinical letters, medical notes, and EHR entries directly from text-based conversations. This capability significantly streamlines documentation. Studies have shown that models like ChatGPT can accurately create patient medical notes, categorize information, and even self-correct without additional prompts. ChatGPT has also proven effective in producing high-quality clinical letters for various communication needs, improving the precision and efficiency of automated text generation [15]. Additionally, research indicates that ChatGPT can draft surgical records faster than humans, with their quality and adherence to guidelines impressing patients and physicians. More advanced models like GPT-4 enhance this capability, even drafting postsurgical discharge summaries [12].

Acknowledging the significant challenges in deploying LLMs in medical settings is crucial. Key concerns include data security and privacy, particularly the risk of inadvertently exposing sensitive patient information, which demands robust protection mechanisms. There is also the danger of LLMs generating incorrect or misleading information, which is a serious risk to healthcare, where errors can cause substantial harm. Issues of fairness and bias are continual, as models trained on internet data might perpetuate online biases, potentially leading to unfair treatment. Furthermore, transparency, explainability, and trustworthiness challenges make it difficult to verify whether LLM outputs align with social norms and regulations. Addressing these hurdles is vital for the responsible and effective integration of LLMs into healthcare. Figure 2.1 represents the benefits and challenges of utilizing LLM-powered systems to optimize healthcare administrative operations. Table 2.1 shows all abbreviation in this chapter.

2.2 ADMINISTRATIVE TASKS

Administrative operations include a wide variety of responsibilities. Healthcare workers establish a reliable connection between clinicians and patients in addition to clinicians and regulations. They ensure the healthcare system is provided smoothly and patients experience the best possible care. Medical centers should be able to quickly respond to recent regulation updates to ensure that their work complies seamlessly with the latest laws governing healthcare. This broad spectrum of duties, from managing medical records to scheduling appointments, aims to enhance healthcare

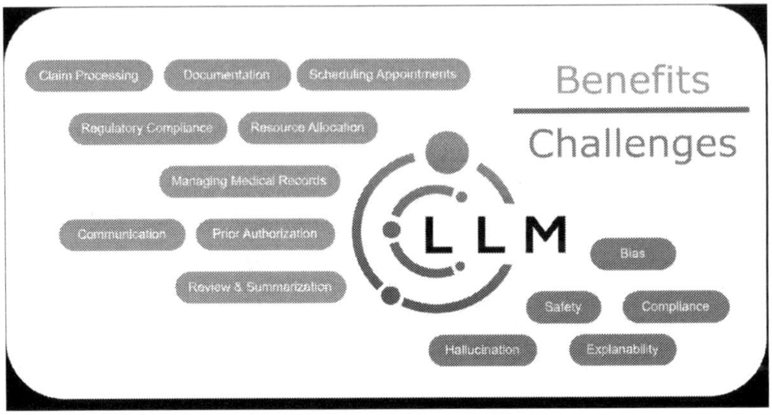

Figure 2.1 Advantages and risks of using LLMs for healthcare administrative efficiency.

Table 2.1 Abbreviations and their definition

Acronym	*Full term*
LLM	Large language model
HITECH	Health Information Technology for Economic and Clinical Health Act
EHR	Electronic health record
AI	Artificial intelligence
ICD	International classification of diseases
NLP	Natural language processing
HIPAA	Health Insurance Portability and Accountability Act
FCA	False Claims Act
GDPR	General Data Protection Regulation
CPT	Current procedural terminology
GLMs	Generative language models
PD	Prompt design
PL	Prompt learning
PT	Prompt tuning
CoT	Chain-of-Thought
RAG	Retrieval-augmented generation
VA	Voice assistant
PEMAT	Patient Education Materials Assessment Tool
ASR	Automated speech recognition
PGHD	Patient-generated health data
SFT	Supervised fine-tuning
PEFT	Parameter efficient fine-tuning
QLoRA	Quantized low-rank adaptation
ICL	In-context learning

delivery. The responsibility set of administrators is mainly determined by the needs of the medical settings. Administrators who work in smaller clinics are usually responsible for a broader range of tasks, and the ones who work for larger hospitals focus on more specialized duties [3]. Therefore, the tasks mentioned here might not be entirely assigned to every medical administrator. Beyond the administrative tasks directly involving LLMs, broader healthcare operations like supply chain management also utilize advanced techniques, such as leveraging blockchain and Adaptive Neuro Fuzzy Inference System (ANFIS), for optimal efficiency [16]. In this section, we will cover different types of administrative operations to get more familiar with the problems that LLMs seek to solve. Table 2.2 provides a summary of key administrative tasks and how LLMs can contribute to their efficiency.

2.2.1 Resource allocation

One of the crucial aspects of providing quality care is the efficient and equitable distribution of resources such as medical supplies and equipment. Hospitals and medical centers often face the challenge of managing a certain amount of resources in the presence of rising patient needs driven by an aging population with growing health issues [17]. This continuous situation makes the problem of resource allocation for healthcare administrators increasingly difficult, especially if they face limited supplies or budgets. Generative AI, for instance, has been explored for its application in optimizing resource allocation within healthcare systems [18]. In this context, the ability to anticipate needs, optimize resource allocation, and improve decision-making processes becomes paramount for healthcare administrators striving to provide quality care amidst rising patient demands and limited resources [9].

2.2.2 Scheduling appointments

A pivotal operation in any medical setting involves facilitating patient access to healthcare providers through efficient appointment scheduling, whether for a preferred physician or the next available specialist. In a busy medical center, scheduling appointments using traditional booking systems can be tedious and time-consuming. Operators must keep track of physicians' work time and occupy time slots to give patients their prioritized appointments. Integrating LLMs into practice management systems can automate routine tasks such as scheduling appointments, sending reminders, and responding to patient inquiries using natural language. By automating assigning patients to the next available slots, staff can be freed up to concentrate on more critical tasks that directly enhance patient care, ultimately optimizing healthcare operations [19]. Figure 2.2 illustrates a sample LLM decision-making process, influenced by various factors originating from patients, physicians, EHRs, and the medical center. It illustrates a conceptual

Table 2.2 Administrative tasks and the possible roles of LLMs

Administrative task	*How LLMs help*
Resource Allocation	Assist in the efficient and equitable distribution of resources by integrating health worker knowledge and translating preferences into models Can help anticipate needs, optimize allocation, and improve decision-making processes
Scheduling Appointments	Automate routine tasks like scheduling, sending reminders, and responding to patient inquiries using natural language Frees up staff time for more critical tasks
Managing Medical Records	Automatically identify contradictions or inconsistencies, alert clinicians to incomplete plans, or highlight important test results Helps ensure patient data is accurate and current, enhancing quality of care
Regulatory Compliance	Proactively maintain legal compliance, especially regarding patient consent and privacy Automatically scrutinize medical record development and alteration to detect and flag potential compliance issues Reduces the burden of manual oversight
Claims Processing	Simplify coding and billing by automatically pulling details, generating codes, confirming insurance eligibility, and ensuring paperwork submission Alleviates administrative burden, speeds reimbursement, and decreases mistakes
Review and Summarization	Automatically or semi-automatically produce high-quality summaries of extensive textual data such as EHRs, diagnostic reports, and patient histories Potential to outperform medical experts in completeness, conciseness, and fewer errors Reduces manual workload and frees time for patient care
Documentation	Automate tasks like transcribing patient notes, updating records, and filling forms Transcribe and structure patient interactions in real-time, generate summaries, update EHRs with structured data Can accurately categorize disorganized information and even self-correct Can draft surgical records and discharge summaries faster than humans
Communication	Make prescreening more efficient by automatically collecting information and providing guidance Make health information easier for patients to understand by translating complex language and providing personalized education Reduces administrative questions due to patient confusion Can use technical language for clinicians and understandable language for patients Aid in conversation summarization
Prior Authorization	Automate compiling necessary information from patient records Insurance companies can automate document review to pinpoint decision-relevant information and determine coverage, and decrease manual review time

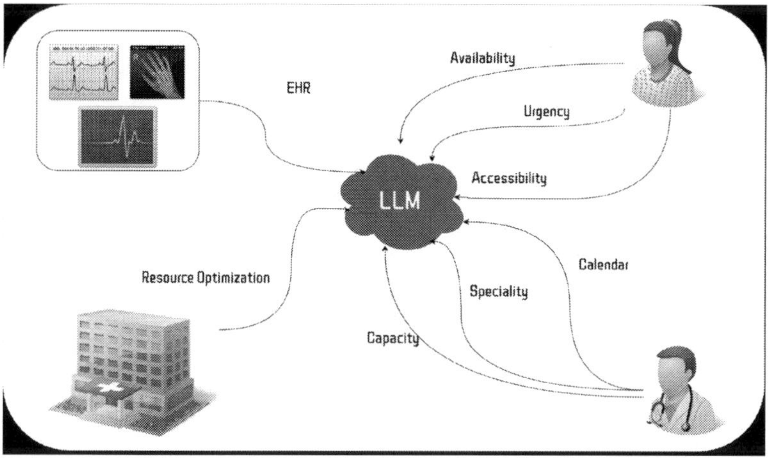

Figure 2.2 LLM-based appointment scheduling and influencing factors in their decision-making.

framework for an LLM-driven appointment scheduling system, highlighting the myriad factors that influence its decision-making process. At the core is the LLM, acting as the intelligent orchestrator. The LLM processes critical data from several sources: it pulls patient information and historical data from the EHR, which can include relevant diagnostic images or test results. Simultaneously, it integrates data concerning resource optimization and overall capacity from the medical facility itself, ensuring efficient utilization of clinical spaces and equipment. From the patient's perspective, factors such as their availability, the urgency of their medical need, and their desired accessibility to care directly inform the LLM. Concurrently, the system considers the physician's calendar and their specific specialty, ensuring appropriate matching. By synthesizing these diverse inputs, the LLM is designed to optimize the scheduling process, leading to efficient and patient-centered appointment allocation.

2.2.3 Managing medical records

Medical records consist of information regarding patients' physical or mental health backgrounds, which helps the continuity of care as different healthcare providers use them. Medical records can be used for future treatments, clinical research, and managerial decision-making. EHRs can enhance patient care by improving the accuracy and clarity of medical records, thereby reducing medical errors and making health information readily available to inform patients, decrease test duplication, and expedite treatment. However, EHR has been recognized as a key factor in administrative burnout and burden [20]. LLMs can manage medical records by automatically identifying potential contradictions or inconsistencies, alerting clinicians to incomplete follow-up plans, or highlighting important test results requiring action. This functionality helps ensure patient data is accurate and current, ultimately enhancing the quality of care and minimizing errors [4].

2.2.4 Regulatory compliance

Healthcare regulatory compliance means following the local and general laws that aim to prevent fraud and misuse in the healthcare system and ensure its integrity. It requires active participation from healthcare providers and administrators. Not following compliance regulations can lead to legal actions, harm to patients, and damage to the reputation of healthcare organizations. Two well-known examples of these laws are the Health Insurance Portability and Accountability Act (HIPAA) and the False Claims Act (FCA) [21]. LLMs offer a proactive solution for healthcare institutions to maintain legal compliance, particularly concerning patient consent and privacy regulations. By automatically scrutinizing the development and alteration of medical records, these models can detect and flag potential compliance issues, enabling providers to remain aligned with regulations. This early identification of risks minimizes the chances of legal liabilities and reduces the burden of manual compliance oversight [19].

2.2.5 Claims processing

The medical payment cycle starts with medical coding and continues to medical billing and claim processing. Medical coding translates medical services into standardized codes such as the ICD or current procedural terminology (CPT). These codes are then used to form claims by medical billers to submit and follow up on claims with payers (insurance and the patient) to receive payment. LLMs can simplify complex coding and billing processes by automatically pulling key details from patient records and claims, generating appropriate billing codes, confirming insurance eligibility, and ensuring all required paperwork is submitted. This automation alleviates the administrative burden for billing departments, speeds up the reimbursement cycle, and decreases mistakes in insurance submissions. Integrating LLMs with digital platforms and centralized databases can further boost operational efficiency and minimize inconsistencies [19].

2.2.6 Review and summarization

Healthcare professionals, such as clinicians, dedicate much of their time to summarizing extensive textual data within EHRs for tasks like diagnostic reports, progress notes, and synthesizing patient histories across specialists.

The documentation burden has increased with EHR adoption, is error-prone even for experienced physicians, and critically detracts from direct patient care. Studies suggest physicians spend up to two hours on documentation for every hour with patients, which can consume up to 60% of nurses' time, contributing to stress. This substantial workload negatively impacts administrative efficiency by consuming valuable clinician time, potentially leading to burnout, decreased job satisfaction, and, ultimately, poorer patient outcomes [22]. LLMs hold the potential to automatically or semi-automatically produce high-quality summaries by leveraging their information retrieval, nuanced comprehension, and text generation abilities.

2.2.7 Documentation

LLMs can automate or streamline tasks such as transcribing patient notes, updating medical records, and filling out forms. They can transcribe and structure patient interactions in real time, generate summaries of diagnoses, and update EHRs using structured data. This process reduces healthcare providers' time on administrative tasks, saving valuable time and minimizing errors associated with manual data entry [19]. ChatGPT has shown potential in aiding the creation of medical notes. When presented with disorganized patient information, it could accurately categorize most parameters into a structured format, even understanding abbreviations without explicit definitions. Notably, it demonstrated the ability to learn from errors and correctly recategorize parameters when prompted. This capability is highly pertinent to improving administrative efficiency in healthcare documentation, potentially automating or significantly speeding up the process of drafting and structuring clinical notes, thereby lessening the administrative workload for clinicians [23]. Leveraging LLMs for medical dialogue summarization offers a promising solution to enhance administrative efficiency in healthcare, especially with the growing demands of telemedicine. A study [24] comparing ChatGPT with fine-tuned models like BERTSUM and BART on medical dialogues revealed a discrepancy between automated and human evaluations. While automated metrics (ROUGE, BERTScore) favored BART, human medical experts consistently preferred ChatGPT's summaries due to their coherence, usefulness, readability, and comprehensive inclusion of key results, often inferring accurate, contextually relevant advice not explicitly stated in the original dialogue. This indicates that automated metrics may not fully capture the practical value of LLM outputs. The study also highlighted that well-designed prompts significantly boost ChatGPT's summarization performance. Despite minor issues like occasional lengthiness, ChatGPT's ability to generate preferred and advantageous summaries, even surpassing human experts in some aspects, suggests its strong potential to alleviate administrative burdens on healthcare professionals by automating tasks like discharge summary generation, freeing up time for patient care and training.

2.2.8 Communication

LLMs can make the prescreening process more efficient by automatically collecting required patient information and providing them with necessary guidance before their appointments [4]. These models can also make health information easier for patients to understand by translating complex medical language and providing personalized education. This improved comprehension can lead to fewer administrative questions and follow-ups due to patient confusion. Patients can learn about their health conditions, treatments, and self-management through LLMs, freeing clinicians' time typically spent on basic explanations. It is vital to emphasize that LLMs should only be used for patient education, not as a source of clinical advice. Their training relies on curated medical datasets to ensure accuracy [4]. A significant advantage of LLMs such as ChatGPT is its ability to summarize. They could use technical language to communicate with clinicians and translate this information into easily understandable language for patients and their families. Efficiently summarizing complex medical information is an administrative task that aids in generating reports, creating patient communication materials, and quickly reviewing patient history, thereby contributing to overall efficiency [23].

Transferring patients from acute care to outpatient settings is a complex process, with patient education being a key component for a smooth transition. However, clinical notes and discharge summaries often contain technical jargon and abbreviations, making them hard for patients and their caregivers to understand. This lack of clarity can delay recommended care or follow-ups and has been linked to adverse outcomes like readmissions. Improving the readability of this information is a significant operational challenge that directly impacts patient engagement and the success of care transitions. The process of simplifying complex medical notes for enhanced patient comprehension is illustrated in Figure 2.3. This process begins with a prompt input that explicitly instructs the LLM to adapt the document's complexity, specifically targeting a sixth-grade reading level to ensure optimal readability for a broad audience. The LLM itself leverages its foundational training on massive general datasets, providing a broad understanding of language and context. Crucially, it has been fine-tuned on specialized medical datasets, allowing it to accurately interpret clinical terminology and nuances while transforming them into easily understandable language without losing critical information.

2.2.9 Prior authorization

Before a healthcare service or medication is covered, prior authorization requires a medical provider to get approval from the patient's health insurer. LLMs offer a solution to the challenging prior authorization process by automatically compiling necessary information from patient records

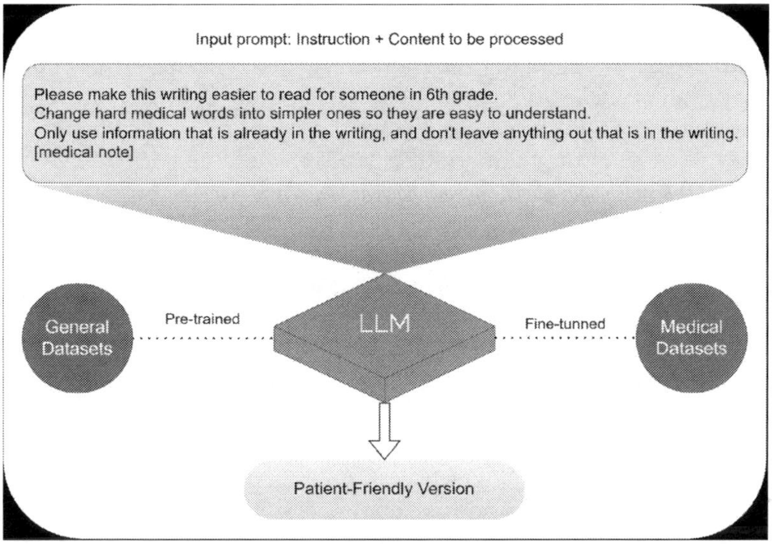

Figure 2.3 Medical note simplification process for enhanced readability.

for complete submissions. Simultaneously, insurance companies can use LLMs to automate their document review, pinpointing decision-relevant information. This analysis of medical records, insurance policies, and other data allows LLMs to determine coverage, significantly decreasing manual review time and alleviating administrative burdens and delays [4].

2.3 PROMPT ENGINEERING

Effectively using LLMs in healthcare operations relies heavily on how instructions are given to them. This is particularly important because medical language is very specific and specialized. Prompt engineering is a structured way of communicating with these models to get the desired results. It essentially programs LLMs through prompts to make them more efficient for specific goals. When prompts are designed well, they lead to good responses, but poorly made prompts result in unsatisfactory outputs. Prompt engineering includes various methods, broadly categorized into prompt design (PD), prompt learning (PL), and prompt tuning (PT) [25]. PD involves creating text prompts manually to guide the LLM's output without changing the model's core settings. Techniques within PD include zero-shot prompting, where an LLM is asked a question without any examples. For instance, an LLM might be asked to "Generate a draft patient discharge summary for a patient with congestive heart failure." One-shot prompting provides a single example within the prompt, while Few-shot prompting gives a small number of examples to guide the LLM. An example would be asking an LLM to "Summarize this patient's progress notes into a SOAP format. Here is an example of a good SOAP note: [example SOAP note]." This can sometimes work better than zero-shot prompting, though its effectiveness varies. Prompts can also be structured into increasing levels of complexity [26]. A simple query like "Summarize the patient's vitals from today" is a Level 1 prompt. Level 2 adds context or assigns a role, such as "You are a seasoned medical coder. Generate the correct ICD-10 codes for this diagnostic report." Level 3 builds on Level 2 by providing examples. Level 4 encourages the LLM to break down the request into steps, like "Think step by step," which improves accuracy for complex tasks such as generating a patient care plan. Iterative prompts involve a collaboration between the user and the LLM to refine the prompt through continuous feedback, clarifying questions, and revised prompts. Chain-of-Thought (CoT) prompting asks the LLM to show its reasoning steps before giving the final answer, which greatly improves complex reasoning. Self-consistency is a more advanced CoT method that further improves performance by using multiple CoT prompts and selecting the most frequent answer [25]. Prompt refinement involves using the LLM to rephrase or translate the prompt itself. Retrieval-augmented generation (RAG) combines an information retrieval component with the LLM. This means relevant information from external sources, such as medical databases, is given to the system along with the prompt, which improves accuracy and reduces incorrect information or hallucinations. PL and PT differ from PD because they involve training only a small part of the LLM's parameters related to the prompt, while keeping the main LLM weights unchanged. These techniques are more computationally efficient than traditional fine-tuning, especially when there is limited training data. PL often adapts masked language model objectives for specific tasks. PT optimizes soft prompts, which are continuous vector representations learned during training. PT is a strong alternative to traditional fine-tuning, requiring significantly fewer parameters to train [25]. Mixed Prompts, which combine manually crafted prompts and trainable prompts, consistently perform better than each type of prompt alone. Applying these prompt engineering techniques in healthcare operations significantly boosts administrative efficiency. They enable LLMs to perform various medical NLP tasks, including medical text classification, named entity recognition, relation extraction, text generation, medical question answering, and summarization. For example, LLMs can efficiently summarize patient histories or create frequently asked questions [26] about hospital procedures, which greatly streamline administrative processes and reduces the workload on healthcare professionals.

2.4 CASE STUDIES

This section delves into specific applications and studies that showcase the practical benefits and outcomes of integrating LLMs into healthcare administration. These examples provide concrete evidence of how LLMs are being used to streamline healthcare operations and potentially reduce administrative burdens. Table 2.3 summarizes several key case studies and applications that demonstrate the practical benefits and outcomes of implementing LLM-powered systems in healthcare administration.

2.4.1 Cardiac discharge note generation

Jung et al. present a method for automating discharge note creation in cardiology using real-world patient progress notes. It employs fine-tuned LLMs for directly addressing manual documentation's administrative inefficiency by demonstrating promising results in generating accurate, complete, and clinically useful notes. These documents ensure quality patient care, seamless continuity, and effective communication among healthcare providers. However, the manual creation process is time-consuming and often leads to inconsistencies and errors, significantly adding to the administrative burden on healthcare professionals. A key innovation in this study is its direct generation of comprehensive discharge records using LLMs, which differs from previous methods that extracted and abstracted key sentences. These models were specifically developed or adapted for cardiac medical terminology and document writing, trained on a large dataset from a real hospital's cardiology department. The study utilized a dataset of 4,588 unique, de-identified patient records, with ethical approval secured and informed consent waived. Progress notes were used for the model's input, detailing patient treatment and sections like RECORD DATE and PROBLEM LIST. The corresponding Discharge Notes, featuring elements such as CHIEF COMPLAINT and HOSPITAL COURSE, served as the target data for training. The researchers employed various pretrained LLMs, including TinyLlama-1.1B, Llama2-7B, Mistral-7B, BioMistral-7B, Meditron-7B, and SOLAR-10.7B. Their core technique for adapting these models was supervised fine-tuning (SFT). It uses labeled discharge notes to train models to generate medically accurate and coherent notes from patient progress notes. To manage the high computational demands of LLMs, they implemented parameter efficient fine-tuning(PEFT), specifically quantized low-rank adaptation (QLoRA), allowing for efficient fine-tuning with fewer parameters, making it feasible even in resource-limited environments. The study's findings highlight the substantial potential of fine-tuned LLMs, especially Mistral-7B, to automate discharge note generation, thereby directly reducing healthcare professionals' administrative workload and potentially freeing up more time for patient care. This represents a crucial advancement

Table 2.3 The investigated case studies along with their approach and outcomes

Application & study focus	*Tasks addressed*	*Approach used*	*Reported outcome*
Cardiac Discharge Note Generation	Documentation, Note Generation	Fine-tuned LLMs	Generates accurate, complete, clinically useful notes, reduces administrative workload.
HEAL	Documentation, Medical Scribing	Domain-specific pretraining on conversations and EHR	Instant, accurate notes surpass human scribes.
Talk2Care	Communication, Information Gathering, Summary	LLM-powered voice assistant & dashboard, Modular reasoning pipeline	Automates data collection from older adults, reducing provider burden and summarizing conversations into concise notes, significantly saving provider time and effort.
Patient-Friendly Discharge Summaries	Communication, Documentation Readability	GPT-4 via Azure OpenAI, Iterative Prompt Engineering	Transforms summaries to significantly more readable and understandable formats.
Structured Data Extraction from Notes	Managing Medical Records and Review & Analysis	Prompt Engineering for JSON output	Outperforms traditional NLP methods; eliminates manual data cleaning.
Clinical Text Summarization	Review & Summarization, Documentation	Various LLMs, ICL, and QLoRA	GPT-4 with ICL on par with medical experts; eases documentation burden.
Polaris	Communication, Workflow Augmentation	Multi-agent LLM constellation architecture	Performs routine, nondiagnostic patient interaction safely and accurately, on par with human nurses for education and conversation quality.
MindfulDiary	Clinical Information Exchange, Monitoring	LLMs in mobile app & web dashboard for summarization and classification	Streamlines PGHD collection, provides structured data, and pre-analyzed insights to clinicians.

(*Continued*)

Table 2.3 (Continued)

Application & study focus	*Tasks addressed*	*Approach used*	*Reported outcome*
Medical Coding (Retrieve-Rank)	Claims Processing, Coding	ColBERT-V2 Retriever + GPT-3.5-turbo Reranker	100% accuracy on single-term conditions, significantly reduces workload, minimizes errors, and enhances quality.
Medical Coding (Prompt Framework)	Claims Processing, Coding	GPT-4o (Azure OpenAI) + smaller open-source LLMs, ICL	Achieved high accuracy and Clinical Trial Coding.
FactsR	Documentation, Note Generation	Modular, LLM-based reasoning pipeline, Real-time processing, Clinician-in-the-loop design	Improves completeness and conciseness of notes, significantly reduces post hoc editing.
PRIORITY2REWARD	Resource Allocation	LLMs to translate natural language preferences into reward functions	Dynamically tailors automated decisions, boosts administrative efficiency, and enhances transparency.
Healthcare Copilot	Documentation, Record Management, and Review	LLM-driven processing component, history memory feature, doctor module	Automates consultation summarization and report generation, manages historical info, and provides structured review and correction.

in healthcare documentation practices. A significant challenge is the lack of standardization in input progress notes, as inconsistencies in formatting and terminology across different physicians can hinder model training and performance.

2.4.2 HEAL

HEAL [27] can automate and improve the process of generating medical documentation, specifically patient notes from conversations. Generating medical notes from conversations is a significant challenge for humans and machines, often involving transcription errors and complex spoken language. Traditionally, this demands substantial time and effort from physicians or human scribes, and even existing medical LLMs or fine-tuned models often fall short, producing incomplete notes or requiring human oversight. This inefficiency in documentation presents a prime opportunity to streamline administrative processes. HEAL is a 13B LLaMA2-based LLM designed for automated medical scribing from doctor–patient conversations. HEAL aims to instantly generate medical notes without human intervention, representing a revolutionary advancement in healthcare NLP. Compared to human scribes, its ability to produce notes almost instantly offers significant time and effort savings. This drastic reduction in documentation time allows healthcare professionals to reallocate time to patient care or other critical tasks, substantially increasing operational efficiency. Beyond just speed, HEAL also enhances note quality. It surpasses human scribes and other comparable models' correctness and completeness, especially in minimizing missed information. It can generate more accurate and complete notes automatically that reduce the time physicians spend reviewing, editing, and adding missing details. HEAL's proficiency stems from its training on diverse medical datasets, including real-world doctor–patient conversations and EHR data. This domain-specific pretraining enables it to better understand the nuances of medical dialogue, producing more accurate and clinically relevant notes than general LLMs. This capability reduces the cognitive load and review time for providers. Notably, HEAL achieves parity with GPT-4 in medical note generation and excels in completeness, outperforming Med-PaLM 2 and other publicly available models of its size, demonstrating its effectiveness as a tool for automating this crucial administrative task. This unique approach, including proprietary instruction data with explanations, significantly improved the model's medical reasoning, vital for high-quality documentation. This highlights why domain-adapted LLMs are essential for specific healthcare administrative tasks.

2.4.3 Talk2Care

The central idea of this system [28] is to harness LLMs' conversational and summarization strengths to simplify communication between patients and providers, especially for older adults receiving home-based care. Healthcare providers are often overwhelmed, finding traditional methods like home visits and phone calls impractical due to the heavy workload. Existing telehealth tools often lack the adaptability and user-friendliness needed, pushing many older adults and providers back to less efficient communication. Providers also contend with unclear patient messages in digital portals and the extra effort required when communicating with older adults with limited health literacy. Talk2Care tackles administrative inefficiencies through two main components: an LLM-powered voice assistant (VA) for older adults and an LLM-based dashboard for healthcare providers. The VA enables natural conversations with older adults at home, gathering detailed health information asynchronously through multi-turn, personalized interactions. This automated data collection reduces the burden on providers, freeing them from inefficient phone calls or processing vague messages, and older adults highly rated its ability to ask clear, understandable questions. The provider dashboard then summarizes these conversations, presenting key health information in a concise clinical note structure via a conversation summary module, highlighting critical details with color-coding in an information highlight module, and suggesting health risk levels through a risk prediction module to aid in task prioritization. User studies demonstrated Talk2Care's potential to significantly save provider time and effort, exhibiting high usability and reducing mental and physical demands while boosting performance. Providers noted that the system was beneficial in offloading their work, with many citing time savings on phone calls and potentially reducing unnecessary in-person visits. More than half of providers found the LLM-powered dashboard aided in triage and task prioritization, boosting efficiency. The summary and highlights features helped organize documentation and speed up review processes. Providers also appreciated that the summaries and conversation logs offered more detailed information than traditional patient portal messages, helping them quickly identify key issues and prepare for future visits, streamlining communication and reducing back-and-forth interactions. The AI-powered VA also eased providers' mental load by acting as an intermediate communication layer. Talk2Care does not have access to EHR and, therefore, cannot provide specific medical advice. In the future, such a system can access the required healthcare data to further enhance processes by analyzing and suggesting primary treatments as a third module, enabling smoother workflows, personalized conversations with access to patient history, and seamless health information updates. In essence, Talk2Care demonstrates how LLMs can significantly enhance administrative efficiency in healthcare operations by automating information gathering and summarizing, offloading routine tasks, facilitating task prioritization, speeding up documentation, and improving communication quality, ultimately saving healthcare professionals time and effort.

2.4.4 ChatGPT

As one of the early and highly influential LLMs, ChatGPT has been extensively utilized and evaluated in numerous studies. GPT-4 holds the potential to transform complex medical notes into a format and language that's easily understandable by patients. Zaretsky et al. [29] investigated whether an LLM could enhance the readability and comprehension of discharge summaries. This involved processing discharge summaries through the Microsoft Azure OpenAI platform, which is secure and HIPAA-compliant and generates patient-friendly versions. The process began by selecting a sample of discharge summaries. Next, a patient family council was consulted to define "patient-friendly" attributes for these summaries. Following this, a multi-week, iterative prompt engineering process was undertaken, involving several physician team members. Finally, the preprocessed summaries were fed into the LLM. Results showed that GPT-4 successfully transformed discharge summaries into a significantly more readable and understandable format for patients. They demonstrated that their patient-friendly discharge summaries consistently achieved a sixth- or seventh-grade reading level, aligning with conventional readability standards. This is a significant improvement over original discharge summaries, which were typically ranked around an eleventh-grade reading level.

Furthermore, using the Patient Education Materials Assessment Tool (PEMAT) instrument, they found these patient-friendly summaries to be highly understandable, which was another improvement compared to their original counterparts. Also, the generated summaries had fewer words overall, which improves accessibility and further improves readability. Despite achieving better readability and understandability, the study revealed significant operational hurdles for LLMs in generating patient-friendly summaries, particularly concerning accuracy, completeness, and safety. Many summaries still contain omissions, inaccuracies, and even hallucinations, with potential safety implications, necessitating robust physician review as a critical safeguard during initial implementation. This highlights a crucial trade-off where readability optimization may compromise detail, requiring further research into prompt strategies and ongoing operational refinement. Finally, the study's single-system focus means generalizability is limited, which emphasizes the need for extensive adaptation and validation in other healthcare settings.

Huang et al. [14] assessed the capacity of ChatGPT to extract structured data efficiently and comprehensively from free-text medical notes. This task is directly relevant to healthcare administrative efficiency because much of the critical information needed for reporting, quality improvement, resource management, and retrospective analysis is locked within these unstructured text documents. The core idea involves leveraging ChatGPT's ability to read and understand clinical notes to automatically transform them into organized data elements, eliminating the need for significant, task-specific human annotation and model training. To evaluate ChatGPT's performance, its generated structured data was compared to expert-validated data, with metrics such as accuracy, F1 score, Kappa coefficient, recall, and precision used for assessment. Its performance was benchmarked against a keyword search and a deep-learning NER model that required weeks of medical expert annotation. ChatGPT demonstrated promising performance and outperformed both traditional NLP methods. The ChatGPT model (GPT-3.5-Turbo) struggled with highly specialized pathology terms and understanding complex, domain-specific medical information, as evidenced by the errors.

Furthermore, in sparse reports, ChatGPT sometimes fabricated information, which suggests the hallucination phenomenon and highlights a broader risk. With typos, missing words, and inconsistent formatting, real-world clinical notes pose challenges for human reviewers and AI models. Successful prompt engineering ensured ChatGPT's output was in JSON format, making the extracted data immediately usable for analysis, reporting, and system integration, thus eliminating manual data cleaning—a typical administrative delay.

Recognizing the significant time and effort clinicians spend on summarization, Van Veen et al. [22] investigated ChatGPT's potential to accelerate the clinical text summarization process. They assessed the performance of two open-source and proprietary LLM groups, including GPT-4, GPT-3.5, FLAN-T5, FLAN-UL2, Alpaca, Med-Alpaca, Vicuna, and Llama-2. They utilized two particular summarization approaches: in-context learning (ICL) and quantized low-rank adaptation (QLoRA). ICL works by directly providing the model with task-specific examples within the prompt without altering the model's weight. On the other hand, QLoRA is a memory-efficient method that alters a small subset of model weights using a training dataset. Standard metrics like BLEU, ROUGE-L, BERTScore, and MEDCON were used to measure syntactic, semantic, and conceptual similarity between generated summaries and reference summaries. In a masked, randomized study, ten physicians assessed summaries. They compared those generated by the top-performing LLM, GPT-4 with ICL, against summaries created by medical experts. The physicians used a five-point Likert scale to evaluate the summaries for completeness (*did it capture important information?*), correctness (*was there minimal false information?*), and conciseness (*was nonessential information minimized?*). Summaries generated by GPT-4 were frequently judged to be equal with or even better than those produced by medical experts. The summaries created by human experts were preferred in only a few instances. This direct comparison, showing LLMs performing comparably to or surpassing human output, is a crucial finding for real-world application. The LLM summaries were more complete and concise and had significantly fewer errors, on average, than medical expert summaries. Integrating LLMs into clinical workflows, given their ability to produce summaries that often match or exceed expert quality, could significantly ease the documentation burden on clinicians. This directly boosts administrative efficiency by allowing healthcare providers to focus more on patient care. They also concluded that despite LLMs' potential in healthcare, they still face challenges like errors, often due to limited clinical knowledge and overly literal interpretation. Concerns also exist regarding proprietary models, data governance, and the risk of bias exacerbating health disparities. Ultimately, evaluating LLM performance remains complex, requiring human oversight beyond traditional metrics, as even ground truth data can contain errors.

2.4.5 Polaris

Mukherjee et al. [13] present a compelling use case for employing LLMs to enhance administrative efficiency and support healthcare operations, particularly through real-time, voice-based patient conversations. Unlike prior LLM applications in healthcare that focused on tasks like question answering or EHR summarization, Polaris specifically targets long, multi-turn voice conversations with patients. This is particularly useful as phone calls are the dominant method for many high-volume healthcare use cases. Developing such a system comes with challenges like detecting and managing erroneous data generated by automated speech recognition and handling different issues during a voice conversation, such as interruptions, response length, and tone. The core objective of Polaris is to perform low-risk, non-diagnostic tasks typically handled by various care team members, such as medical assistants. By automating these tasks, Polaris aims to provide workforce augmentation, which allows human healthcare providers to concentrate on higher-level diagnostic and clinical duties. Polaris is designed to be a scalable and safe system for handling nondiagnostic communications to improve patient outcomes and reduce the extra burden. Polaris utilizes a multi-agent LLM constellation architecture composed of a primary conversational agent and several specialist support agents. This architecture is optimized for real-time healthcare conversations and designed for better domain-specific interactions than a single general-purpose LLM.

The primary agent focuses on driving engaging, patient-friendly conversations, while the specialist support agents handle specific healthcare tasks requiring high accuracy. This division of labor increases safety and reduces hallucinations by allowing specialists to focus on their specific areas of expertise. The constellation also aids in keeping latency low for real-time interactions. This automation of documentation significantly streamlines the post-call administrative workload. The evaluation of Polaris involved over 1100 nurses and 130 physicians. On average, Polaris performed on par with human nurses across dimensions, including patient education and conversational quality. In conclusion, Polaris demonstrates the potential of a specialized, multi-agent LLM system to improve administrative efficiency and enhance healthcare operations by safely and accurately performing routine, nondiagnostic patient interaction tasks. These high-volume activities mitigate staffing shortages and allow human caregivers to focus on more complex clinical work, potentially improving healthcare delivery and patient outcomes.

2.4.6 MindfulDiary

MindfulDiary [30] introduces an LLM-powered journaling app to support psychiatric patients and improve their communication with mental health professionals. While its primary focus is on enhancing patient journaling and clinical communication, its use of LLMs within a healthcare context offers insights into the operational applications of these models, even if it leans more towards patient-facing clinical operations than strict administrative tasks like billing or scheduling. This study offers valuable insights into how LLMs can enhance clinical information exchange and patient monitoring efficiency and quality. This represents a distinct form of operational improvement within the larger healthcare system. It enhances mental healthcare through its patient interface and clinician dashboard. The mobile app uses LLMs to facilitate conversational journaling, prompting patients for richer daily records, making the process less daunting and more engaging than traditional methods. The web dashboard, powered by LLMs for summarization and classification, visualizes key insights from mental health professionals' patient records, including engagement metrics and emotional trends. Studies with patients experiencing major depressive disorder and psychiatrists showed that patients consistently provided more detailed and diverse daily records. At the same time, clinicians gained more profound understanding and empathy, even eliciting candid thoughts that were difficult to obtain otherwise. From an operational perspective, MindfulDiary streamlines patient-generated health data collection, provides structured patient data to clinicians for more efficient consultations, and enhances communication quality by offering pre-analyzed insights, ultimately improving the efficiency and effectiveness of clinical interactions.

2.4.7 Coding

LLMs initially faced significant hurdles in accurately generating medical codes. Early evaluations of prominent LLMs revealed low exact match rates for ICD-10-CM codes, leading to the initial conclusion that they were unsuitable for direct use in this critical administrative task. However, researchers proved that providing LLMs with appropriate tools and retrieval mechanisms could dramatically improve their performance, aligning with advancements in retrieval-augmented generation and the use of external knowledge bases. Kwan [31] developed a novel two-stage retrieve-rank system for automated ICD-10-CM coding. This system employs a ColBERT-V2 retriever to identify relevant codes from a trained index, followed by GPT-3.5-turbo for reranking to select the most probable code. This innovative approach yielded a dramatic improvement in accuracy. On a dataset of 100 single-term medical conditions, the Retrieve-Rank system achieved 100% accuracy, a stark contrast to the mere 6% accuracy of a vanilla LLM (GPT-3.5-turbo). The Retrieve-Rank system's superior accuracy stems from its remarkable precision in capturing crucial medical details often missed by vanilla LLMs, such as specific anatomical locations, encounter types, and complex medical conditions, while demonstrating consistency across various medical specialties. The implications for administrative efficiency are substantial: An accurate, automated coding system could significantly reduce the workload on medical coders, minimize errors, and enhance the overall quality of medical records. This, in turn, promises more efficient healthcare administration, more accurate billing processes, and improved data quality for research and decision-making.

A recent study [32] investigated the effectiveness of LLMs, specifically GPT, for medical coding. Recognizing the limitations of basic LLM prompting for complex coding tasks, the research introduces a novel prompt framework designed to significantly enhance performance. This innovative framework incorporates advanced prompt engineering techniques, including a meta prompt to extract task-specific knowledge and guidelines, multi-shot learning, and dynamic in-context learning that retrieves examples semantically similar to the input. The framework's efficacy was assessed across three medical coding tasks: semantic coding, clinical trial criteria coding, and MS-DRG coding. For the complex MS-DRG coding task on the MIMIC-IV dataset, the prompt-based method achieved 68.1% accuracy for the 30 most frequent codes. This performance is notably comparable to the state-of-the-art supervised model DRG-LLaMA. Similarly, for the complex clinical trial criteria coding task, the method attained a macro F1 score of 68.4, closely matching the best-supervised model. The study concludes that meticulously designed prompt-based learning with LLMs can achieve accuracy on par with state-of-the-art supervised models for complex medical coding. While LLMs currently function as highly effective assistants, their potential to reliably automate complex medical coding is substantial, particularly as their context window sizes expand.

2.4.8 FactsR

Generating clinical notes is a significant administrative burden for healthcare professionals, consuming valuable time that could otherwise be spent with patients. This pressure can compromise the thoroughness of medical records, yet accurate and concise documentation is crucial for effective patient handovers and legal compliance. Ambient Scribes, powered by LLMs, have emerged as a promising solution to automate the abstractive summarization of medical dialogues, aiming to reduce this administrative overhead and enhance documentation quality. Despite their promise, traditional LLM-based scribes face challenges. Summarizing complex medical consultations is difficult due to specialized terminology, diverse language, and unstructured dialogue, where clinically relevant information is often sparse. Many existing AI scribing solutions process the entire consultation transcript only after it ends, typically using one-shot or few-shot prompts. This post hoc approach can lead to lengthy notes, increased hallucinations, misrepresentation of clinician intent, and a substantial need for extensive proofreading. Such reliance on manual review, combined with clinician workload and fatigue, risks patient safety. Furthermore, simple few-shot prompts often yield suboptimal results, while complex prompts can become unwieldy and fragile. Even fine-tuning LLMs may not fully address the complexities of intricate consultations.

FactsR [33] introduces a novel, more secure, and efficient approach to healthcare documentation in response to these limitations. FactsR operates in real-time during the consultation, employing a modular, LLM-based reasoning pipeline to continuously extract crucial clinical information, referred to as facts, as the dialogue unfolds. The system works by extracting facts from segmented, overlapping windows of the transcript. It utilizes a set of specialized LLMs: a draft model to initialize facts, an evaluator model to check their validity against criteria, and a refinement model to correct any facts that fail evaluation through an agentic self-refinement algorithm. After the consultation, the finalized set of extracted Facts is used by a separate instruction-tuned LLM and a clinical note template to generate the final document. A key innovation of FactsR is its clinician-in-the-loop design, making these intermediate Facts interpretable. This allows clinicians to interactively refine or validate information on the fly, mirroring traditional note-taking processes. FactsR's effectiveness was evaluated using a Model-as-a-Judge approach, assessing generated notes against human-written notes and the transcript for completeness, and conciseness. Compared to traditional ambient scribe baselines, FactsR improved completeness and conciseness. Crucially, simulating clinician interaction with the extracted Facts resulted in significant boosts, bringing the AI-generated notes much closer to ideal human-written notes. This demonstrates that breaking down the summarization task into interpretable reasoning steps and actively involving clinicians substantially enhances note quality, yielding more complete and concise documentation. By extracting salient information in real-time and producing more accurate and concise notes through structured reasoning and clinician guidance, FactsR significantly reduces the need for extensive post-consultation editing and proofreading inherent in less reliable traditional methods. This directly contributes to administrative efficiency by minimizing clinicians' time on documentation. Moreover, the real-time extraction of facts opens doors for AI-driven decision support at the point of care, further optimizing clinical workflows. This approach underscores the critical value of integrating clinicians into AI workflows to ensure safety and clinical fidelity in healthcare documentation.

2.4.9 PRIORITY2REWARD

PRIORITY2REWARD [31] is an AI-powered application that leverages LLMs to streamline resource allocation in public health. This tool tackles the essential administrative challenge of distributing limited resources, such as staff time or interventions, by effectively integrating the on-the-ground knowledge of health workers. It enables these frontline staff to express their allocation preferences in natural language, which the LLM then translates into specific reward functions for a resource distribution model. This dynamic tailoring of automated decisions, guided by local insights, significantly boosts administrative efficiency by creating more responsive and impactful policies at the community level. The application's effectiveness has been demonstrated in a simulated mobile health program in India, where it helped determine which beneficiaries should receive calls based on health worker priorities to maximize engagement within budget constraints. Furthermore, PRIORITY2REWARD enhances administrative transparency by visually showcasing how LLM-generated reward functions influence resource distribution and engagement outcomes, allowing for quicker adaptation to evolving needs. The system also incorporates computational efficiencies to ensure practical usability, making the tool responsive for frontline staff.

2.4.10 Healthcare Copilot

The Healthcare Copilot [34] streamlines healthcare operations through several key administrative efficiency features. It automates consultation summarization and report generation via an LLM-driven processing component, creating medical reports that offer an overview of conditions, diagnostics, and recommendations for patients and doctors. This directly automates a common documentation requirement. Additionally, the system efficiently manages historical patient information by summarizing past conversations into a concise history memory after each consultation. This ensures essential data is retained while saving space and improving accessibility for subsequent interactions, making historical data more manageable for the LLM and potentially human clinicians. Finally, a doctor's module streamlines doctor review and intervention, allowing healthcare professionals to easily modify AI-generated responses with simple guidance. While primarily for safety, this feature also boosts administrative efficiency by providing a structured, less burdensome method for doctors to review and correct AI outputs, making AI integration into workflows more feasible. In essence, the Healthcare Copilot automates key information management, reporting, and review functions, significantly improving the efficiency of operational workflows.

2.5 CHALLENGES AND LIMITATIONS

Integrating LLMs necessitates careful consideration of security and privacy, including protecting patient data and adhering to regulations like HIPAA. Utilizing advanced LLMs like GPT-4 with sensitive healthcare information raises significant concerns regarding patient privacy and cybersecurity. Healthcare organizations must ensure that their data-handling practices comply with relevant laws. The deployment of AI introduces new avenues for cyberattacks, potentially compromising patient data's confidentiality, integrity, and availability. Securely integrating LLMs with EHRs could establish a HIPAA-compliant environment. Ultimately, healthcare providers are responsible for ensuring the appropriate use of new technologies and prioritizing the safety and security of patient data [4]. While LLMs can aid in regulatory compliance and streamline claims processing to prevent fraud and misuse, other AI techniques like bidirectional encoder representations from transformers (BERT), sometimes enhanced with technologies such as blockchain are also being explored for specific tasks like health insurance fraud detection [35]. Therefore, integrating LLMs with such systems might be a step forward in tasks where adequate accuracy has not been reached by LLMs.

Due to the potential for insufficient training on reliable medical data, the dependability of LLMs in healthcare is uncertain. Models not trained on carefully selected medical datasets might provide incorrect information or even fabricate details. To address these shortcomings, it is crucial to train LLMs on trustworthy medical sources, conduct rigorous validation, minimize bias in the data, use domain-specific and diverse datasets, and establish continuous learning and validation cycles involving human expertise [4].

Proprietary LLMs such as ChatGPT have great potential in reducing and addressing administrative burdens without much fine-tuning. Although ChatGPT showed promise in structuring and summarizing medical information, it was not developed to answer medical questions. It lacks the specialized medical knowledge and context to fully comprehend intricate connections between conditions and treatments. While it can effectively organize information, its ability for complex reasoning, particularly involving causal relationships, is limited. This suggests that while LLMs can help structure and summarize tasks, they may not be dependable for tasks requiring in-depth medical understanding or inference without human supervision [23].

A significant challenge with LLMs is their tendency to hallucinate, generating incorrect or nonsensical yet plausible-sounding answers. Given the critical nature of healthcare, where administrative processes impact patient care and billing, inaccurate information from an LLM could lead to serious consequences. Furthermore, LLMs can replicate biases present in their training data. This could manifest in administrative tasks by perpetuating biases in scheduling priorities or documentation style, necessitating careful monitoring and mitigation strategies [23].

LLMs primarily function by recognizing and matching patterns in their training data rather than possessing human-like reasoning. While they are adept at generating text, their understanding lacks inherent meaning. This can limit their effectiveness in complex administrative tasks that demand nuanced interpretation, problem-solving beyond established patterns, or handling unfamiliar situations not adequately present in their training data. Even in patient interactions, LLM chatbots may struggle with complex queries due to a lack of deep knowledge and the inability to interpret emotional cues. This suggests that while LLMs can manage routine inquiries, more intricate administrative tasks requiring subtle interpretation or highly specialized information may exceed their current capabilities.

Furthermore, various forms of bias exist, with training data bias being particularly critical as it can perpetuate inequities against underrepresented groups, exacerbating health disparities. This bias could inadvertently be reproduced in administrative tasks if LLMs are used without careful oversight, for instance, in resource allocation or automated communication. Off-the-shelf LLM products often fail to meet regulatory requirements, especially concerning data privacy, and may lack healthcare-specific training. Their pricing structures are complex and variable, often excluding essential costs like implementation, training, customization, validation, monitoring, and maintenance. The infrastructure relies on expensive cloud servers, and rigorous regulatory review by experts is necessary due to data privacy laws (HIPAA, General Data Protection Regulation [GDPR]) and medical malpractice law, potentially causing project delays and increased initial expenses [36].

To mitigate the limitations of LLMs in healthcare administration, including hallucinations and lack of specific medical knowledge, RAG can be employed to add relevant context from external knowledge bases like medical databases, providing access to up-to-date guidelines and policies for accuracy; furthermore, LLM fine-tuning can enhance performance in specific administrative tasks like information extraction and report generation. Scaling LLMs with better-curated medical pretraining data is also expected to improve performance across administrative benchmarks. At the same time, proactive fairness approaches are crucial to prevent the exacerbation of health inequities due to bias. The broader consensus emphasizes that safe and effective implementation across all domains necessitates thorough validation and robust human oversight [37]. Table 2.4 provides a categorized summary of the key benefits and challenges involved in the integration of LLMs within healthcare administration.

Table 2.4 Benefits and considerations of using LLMs for streamlining healthcare administration

Category	*Benefits*	*Challenges*
Efficiency	• Automates tasks • Reduces clinician time • Streamlines documentation • Speeds up records • Automates patient interaction • Improves billing • Less manual workload • Boosts prescreening efficiency • Decreases prior authorization review time • Instant note generation • Saves provider effort • Offloads routine tasks	• Significant initial effort for annotation/training • Complex prompts can be fragile • Requires adaptation across settings • Clinical notes issues such as typos, missing words, inconsistent formatting • Evaluation metrics may lack nuance
Quality	• Enhances medical record clarity and accuracy • Minimizes documentation errors • Accurately categorizes patient information • Summaries preferred by human experts • More accurate and clinically relevant notes • Improves correctness and completeness of notes • Summaries on par with or better than human experts • Improves completeness and conciseness of notes	• Risk of generating incorrect or misleading information • May misrepresent clinician intent Struggles with specialized terminology and complex information • May fabricate information in sparse reports • Accuracy concerns in patient-friendly summaries • Limitations due to insufficient training on reliable medical data • Lack of specialized medical knowledge and context • May struggle with complex patient queries • Evaluation remains complex, needing human oversight

(Continued)

Table 2.4 (Continued)

Category	*Benefits*	*Challenges*
Safety	• Reduces medical errors • Potential safety implications from hallucinations and inaccuracies • Requires robust physician review • Needs thorough validation and human oversight • Risk of misrepresenting clinician intent • Reliance on proofreading with workload can be dangerous • Designed for safety • Clinician-in-the-loop design enhances safety and fidelity	• Data security and privacy concerns • Requires robust protection mechanisms and HIPAA compliance • New avenues for cyberattacks
Bias & Equity	• Proactive fairness approaches crucial	• Fairness and bias issues • Perpetuation of biases from internet data • Potential for inequitable treatment • Training data bias perpetuates inequities • Bias reproduced in administrative tasks without oversight
Technical & Operational	• Flexible integration with practice management systems • Domain-specific pretraining for medical dialogue understanding • Specialized training and proprietary data for improved medical reasoning • Designed for easy integration into existing workflows • Efficient data extraction in usable formats • Prompt engineering enhances performance RAG and fine-tuning mitigates limitations • Computational efficiencies for usability • Multi-agent architecture for safety/low latency	• Transparency, explainability, and trustworthiness issues • Lack of true reasoning or deep knowledge • Struggle with nuanced interpretation and unfamiliar situations • Limited context window sizes • Lack of standardization in input data • Cannot provide specific medical advice without data access • Single system focus limits generalizability • Concerns regarding proprietary models and data governance • Off-the-shelf products may lack regulations • Complex and variable pricing • Rigorous regulatory review required

2.6 CONCLUSION

LLMs hold immense potential for transforming healthcare administration, promising significant gains in efficiency and enhancing patient care. Trained on massive datasets, LLMs excel at processing natural language and generating human-like text, making them well-suited to automate routine and repetitive tasks that currently consume a substantial amount of clinicians' and administrators' time. This administrative burden not only detracts from direct patient interaction and care quality but also contributes to physician and healthcare provider burnout. LLMs can streamline a wide range of administrative duties, from automating scheduling and patient inquiries to managing medical records, ensuring regulatory compliance, simplifying claims processing and coding, generating clinical documentation and summaries, and improving communication. By automating these tasks, LLMs can free up staff time for more critical patient-facing activities, expedite processes like reimbursement, reduce errors associated with manual methods, and make health information more accessible and understandable for patients. The investigated case studies for patient communication and summarization, and applications for discharge note generation and structured data extraction, highlight the practical effectiveness and time-saving potential of LLM-powered systems in real-world healthcare scenarios. Techniques like prompt engineering, including various methods, are crucial for effectively guiding LLMs to perform specific medical NLP tasks with greater accuracy and reliability. However, integrating LLMs into medical settings presents significant challenges and crucial ethical considerations. Ensuring data security and patient privacy, particularly adherence to regulations like HIPAA and GDPR, is paramount. A major concern is the risk of LLMs generating incorrect or misleading information, which is known as hallucinations. Hallucinations can have serious consequences in healthcare. Furthermore, issues of fairness and bias inherent in training data could perpetuate inequities if not carefully mitigated. LLMs primarily function by pattern matching rather than true medical reasoning or possessing deep domain knowledge, which limits their dependability for tasks requiring nuanced interpretation or causal understanding without human supervision. Technical and operational hurdles include the need for robust validation, adaptation to varied clinical settings and data formats, complex pricing structures, and navigating rigorous regulatory reviews. Despite these challenges, the future of LLMs in enhancing healthcare administrative efficiency appears exceptionally bright. Ongoing advancements, such as the development of domain-specific LLMs, the use of techniques like RAG and fine-tuning to improve accuracy and relevance, and the integration of human oversight through clinician-in-the-loop designs, are actively addressing current limitations. As demonstrated different systems, the ability to process information in real-time, provide structured summaries, and allow for easy clinician review offers pathways to safer and more effective integration. Ultimately, the responsible and effective integration of LLMs into healthcare administration necessitates continuous validation, robust human oversight, and a focus on designing systems that are not only efficient but also safe, fair, and trustworthy, thereby maximizing their potential to alleviate administrative burdens and allow healthcare professionals to focus on what matters most.

REFERENCES

1. Cantlupe, J. *Expert Forum: How hospital admin boom could reduce burnout.* 2017 [cited 10 May 2025]; Available from: https://www.athenahealth.com/resources/blog/expert-forum-rise-and-rise-healthcare-administrator.
2. Alder, S. *What is the HITECH Act?* 2025 [cited 10 May 2025]; Available from: https://www.hipaajournal.com/what-is-the-hitech-act/.
3. CHCP. *Medical Administrative Assistant Career Guide.* 2025 [cited 12 May 2025]; Available from: https://www.chcp.edu/blog/what-does-a-medical-administrative-assistant-do/.
4. Tripathi, S., R. Sukumaran, and T. S. Cook, Efficient healthcare with large language models: optimizing clinical workflow and enhancing patient care. *Journal of the American Medical Informatics Association*, **31**(6): 1436–1440, 2024.
5. Mahalegi, H. S. M., et al. Generative Adversarial Networks for Heterogeneous Unsupervised Domain Adaptation Detection. In *2024 IEEE 28th International Conference on Intelligent Engineering Systems (INES)*, 2024. IEEE.
6. Xing, F., Designing heterogeneous LLM agents for financial sentiment analysis. *arXiv preprint arXiv:2401.05799*, 2025.
7. Jahanmanesh, P., A. Farhadi, and A. Zamanifar, Mobility management with AI. *IEEE Access*, 2025
8. Zeng, Y., et al., Integrating type-2 fuzzy logic controllers with digital twin and neural networks for advanced hydropower system management. *Scientific Reports*, **15**(1): 5140, 2025.
9. Kalinin, K. *Automation in Healthcare Administration: A Complete Guide.* 2025 [cited 12 May 2025]; Available from: https://topflightapps.com/ideas/automation-healthcare-administration/.
10. Farhadi, A. and A. Taheri, Application of GenAI in Synthetic Data Generation in the Healthcare System, in *Application of Generative AI in Healthcare Systems* (pp. 67–89). Springer, 2025.
11. Rashidieranjbar, F., A. Farhadi, and A. Zamanifar, Revolutionizing Healthcare with Generative Artificial Intelligence Technologies, in *Generative Artificial Intelligence (AI) Approaches for Industrial Applications* (pp. 189–221). Springer, 2025.
12. Wang, D. and S. Zhang, Large language models in medical and healthcare fields: applications, advances, and challenges. *Artificial Intelligence Review*, **57**(11): 299, 2024.

13. Mukherjee, S., et al., Polaris: A safety-focused llm constellation architecture for healthcare. *arXiv preprint arXiv:2403.13313*, 2024.
14. Huang, J., et al., A critical assessment of using ChatGPT for extracting structured data from clinical notes. *npj Digital Medicine*, 7(1): 106, 2024.
15. Taheri, A., A. Farhadi, and A. Zamanifar, Application of GenAI in Clinical Administration Support, in *Application of Generative AI in Healthcare Systems* (pp. 91–117). Springer, 2025.
16. Farhadi, A., et al., Leveraging Blockchain and ANFIS for Optimal Supply Chain Management. *arXiv preprint arXiv:2408.17161*, 2024.
17. Bodina, A., A. Pavan, and S. Castaldi, Resource allocation criteria in a hospital. *Journal of Preventive Medicine and Hygiene*, **58**(2): E184, 2017.
18. Mahalegi, H. S. M., et al., Application of Generative AI in Resource Optimization in Healthcare Systems, in *Application of Generative AI in Healthcare Systems* (pp. 175–195). Springer, 2025.
19. Lorencin, I., N. Tankovic, and D. Etinger. Optimizing Healthcare Efficiency with Local Large Language Models. Advances in Human Factors and Ergonomics, In *Intelligent Human Systems Integration*. 2025.
20. Tajirian, T., et al., Assessing the Impact on Electronic Health Record Burden After Five Years of Physician Engagement in a Canadian Mental Health Organization: Mixed-Methods Study. *JMIR Human Factors*, **12**: e65656, 2025.
21. Feder, M. *Exploring healthcare compliance as a career.* 2024 [cited 15 May 2025]; Available from: https://www.phoenix.edu/blog/what-is-healthcare-compliance.html.
22. Van Veen, D., et al., Adapted large language models can outperform medical experts in clinical text summarization. *Nature Medicine*, **30**(4): 1134–1142, 2024.
23. Cascella, M., et al., Evaluating the feasibility of ChatGPT in healthcare: an analysis of multiple clinical and research scenarios. *Journal of Medical Systems*, **47**(1): 33, 2023.
24. Liu, Y., S. Ju, and J. Wang, Exploring the potential of ChatGPT in medical dialogue summarization: a study on consistency with human preferences. *BMC Medical Informatics and Decision Making*, **24**(1): 75, 2024.
25. Zaghir, J., et al., Prompt engineering paradigms for medical applications: scoping review and recommendations for better practices. *arXiv preprint arXiv:2405.01249*, 2024.
26. Heston, T. F. and C. Khun, Prompt engineering in medical education. *International Medical Education*, **2**(3): 198–205, 2023.
27. Yuan, D., et al., A continued pretrained llm approach for automatic medical note generation. *arXiv preprint arXiv:2403.09057*, 2024.
28. Yang, Z., et al., Talk2care: An llm-based voice assistant for communication between healthcare providers and older adults. *Proceedings of the ACM on Interactive, Mobile, Wearable and Ubiquitous Technologies*, **8**(2): 1–35, 2024.
29. Zaretsky, J., et al., Generative artificial intelligence to transform inpatient discharge summaries to patient-friendly language and format. *JAMA Network Open*, 7(3): e240357, 2024.

30. Kim, T., et al. MindfulDiary: Harnessing Large Language Model to Support Psychiatric Patients' Journaling. in *Proceedings of the 2024 CHI Conference on Human Factors in Computing Systems, ACM*. 2024.
31. Verma, S., et al. PRIORITY2REWARD: Incorporating Healthworker Preferences for Resource Allocation Planning. In *Proceedings of the AAAI Conference on Artificial Intelligence*, Association for the Advancement of Artificial Intelligence (AAAI), 2025.
32. Feng, Y., *Can Large Language Models Replace Coding Specialists? Evaluating GPT Performance in Medical Coding Tasks, SAGE* . 2025.
33. Hansen, V. P. B., et al., FactsR: A Safer Method for Producing High Quality Healthcare Documentation. *arXiv preprint arXiv:2505.10360*, 2025.
34. Ren, Z., et al., Healthcare copilot: Eliciting the power of general llms for medical consultation. *arXiv preprint arXiv:2402.13408*, 2024.
35. Lataran, P. N., et al., Developing a BERT-Enhanced Blockchain Model for HealthInsurance Fraud Detection. *Journal of Information Systems Research and Practice*, 2(3): 56–61, 2024.
36. Moura, L., et al., Implications of large language models for quality and efficiency of neurologic care: emerging issues in neurology. *Neurology*, **102**(11): e209497, 2024.
37. Vrdoljak, J., et al. A review of large language models in medical education, clinical decision support, and healthcare administration. In *Healthcare*. MDPI, 2025.

Chapter 3

LLMs in drug discovery, clinical trial analysis, and medical literature review

Sina Abbaskhani, Deniz NoorMohammadzadeh Maleki, Amirfarhad Farhadi, and Azadeh Zamanifar

3.1 OVERVIEW OF LLM APPLICATIONS IN DRUG DISCOVERY AND CLINICAL RESEARCH

Large language models (LLMs) have emerged as transformative tools in biomedical research, particularly in drug discovery, clinical trial analysis, and medical literature review. Their ability to process and generate human-like text enables researchers to navigate complex biomedical data efficiently. In drug discovery, LLMs facilitate the identification of novel drug targets, predict drug–drug interactions (DDIs), and even propose molecular scaffolds in early-stage compound design. A comprehensive study evaluated 18 different LLMs, including GPT-4 and open-source variants, for their capability to predict DDIs by processing molecular structures and gene interaction data [1]. Beyond predictive analytics, newer LLM-integrated frameworks now combine chemical language representations with protein structures, enabling cross-modal learning and functional annotation for uncharacterized proteins, pushing boundaries in de novo drug development. LLMs also contribute in preclinical stages, where they analyze omics data (e.g., transcriptomics, proteomics) and extract mechanistic insights from preclinical models. This helps in hypothesis generation and identifying off-target effects early, reducing downstream attrition rates. In clinical trial analysis, LLMs have been employed to match patients to appropriate trials by assessing eligibility criteria against patient summaries, demonstrating performance parity with proprietary models when fine-tuned on synthetic datasets [2]. These models are also being integrated into protocol optimization, helping design trials with more inclusive eligibility criteria and fewer redundancies.

A notable new trend is the application of LLMs to assess real-world data (RWD) such as electronic health records (EHRs), patient registries, and insurance claims to predict trial results or analyze post-marketing safety. These abilities are becoming more popular in regulatory decision-making, as LLMs help to draft documents and spot deficiencies in trial evidence.

For medical literature review, LLMs expedite the screening and summarization of scientific publications. In cardiovascular drug development, a cross-sectional study investigated the performance of LLMs in accelerating

DOI: 10.1201/9781003665083-3

literature screening processes, highlighting their potential to reduce the manual burden on researchers [3]. Moreover, LLMs can swiftly retrieve and organize crucial information from vast biomedical literature, aiding researchers in synthesizing the latest findings on specific drugs, diseases, or genes [4]. Recent advances are also exploring the integration of knowledge graphs and biomedical ontologies into LLMs, enhancing their factual accuracy and enabling reasoning over heterogeneous data sources. These hybrid systems promise to further elevate the role of LLMs from passive summarizers to active research co-pilots in biomedical science.

This chapter presents in-depth and systematic review of the application of large language models (LLMs) in drug discovery, clinical trial evaluation, and assessment of medical literature. It aimed to elucidate the biomed research and clinical workflow enhancement through LLMs by automating intricate language and reasoning tasks with higher precision, efficiency, and scalability. The chapter, through an extensive range of case studies and empirical assessments, demonstrates the pivotal role of LLMs in identifying novel therapeutic targets, optimizing trial designs, detecting adverse events (AEs) in real time, and synthesizing scientific texts at remarkable speeds. At the same time, it also critically addresses fundamental data quality, model interpretation, ethical, and regulatory compliance issues. Evidence collected corroborates that with responsible development and careful stewardship, LLMs can profoundly transform the enhancement of evidence-based medicine (EBM), acceleration of drug development processes, and delivery of medicine in a more equitable and individualized manner.

3.2 LLMS IN DRUG DISCOVERY

Large language models (LLMs) are transforming drug discovery through the automated, scalable, and smart analysis of biomedical data to pinpoint possible drug targets and forecast intricate molecular interactions. These models, developed on extensive datasets of scientific literature, molecular information, and biological sequences, can understand and produce significant representations of chemical structures and protein–ligand interactions. LLMs enhance the retrieval of new therapeutic insights, assist in creating target-specific ligands, and speed up the optimization of binding affinity and pharmacokinetic characteristics. Through the integration of various types of information such as molecular graphs, SMILES (Simplified Molecular Input Line Entry System) strings, and protein sequences, LLMs can aid comprehensive drug discovery processes, lessen reliance on manual feature engineering, and improve the clarity of prediction results. This establishes LLMs as key instruments in contemporary computational pharmacology, playing a crucial role in hypothesis generation and experimental design during the initial phases of drug development.

Building upon this foundation, we have conducted a comprehensive review of studies and peer-reviewed articles published between 2022 and 2025, focusing on the application of large language models (LLMs) in drug discovery. The findings underscore the increasingly pivotal role of LLMs across various stages of drug development, from target identification to molecular optimization.

Wang et al. (2022) introduced an innovative approach for predicting drug-target interactions utilizing a graph transformers model. This method utilizes the power of graph attention networks to understand complex connections between drugs and targets, improving the precision of interaction forecasts [5]. Moreover, Li et al. (2023) created MolReGPT, a system based on LLM that can convert molecule descriptions into natural language. Utilizing a retrieval-based prompt approach via in-context learning, MolReGPT enables both molecule description and text-driven molecule creation. This system marks major progress in molecular discovery, allowing for the creation of new molecules without requiring extensive adjustments [6].

Additionally, Cao et al. (2023) presented InstructMol, a multimodal LLM that successfully aligns molecular structures with natural language through an instruction-tuning method. Employing a two-phase training approach that integrates restricted domain-specific data alongside molecular and textual insights, InstructMol demonstrates significant advancements in molecular tasks related to drug discovery. It outperforms top LLMs and greatly narrows the difference with specialized models, creating a strong base for a flexible and reliable drug discovery helper [7].

Ultimately, Gao et al. (2025) presented PharmAgents, a virtual pharmaceutical environment driven by LLM-based collaboration among multiple agents. This system replicates the complete drug discovery process from target identification to preclinical assessment by combining explainable, LLM-based agents armed with specialized machine learning models and computational resources. By means of organized knowledge sharing and automated enhancements, PharmAgents pinpoints potential therapeutic targets, uncovers promising lead compounds, boosts binding affinity and essential molecular characteristics, and conducts in silico assessments of toxicity and synthetic viability. The design of the system prioritizes interpretability, interaction with agents, and self-evolution, allowing it to enhance future drug designs using past experiences. This research introduces a new framework for autonomous, transparent, and scalable pharmaceutical exploration, with future developments aimed at complete drug lifecycle management [8].

In the same vein, Singh et al. (2025) created Chem42, a group of chemical language models aimed at generating ligands with specified targets. By combining atomic-level interactions with various inputs from Prot42, a supportive protein language model, Chem42 establishes an advanced cross-modal depiction of molecular structures, interactions, and binding patterns. This cutting-edge framework facilitates the development of structurally sound, synthetically obtainable ligands with improved target specificity. Assessments on various protein targets show that Chem42 exceeds current methodologies in chemical authenticity, target-focused design, and anticipated binding strength, possibly speeding up the drug discovery process [9].

Furthermore, De Vito et al. (2025) performed an extensive study assessing the abilities of LLMs to predict drug–drug interactions (DDIs). The research evaluated 18 various LLMs, encompassing both proprietary and open-source types, by analyzing molecular structures, target organisms, and gene interaction information presented as raw text input. The results indicated that fine-tuned LLMs showed enhanced performance in DDI prediction, successfully identifying intricate molecular interaction patterns and situations where drug pairs affect shared genes. This highlights the capability of LLMs as essential resources in pharmaceutical research and clinical environments [1]. Farhadi et al. provide an in-depth overview of how generative artificial intelligence (GenAI) techniques are reshaping the landscape of drug discovery by addressing key challenges such as design complexity, time constraints, and development costs. Their work highlights the transformative potential of various GenAI architectures, including Generative Adversarial Networks (GANs), Variational Autoencoders (VAEs), diffusion models, and transformer-based frameworks, in de novo molecular generation and optimization. The authors emphasize that these models, through their ability to generate novel and chemically valid compounds, have become pivotal in expanding the searchable chemical space and automating early-stage drug design tasks. Moreover, they explore the application of reinforcement learning and sequence-based neural networks in refining candidate selection strategies, thereby underscoring the interdisciplinary nature of modern AI-driven pharmaceutical research. The chapter presents GenAI not only as a technological innovation but also as a strategic shift in drug development pipelines, offering new avenues for scalable, precise, and cost-effective solutions in medicinal chemistry [10].

Table 3.1 summarizes cutting-edge AI models developed for healthcare and biomedical applications between 2017 and 2025, highlighting their primary tasks, affiliated institutions, and accessibility. The models span diverse functionalities, from explainable drug recommendations and multimodal medical reasoning to specialized tasks like radiology report generation and hallucination detection in medical texts. While some models offer open-source access for community use, others remain proprietary, reflecting the balance between academic transparency and commercial development in AI-driven healthcare innovation.

Table 3.1 Summary of large language models in healthcare

Model name	*Year*	*Primary task(s)*	*Institution(s)*	*Source code/Access link*
KEDRec-LM [11]	2025	Explainable Drug Recommendation	Indiana University, Emory University	Not yet released (planned for public release)
Gemini 2.5 Pro	2025	Multimodal Reasoning in Healthcare	Google DeepMind	https://deepmind.google/models/gemini/pro/
Velvet AI	2025	Multilingual Medical Applications	Almawave	https://huggingface.co/Almawave/Velvet-14B
Med42-v2 [12]	2024	Clinical Decision Support	M42 Health	https://github.com/m42-health/med42
BioMistral [13]	2024	Biomedical Question Answering	Avignon Université, Nantes Université	https://huggingface.co/BioMistral/BioMistral-7B
Med-PaLM 2 [14]	2023	Medical Question Answering	Google Research, DeepMind	Not Available
Radiology-Llama2 [15]	2023	Radiology Report Generation	University of Georgia	Not Available
DeID-GPT [16]	2023	De-identification of Medical Records	University of Georgia	https://github.com/yhydhx/ChatGPT-API
Med-HALT [17]	2023	Hallucination Detection in Medical Text	Saama AI Research	https://github.com/medhalt/medhalt
ChatCAD [18]	2023	Computer-Aided Diagnosis	Shanghai Tech University	https://github.com/zhaozh10/ChatCAD
BioGPT [19]	2023	Biomedical Text Processing	Microsoft Research	https://github.com/microsoft/BioGPT
GatorTron [20]	2022	Clinical Text Analysis	University of Florida	https://github.com/uf-hobi-informatics-lab/GatorTron
BioMedLM [21]	2022	Biomedical Question Answering	Stanford CRFM, MosaicML	https://github.com/stanford-crfm/BioMedLM
BioBART [22]	2022	Biomedical Text Summarization and NER	Tsinghua University, IDEA	https://github.com/GanjinZero/BioBART

(Continued)

Table 3.1 (Continued)

Model name	*Year*	*Primary task(s)*	*Institution(s)*	*Source code/Access link*
ClinicalT5 [23]	2022	Clinical Text Classification and NER	University of Oregon, Baidu Research	https://huggingface.co/xyla/Clinical-T5-Large
CRNN [24]	2017	Relation Classification in Clinical Text	Indian Institute of Technology	https://github.com/desh2608/crnn-relation-classification
LSTM RNN [25]	2017	Named Entity Recognition in Biomedical Text	Wuhan University	https://github.com/lvchen1989/BNER

3.2.1 LLMs for drug screening and repurposing

Implementation of computer strategies in discovering new drugs transformed conventional models of drug discovery through virtual screening, lead optimization, and drug repurposing. Virtual screening helps identify large datasets of active compounds quickly and inexpensively by automated docking simulations. Moreover, this technique minimizes the experimental workload in addition to several months of time during the drug discovery process. Likewise, lead optimization augments experimental hits into viable candidates by improving their potency, selectivity, and pharmacokinetics using computer simulations of biological systems and structure-activity relationship models. The second approach complements the first by using known drugs to improve their time-to-market through novel therapeutic indications, translating to lower costs and faster availability.

With the new addition of AI and deep learning algorithms, virtual screening underwent significant development due to their ability to accurately identify valuable hits. Traditional docking pipelines suffer from poor hit enrichment compared to new techniques like SPRINT, which allow structure-aware screening of billions of compounds in unmatched timeframes. These techniques made Sirtuin-1 deacetylase inhibitor discovery easier by aiding in the search for compounds that target aging and metabolic disorder areas. Along with the methods mentioned, prioritization based on ADMET and pharmacophoric features profile becomes possible, streamlining validation effort optimization.

Lead optimization applies computer-aided molecular design and chemistry, enhancing the sought properties of a compound using molecular docking, free energy perturbation, and molecular dynamics simulations.

In the particular case of LY2023-001, a lead compound developed for the selectively inhibitory G2019S LRRK2 Parkinson's mutation, a structure-based design method was applied. Additionally, the electronic and steric parameters of the ligands were modified using density functional theory (DFT) calculations, which enhanced their binding affinities and metabolic stability [26]. The application of these techniques enhances the compound's attrition rates in clinical trials by optimizing quality at the compound level prior to the trial.

Drug repurposing is particularly effective in advancing drug development by utilizing AI-powered virtual screenings and network pharmacology. An example is Aristospan, an anti-inflammatory corticosteroid that was recently repurposed to serve as a β-lactamase inhibitor for resistant strains of Gram-negative bacteria (Frontiers in Pharmacology, 2024). In the same way, some FDA-validated compounds were tested against hTERT, and several potential candidates for oncological indications were found [27].

Such structural databases and virtual screening platforms enable the retrieval of innovative therapeutic approaches using existing molecules. The function of Large Language Models (LLMs) in drug discovery processes in Figure 3.1, such as virtual screening, lead optimization, and drug

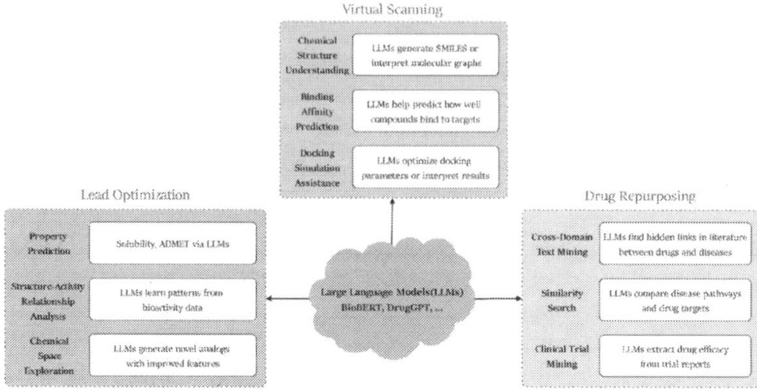

Figure 3.1 Integration of large language models (LLMs) such as BioBERT and DrugGPT in drug discovery workflows.

repurposing, is demonstrated. LLMs like BioBERT (Bidirectional Encoder Representations from Transformers for Biomedical Text Mining) and DrugGPT play roles at different phases: during virtual screening, they assist in comprehending chemical structures, predicting binding affinities, and conducting docking simulations; in lead optimization, they support property forecasts (e.g., solubility, ADMET), analyze structure-activity relationships, and generate new analogs; and in drug repurposing, they execute cross-domain text mining, similarity assessments, and mining of clinical trials. This versatile integration of LLMs improves the accuracy, rapidity, and effectiveness of pinpointing and fine-tuning therapeutic candidates.

3.2.2 Applications and challenges in drug development with LLMs

The integration of large language models (LLMs) in drug development pipelines has profoundly changed the pharmaceutical research environment, enhancing the accuracy and efficiency of various steps, from target identification through lead optimization. More specifically, models such as AlphaFold and BioBERT have demonstrated immense potential in addressing age-old challenges in structural biology and biomedical text mining, respectively. Such advancements underscore the growing contribution of artificial intelligence (AI) in accelerating drug discovery processes [28].

AlphaFold by DeepMind has changed protein structure prediction with never-before-seen accuracy through the use of deep learning methods. Researchers in a pioneering research paper utilized structures predicted using AlphaFold in combination with Insilico Medicine's AI platforms,

PandaOmics and Chemistry42, to identify a new inhibitor for cyclin-dependent kinase 20 (CDK20) against hepatocellular carcinoma. AlphaFold's journey started with the launch of its initial release, AlphaFold 1, at the 13th Critical Assessment of Techniques for Protein Structure Prediction (CASP13) back in 2018. Its performance utilized deep learning to predict amino acid residue distance maps and obtained a median Global Distance Test (GDT) score of 68.5 across all targets, which was greater than other methods available then [29].

AlphaFold 2, unveiled in 2020 at CASP14, was a vast improvement in accuracy. It introduced the Evoformer architecture by merging numerous sequence alignments and residue pair interactions into near-experimental accuracy in protein structure prediction. AlphaFold 2 attained a median GDT score of 92.4, surpassing all other competitors, and a new benchmark in the business [30].

DeepMind and Isomorphic Labs issued AlphaFold 3 in May 2024, which takes the model's capabilities from protein structures to interaction with deoxyribonucleic acid (DNA), ribonucleic acid (RNA), small molecules, ions, and post-translational modifications. AlphaFold 3 is a diffusion-based architecture and can accurately predict the joint structure of complex biomolecular assemblies [31]. The AlphaFold Protein Structure Database, launched in July 2021, has been central to demystifying access to predicted protein structures. As of July 2022, the database contained over 200 million predictions for nearly every known protein sequence, thus accelerating research into numerous fields [32]. In a groundbreaking research study, researchers have utilized AlphaFold-predicted structures and Insilico Medicine's AI-driven platforms, PandaOmics and Chemistry42, for the discovery of a novel cyclin-dependent kinase 20 (CDK20) inhibitor for hepatocellular carcinoma [33].

This approach led to the identification of a high-potency molecule, ISM042-2-048 with IC_{50} = 33.4 ± 22.6 nM, within 30 days and following the synthesis of only 13 compounds. Such efficacy indicates AlphaFold's capability to accelerate the hit identification phase in drug discovery [34, 35]. Complementing structural prediction tools, BioBERT, a biomedical text mining domain adaptation of bidirectional encoder representations from transformers (BERT), has also enhanced the retrieval of valuable information from vast biomedical literature. In a recent study, BioBERT was applied to increase relation extraction processes by uniting the ChemProt (Chemical-protein) and DrugProt datasets and recording significant performance improvements in chemical-gene interaction detection. This is useful in facilitating the effective curation of potential drug-target relations, speeding up the early stages of drug discovery [36, 37]. The complementarity of AlphaFold and BioBERT is a testbed of the groundbreaking impact of LLMs in drug discovery. While AlphaFold accelerates the prediction of protein structures, facilitating easier structure-based drug design, BioBERT enhances literature-based retrieval of useful biomedical data, informing target identification and validation. The complementarity of the two models adds strength to a more streamlined and efficient drug discovery pipeline, which will facilitate the rapid development of new drugs [35].

The use of large language models (LLMs) for drug discovery, interpretation of clinical trials, and review of medical literature is fraught with significant data quality, model interpretability, and validation issues. Of primary concern among these are the quality and representativeness of training data. LLMs are typically derived from large databases that may hold unvalidated or skewed information and generate "hallucinations" of credible but incorrect outputs. This issue is particularly vital within healthcare, where decisions made based on false data can lead to grave consequences. In addition, the pervasive prevalence of data originating from high-income English-speaking regions introduces biases that might affect the objectivity and generalizability of LLMs in different populations [38]. Model interpretability is another crucial issue. LLMs, especially deep learning models, are "black boxes," and therefore it is difficult to understand the rationale for their output [39]. Such a lack of transparency poses a threat to trustworthiness and acceptability among clinicians who require explainable and transparent models for making clinical decisions. Work on enhancing interpretability, such as the integration of explainable AI (XAI) methods like SHapley Additive exPlanations (SHAP) and local interpretable model-agnostic explanations (LIME), is underway but far from solving these problems in totality [40].

Validation of LLM output continues to be a significant bottleneck. Studies have shown that different LLMs, or even the same model on different instances, can provide different analyses of identical clinical trial data due to model drift and differences in data preprocessing. The fluctuation creates challenges for reproducibility and dependability of LLM-facilitated analyses, pointing out the need for standard validation systems and continuous monitoring to ensure consistent performance in high-stakes healthcare use cases [41].

Figure 3.2 illustrates a modern drug discovery pipeline enhanced by AI models, emphasizing the roles of AlphaFold and BioBERT in streamlining various stages from target identification to clinical deployment. BioBERT, trained on biomedical text and datasets like ChemProt and DrugProt, enables efficient extraction of drug-target relationships from scientific literature. These insights feed into AlphaFold for protein structure prediction, guiding structure-based drug design. The pipeline progresses through lead optimization and clinical trials review, ultimately leading to validation and deployment. The diagram also highlights a successful application: the AI-driven discovery of a potent CDK20 inhibitor (ISM042-2-048) for hepatocellular carcinoma, achieved with minimal synthesis and within 30 days, demonstrating the rapid, cost-effective impact of AI in accelerating therapeutic development.

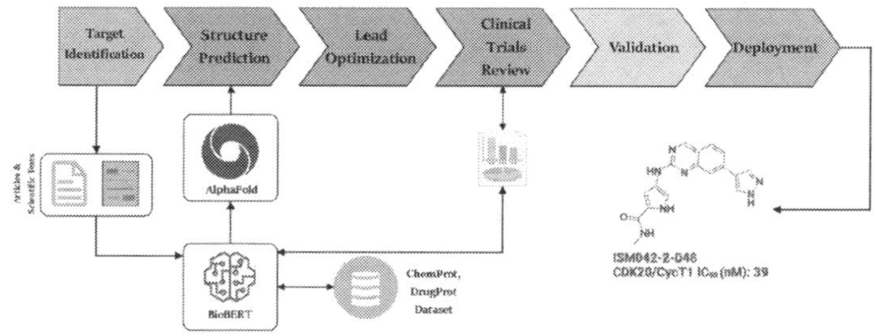

Figure 3.2 Modern drug discovery pipeline enhanced by AI models, emphasizing the roles of AlphaFold and BioBERT.

Table 3.2 provides a comprehensive overview of cutting-edge explainable AI (XAI) frameworks applied in healthcare. Notably, newer frameworks (2024–2025) emphasize human-AI collaboration, integrating LLMs with SHAP/LIME for transparent reasoning, while earlier approaches (2019–2023) relied on attention mechanisms or saliency maps. Evaluation strategies also evolved from qualitative expert reviews to quantitative metrics like formal verification (VERIFAI-LORE) and user-guided justification (Biomedical Claim Verification System). This progression reflects the field's shift toward clinician-centric interpretability and real-world usability in high-stakes medical AI.

3.3 LLMS IN CLINICAL TRIAL ANALYSIS

3.3.1 LLMs in trial design and patient recruitment

The use of large language models (LLMs) in clinical trial design has greatly enhanced efficiency and quality in the extraction of eligibility criteria. For instance, AutoCriteria uses GPT-based models to extract eligibility criteria from clinical trial text for contextual aspects such as negation, temporal relations, and entity typing. This approach has proven to generalize across other disease domains, including oncology and neurodegenerative conditions, to facilitate easier analysis of eligibility criteria and improve interoperability [57]. Similarly, Criteria2Query 3.0 uses GPT-4 to transform eligibility criteria into executable database queries with high fidelity in concept extraction and SQL generation to enable patient eligibility determination automation [58]. Within patient recruitment, LLMs have played a pivotal role in the automation of patient matching with suitable clinical trials.

Table 3.2 Summary of recent XAI methods for LLMs in healthcare

Framework	*Year*	*Application domain*	*Key features*	*Evaluation metric*
Biomedical Claim Verification System [42]	2025	Biomedical Claim Verification	Integrates LLMs with SHAP values for transparent reasoning in claim verification tasks.	SHAP-based word-level attribution, user-guided justification, and consensus-based narrative summaries.
Clinician XAI Survey	2025	Clinical Outcome Prediction	Surveys clinician preferences on XAI techniques like LIME, SHAP, and attention mechanisms.	Clinician preference rankings, interpretability ratings, and usability feedback.
TranspNet [43]	2024	Trustworthy AI Systems	Combines LLMs with ontologies and logical reasoning to enhance transparency in AI systems.	Semantic and structural similarity metrics for ontology evaluation.
XAI4LLM [44]	2024	Clinical Decision Support	Integrates ML models and LLMs for enhanced in-context learning in healthcare diagnostics.	Prediction accuracy, cost-sensitivity analysis, and clinical decision-making effectiveness.
Storytelling XAI Framework [45]	2024	Healthcare Narrative Explanations	Utilizes narratives and knowledge distillation for concept-based explanations in healthcare.	Human-centered evaluations focusing on interpretability and trustworthiness.
VERIFAI-LORE	2024	Cardiac Risk Evaluation	Employs local rule-based explanations with formal verification for trustworthy AI predictions.	Formal verification metrics and local rule-based explanation assessments.
MentalLLaMA [46]	2024	Mental health analysis	Prompt-based (ChatGPT with task-specific instructions)	BART-score, Human Eval

(*Continued*)

Table 3.2 (Continued)

Framework	*Year*	*Application domain*	*Key features*	*Evaluation metric*
ArgMed-Agents [47]	2024	Clinical decision reasoning	Prompt-based (self-argumentation iterations + symbolic solver)	Prediction accuracy with LLM evaluator
Diagnostic reasoning prompts [48]	2024	Medical Question Answering (MedQA)	Prompt-based (Bayesian, differential, analytical, intuitive reasoning)	Expert Evaluation, Inter-rater Agreement
SkinGEN [49]	2024	Dermatological diagnosis	Visual explanations (Stable Diffusion), interactive UI	Perceived explainability ratings
DR. KNOWS [50]	2023	Automated diagnosis generation	Knowledge Graph (explainable diagnostic pathway)	Qualitative Review
Human-AI Collaboration [51]	2023	Clinical decision-making	Salient features, counterfactual explanations	Agreement Level, Usability Questionnaires
ChatGPT (mental health) [52]	2023	Mental health analysis	Prompt-based (emotional cues + few-shot expert-written examples)	BART-score, Human Evaluation
CHiLL [53]	2023	Clinical prediction (X-ray, report classification)	Interpretable features, linear models	Expert Eval, Clinical Judgement Alignment
Trap-VQA [54]	2022	Pathology Visual QA	Grad-CAM, SHAP	Qualitative Evaluation
Vision Transformer [55]	2021	Covid-19 diagnosis	Saliency maps	Visualization
ClinicalBERT [56]	2019	Predicting hospital readmission	Attention weights	Visualization

The TrialGTP model, for example, employs a three-module methodology to select candidate trials, predict patient eligibility, and rank the trials. Trials have been found to be capable of recalling more than 90% of the corresponding trials with 87.3% accuracy in matching patients with criteria, greatly reducing time for patient screening [59]. Furthermore, the RECTIFIER tool demonstrated that manual screening can be beaten by LLM-enabled prescreening in terms of sensitivity, specificity, and accuracy, attesting to the potential of LLMs in making clinical trial recruitment processes more efficient [60]. Apart from eligibility criteria extraction and patient recruitment, LLMs have also been employed in the development of clinical trial protocols.

The AutoTrial system, for instance, facilitates the generation of eligibility criteria through the generation of understandable and fluent texts representing pertinent clinical concepts. The method has been validated against a large set of clinical trials and has demonstrated its capability to generate high-quality criteria in line with up-to-date clinical standards [61]. In addition, studies have proven that LLMs are able to effectively evaluate multi-aspect eligibility criteria, both with intricate semantic connections and with modifiers, thereby supporting the development of more precise and detailed trial protocols [62].

3.3.2 LLMs for extraction clinical trial data

Recently, the rise of large language models (LLMs) has indicated a major shift in biomedical informatics, particularly in automating data extraction from clinical trial reports and protocols. This alteration is especially important as the volume and complexity of clinical data continue to increase, placing greater demands on researchers and regulators. By utilizing the natural language processing abilities of LLMs, researchers can now handle unstructured text more effectively, thereby speeding up processes in drug discovery, clinical trial evaluation, and medical literature assessment. These progressions are not just theoretical; empirical research has shown that LLMs effectively enhance accuracy and throughput at various stages of clinical studies [63].

A key application of LLMs lies in generating and standardizing clinical trial protocols, a historically labor-intensive process. Specifically, recent implementations of GPT-4 have demonstrated the capacity to author entire protocol sections from structured study-level metadata, thereby reducing both the cognitive load on clinical researchers and the time to protocol finalization [63]. The automation of protocol creation accelerates trial commencement and promotes regulatory adherence by guaranteeing uniformity and traceability in the records. Consequently, LLMs are progressively incorporated into clinical trial management systems to facilitate scalable, high-accuracy documentation processes. Moreover, LLMs have been utilized with notable effectiveness in retrieving structured data through the PICO (Population, Intervention, Comparator, Outcome) framework, which is essential to evidence-based medicine. For example, the GPT-4o model was utilized to retrieve more than 680,000 PICO elements from abstracts of randomized clinical trials, demonstrating the scalability and accuracy of extraction pipelines powered by LLMs [64].

In a complementary effort, the AlpaPICO framework introduced a novel architecture incorporating instruction tuning and in-context learning, resulting in state-of-the-art performance on EBM-NLP datasets [65]. These developments collectively underscore the role of LLMs in translating free-text clinical evidence into analyzable datasets.

Building upon this, LLMs have shown considerable promise in automating systematic literature reviews (SLRs), a critical step in synthesizing clinical evidence. A notable study evaluating GPT-4-assisted data extraction from randomized controlled trials (RCTs) reported an average accuracy of 84%, superior in capturing patient characteristics compared to other data fields [66]. Moreover, introducing the LEADS foundation model marked a significant advancement, outperforming generic LLMs in tasks such as article screening, evidence tagging, and structured data extraction [67]. These findings affirm the utility of domain-specific fine-tuning in improving model reliability across diverse review tasks.

In addition to standard trial analysis, LLMs have also facilitated the automation of complex methodologies such as network meta-analyses (NMA). By employing GPT-4 for data extraction, R script generation, and output interpretation, researchers have demonstrated the feasibility of near-complete automation of NMA workflows [68]. This approach enhances reproducibility and reduces the technical expertise required to perform high-quality NMAs, thereby democratizing access to advanced evidence synthesis methods. Such capabilities position LLMs as indispensable tools in the evolving ecosystem of clinical decision support.

Figure 3.3 presents a hybrid trial-matching framework that leverages GPT-4o and a combination of No-SQL and vector databases (MongoDB and Chroma DB) to streamline the matching of clinical trials to patient records. Starting with metadata from over 110,600 esophageal cancer-related trials on PubMed, the system extracts and embeds textual features using models like "**bge-large-en-v1.5.**" These embeddings populate a hybrid database, enabling efficient semantic search. Physicians input patient-specific criteria, which are converted into structured queries. GPT-4o assists by filtering and generating vector-based search queries, retrieving the most relevant clinical trials using cosine similarity. The system then presents full trial descriptions, checks eligibility and exclusion criteria, and categorizes trials as eligible, ineligible, or unknown supporting clinicians in making the final inclusion decision. This pipeline exemplifies the transformative

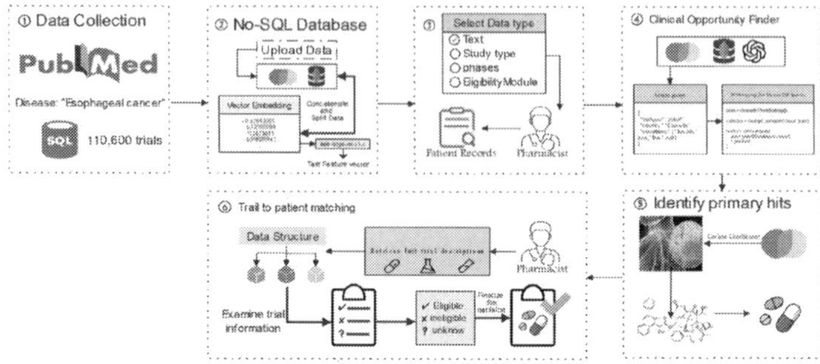

Figure 3.3 GPT-4o-enabled hybrid pipeline for automated clinical trial matching using structured queries and vector search.

potential of LLMs in optimizing clinical trial recruitment with speed, precision, and scalability.

3.3.3 LLMs in real-time clinical monitoring

The integration of large language models (LLMs) in clinical studies and pharmacovigilance has revolutionized real-time monitoring and adverse event (AE) detection. With the help of the power of LLMs, researchers and doctors are now able to analyze humongous amounts of unstructured data, enabling early detection of possible safety issues. It is most significant in drug discovery, monitoring of clinical trials, and analysis of medical literature, where the speedy and accurate detection of AE is crucial.

The advent of immune checkpoint inhibitors (ICIs) revolutionized cancer therapy at the cost of potentially life-threatening and severe immune-related adverse events (irAEs). Traditional detection methods are very insensitive and only sensitive to rough clinical expression of irAEs, relying primarily on International Classification of Diseases (ICD) codes.

Recent advancements in artificial intelligence, particularly the application of large language models (LLMs), have been promising to enhance the identification and monitoring of irAEs by effectively processing unstructured clinical data. A seminal paper by Sun et al. (2024) compared the performance of an LLM that had been augmented with retrieval-augmented generation (RAG) to identify irAEs among patients undergoing ICI therapy [69]. The study compared 7,555 hospitalizations, looking for common irAEs such as colitis, hepatitis, pneumonitis, and myocarditis. The LLM demonstrated 94.7% sensitivity in detecting irAEs, more than double the 68.7% sensitivity of ICD codes with comparable specificity (93.7% vs. 92.4%)

[70]. This significant improvement illustrates the capability of LLMs to identify adverse events not captured by standard coding systems.

Apart from accuracy, the speed at which LLMs process clinical data is impressive. According to the same study, the LLM took an average of only 9.53 s per chart in identifying irAEs, which is much better than the estimated 15 min of manual chart review. Such processing speed enables real-time surveillance and prompt intervention, which in the management of serious adverse events and the improvement of patient outcomes, is crucial. The LLM's robustness was further validated in an external dataset of 1,270 hospital admissions from a different institution. In the validation cohort, the LLM exhibited a mean sensitivity of 98.1% and specificity of 95.7%. This reinforces the LLM's generalizability and reliability across various clinical settings. Such consistency is vital for the broader application of LLMs in heterogeneous healthcare environments [71]. Moreover, LLM's ability to identify more cases of irAEs in addition to manual adjudication highlights its promise to aid the identification of subtle clinical patterns beyond human reviewers. This is particularly valuable in complex cases in which irAEs present with unexpected symptoms or with other disorders. Through a more complete detection process, LLMs can enhance patient safety and inform more successful treatments [72]. Applications of LLMs are also valuable in aspects of accessibility and scalability. As open-source models, they may be deployed on existing electronic health record platforms, so there is the potential for institutions with any size and capability to deploy advanced monitoring tools without significant financial or technical barriers. Technology openness provides more patients with access to improved surveillance and care.

Systematic surveillance of chemotherapy-induced toxicities in oncology is mandated to guarantee patient safety as well as optimize treatment effectiveness. Traditional methods of surveillance using standard clinical assessment and self-reporting by the patient are time-consuming and can do little to capture real-time patient experience [73]. The integration of large language models (LLMs) in clinical practice offers an appealing option for the optimization of detecting and classifying subjective toxicities, allowing 24/7 monitoring and early intervention [74].

A recent pilot study evaluated the efficacy of LLMs in classifying subjective toxicities experienced by patients undergoing chemotherapy. The study involved 13 oncologists who assessed 30 fictitious cases created using expert knowledge and OpenAI's GPT-4. Based on the Common Terminology Criteria for Adverse Events (CTCAE v.5), the evaluations were compared to those of a contextualized LLM model. The LLM achieved an accuracy of 85.7% in general toxicity categories and 64.6% in specific categories, demonstrating performance comparable to that of expert oncologists in general classifications [74]. Monitoring in real-time by LLMs is key in the prevention of higher degrees of toxicity that can lead to changes in treatment or hospitalization. The continuous monitoring of patient reports and clinical data by LLMs enables them to detect adverse events early enough so that early intervention by clinicians can be made.

LLMs' real-time monitoring capabilities are essential in preventing the advanced levels of toxicity that could lead to treatment adjustments or hospitalization. With continuous assessment of patient-reports and clinical data, LLMs are able to detect adverse events promptly, enabling clinicians to initiate timely interventions. Early intervention enhances patient protection and maximizes the overall quality of oncology care provision. The evaluation also noted the range of oncologists' ratings from 66.7% to 89.2% for broad categories and from 57.0% to 76.0% for specific categories. The LLM's performance in broad categories fell within this range, attesting to its usefulness as a potential tool for toxicity classification. However, the lower accuracy for specific categories indicates that LLMs must be improved and further trained to enhance specificity in toxicity detection. The use of LLMs in clinical practice has multiple advantages, such as reduced clinician workload, enhanced monitoring of patients, and more personalized care as a potential benefit. By facilitating automated classification of subjective toxicities, LLMs can reduce the workload of the oncologists to enable them to undertake more sophisticated decision-making processes.

The LLMs' real-time monitoring can also lead to earlier detection of side effects and accordingly better patient outcomes. Although the pilot study provides heartening facts about the potential of LLMs, it also highlights certain restrictions. Use of simulated scenarios and lack of patient interaction may not fully capture the complexity of clinical scenarios in real practice. Future research should focus on training LLMs with real patient data, incorporating interactive evaluations, and expanding sample sizes to ensure robustness and generalizability across diverse clinical settings [74]. Its rapid growth creates serious challenges for pharmacovigilance, particularly for the timely detection of safety signals. Human screening processes are slow and susceptible to bias, with the potential to delay interventions for safety. The recent development of large language models (LLMs) such as GPT-3.5, GPT-4, and Claude2 has demonstrated promising potential in computerized literature screening, which can streamline pharmacovigilance activities and improve accuracy [75].

According to research from Guo et al. (2023) introduced a novel workflow utilizing GPT-3.5 and GPT-4 APIs for screening titles and abstracts in clinical reviews. The models were evaluated against human-reviewed papers across six reviews, screening over 24,000 titles and abstracts. The results indicated an overall accuracy of 91%, with a sensitivity of 91% for excluded documents and 76% for included documents, highlighting the potential of LLMs to streamline the clinical review process [75]. Farhadi and Taheri (2025) emphasized the vital role of Generative AI (GenAI) in addressing data shortages and privacy limitations in healthcare systems by generating synthetic clinical data. Their study investigates how strict regulatory frameworks, such as Health Insurance Portability and Accountability Act (HIPAA) and General Data Protection Regulation (GDPR), often limit access to real medical records, obstructing research, innovation, and educational efforts [76].

By generating synthetic datasets that emulate the statistical patterns and contextual meanings of actual patient records, GenAI models provide a scalable option that protects patient privacy while maintaining data usability. The authors emphasize that synthetic data produced by GenAI can effectively replace real data in training machine learning models, evaluating healthcare applications, and creating AI prototypes while upholding ethical and legal standards. Their analysis further examines the existing methods and frameworks for generating synthetic data, focusing on the technical difficulties and possible risks, such as model fidelity, overfitting, and identity disclosure via inversion attacks. This research makes a notable contribution to the current conversation surrounding ethical AI use in healthcare by introducing synthetic data as a link between innovation and regulation.

Additionally, Taheri et al. investigated the impactful potential of generative artificial intelligence (GenAI) in reducing the administrative workload encountered by clinicians, especially in relation to electronic health records and documentation processes. Their research highlights that repetitive activities like medical coding, summarizing notes, and managing records often interfere with providing personalized patient care. GenAI models, due to their capacity to generate coherent and contextually appropriate responses, are seen as effective tools for automating or optimizing these tasks, allowing clinicians to shift their attention to more essential healthcare duties. The authors provide multiple case-based examples illustrating how GenAI can be incorporated into clinical settings to enhance operational efficiency. Their evaluation also highlights crucial aspects concerning the secure implementation of these systems, such as matters related to bias, transparency, and ethical accountability. In summary, the research offers a persuasive perspective on how GenAI can transform clinical processes, reduce burnout, and enhance the quality of patient care by providing smart administrative assistance [77].

Figure 3.4 illustrates a comprehensive pipeline leveraging LLMs and retrieval-augmented generation (RAG) for real-time adverse event (AE) detection in clinical settings. Input data is sourced from various clinical records, including EHR systems, patient self-reports, imaging reports, clinical notes, drug logs, and lab results. This unstructured data undergoes preprocessing text extraction, de-identification, noise removal, standardization, and structuring before being analyzed by an LLM–RAG framework. The model outputs AE type, severity, and confidence score, which subsequently trigger actions such as real-time alerts to clinicians, automatic

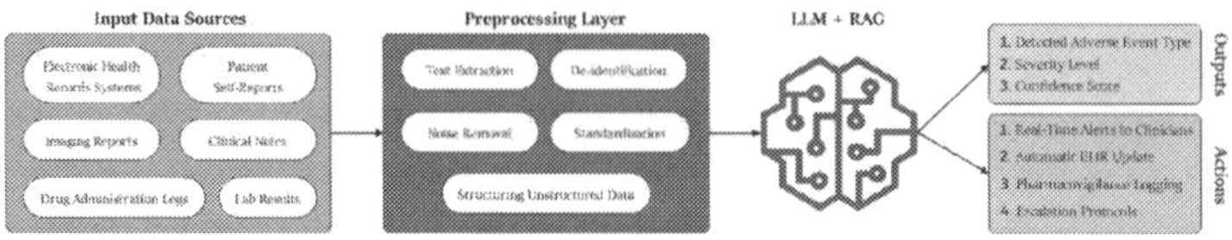

Figure 3.4 Real-time monitoring and adverse event detection using large language models (LLMs).

EHR updates, pharmacovigilance logging, and escalation protocols, thereby enabling timely and accurate clinical decision-making.

3.4 KEY LIMITATIONS

Incorporating large language models (LLMs) into the biomedical research workflow has sparked a transformative change in the automation of systematic reviews and meta-analyses, particularly in areas such as drug discovery, clinical trial synthesis, and the extensive evaluation of medical literature. Historically, these tasks require careful manual organization, specialized knowledge, and prolonged timelines.

LLMs, trained on vast biomedical corpora and enhanced through techniques like retrieval-augmented generation (RAG), are increasingly capable of parsing, summarizing, and contextualizing clinical findings at scale [78]. These models can streamline identifying relevant studies, extract key trial metrics, and generate comprehensive narratives while maintaining consistency across heterogeneous datasets. In drug discovery, LLMs support meta-analytical synthesis by evaluating treatment efficacy across multiphase trials, identifying off-target effects, and correlating biomolecular interactions with clinical endpoints. For instance, the ability of LLMs to structure findings from HER2-targeted therapies in biliary tract cancers has highlighted promising response rates and survival outcomes from early-phase trials [78]. Likewise, in clinical trial analysis, LLMs can automate the comparison of survival metrics and adverse event profiles as demonstrated in analyses of immunotherapies like pembrolizumab in esophageal carcinoma, thus reducing researcher bias and enhancing reproducibility [79]. Furthermore, when integrated with robust misinformation mitigation frameworks, LLMs show improved resistance to generating misleading medical narratives, an essential safeguard for high-stakes decision-making in evidence-based medicine [80]. Ultimately, LLMs' utility in automating meta-analytical tasks extends beyond efficiency; they enable a new standard of data integrity, scalability, and interdisciplinary synthesis. However, their successful deployment requires stringent safety measures, domain-adapted tuning, and transparent validation protocols to ensure that outputs remain clinically actionable and free of epistemic bias. Continued advancements in prompt engineering and alignment techniques will make LLMs a reliable tool for biomedical evidence synthesis [78]. Lataran et al. propose an integrated approach to tackling healthcare fraud by combining the semantic power of transformer-based models with the security of blockchain technology. Their model, HI-BERT, modifies the BERT architecture to align more closely with healthcare-specific vocabulary and diagnostic classification standards, thereby improving the system's ability to detect fraudulent medical prescriptions. The authors also incorporate Naive Bayes classification to label prescriptions according to disease categories and measure their semantic similarity to ICD codes, enhancing interpretability and trust in model outputs. In parallel, the use of a hybrid blockchain infrastructure ensures the secure storage and access of medical records, addressing longstanding concerns about data privacy and system transparency. The study demonstrates how the convergence of language models and blockchain technology can create robust infrastructures for safeguarding healthcare systems while enabling more intelligent fraud detection mechanisms [81].

3.4.1 Medical text mining for evidence and hypothesis generation

The difficulty of extracting practical insights from unstructured medical documents like clinical notes, PubMed abstracts, and electronic health records (EHRs) has been greatly reduced by the emergence of large language models (LLMs).

These models can parse complex medical narratives through their contextual understanding and zero-shot reasoning abilities, enabling structured information extraction at scale. A study using EHR data from Mass General Brigham demonstrated that open-source LLMs outperformed traditional pattern-matching algorithms in extracting social determinants of health (SDoH), with accuracy gains of up to 40% for the mentioned elements, showcasing their robustness across heterogeneous clinical narratives [82]. This capacity to automate labor-intensive annotation tasks holds transformative potential for epidemiological studies, cohort selection, and predictive modeling. In drug discovery and clinical trial analysis, LLMs are increasingly leveraged to extract and contextualize mechanistic details, therapeutic outcomes, and biomarker associations from publications and reports. For example, hallucination-tolerant LLMs counterintuitively have demonstrated improved ROC–AUC in molecule classification tasks when their generated molecular descriptions are integrated into prompts, indicating that controlled semantic generation may augment downstream performance [83]. Furthermore, in systematic reviews across gastroenterology and hepatology, LLM-based models enhanced the precision of disease feature extraction from endoscopy notes and radiology reports, contributing to clinical decision support with evidence-backed confidence [84].

Large language models (LLMs) are redefining the epistemic architecture of evidence-based medicine (EBM) by automating the synthesis, evaluation, and generation of clinical evidence from diverse sources. Traditional EBM relies heavily on meta-analyses and randomized controlled trials (RCTs), often lacking real-world applicability due to narrow patient populations and rigid experimental constraints. LLMs can bridge this gap by enabling high-throughput literature synthesis, extracting heterogeneous clinical endpoints, and aligning them with patient-centered outcomes. For instance, the EvidenceMap framework uses small language models to enhance biomedical question answering through structured evidence mapping and reasoning, significantly outperforming conventional LLM approaches in logical coherence and factual accuracy [85]. LLMs offer a computational scaffold for ideating novel therapeutic directions and trial designs in hypothesis generation. Recent studies have demonstrated that LLMs can be trained to operate under domain-specific constraints to generate scientifically plausible hypotheses that align with real-world research objectives. For example, in materials and drug discovery, LLM-driven agents have produced context-aware hypotheses by synthesizing goal-directed prompts with constraint logic, emulating expert reasoning processes [86]. This generative capability is further complemented by Bayesian statistical models and pragmatic trial designs, which, when integrated with LLM outputs, create a robust framework for exploratory and confirmatory research in clinical settings [87]. Such integration enhances translational fidelity and accelerates the iterative feedback loop between data generation and hypothesis refinement in biomedical sciences.

3.4.2 Challenges in contradiction detection and accuracy

Despite the remarkable utility of large language models (LLMs) in streamlining medical literature reviews, significant challenges remain in handling contradictory findings and maintaining factual accuracy. The inherently probabilistic nature of LLMs renders them susceptible to "hallucinations" fabricated content that appears plausible yet lacks factual grounding. In medical contexts, this vulnerability becomes a critical concern. A recent study found that even top-tier models like GPT-4o and LLaMA3-70B generated misleading medical content in over half of test scenarios when prompted with illogical requests, underscoring their limited capacity to detect inconsistencies across literature sources without dedicated safety tuning [80].

Additionally, LLMs often struggle with conflicting evidence, particularly when synthesizing findings from heterogeneous study designs or populations. This is exemplified in systematic review tasks, where models like GPT-3.5 and GPT-4o showed varying sensitivity and specificity in classifying randomized controlled trials, suggesting an inconsistent ability to discern methodological quality or reconcile divergent results [88]. Moreover, while fine-tuning and retrieval-augmented generation have improved factual alignment, challenges persist in adapting LLM outputs to real-world clinical contexts, especially when those involve nuanced reasoning or ambiguous clinical presentations [78]. Addressing these limitations necessitates advanced model architectures and robust evaluation pipelines that incorporate domain-specific logic verification and contradiction detection to safeguard against erroneous conclusions in evidence-based medicine.

3.5 CONCLUSION AND FUTURE DIRECTIONS

The use of large language models (LLMs) in medicine has revolutionized drug discovery, clinical trial analysis, and review of medical literature. LLMs assist in the identification of new drug targets and drug efficacy prediction with massive biomedical data. LLMs, for example, can predict the activity, toxicity, and pharmacokinetic properties of new chemicals and thereby improve early-stage drug screening processes. In the analysis of clinical trials, LLMs enable trial matching for patients by interpreting intricate eligibility criteria and unstructured patient information, thus improving trial recruitment efficiency and accuracy. Research has shown that LLMs exceed traditional methods in matching patients with suitable clinical trials, surpassing human specialists in certain situations. In terms of medical literature review, LLMs facilitate the integration of research results, allowing for quick absorption of new information.

They are able to successfully identify applicable literature, gather required information, and prepare elaborate summaries, and hence accelerate the process of literature review for clinicians and researchers alike [4]. Some of the current trends of interacting with LLMs in healthcare are the creation of multimodal models that combine textual data with medical imaging and other forms of information for enhancing diagnostic accuracy. Integration of real-world evidence, e.g., electronic health records, into LLMs makes them more practical in clinical environments, as it offers context-rich information.

Moreover, LLMs that customize suggestions based on specific patient data advance the personalization of medicine, resulting in more accurate and efficient therapies [89]. These developments highlight the transformative capabilities of LLMs in revolutionizing healthcare methods and enhancing patient results. Combining large language models (LLMs) with multimodal competence is transforming radiology and medicine by preparing them to perform simultaneous interpretation of images, text, and structured clinical data. Multimodal models are particularly potent in clinical uses of radiographic imaging, histopathology, and electronic health records.

For instance, research on compositional generalization has demonstrated that multimodal LLMs (MLLMs) trained across various imaging modalities and anatomical regions can generalize better across unseen clinical tasks, enhancing diagnostic scalability and reducing dependency on large labeled datasets [90]. This framework enables richer semantic reasoning and cross-modal knowledge transfer, which is vital in drug discovery processes that depend on both molecular imaging and clinical text synthesis. Parallelly, the application of real-world evidence (RWE) in clinical trials and drug development is increasingly gaining popularity through the deployment of LLMs. Through the capacity to extract unstructured medical data like physician feedback, patient-reported outcomes, and diagnostic codes, LLMs are able to identify treatment outcomes and side effects in heterogeneous populations.

This capacity supports pragmatic trial emulation and enhances the generalizability of clinical findings [91]. Moreover, these models empower personalized medicine by synthesizing an individual's genomic, phenotypic, and lifestyle data to predict disease risk and tailor therapeutic strategies. For example, LLMs have been successfully applied to detect early signs of chronic conditions like diabetes and cardiovascular disease by correlating patient symptoms, lab results, and literature-based risk factors [92]. These developments mark a significant shift from population-level analyses to patient-specific clinical decision support.

Also, Mahalegi et al. explore how Generative AI can be a powerful tool in addressing the persistent challenge of resource optimization within modern healthcare systems. Their research explores the application of sophisticated generative models, such as variational autoencoders and generative adversarial networks, to generate high-quality synthetic medical data, enabling better predictive analytics, enhanced personalization, and optimal distribution of clinical resources. The writers emphasize how these models tackle significant challenges like limited data and privacy issues, which frequently obstruct data-driven healthcare solutions. Furthermore, the study emphasizes the utility of transformer-based generative models for extracting actionable insights from complex electronic health records, thereby improving operational foresight and responsiveness. By demonstrating the potential of GenAI to elevate the efficiency and precision of healthcare delivery systems, the chapter contributes a forward-looking perspective on integrating AI-driven tools into systemic healthcare reform and intelligent resource management [93].

As large language models (LLMs) gain traction in medical literature review, drug discovery, and clinical trial interpretation, the imperative for responsible AI development and active collaboration with domain experts has become increasingly evident. The sophisticated outputs of LLMs while linguistically coherent can obscure underlying inaccuracies or biases if not subjected to expert scrutiny. A comprehensive review of medical peer review practices found that LLMs such as ChatGPT could assist with linguistic editing and reviewer triage. However, it underscored their limitations in evaluating clinical validity and ethical appropriateness, advocating for structured human oversight in all high-stakes applications [94]. This necessity is especially pronounced in biomedical settings, where clinical decision-making depends on nuanced interpretation of heterogeneous data. Responsible AI frameworks must emphasize co-design with medical professionals to ensure models are technically robust and contextually aligned with clinical realities. As emphasized in the broader literature on AI deployment in drug development, the effectiveness of LLMs is contingent upon interdisciplinary validation pipelines where outputs are continuously evaluated against evolving therapeutic standards and regulatory expectations [95]. Such collaboration enables iterative refinement of LLM applications, from hypothesis generation to cohort selection, fostering transparency, accountability, and equity in real-world use.

Furthermore, Rashidieranjbar et al. offer an extensive outlook on the revolutionary impact of generative artificial intelligence on various facets of healthcare delivery and innovation. Their research examines how GenAI technologies able to create multimodal content like text, images, and code can be customized to tackle various medical issues, including medical imaging, pandemic prediction, synthetic data creation, clinical documentation, and patient interaction. The writers emphasize GenAI's ability to adapt to particular clinical requirements, framing it as a potentially essential part of contemporary healthcare teams. Simultaneously, they highlight the ethical, legal, and privacy concerns that could impede the broad implementation of these technologies without strong governance structures being developed. By presenting GenAI as a facilitator of medical advancement and a driver of organizational change, their efforts highlight the necessity of assessing and incorporating these tools thoughtfully into healthcare systems [96].

REFERENCES

1. De Vito, G., Ferrucci, F., & Angelakis, A. (2025). LLMs for Drug-Drug Interaction Prediction: A Comprehensive Comparison. *arXiv preprint arXiv:2502.06890*. https://arxiv.org/abs/2502.06890
2. Nievas, M., Basu, A., Wang, Y., & Singh, H. (2023). Distilling Large Language Models for Matching Patients to Clinical Trials. *arXiv preprint arXiv:2312.09958*. https://arxiv.org/abs/2312.09958
3. Ronquillo, J., Ye, J., Gorman, D., Lemeshow, A., & Watt, S. (2024). Practical Aspects of Using Large Language Models to Screen Abstracts for Cardiovascular Drug Development: Cross-Sectional Study. *JMIR Med Inform*, *12*, e64143. https://doi.org/10.2196/64143

4. Zhang, K., Meng, X., Yan, X., Ji, J., Liu, J., Xu, H., Zhang, H., Liu, D., Wang, J., Wang, X., Gao, J., Wang, Y., Shao, C., Wang, W., Li, J., Zheng, M., Yang, Y., & Tang, Y. (2025). Revolutionizing Health Care: The Transformative Impact of Large Language Models in Medicine. *J Med Internet Res*, *27*, e59069. https://doi.org/10.2196/59069
5. Wang, H., Guo, F., Du, M., *et al.* (2022). A novel method for drug-target interaction prediction based on graph transformers model. *BMC Bioinf*, *23*, 459. https://doi.org/10.1186/s12859-022-04812-w
6. Liu, X., Lu, Z., Wang, T., & Liu, F. (2024). Large language models facilitating modern molecular biology and novel drug development. *Front Pharmacol*, *15*, 1458739. https://doi.org/10.3389/fphar.2024.1458739
7. Cao, H., Liu, Z., Lu, X., Yao, Y., & Li, Y. (2023). InstructMol: Multi-Modal Integration for Building a Versatile and Reliable Molecular Assistant in Drug Discovery. *arXiv preprint arXiv:2311.16208*. https://arxiv.org/abs/2311.16208
8. Gao, B., Huang, Y., Liu, Y., Xie, W., Ma, W., Zhang, Y., & Lan, Y. (2025). PharmAgents: Building a Virtual Pharma with Large Language Model Agents. *arXiv preprint arXiv:2503.22164*. https://arxiv.org/abs/2503.22164
9. Singh, A., Tekin, E., Nadeem, M., ElNaker, N. A., Sayeed, M. A., Vassilieva, N., & Amor, B. B. (2025). Chem42: A Family of chemical Language Models for Target-aware Ligand Generation. *arXiv preprint arXiv:2503.16563*. https://arxiv.org/abs/2503.16563
10. Farhadi, A., Zamanifar, A., & Faezipour, M. (2025). Application of Generative AI in Drug Discovery. In: Zamanifar, A., Faezipour, M. (Eds.), *Application of Generative AI in Healthcare Systems*. Springer, Cham. https://doi.org/10.1007/978-3-031-82963-5_6
11. Zhang, K., Zhu, R., Ma, S., Xiong, J., Kim, Y., Murai, F., & Liu, X. (2025). KEDRec-LM: A Knowledge-distilled Explainable Drug Recommendation Large Language Model. *arXiv preprint arXiv:2502.20350*. https://arxiv.org/abs/2502.20350
12. Christophe, C., Kanithi, P. K., Raha, T., Khan, S., & Pimentel, M. A. (2024). Med42-v2: A Suite of Clinical LLMs. *arXiv preprint arXiv:2408.06142*. https://arxiv.org/abs/2408.06142
13. Labrak, Y., Bazoge, A., Morin, E., Gourraud, P. A., Rouvier, M., & Dufour, R. (2024). BioMistral: A Collection of Open-Source Pretrained Large Language Models for Medical Domains. *arXiv preprint arXiv:2402.10373*.
14. Singhal, K., Tu, T., Gottweis, J., Sayres, R., Wulczyn, E., Hou, L., Clark, K., Pfohl, S., Cole-Lewis, H., Neal, D., et al. (2024). Towards expert-level medical question answering with large language models. *arXiv preprint arXiv:2305.09617*.
15. Liu, Z., Li, Y., Shu, P., Zhong, A., Yang, L., Ju, C., Wu, Z., Ma, C., Luo, J., Chen, C., et al. (2023). Radiology-Llama2: Best-in-Class Large Language Model for Radiology. *arXiv preprint arXiv:2309.06419*.
16. Liu, Z., Yu, X., Zhang, L., Wu, Z., Cao, C., Dai, H., Zhao, L., Liu, W., Shen, D., Li, Q., et al. (2023). Deid-gpt: Zero-shot medical text de-identification by gpt-4. *arXiv preprint arXiv:2303.11032*.

17. Umapathi, L. K., & Pal, A. (2023). Sankarasubbu, M. Med-halt: Medical domain hallucination test for large language models. *arXiv preprint arXiv:2307.15343.*
18. Zhao, Z., Wang, S., Gu, J., Zhu, Y., Mei, L., Zhuang, Z., Cui, Z., Wang, Q., & Shen, D. (2023). ChatCAD+: Towards a Universal and Reliable Interactive CAD using LLMs. *arXiv preprint arXiv:2305.15964.*
19. Luo, R., Sun, L., Xia, Y., Qin, T., Zhang, S., Poon, H., & Liu, T. Y. (2022). BioGPT: Generative pre-trained transformer for biomedical text generation and mining. *Briefings Bioinform*, 23, bbac409.
20. Yang, X., Chen, A., PourNejatian, N., Shin, H. C., Smith, K. E., Parisien, C., Compas, C., Martin, C., Flores, M. G., Zhang, Y., et al. (2022). Gatortron: A large clinical language model to unlock patient information from unstructured electronic health records. *arXiv preprint arXiv:2203.03540.*
21. Yuan, H., Yuan, Z., Gan, R., Zhang, J., Xie, Y., Yu, S. (2022). BioBART: Pretraining and evaluation of a biomedical generative language model. *arXiv preprint arXiv:2204.03905.*
22. Lu, Q., Dou, D., & Nguyen, T. (2022). ClinicalT5: A generative language model for clinical text. In *Proceedings of the Findings of the Association for Computational Linguistics: EMNLP, Abu Dhabi, United Arab Emirates*, 7–11 December 2022; pp. 5436–5443.
23. Yuan, Z., Liu, Y., Tan, C., Huang, S., & Huang, F. (2021). Improving biomedical pretrained language models with knowledge. *arXiv preprint arXiv:2104.10344.*
24. Raj, D., Sahu, S., & Anand, A. (2017). Learning local and global contexts using a convolutional recurrent network model for relation classification in biomedical text. In *Proceedings of the 21st Conference on Computational Natural Language Learning (CoNLL 2017)*, Vancouver, BC, Canada, 3–4 August 2017; pp. 311–321.
25. Lyu, C., Chen, B., Ren, Y., & Ji, D. (2017). Long short-term memory RNN for biomedical named entity recognition. *BMC Bioinform*, 18, 462.
26. Vuppala, S., Kim, J., Joo, B.-S., Choi, J.-M., & Jang, J. (2022). A Combination of Pharmacophore-Based Virtual Screening, Structure-Based Lead Optimization, and DFT Study for the Identification of *S. epidermidis* TcaR Inhibitors. *Pharmaceuticals*, *15*(5), 635. https://doi.org/10.3390/ph15050635
27. Afzaal, H., Altaf, R., Ilyas, U., Zaman, S. U., Abbas Hamdani, S. D., Khan, S., Zafar, H., Babar, M. M., & Duan, Y. (2022). Virtual screening and drug repositioning of FDA-approved drugs from the ZINC database to identify the potential hTERT inhibitors. *Front Pharmacol*, *13*, 1048691. https://doi.org/10.3389/fphar.2022.1048691
28. Lee, J., Yoon, W., Kim, S., Kim, D., Kim, S., So, C. H., & Kang, J. (2019). BioBERT: A pre-trained biomedical language representation model for biomedical text mining. *Bioinformatics*, *36*(4), 1234–1240.. https://doi.org/10.1093/bioinformatics/btz682
29. Senior, A. W., Evans, R., Jumper, J., Kirkpatrick, J., Sifre, L., Green, T., Qin, C., Žídek, A., R. Nelson, A. W., Bridgland, A., Penedones, H., Petersen, S., Simonyan, K., Crossan, S., Kohli, P., Jones, D. T., Silver, D., Kavukcuoglu, K., & Hassabis, D. (2019). Protein structure prediction using multiple deep neural

networks in the 13th Critical Assessment of Protein Structure Prediction (CASP13). *Proteins Struct Funct Bioinf*, *87*(12), 1141–1148. https://doi.org/10.1002/prot.25834

30. Jumper, J., Evans, R., Pritzel, A., Green, T., Figurnov, M., Ronneberger, O., Tunyasuvunakool, K., Bates, R., Žídek, A., Potapenko, A., Bridgland, A., Meyer, C., Kohl, S. A., Ballard, A. J., Cowie, A., Nikolov, S., Jain, R., Adler, J., Back, T., . . . Hassabis, D. (2021). Highly accurate protein structure prediction with AlphaFold. *Nature*, *596*(7873), 583–589. https://doi.org/10.1038/s41586-021-03819-2
31. Abramson, J., Adler, J., Dunger, J., Evans, R., Green, T., Pritzel, A., Ronneberger, O., Willmore, L., Ballard, A. J., Bambrick, J., Bodenstein, S. W., Evans, D. A., Hung, C. C., O'Neill, M., Reiman, D., Tunyasuvunakool, K., Wu, Z., Žemgulytė, A., Arvaniti, E., Beattie, C., Bertolli, O., Bridgland, A., Cherepanov, A., Congreve, M., Cowen-Rivers, A. I., Cowie, A., Figurnov, M., Fuchs, F. B., Gladman, H., Jain, R., Khan, Y. A., Low, C. M. R., Perlin, K., Potapenko, A., Savy, P., Singh, S., Stecula, A., Thillaisundaram, A., Tong, C., Yakneen, S., Zhong, E. D., Zielinski, M., Žídek, A., Bapst, V., Kohli, P., Jaderberg, M., Hassabis, D., Jumper, J. M. (2024). Accurate structure prediction of biomolecular interactions with AlphaFold 3. *Nature*, *630*(8016), 493–500. https://doi.org/10.1038/s41586-024-07487-w. Epub 2024 May 8. PMID: 38718835; PMCID: PMC11168924.
32. Elofsson, A. (2022). Protein Structure Prediction until CASP15. *arXiv preprint arXiv:2212.07702.*
33. Wee, J., & Wei, G. (2024). Benchmarking AlphaFold3's protein-protein complex accuracy and machine learning prediction reliability for binding free energy changes upon mutation. *arXiv preprint arXiv:2406.03979.* https://arxiv.org/abs/2406.03979
34. Ren, F., Ding, X., Zheng, M., Korzinkin, M., Cai, X., Zhu, W., Mantsyzov, A., Aliper, A., Aladinskiy, V., Cao, Z., Kong, S., Long, X., Man Liu, B. H., Liu, Y., Naumov, V., Shneyderman, A., Ozerov, I. V., Wang, J., Pun, F. W., . . . Zhavoronkov, A. (2023). AlphaFold accelerates artificial intelligence powered drug discovery: Efficient discovery of a novel CDK20 small molecule inhibitor. *Chem Sci*, *14*(6), 1443. https://doi.org/10.1039/d2sc05709c
35. F. Ren *et al.* (2023). AlphaFold accelerates artificial intelligence powered drug discovery: efficient discovery of a novel CDK20 small molecule inhibitor. *Chem Sci*, 14(6), 1443–1452. https://doi.org/10.1039/D2SC05709C.
36. Lee, J., Yoon, W., Kim, S., Kim, D., Kim, S., So, C. H., & Kang, J. (2019). BioBERT: A pre-trained biomedical language representation model for biomedical text mining. *Bioinformatics*, *36*(4), 1234–1240. https://doi.org/10.1093/bioinformatics/btz682
37. McInnes, B. T., Tang, J., Mahendran, D., & Nguyen, M. H. (2024). BioBERT-based Deep Learning and Merged ChemProt-DrugProt for Enhanced Biomedical Relation Extraction. *arXiv preprint arXiv:2405.18605.* https://arxiv.org/abs/2405.18605
38. Zhang, L., Zhao, Q., Zhang, D., Song, M., Zhang, Y., & Wang, X. (2025). Application of large language models in healthcare: A bibliometric analysis. *Digital Health*, *11*, 20552076251324444. https://doi.org/10.1177/20552076251324444

39. Hartung, T., & Kleinstreuer, N. (2025). Challenges and opportunities for validation of AI-based new approach methods. *ALTEX*, *42*(1), 3–21. . https://doi.org/10.14573/altex.2412291
40. Nazi, Z. A., & Peng, W. (2024). Large Language Models in Healthcare and Medical Domain: A Review. *Informatics*, *11*(3), 57. https://doi.org/10.3390/informatics11030057
41. Komandur, R., McDunn, J., Nair, N., Fall, B., Dicker, A. P., & Khozin, S. (2025). Artificial intelligence in biomedical data analysis: a comparative assessment of large language models for automated clinical trial interpretation and statistical evaluation. *medRxiv* 2025.02.05.25321607. https://doi.org/10.1101/2025.02.05.25321607
42. Liang, S., & Sonntag, D. (2025). Explainable Biomedical Claim Verification with Large Language Models. *arXiv preprint arXiv:2502.21014*. https://arxiv.org/abs/2502.21014
43. Machot, F. A., Horsch, M. T., & Ullah, H. (2024). Building Trustworthy AI: Transparent AI Systems via Large Language Models, Ontologies, and Logical Reasoning (TranspNet). *arXiv preprint arXiv:2411.08469*. https://arxiv.org/abs/2411.08469
44. Nazary, F., Deldjoo, Y., Di Noia, T., & Di Sciascio, E. (2024). XAI4LLM. Let Machine Learning Models and LLMs Collaborate for Enhanced In-Context Learning in Healthcare. *arXiv preprint arXiv:2405.06270*. https://arxiv.org/abs/2405.06270
45. Dubey, A., Yang, Z., & Hattab, G. (2024). AI Readiness in Healthcare through Storytelling XAI. *arXiv preprint arXiv:2410.18725*. https://arxiv.org/abs/2410.18725
46. Yang, K., Zhang, T., Kuang, Z., Xie, Q., Huang, J., & Ananiadou, S. (2024). MentaLLaMA: Interpretable mental health analysis on social media with large language models. In *Proceedings of the ACM on Web Conference 2024*, Singapore, 13–17 May 2024; pp. 4489–4500.
47. Hong, S., Xiao, L., Zhang, X., & Chen, J. (2024). ArgMed-Agents: Explainable Clinical Decision Reasoning with Large Language Models via Argumentation Schemes. *arXiv preprint arXiv:2403.06294*.
48. Savage, T., Nayak, A., Gallo, R., Rangan, E., & Chen, J. H. (2024). Diagnostic reasoning prompts reveal the potential for large language model interpretability in medicine. *NPJ Digit Med*, *7*, 20.
49. Lin, B., Xu, Y., Bao, X., Zhao, Z., Zhang, Z., Wang, Z., Zhang, J., Deng, S., & Yin, J. (2024). SkinGEN: An explainable dermatology diagnosis-to-generation framework with interactive vision-language models. *arXiv preprint arXiv:2404.14755*.
50. Gao, Y., Li, R., Caskey, J., Dligach, D., Miller, T., Churpek, M. M., & Afshar, M. (2023). Leveraging a medical knowledge graph into large language models for diagnosis prediction. *arXiv preprint arXiv:2308.14321*.
51. Lee, M. H., & Chew, C. J. (2023). Understanding the effect of counterfactual explanations on trust and reliance on ai for human-AI collaborative clinical decision making. *Proc. ACM Hum Comput Interact*, *7*, 369.
52. Yang, K., Ji, S., Zhang, T., Xie, Q., Kuang, Z., & Ananiadou, S. (2023). Towards interpretable mental health analysis with large language models. *arXiv preprint arXiv:2304.03347*.

53. McInerney, D. J., Young, G., van de Meent, J. W., & Wallace, B. C. (2023). Chill: Zero-shot custom interpretable feature extraction from clinical notes with large language models. *arXiv preprint arXiv:2302.12343*.
54. Naseem, U., Khushi, M., & Kim, J. (2022). Vision-language transformer for interpretable pathology visual question answering. *IEEE J Biomed Health Inform*, *27*, 1681–1690.
55. Park, S., Kim, G., Oh, Y., Seo, J., Lee, S., Kim, J., Moon, S., Lim, J., & Ye, J. (2021). Vision Transformer for COVID-19 CXR Diagnosis using Chest X-ray Feature Corpus. *arXiv preprint arXiv:2103.07055*.
56. Huang, K., Altosaar, J., & Ranganath, R. (2024). Clinicalbert: Modeling clinical notes and predicting hospital readmission. *arXiv preprint arXiv:1904.05342*.
57. Datta, S., Lee, K., Paek, H., Manion, F. J., Ofoegbu, N., Du, J., Li, Y., Huang, L. C., Wang, J., Lin, B., Xu, H., & Wang, X. (2024). AutoCriteria: a generalizable clinical trial eligibility criteria extraction system powered by large language models. *J Am Med Inform Assoc* , 31(2), 375–385. https://doi.org/10.1093/jamia/ocad218. PMID: 37952206; PMCID: PMC10797270.
58. Park, J., Fang, Y., Ta, C., Zhang, G., Idnay, B., Chen, F., Feng, D., Shyu, R., Gordon, E. R., Spotnitz, M., & Weng, C. (2024). Criteria2Query 3.0: Leveraging generative large language models for clinical trial eligibility query generation. *J Biomed Inform*, *154*, 104649. https://doi.org/10.1016/j.jbi.2024.104649
59. Jin, Q., Wang, Z., Floudas, C. S., Chen, F., Gong, C., Xue, E., Yang, Y., Sun, J., & Lu, Z. (2023). Matching Patients to Clinical Trials with Large Language Models. *Nat Commun*, *15*(1), 9074.https://doi.org/10.1038/s41467-024-53081-z
60. Unlu, O., Varugheese, M., Shin, J., et al. (2025). Manual vs AI-Assisted Prescreening for Trial Eligibility Using Large Language Models—A Randomized Clinical Trial. *JAMA*, *333*(12), 1084–1087. https://doi.org/10.1001/jama.2024.28047
61. Wang, Z., Xiao, C., & Sun, J. (2023). AutoTrial: Prompting Language Models for Clinical Trial Design. *arXiv preprint arXiv:2305.11366*. https://arxiv.org/abs/2305.11366
62. Lee, K., Liu, Z., Mai, Y., Jun, T., Ma, M., Wang, T., Ai, L., Calay, E., Oh, W., Stolovitzky, G., Schadt, E., & Wang, X. (2024). Optimizing Clinical Trial Eligibility Design Using Natural Language Processing Models and Real-World Data: Algorithm Development and Validation. *JMIR AI*, *3*, e50800. https://ai.jmir.org/2024/1/e50800; DOI: 10.2196/50800
63. Maleki, M., & Ghahari, S. (2024). Clinical Trials Protocol Authoring using LLMs. *arXiv preprint arXiv:2404.05044*. https://arxiv.org/abs/2404.05044
64. Reason, T., Langham, J. & Gimblett, A. (2024). Automated Mass Extraction of Over 680,000 PICOs from Clinical Study Abstracts Using Generative AI: A Proof-of-Concept Study. *Pharm Med*, *38*, 365–372. https://doi.org/10.1007/s40290-024-00539-6
65. Ghosh, M., Mukherjee, S., Ganguly, A., Basuchowdhuri, P., Naskar, S. K., & Ganguly, D. (2024). AlpaPICO: Extraction of PICO Frames from Clinical Trial Documents Using LLMs. *Methods*, *226*, 78–88. https://doi.org/10.1016/j.ymeth.2024.04.005

66. ISPOR. (2025). Automated Data Extraction in Systematic Literature Reviews (SLRs): Assessing the Accuracy and Reliability of a Large Language Model (LLM). ISPOR | International Society For Pharmacoeconomics and Outcomes Research. Accessed: May 07, 2025. Available at: https://www.ispor.org/heor-resources/presentations-database/presentation/euro2024-4018/146845
67. Wang, Z., Cao, L., Jin, Q., Chan, J., Wan, N., Afzali, B., Cho, H., Choi, C., Emamverdi, M., Gill, M. K., Kim, S., Li, Y., Liu, Y., Ong, H., Rousseau, J., Sheikh, I., Wei, J. J., Xu, Z., Zallek, C. M., . . . Sun, J. (2025). A foundation model for human-AI collaboration in medical literature mining. *arXiv preprint arXiv:2501.16255*. https://arxiv.org/abs/2501.16255
68. Reason, T., Benbow, E., Langham, J. *et al.* (2024). Artificial Intelligence to Automate Network Meta-Analyses: Four Case Studies to Evaluate the Potential Application of Large Language Models. *PharmacoEconomics Open*, *8*, 205–220. https://doi.org/10.1007/s41669-024-00476-9
69. Nashed, A., Zhang, S., Chiang, C. W. *et al.* (2021). Comparative assessment of manual chart review and ICD claims data in evaluating immunotherapy-related adverse events. *Cancer Immunol Immunother*, *70*, 2761–2769. https://doi.org/10.1007/s00262-021-02880-0
70. https://doi.org/10.1200/JCO.24.00326
71. Sun, V. H., Heemelaar, J. C., Hadzic, I., Raghu, V. K., Wu, C. Y., Zubiri, L., Ghamari, A., LeBoeuf, N. R., Abu-Shawer, O., Kehl, K. L., Grover, S., Singh, P., Suero-Abreu, G. A., Wu, J., Falade, A. S., Grealish, K., Thomas, M. F., Hathaway, N., Medoff, B. D., Gilman, H. K., Villani, A. C., Ho, J. S., Mooradian, M. J., Sise, M. E., Zlotoff, D. A., Blum, S. M., Dougan, M., Sullivan, R. J., Neilan, T. G., Reynolds, K.L. (2024). Enhancing Precision in Detecting Severe Immune-Related Adverse Events: Comparative Analysis of Large Language Models and International Classification of Disease Codes in Patient Records. *J Clin Oncol*, *42*(35), 4134–4144. https://doi.org/10.1200/JCO.24.00326
72. Sun, V. H., Heemelaar, J. C., Hadzic, I., Raghu, V. K., Wu, C. Y., Zubiri, L., Ghamari, A., LeBoeuf, N. R., Abu-Shawer, O., Kehl, K. L., & Grover, S. (2024). Enhancing Precision in Detecting Severe Immune-Related Adverse Events: Comparative Analysis of Large Language Models and International Classification of Disease Codes in Patient Records. *JCO*, *42*, 4134–4144. https://doi.org/10.1200/JCO.24.00326
73. https://doi.org/10.1101/2023.11.04.23298081
74. Ruiz Sarrias, O., Martínez del Prado, M.P., Sala Gonzalez, M.Á., Azcuna Sagarduy, J., Casado Cuesta, P., Figaredo Berjano, C., Galve-Calvo, E., López de San Vicente Hernández, B., López-Santillán, M., Nuño Escolástico, M. and Sánchez Togneri, L., Sande Sardina, L., Pérez Hoyos, M. T., Abad Villar, M. T., Zabalza Zudaire, M., & Sayar Beristain, O. (2024). Leveraging Large Language Models for Precision Monitoring of Chemotherapy-Induced Toxicities: A Pilot Study with Expert Comparisons and Future Directions. *Cancers (Basel)*, *16*(16), 2830. https://doi.org/10.3390/cancers16162830
75. Guo, E., Gupta, M., Deng, J., Park, Y., Paget, M., & Naugler, C. (2023). Automated Paper Screening for Clinical Reviews Using Large Language Models. *JMIR*, *26*, e48996. https://doi.org/10.2196/48996

76. Farhadi, A., & Taheri, A. (2025). Application of GenAI in Synthetic Data Generation in the Healthcare System. In: Zamanifar, A., Faezipour, M. (Eds), *Application of Generative AI in Healthcare Systems*. Springer, Cham. https://doi.org/10.1007/978-3-031-82963-5_3
77. Taheri, A., Farhadi, A., & Zamanifar, A. (2025). Application of GenAI in Clinical Administration Support. In: Zamanifar, A., Faezipour, M. (Eds), *Application of Generative AI in Healthcare Systems*. Springer, Cham. https://doi.org/10.1007/978-3-031-82963-5_4
78. Vercaempst, V. (2025). A Review of Large Language Models in Medical Education, Clinical Decision Support, and Healthcare Administration. In *Healthcare* (Vol. 13, No. 6, p. 603). MDPI. https://doi.org/10.3390/healthcare13060603
79. Hussaini, H., Anjum, Z., Mandal, S., Noori, N., Masood, M. M., Tariq, M., Memon, B., Rasheed, A., Patel, M. P., Samreen, I., Ahmed, Z., & Chou, B. (2025). Efficacy of pembrolizumab in advanced esophageal carcinoma: A systematic review and meta-analysis. *J Clin Oncol*, *43*(4_suppl), 438. https://doi.org/10.1200/jco.2025.43.4_suppl.438
80. Chen, S., Gao, M., Sasse, K., Hartvigsen, T., Anthony, B. W., Fan, L., Gallifant, J., & Bitterman, D. S. (2025). Abstract IA04: Evaluating and mitigating medical misinformation risk in large language models. *Clin Cancer Res*, *31*(2_Supplement), IA04. https://doi.org/10.1158/1557-3265.targeted-therap-ia04
81. Lataran, P. N., Farhadi, A., Zamanifar, A., & Taheri, A. (2024). Developing a BERT-Enhanced Blockchain Model for HealthInsurance Fraud Detection. *J Inf Syst Res Pract*, *2*(3), 56–61.
82. Gu, B., Shao, V., Liao, Z., Carducci, V., Romero-Brufau, S., Yang, J., & Desai, R. (2025). Scalable information extraction from free text electronic health records using large language models. *BMC Med Res Methodol*, *25*(1). https://doi.org/10.1186/s12874-025-02470-z
83. Yuan, S., & Färber, M. (2025). Hallucinations Can Improve Large Language Models in Drug Discovery. *arXiv preprint arXiv:2501.13824*. https://doi.org/10.48550/arxiv.2501.13824
84. Omar, M., Nassar, S., Sharif, K., Glicksberg, B. S., Nadkarni, G. N., & Klang, E. (2025). Emerging applications of NLP and large language models in gastroenterology and hepatology: a systematic review. *Front Med*, *11*, 1512824. https://doi.org/10.3389/fmed.2024.1512824
85. Zong, C., Wan, J., & Zhang, L. (2025). EvidenceMap: Unleashing the Power of Small Language Models with Evidence Analysis for Biomedical Question Answering. *arXiv preprint arXiv:2501.12746*. https://doi.org/10.48550/arxiv.2501.12746
86. Kumbhar, S., Mishra, V., Coutinho, K., Handa, D., Iquebal, A. S., & Baral, C. (2025). Hypothesis Generation for Materials Discovery and Design Using Goal-Driven and Constraint-Guided LLM Agents. *arXiv preprint arXiv:2501.13299*. https://doi.org/10.48550/arxiv.2501.13299
87. Porzsolt, F. (2025). The Call for Progress in Evidence-Based Medicine. J Family Med Prim Care Open Acc.; 9: 278https://doi.org/10.32388/3tdwgw

88. Galli, C., Colangelo, M. T., Guizzardi, S., Meleti, M., & Calciolari, E. (2025). A Zero-Shot Comparison of Large Language Models for Efficient Screening in Periodontal Regeneration Research., decision-making, 3, 4. https://doi.org/10.20944/preprints202501.2029.v1
89. Yuan, J., Tang, R., Jiang, X., & Hu, X. (2023). Large Language Models for Healthcare Data Augmentation: An Example on Patient-Trial Matching. *arXiv preprint arXiv:2303.16756* https://arxiv.org/abs/2303.16756
90. Cai, Z., Chen, J., Wang, R., Wang, W., Deng, Y., Song, D., Chen, Y., Zhang, Z. T., & Wang, B. (2024). On the Compositional Generalization of Multimodal LLMs for Medical Imaging. https://doi.org/10.48550/arxiv.2412.20070
91. Pitt, W. R., Bentley, J., Boldron, C., Colliandre, L., Esposito, C., Frush, E. H., Kopec, J., Labouille, S., Meneyrol, J., Pardoe, D., Palazzesi, F., Pozzan, A., Remington, J. M., Rex, R., Southey, M., Vishwakarma, S., & Walker, P. (2025). Real-World Applications and Experiences of AI/ML Deployment for Drug Discovery. *J Med Chem.* https://doi.org/10.1021/acs.jmedchem.4c03044
92. Panguraj, A. R. R. (2025). Exploring how LLMs can analyse patient data, medical literature, and symptoms to assist in the early detection of chronic conditions like diabetes, cancer, or cardiovascular diseases. *Indian Sci J Res Eng Manag, 09*(01), 1–7. https://doi.org/10.55041/ijsrem22924
93. Mahalegi, H.S.M., Farhadi, A., Balogh, G., & Nagy, E. (2025). Application of Generative AI in Resource Optimization in Healthcare Systems. In: Zamanifar, A., Faezipour, M. (Eds), *Application of Generative AI in Healthcare Systems.* Springer, Cham. https://doi.org/10.1007/978-3-031-82963-5_7
94. Lee, J., Lee, J., & Yoo, J. (2025). The role of large language models in the peer-review process: opportunities and challenges for medical journal reviewers and editors. *J Educ Eval Health Prof*, 22, 4. https://doi.org/10.3352/jeehp.2025.22.4
95. Pandey, A., & Singh, D. (2025). Revolutionizing Drug Discovery and Development. In *Technologies and Innovations for Sustainable Development* (pp. 16–17). https://doi.org/10.1201/9781003487012-4
96. Rashidieranjbar, F., Farhadi, A., & Zamanifar, A. (2025). Revolutionizing Healthcare with Generative Artificial Intelligence Technologies. In: Vajjhala, N.R., Roy, S.S., Taşcı, B., Hoque Chowdhury, M.E. (Eds), *Generative Artificial Intelligence (AI) Approaches for Industrial Applications. Information Systems Engineering and Management*, Vol 24. Springer, Cham. https://doi.org/10.1007/978-3-031-76710-4_10

Chapter 4

LLMs for personalized medicine and treatment planning

Amirfarhad Farhadi and Nasser Mozayeni

4.1 INTRODUCTION

Today, personalized medicine is gaining attention as a modern approach to healthcare that recognizes the differences among individuals [1]. Instead of using the same treatment for everyone, it focuses on what makes each patient unique, such as their genes, lifestyle, environment, and personal preferences. The goal is to provide the right treatment to the right person at the right time. This approach is already making progress in areas like cancer and autoimmune diseases, where patients often respond differently to the same drugs [2, 3].

Some patients have specific antibodies or genetic patterns that suggest one drug might work better than another. Personalized medicine aims to match these biological signals with the most effective treatments. But making these decisions isn't easy [4]. There is a large volume of data, and new drugs receive approval each year. Medical professionals are confronted with an overwhelming number of options, and testing is often expensive [5]. This makes it difficult to provide personalized care to everyone. We need tools that can process and analyze this information to suggest the most suitable treatments for each patient. Recently, large language models (LLMs) have shown promise in this area [6]. LLMs are advanced artificial intelligence (AI) models trained on vast amounts of text data. They can understand medical notes, summarize patient histories, and provide advice based on clinical guidelines or the latest research. Since the release of ChatGPT in 2022, interest in applying LLMs to healthcare has grown rapidly [7]. LLMs are skilled not only in language tasks like reading and writing but also in reasoning. They can generate accurate answers to medical questions. LLMs have been shown to predict patient risks more effectively than traditional methods. For example, one study found that LLMs could better predict surgery-related risks by analyzing clinical notes [8].

 DOI: 10.1201/9781003665083-4

4.2 PERSONALIZED MEDICINE AND AI

One of the biggest ways AI helps in personalized medicine is through predictive modeling. This means using data and smart algorithms to guess what might happen in a patient's health. AI can look at complex medical data, like electronic health records (EHRs), lab results, and even medical images, and predict how diseases may develop or how a patient may respond to treatment [9]. For example, at Vanderbilt University, researchers used years of patient data and genetic information to predict the risk of heart disease over ten years [9]. Their AI models, including deep learning and decision tree methods, were more accurate than older methods. They could find people at high risk who might have been missed otherwise. This shows how AI can discover latent patterns and help doctors act early. In cancer care, AI helps predict which patients might respond well to certain treatments or who might have strong side effects. One large review of AI in oncology found that many models focus on predicting treatment success or survival [10]. This helps doctors choose the best therapy for each patient. AI can also track live health data from intensive care unit (ICU) monitors or wearable devices. For instance, AI in smartwatches can spot small changes in heart rate or glucose levels and warn users before a serious problem happens. This kind of early warning is a major step from reactive care to proactive care, treating before things get worse. Genetic data plays a key role in personalized medicine [11]. AI is now essential in understanding this complex information. With the rise of genome sequencing, we have tons of data, but it's hard to make sense of it without AI. Machine learning and deep learning tools can find patterns in deoxyribonucleic acid (DNA) that tell us about disease risks or treatment options. For instance, Google's DeepVariant uses deep learning to read raw genetic data and find important mutations. This helps identify genetic problems that might cause disease or affect how a patient responds to a drug. AI also supports pharmacogenomics, which is about matching drug treatments to a person's genetic profile. Some people have gene variants that change how their body processes drugs. As shown in Figure 4.1, the role of pharmacogenomics in personalized medicine. AI models can find these genes and suggest safer or more effective medication. For example, if a patient has a gene that slows drug metabolism, the system may suggest a different drug or a lower dose. In real-world settings, advanced clinical tools now connect genetic test results with drug information. If a risk is found, the AI gives alerts and advice to the doctor. In cancer care, AI looks at a tumor's genetic data to help pick the best targeted treatment. Deep learning can compare a patient's tumor profile with many past cases to find the most promising therapy. These tools help doctors treat patients based on their unique biology.

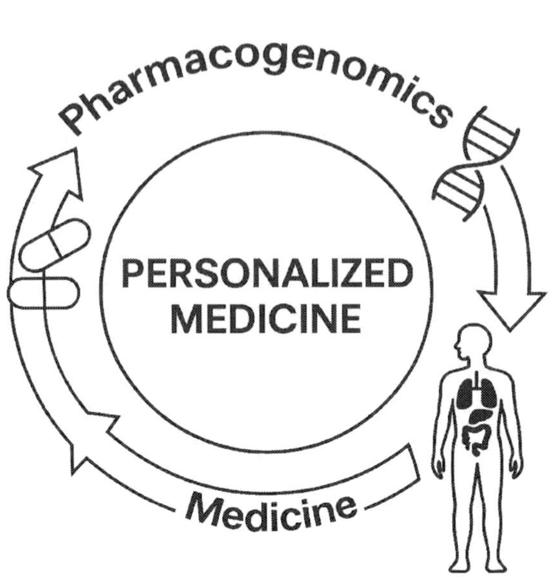

Figure 4.1 The role of pharmacogenomics in personalized medicine.

4.3 PERSONALIZED MEDICINE AND LARGE LANGUAGE MODELS (LLMS)

One of the most promising uses of LLMs in personalized medicine is helping with disease diagnosis. Diagnosing a patient usually means looking at many pieces of information symptoms, test results, and past medical history. Much of this data is stored in unstructured text. LLMs are good at reading and understanding such medical texts. They can suggest possible diagnoses by comparing the patient's information to what they've learned from large medical datasets. In practice, a doctor might give a patient case to an LLM, and the model can return a list of likely diagnoses. Studies have already tested how well general LLMs, like ChatGPT-4, perform in diagnostic tasks. In one study, GPT-4 was given real clinical case reports and asked to suggest possible diagnoses. The correct diagnosis appeared in the model's top five suggestions 81% of the time, better than a group of physicians, who scored 67% on the same task [12]. This shows LLMs are approaching expert-level diagnostic performance. GPT-4 also outperformed earlier versions like GPT-3.5, showing how improvements in model size and training have increased medical reasoning skills [13]. Some models are even fine-tuned for medicine. For example, Med-PaLM was the first LLM to score above the USMLE pass mark, a key medical licensing exam, proving it can reason like a new physician [14]. LLMs are also being used in real-time medical practice. Some diagnostic chatbots allow patients to enter symptoms and receive possible conditions or follow-up questions. In emergency care settings, GPT models have helped doctors identify rare diagnoses that might otherwise be missed [15]. Another key role for LLMs is organizing complex patient records. Instead of reading through many pages of health records, doctors can use LLMs to get clear summaries. A recent study showed that physicians preferred LLM-generated summaries over human-written ones when reviewing medical documents [16]. As shown in Figure 4.2, the schematic illustrates LLM-enabled personalized medicine. The strength of these models comes from two things: their training on massive datasets (including textbooks and clinical notes) and their ability to attend to key details in long texts using the Transformer architecture. Some setups use step-by-step (chain-of-thought) prompting to guide the model's reasoning, like how a real doctor thinks through a case. Of course, these models aren't perfect. Sometimes they generate errors or hallucinate facts. But even now, models like GPT-4 and Med-PaLM are powerful diagnostic assistants. With more fine-tuning and access to real-time data, they could become essential tools.

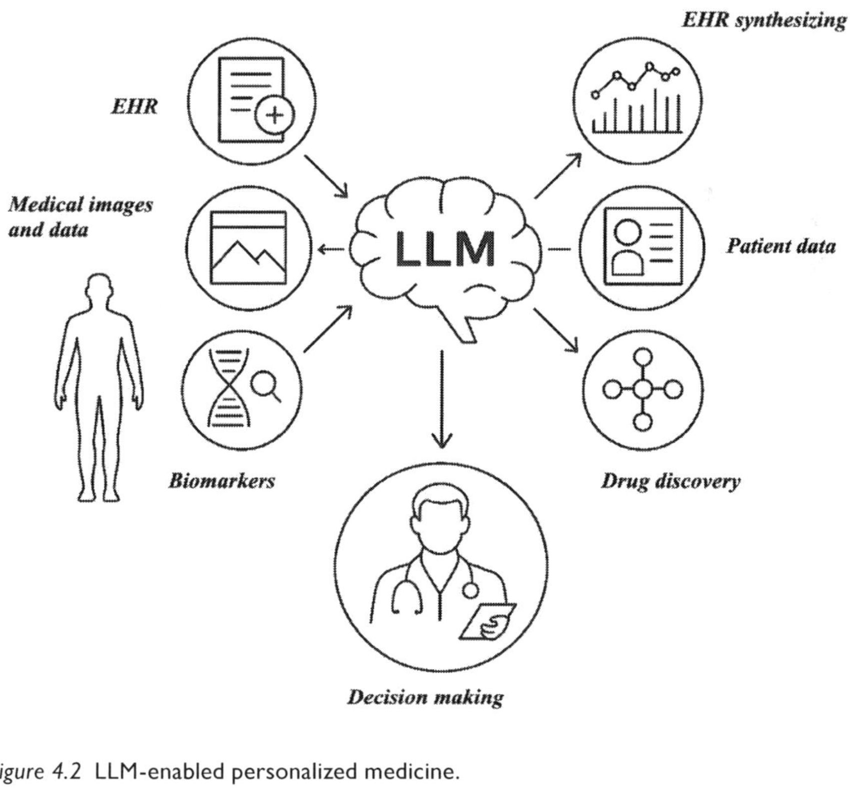

Figure 4.2 LLM-enabled personalized medicine.

4.4 LLMS IN DISEASE PREDICTION

Personalized medicine is not just about treating disease; it's also about predicting it. By anticipating future health risks, doctors can take action early. LLMs are becoming useful for this, especially when working with electronic health records (EHRs). These records include time-based data like diagnoses, lab tests, and hospital visits. Predicting future conditions from this data is a complex task. But LLMs can handle it by treating a patient's history like a story. One strong example is TransformEHR, a Transformer-based model that predicts future diagnoses from a patient's EHR timeline [17]. It uses an encoder–decoder structure: it reads past events and generates likely future outcomes. Compared to older models like logistic regression or even fine-tuned bidirectional encoder representations from transformers (BERT), TransformEHR performed better. It improved AUROC by 5.9% for rare outcomes and about 4% for common ones [18]. In some high-risk tasks the improvements were even more.

Another recent method is clinical prediction with LLMs (CPLLM), which adapts a general language model using clinical prompts. Patient history is converted into a prompt, and the model predicts outcomes such as hospital readmission. Even without specialized pretraining, CPLLM outperformed models like Med-BERT and Retain on several tasks [19]. A major benefit was that it didn't need huge amounts of medical training data. These methods work well because LLMs can keep track of long-term connections in a patient's story. They use self-attention to focus on key past events that may affect future outcomes. Time-aware encoding and structured data (like lab results) can also be added to improve accuracy. In practice, this could mean a doctor gets an alert: "This patient has an 85% chance of hospital readmission in 3 months. With that information, they can plan a preventive treatment. Researchers are also building ways to make these predictions explainable, showing which past events influenced the model's decisions. This transparency helps build trust in AI systems and supports clinical decisions.

4.5 LLMS FOR PERSONALIZED TREATMENT

Treatment is the heart of personalized medicine; it means choosing the right therapy for the right person. Every patient is different. They may have other illnesses, specific genes, and personal preferences. Doctors usually rely on guidelines and experience, but the amount of medical knowledge is growing too fast for any one person to handle. LLMs can help here. With their ability to read and reason over huge amounts of data, they can suggest tailored treatment plans. In oncology, for example, LLMs are already helping oncologists design custom therapies. One system called MEREDITH (built on Google's Gemini Pro) combines LLMs with medical databases to help plan cancer treatment [20]. It uses retrieval-augmented generation (RAG) and then suggests treatments based on a patient's tumor profile. In testing, MEREDITH gave more treatment options than tumor boards and matched expert opinions 94.7% of the time [21]. It even suggested newer treatments that doctors hadn't thought of, but still found helpful. LLMs can also assist in managing chronic diseases. For example, if a patient with diabetes and high blood pressure is not responding to treatment, an LLM could suggest a different drug or lifestyle change, based on clinical guidelines. GPT-4 has shown it can produce such treatment plans and explain the reasons behind them. Patient communication is another area where LLMs shine. They can adjust explanations based on who they're talking to a doctor, a nurse, or a patient. The same treatment plan can be explained in simple language to the patient and in detailed terms to the specialist. Behind the scenes, safe treatment support from LLMs depends on extra tools. Retrieval systems can keep the model's answers current. Fine-tuning with expert examples teaches the model how doctors make decisions. Safety checks (like drug interaction warnings) help avoid harmful suggestions. Although clinical approval and oversight are essential, the future is clear. LLMs are becoming trusted partners in clinical decision-making. We may soon see doctors use them directly in electronic health records, asking for help with complex treatment questions and getting personalized, evidence-based answers [22].

4.6 LLMS IN CLINICAL DECISION SUPPORT SYSTEMS (CDSS)

AI-powered clinical decision support systems (CDSS) help doctors make better, faster, and more personalized choices. These systems bring together all kinds of patient data, like health history, lab tests, images, genes, and even lifestyle. AI can connect all these pieces and give clear advice at the point of care. For example, an AI system might notice that a patient has a family history of cancer and a risky gene variant. It can then recommend earlier cancer screening. Or, it might check drug-gene interactions and suggest which antidepressant is best for the patient.

Here are some real uses:

- **Diagnosis:** AI looks at symptoms, tests, and scans to suggest likely diagnoses. In radiology, AI can spot tiny signs in images that may be linked to certain diseases or mutations.
- **Treatment Advice:** AI can scan a patient's full profile and suggest treatments based on clinical guidelines and past cases. In diabetes care, smart insulin pumps use AI to adjust doses based on real-time data.
- **Prevention:** AI tools can predict when a patient is at risk of a health crisis, like sepsis. Hospitals now use AI alerts to catch early signs of trouble. AI in wearables also gives daily advice and health warnings based on live data.

One of AI's greatest strengths is merging different types of data. For example, understanding how a patient's genes and lifestyle together affect their health. AI can balance all these factors and offer more accurate advice than rule-based systems. Today, many hospitals use AI systems that alert doctors about drug risks based on genetics. In cancer centers, AI tools are used in tumor boards to recommend therapies. As AI continues to learn and include more data, like social conditions or patient-reported outcomes, its guidance will get even more personal and powerful.

Recent studies have tested how well LLMs can support clinical decision-making. Many of these works focus on diagnosis, triage, treatment planning, and doctor support. Some use real patient data to compare model decisions with those of experienced physicians. Others build prototype tools to integrate LLMs into clinical workflows. One important study by Gaber et al. [23] used an LLM-based system with retrieval-augmented generation (RAG) to help with triage and diagnosis in ICU patients. They tested the model on 2,000 real cases from the MIMIC-IV database. The model (based on Anthropic Claude) helped decide triage levels, predict diagnoses, and suggest specialist referrals. It showed good performance for classifying urgent cases and selecting likely conditions. However, not all results were positive. Hager et al. [24] created a test set with 2,400 ICU patients and found that open-source LLMs (like LLaMA-2 and Claude-2) performed much worse than physicians. Models missed important lab data, ignored medical guidelines, and gave many incorrect diagnoses. This shows that while LLMs have potential, they are not yet safe to replace expert clinicians. Some tools are designed to help—not replace—doctors. For example, McDuff et al. [25] developed AMIE, an LLM trained for diagnostic reasoning. When doctors used AMIE, their list of possible diagnoses (called "differential diagnoses") improved. The model alone even outperformed unaided doctors in identifying the correct condition. This shows that LLMs can act as useful partners in diagnostic thinking. Zhu et al. [26] explored whether adding lab test results to clinical descriptions helps LLMs. They tested GPT-4, Claude-2, LLaMA-70B, and Mixtral. Including lab data improved the models' diagnosis accuracy by around 30%. GPT-4 achieved the best results, with a top-1 accuracy of around 55%. This proves that richer input improves LLM decision quality.

LLMs have also been tested in emergency departments. Williams et al. [27] evaluated GPT-4 Turbo and GPT-3.5 Turbo on 10,000 real ED cases. Tasks included deciding on patient admission, imaging orders, and antibiotics. The models performed worse than residents—GPT-4 was about 8% less accurate. Models tended to give safe but overly cautious advice. This suggests that LLMs need improvement before they can guide emergency care. In another case, Giaj Levra et al. [28] built a tool for detecting syncope (fainting) using BERT-based models trained on 15,000 Italian emergency records. The models reached very high accuracy (AUC 0.94–0.98), even spotting syncope when not mentioned directly. This could help alert doctors early to hidden warning signs. LLMs are also being used in treatment decisions. Ah-Thiane et al. [29] tested three models (Claude 3-Opus, GPT-4 Turbo, and LLaMA-3 70B) on 112 real breast cancer cases. Claude and GPT-4 correctly matched expert decisions about 86% of the time, better than LLaMA. They were especially good at endocrine and targeted therapy suggestions, though less reliable for radiotherapy and chemotherapy advice. Shelly et al. [30] tested In the area of stroke care, GPT-4 was tested by Shelly et al. The model was given real patient histories, imaging, and exams. It made recommendations about thrombolysis and thrombectomy. The results were close to expert opinions, with strong agreement (AUC around 0.85–0.94). Though GPT-4 sometimes leaned toward more aggressive treatment, it showed promise as a support tool in stroke decisions. Some studies focus on comparing different LLMs. Sandmann et al. [31] benchmarked open models like DeepSeek against commercial ones like GPT-4o and Gemini. They found that new open-source models can match top proprietary systems, offering a cost-effective path for hospitals to train their own secure models. A randomized trial by Goh et al. [32] tested how much LLMs improve doctors' reasoning. Fifty physicians worked on complex cases, with or without LLM help. Surprisingly, the LLM alone scored higher than the doctors, but having the LLM didn't help the doctors much. This shows that better design is needed for human-AI collaboration in real clinics. LLMs are being tested in many areas of clinical decision support, including emergency triage, ICU diagnosis, oncology treatment, and stroke management. They use various models, GPT-4, Claude, LLaMA, BERT, and are evaluated on real patient data or expert-designed vignettes [33]. LLMs can support diagnosis and treatment planning, especially when given a complete clinical context. In some cases, LLMs help doctors improve accuracy. But they still make dangerous errors and often ignore clinical guidelines. LLMs work better as support tools than autonomous decision-makers. Open-source models are catching up in quality, offering cheaper and safer deployment options. Overall, LLMs show strong potential to support CDSS, but they are not ready for full independence when used in critical situations, where errors can lead to serious harm.

4.7 MULTIMODAL LARGE LANGUAGE MODELS IN PERSONALIZED MEDICINE

Personalized medicine depends on many types of patient data. These include clinical notes, electronic health records (EHRs), medical images, lab results, genomics, and data from wearable devices. Multimodal large language models (M-LLMs) are designed to bring all these sources together. Unlike traditional models that only work with text, M-LLMs can understand images, structured data, and even time-series signals. This is important because medical decisions often rely on combining different kinds of information. For example, a skin condition may require both an image and a written note. A heart problem may involve ECG waveforms and past health records. M-LLMs make it possible to process this variety in one model. Some examples show how this works in practice. SkinGPT-4 combines a vision transformer with a language model (LLaMA2-13B) to analyze skin images along with doctor notes. It can generate accurate diagnoses and treatment suggestions. ChestX-Transcribe uses X-ray images and language data to create full radiology reports. It uses Swin Transformer for vision and DistilGPT-2 for text. Both models have shown strong performance compared to earlier methods. Other systems also show the power of combining data. Merlin processes 3D CT scans, diagnosis codes, and radiology reports. It can detect abnormalities, segment organs, and predict future disease risk. M-BEHRT focuses on EHR data, mixing structured features like lab results with free-text notes. It helped breast cancer patients at risk with higher accuracy than traditional methods. Wearable data is another important source. PhysioLLM connects Fitbit data with language-based advice. Users found it more helpful than the original Fitbit app or a general chatbot. MedTsLLM takes in waveforms like electrocardiogram (ECG) or ventilator pressure and connects them with patient text data. It showed top results on signal segmentation and beat detection tasks. Genomics and other omics data are also being used. Precious2GPT is a model trained on DNA methylation data. It generates realistic biological data that help predict aging and discover new disease markers. This kind of model can assist in drug discovery and personalized treatment by simulating data and identifying useful targets.

Overall, M-LLMs help with many tasks: diagnosis, treatment planning, drug discovery, and patient stratification. They support doctors by combining data sources in a smart way. For diagnosis, they interpret both images and notes. For treatment, they analyze patient history and suggest care plans. In drug development, they simulate genetic data to find new drugs. For patient grouping, they identify health patterns to guide personalized care. Still, there are challenges. Medical data come in many formats. It's hard to align them in time and space. Public datasets are limited, and training large models needs a lot of computing power. Also, these models can make mistakes or show bias, and privacy is a major concern. If patient data is not protected, it could leak. Trust, safety, and fairness must be built into every step. To solve these problems, researchers are working on several solutions. Smaller models with efficient tuning methods are being developed. Synthetic data and federated learning (FL) help when data sharing is not allowed. New training methods help models stay up-to-date. Compression and edge computing allow deployment in resource-limited settings. Most importantly, new standards and tests are needed before using M-LLMs in clinics.

In the future, these models could become part of digital health systems. They might act as clinical assistants, digital twins, or tools for early diagnosis. With better design, validation, and safeguards, M-LLMs may truly transform personalized healthcare.

4.7.1 Electronic health record (EHR) integration

A key step in using LLMs for personalized medicine is the ability to work with patient-specific data. This includes electronic health records (EHRs), lab tests, medical images, and genomic information. Early LLM applications focused mainly on written text like doctor's notes or scientific articles. But newer systems can now combine many kinds of data. EHRs hold a huge amount of information. They include patient histories, lab results, medications, and clinical notes. LLMs are now helping to summarize this data and highlight key points for doctors. For example, Epic Systems, a major EHR platform, partnered with Microsoft to bring GPT-4 into clinics. These tools help doctors by summarizing a patient's full chart, drafting replies to patient messages, highlighting urgent findings like abnormal labs or new symptoms.

One example showed GPT-4 listening to a conversation between a doctor and patient, then producing a draft clinical note in seconds. The doctor only needed to review and edit. This saves time and ensures nothing important is missed when planning care. LLMs can also bring in data from other similar patients or treatment-based suggestions tailored to the current case.

4.7.2 Genomic and multi-omics data integration

Personalized medicine often depends on a person's genes. But DNA is not written in natural language. So, how can LLMs help? Scientists now treat gene sequences like a special kind of language. Models such as DNABERT and BERT-genome learn patterns in DNA like words and grammar. These models can find mutations and predict their impact on health.

Researchers are also working on multi-omics integration, combining DNA data with other layers like proteins or gene activity. Models like GROVER and DeepMAPs use transformers to understand these complex datasets. Though not all are classic LLMs, they show how AI can read biological data and produce useful, readable outputs.

In the future, an LLM system might review all a patient's data, such as DNA, labs, imaging, and more and say: "This tumor has a mutation in gene X; drug Y is effective; gene A shows high activity, which is a good sign; consider checking marker B in two months." All written in plain, clinical language. To make this vision real, LLMs need to handle many types of data at once. GPT-4 now has a vision-enabled version (GPT-4) that can look at images. In medicine, this has been used for radiology. One system,

GPT-RadPlan, uses GPT-4 Vision to examine radiation dose charts and write feedback. More broadly, these models can review a patient's imaging and compare it to their symptoms or lab results. Some projects feed both radiology reports and the matching images into a model. This lets the AI check if the text matches the image. Other efforts include using signals like heart sounds or EKGs, turning them into text, and then letting the LLM reason about them. Despite these gains, full multimodal models are still new. A 2023 study said these systems are "still in the early stages." Challenges include data size and logical answers across all types of data. One current solution is to split the task: use different models for imaging, genomics, etc.

4.8 THE ROLE OF LLMS IN DRUG DISCOVERY

LLMs, especially those based on transformer architectures, are transforming how we approach drug discovery and personalized treatment. These AI systems are trained on vast biomedical texts, clinical records, and scientific data. They help identify drug targets, suggest repurposed drugs, discover biomarkers, and group patients into subtypes for more precise care. By understanding patterns in both research literature and patient records, LLMs support faster and more accurate decision-making in medicine.

One major application is drug repurposing. LLMs can read thousands of studies and suggest existing drugs that may work for other diseases. For example, researchers used ChatGPT-4 to generate a list of possible drugs for Alzheimer's disease. Among the top suggestions were metformin, simvastatin, and losartan. Later, analysis of real-world patient data showed that these drugs were indeed linked to a lower risk of Alzheimer's, confirming the model's potential to speed up hypothesis generation. LLMs also assist in biomarker discovery. By mining genomics data and medical publications, they can extract biomarkers like specific gene mutations or expression patterns. These markers help classify disease types and choose the right treatment. In oncology, for example, AI systems are already matching patients to clinical trials based on their biomarker profiles. Another key use is in target prediction. LLMs can analyze biomedical text to suggest new genes or proteins involved in disease. A notable example is BioGPT (Biomedical Generative Pre-trained Transformer), a GPT-style model trained specifically on biomedical literature. When fine-tuned on aging-related content, BioGPT was able to rank genes by their relevance to aging, recovering known targets and even suggesting new ones, such as CCR5 and PTH. In patient stratification, LLMs can read clinical notes and unstructured health records to identify patient subgroups. These groups may respond differently to the same treatment, so identifying them helps in planning personalized care. In one study, a fine-tuned Flan-T5 XL model analyzed patient records and identified nearly 94% of individuals with social risk factors, while traditional structured data only captured 2%. This shows the strength of LLMs in uncovering hidden patient features from free text.

Importantly, modern LLMs are evolving to handle more than just text. Some models are now trained on multimodal biomedical data, combining language with structured data, chemical formulas, gene sequences, or imaging features. For instance, Meta's Galactica model was trained on scientific articles, chemical structures Simplified Molecular Input Line Entry System (SMILES), and protein sequences. Researchers can now ask Galactica to name a compound, predict a reaction, or design a molecule, using natural language. These capabilities help bridge the gap between chemistry, biology, and clinical care. Other systems combine LLMs with structured data to improve predictions. One study joined LLM-generated embeddings from clinical notes with lab test values to classify patients into risk categories. Similarly, transformer-based graph models are used to predict drug responses or side effects by linking different biomedical features. These integrated approaches allow for richer, more personalized insights. Several specialized LLMs have been developed for medicine. BioGPT focuses on biomedical texts. Google's Med-PaLM 2, trained for medical question-answering, scored 86.5% on the MedQA benchmark. Galactica connects natural language with molecular and protein data. PubMedBERT and NVIDIA's BioNeMo are also used in biomedical research. They help with molecule design, disease mechanism exploration, and protein modeling. These tools support tasks ranging from summarizing literature to generating treatment hypotheses and designing experiments. As shown in Figure 4.3, the schematic illustrates LLM-based drug discovery. In summary, LLMs are powerful tools for drug discovery and personalized medicine. They can read and reason over scientific data, find hidden patterns, and support complex medical decisions. With continued development and careful validation, they can become key partners in creating safer, faster, and more effective healthcare solutions.

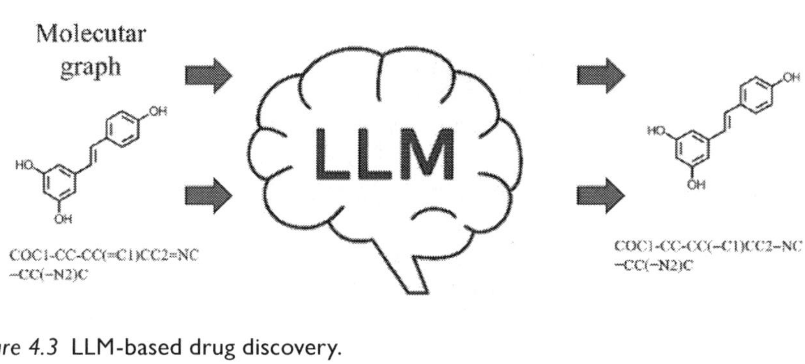

Figure 4.3 LLM-based drug discovery.

4.9 PRIVACY AND SECURITY THREATS OF LLMS IN PERSONALIZED MEDICINE

LLMs offer powerful tools for personalized medicine. They can analyze patient records, suggest treatments, and assist in diagnosis. But these models raise serious privacy concerns. Patient data is highly sensitive. If not protected, models can leak personal health information (PHI). LLMs can memorize parts of electronic health records (EHRs), even without overfitting. When queried, they might reveal private details. Two major attack types are membership inference and model inversion, where outputs are used to guess sensitive data such as disease status. Adversarial prompts can also be used to extract hidden data, violating Health Insurance Portability and Accountability Act (HIPAA), General Data Protection Regulation (GDPR), and other privacy laws. Studies show models like GPT-2 and BERT can memorize unique phrases from their training sets. As model sizes grow, these risks increase. Techniques such as model distillation and complex querying further heighten leakage threats. To address these risks, several privacy-preserving methods are emerging. Differential privacy (DP) is a key approach. It adds controlled noise during training or to model outputs, making it hard to tell if any one patient's data influenced the model. A common DP method, Differentially Private Stochastic Gradient Descent (DP-SGD), clips individual gradients and adds noise. This protects privacy but may lower model accuracy, which is especially concerning in clinical settings. Researchers are actively optimizing DP approaches to reduce this trade-off. Federated learning (FL) is another strategy. It allows hospitals to collaborate on training a global model without sharing raw patient data. Each hospital trains the model locally and sends only encrypted updates to a central server. This helps protect local EHRs. However, even model updates can leak information through techniques like gradient inversion. Cryptographic tools offer strong data protection. Homomorphic encryption (HE) enables computations directly on encrypted data. Secure multiparty computation (SMPC) splits data into secret shares processed across different parties. These techniques prevent raw data exposure even if servers are attacked. Still, they are computationally expensive and hard to scale, especially for large models.

De-identification techniques, like removing names and dates from medical notes, are often used before model training. More advanced methods replace identifiers with simple fake names or codes. However, de-identification alone leaves residual risks, so it is often paired with differential privacy. Synthetic data generation is another method. Generative models can create artificial patient records that resemble real ones. When built with DP, these synthetic records have a low chance of exposing private patient information. Still, synthetic data must be checked to make sure they look real and are fair. Strong monitoring and auditing are essential for following data protection rules. Hospitals and developers should log all training runs and model queries. Privacy testing tools help detect memorization. Newer auditing methods like "Noisy Neighbors" perform privacy checks using only black-box model access. Regulations such as HIPAA and the EU AI Act require documentation and regular checks for safety and risk in AI systems. This includes model cards, datasheets, and third-party audits. Using laws, technical tools, and regular checks together helps make sure LLMs are safe and reliable in personalized medicine.

4.10 CASE STUDIES: LLMS IN PERSONALIZED MEDICINE

4.10.1 Cancer

Cancer care needs personalized treatment. Doctors must look at complex data, like genetic mutations and tumor markers, to decide what therapies to give. LLMs help by reading this data and suggesting treatment options based on medical literature. One system, called MEREDITH, was developed in Germany using Google Gemini Pro. It supports cancer tumor boards by analyzing patient files and offering therapy suggestions. In another example, a breast cancer team in Hannover tested ChatGPT on 30 real patient cases. The LLM's treatment plans were compared to those of expert doctors. MEREDITH gave more therapy suggestions per patient (average 4) compared to experts (average 2). It matched expert choices in 94.7% of cases. In the breast cancer study, ChatGPT's advice was considered useful, especially for HER2-positive cancers and initial treatment decisions. But there were problems. Some LLM suggestions lacked strong evidence and were easy to spot as AI-generated. A separate study showed that LLM treatment suggestions often didn't match gold-standard answers (F1 scores around 0.2). Still, LLMs often result in at least one novel or helpful idea per case. LLMs can hallucinate or give outdated information. Their reasoning is not always clear. Doctors must review all AI suggestions. Privacy, bias in training data, and legal responsibility are also concerns. Guidelines like TRIPOD-LLM are needed before real-world deployment.

4.10.2 Rare diseases

Rare diseases are hard to diagnose. Symptoms are vague, and most doctors haven't seen these cases before. Some patients wait years to get a correct diagnosis. LLMs are now helping shorten this "diagnostic odyssey." One study from China tested four top LLMs, ChatGPT-4o, Claude 3.5 Sonnet, Gemini Advanced, and LLaMA 3, using 152 real rare disease case reports. The models were asked to find the correct disease. In another approach,

LLMs were combined with rare disease ontologies like Orphanet. These systems scan unstructured clinical notes to highlight possible rare conditions for follow-up. In the Chinese study, Claude 3.5 Sonnet correctly identified the rare disease in nearly 79% of cases, far better than doctors (26.3%). But another benchmark showed GPT-4o got only 24% of diagnoses right, compared to 36% for a genetics tool (Exomiser). For phenotyping, LLMs improved extraction accuracy from 0.49 to 0.69 (F1 score), showing real gains in identifying undiagnosed rare conditions. LLMs may still miss rare mutations or suggest unlikely diagnoses. Privacy of genomic data is a major concern. These systems can also reflect biases from their training data. LLMs should assist, not replace, expert review. Hybrid systems and secure cloud environments are recommended.

4.10.3 Mental health

Mental health care is under pressure globally. There aren't enough therapists, and many people struggle in silence. LLMs offer support in two ways: (i) as chatbots offering therapy-like interactions and (ii) as tools for analyzing patient language. In the United States, researchers built Therabot, a chatbot trained on therapy content. In a clinical trial, 106 patients with depression, anxiety, or eating issues used the app for eight weeks. In Korea, another team used GPT models to read emotional diary entries and predict depression scores (PHQ-9). Therabot users showed big improvements. Depression scores dropped by 51%, and anxiety by 31%. Users felt connected to the chatbot, sometimes more than to real therapists. The Korea study showed 90% accuracy in detecting depression using fine-tuned GPT-3.5, even higher with full diary data. AI chatbots can still give wrong or generic advice. They must not be used without human backup. Data privacy is critical, especially for mental health records. LLMs can also carry cultural bias. Clear safety measures and informed consent are essential. Across cancer, rare diseases, and mental health, LLMs show real potential in personalized medicine. They help doctors consider more options, spot hidden conditions, and support mental health care. But they are not perfect. Clinical oversight, ethical safeguards, and stronger evidence standards are needed before full deployment.

4.11 COMPARING LLM-BASED AND TRADITIONAL TREATMENT PLANNING METHODS

To understand the real value of LLMs in clinical care, it's helpful to compare them with traditional methods of treatment planning and clinical decision support. In the past, doctors have used a mix of medical guidelines, personal experience, and basic prediction tools to plan treatments. For example, cancer specialists often follow protocols like the NCCN guidelines and look at results from clinical trials. In more complex or rare cases, they might search the literature or check specialized databases manually. Older CDSS were mostly rule-based. They gave alerts, for example, if a drug dose was too high or if a patient had a high risk of a side effect. But these systems only worked with structured data and needed experts to build and maintain the rules. They could not understand free-text notes or adapt to unusual cases.

4.11.1 Enhancements enabled by LLMs

LLMs offer new capabilities that go far beyond these older methods:

- LLMs can read and use knowledge from textbooks, research papers, and clinical notes. So, if a patient has a rare gene mutation or multiple conditions, an LLM might still find relevant studies and similar past cases. Traditional methods might miss these cases due to time limits or narrow rules.
- LLMs can read physician notes, patient stories, or consult letters. They can "understand" unstructured text and use it to build a full picture of the patient's condition. Older systems often ignore this kind of data.
- LLMs can explain their suggestions in plain language. For example, they can say, "We recommend Treatment X because this patient has biomarker Y, and a study showed good results for similar patients." This helps both doctors and patients understand the reasons behind the plan. Older systems rarely provide this kind of explanation.
- LLMs can quickly write clinical summaries, suggest treatment options, or find relevant research. This saves doctors time and allows them to focus on talking with patients and making tough decisions. Traditional planning is more manual and slower.
- Traditional systems only update when a human changes them. But LLMs can be trained on new research or connect to live sources of knowledge. This means they can stay current with medical advances much more easily.

4.11.2 Limitations of LLMs

Despite these strengths, LLMs also have important challenges:

- LLMs can make mistakes or "hallucinate" fake facts. For example, they might suggest a wrong drug dose or refer to a study that doesn't exist. In contrast, traditional systems only give answers based on known rules and data.

- LLMs are like black boxes; they don't always show how they came to a conclusion. This makes it hard for doctors to trust their suggestions. Traditional tools often have clear rules or thresholds that are easier to understand.
- LLMs might give different answers if you change how the question is asked. Even small differences in wording can change the response. Traditional systems are more consistent; the same input always gives the same output.
- A general LLM may not know enough about specific medical fields. For example, it might not know the latest cancer treatment protocol unless it was trained on that exact data. Traditional tools, although narrow, are often built by experts for specific areas.
- LLMs learn from data that may contain bias. This could lead to unequal treatment recommendations for different groups. Traditional methods are usually tested for fairness or at least applied the same way to all patients.
- Unlike many approved clinical tools, LLMs have not been fully validated or approved by health regulators. If an LLM gives a wrong suggestion that harms a patient, it's unclear who is legally responsible. That's why most hospitals use LLMs only in low-risk tasks or research settings.

4.12 CONCLUSION AND FUTURE WORKS

LLMs are becoming powerful tools in personalized medicine. They help process huge amounts of medical information and turn it into useful insights. From cancer care to rare diseases and mental health, LLMs can support more accurate and personalized treatment. One big strength of LLMs is their ability to connect different kinds of knowledge, clinical guidelines, research papers, and patient data. They can then present this information in a clear and human-readable way. This helps doctors make more informed choices, matching care to the unique needs of each patient. Still, LLMs are not perfect. They are good at generating realistic suggestions, but their answers are not always correct. They can also lack transparency in how they reach a decision. So, they cannot be trusted to make critical medical decisions on their own. For now, the most practical use of LLMs is as advanced assistants. They can help with second opinions, write medical notes, find evidence, and manage routine tasks.

There are already real examples. Some LLM-based tools for radiotherapy planning have performed as well as human experts. GPT-4 has passed medical board exams. These are early signs of how powerful LLMs can be when used properly.

Looking ahead, three key trends are emerging:

1. **More Specialized LLMs:** Future systems will likely combine text, images (like X-rays), and omics data (like genomics). An LLM could be at the center, pulling insights from all sources to give full, personalized care from diagnosis to treatment and follow-up.
2. **Better Control and Safety:** Researchers and policy makers are working on ways to improve trust in LLMs. These include using medical knowledge graphs, fact-checking answers, and adding clear citations. In time, some LLMs may be certified like medical devices, giving doctors more confidence to use them.
3. **Wider Access to Expertise:** LLMs could help close the healthcare gap. A doctor in a remote or under-resourced area could use an LLM to get expert-level treatment advice. This could make advanced care more widely available.

As LLMs become part of clinical work, the role of doctors may change. Physicians will need new skills: asking good questions, reviewing AI output carefully, and correcting it when needed. Medical education may also change, focusing more on ethics, empathy, and how to work with AI. In this new setup, doctors will be like curators—using both AI and their own judgment to guide care. In summary, LLMs are a major step forward for personalized medicine. They can digest complex data and give useful insights tailored to the patient. While there are still problems to solve, early results are promising. With careful development and ethical use, LLMs can support doctors, not replace them. They can help make medicine more precise, personal, and effective. The next decade will be key. With the right collaboration between clinicians, AI experts, and regulators, we can move from hype to real impact. LLMs could soon help deliver on the promise of precision health: giving the right treatment to the right person at the right time.

REFERENCES

1. Taheri, A., Zamanifar, A., & Farhadi, A. (2024). Enhancing aspect-based sentiment analysis using data augmentation based on back-translation. *International Journal of Data Science and Analytics*, 1–26.
2. Farhadi, A., Mahalegi, H. S. M., Firouzabad, A. P., Zamanifar, A., & Sorouri, M. (2024). Leveraging Blockchain and ANFIS for Optimal Supply Chain Management. *arXiv preprint arXiv:2408.17161.*
3. Zeng, Y., Hussein, Z. A., Chyad, M. H., Farhadi, A., Yu, J., & Rahbarimagham, H. (2025). Integrating type-2 fuzzy logic controllers with digital twin and neural networks for advanced hydropower system management. *Scientific Reports*, *15*(1), 5140.
4. Farhadi, A., Zamanifar, A., & Faezipour, M. (2025). Application of generative AI in drug discovery. In *Application of Generative AI in Healthcare Systems* (pp. 155–174). Cham: Springer Nature Switzerland.

5. Taheri, A., Farhadi, A., & Zamanifar, A. (2025). Application of GenAI in clinical administration support. In *Application of Generative AI in Healthcare Systems* (pp. 91–117). Cham: Springer Nature Switzerland.
6. Jahanmanesh, P., Farhadi, A., & Zamanifar, A. (2025). Mobility management with AI. *IEEE Access,13*, 83022–83060.
7. Farhadi, A., & Taheri, A. (2025). Application of GenAI in synthetic data generation in the healthcare system. In *Application of Generative AI in Healthcare Systems* (pp. 67–89). Cham: Springer Nature Switzerland.
8. Rashidieranjbar, F., Farhadi, A., & Zamanifar, A. (2025). Revolutionizing Healthcare with Generative Artificial Intelligence Technologies. In *Generative Artificial Intelligence (AI) Approaches for Industrial Applications* (pp. 189–221). Cham: Springer Nature Switzerland.
9. Topol, E. J. (2019). High-performance medicine: the convergence of human and artificial intelligence. *Nature Medicine*, 25(1):44–56. DOI: 10.1038/s41591-018-0300-7.
10. Zhao, J., Feng, Q., Wu, P., *et al.* (2019). Learning from longitudinal data in electronic health records and genetic data to improve cardiovascular event prediction. *Scientific Reports*, 9:717. DOI: 10.1038/s41598-018-36769-5.
11. Perez, M. V., Mahaffey, K. W., Hedlin, H., *et al.* (2019). Large-scale assessment of a smartwatch to identify atrial fibrillation. *New England Journal of Medicine*, 381(20):1909–1917. DOI: 10.1056/NEJMoa1901183.
12. Piwek, L., Ellis, D. A., Andrews, S., Joinson, A. (2016). The rise of consumer health wearables: promises and barriers. *PLoS Medicine, 13*(2):e1001953. DOI: 10.1371/journal.pmed.1001953.
13. Poplin, R., Chang, P. C., Alexander, D., *et al.* (2018). A universal SNP and small-indel variant caller using deep neural networks. *Nature Biotechnology*, 36(10):983–987. DOI: 10.1038/nbt.4235.
14. Adam, G., Rampášek, L., Safikhani, Z., *et al.* (2020). Machine learning approaches to drug response prediction: challenges and recent progress. *NPJ Precision Oncology*, 4:19. DOI: 10.1038/s41698-020-0122-1.
15. Singhal, K., *et al.* (2023). Large language models encode clinical knowledge. *Nature*, 620:172–180.
16. Nori, H., *et al.* (2023). Capabilities of GPT-4 on medical challenge problems. *arXiv preprint arXiv:2303.13375*.
17. Jiao, J., *et al.* (2023). ChatGPT-generated differential diagnosis lists for complex clinical vignettes: diagnostic accuracy evaluation. *JMIR Medical Education*, 9(1):e48808.
18. Microsoft Research. (2023). BioGPT: Generative pre-trained transformer for biomedical text. *Clinical Trials Arena News*, Feb 9, 2023.
19. Van Veen, D., *et al.* (2024). Adapted large language models can outperform medical experts in clinical text summarization. *Nature Medicine*, 30(4):555–561
20. Zhang, Y., *et al.* (2023). TransformEHR: transformer-based generative model for EHR outcome prediction. *Nature Communications*, 14:6445.
21. Ben Shoham, O. & Rappoport, N. (2024). CPLLM: Clinical prediction with large language models. *PLOS Digital Health*, 3(12):e0000680.
22. Lammert, J., *et al.* (2024). Expert-guided LLMs for clinical decision support in precision oncology. *JCO Precision Oncology*, 8:e2400478.

23. Gaber, F., Shaik, M., Allega, F., *et al.* Evaluating large language model workflows in clinical decision support for triage and referral and diagnosis. *npj Digital Medicine, 8(1), 263.*
24. Hager, P., Jungmann, F., Bhagat, K., Hubrecht, I., Knauer, M., Vielhauer, J., ... & Rueckert, D. (2024). Evaluating and mitigating limitations of large language models in clinical decision making. *medRxiv*, 2024-01.
25. McDuff, D., Schaekermann, M., Tu, T., Palepu, A., Wang, A., Garrison, J., ... & Natarajan, V. (2025). Towards accurate differential diagnosis with large language models. *Nature, 642*, 1–7.
26. Zhu, J., & Wu, J. (2025). Ask patients with patience: enabling LLMs for human-centric medical dialogue with grounded reasoning. *arXiv preprint arXiv:2502.07143.*
27. Williams, C. Y., Bains, J., Tang, T., Patel, K., Lucas, A. N., Chen, F., ... & Kornblith, A. E. (2024). Evaluating large language models for drafting emergency department discharge summaries. *medRxiv.*
28. Levra, A. G., Gatti, M., Mene, R., Shiffer, D., Costantino, G., Solbiati, M., ... & Dipaola, F. (2025). A large language model-based clinical decision support system for syncope recognition in the emergency department: A framework for clinical workflow integration. *European Journal of Internal Medicine, 131*, 113–120.
29. Ah-Thiane, L., Heudel, P. E., Campone, M., Robert, M., Brillaud-Meflah, V., Rousseau, C., ... & Frenel, J. S. (2025). Large language models as decision-making tools in oncology: Comparing artificial intelligence suggestions and expert recommendations. *JCO Clinical Cancer Informatics*, 9, e2400230.
30. Shmilovitch, A. H., Katson, M., Cohen-Shelly, M., Peretz, S., Aran, D., & Shelly, S. (2025). GPT-4 as a clinical decision support tool in ischemic stroke management: evaluation study. *JMIR AI*, *4*(1), e60391.
31. Sandmann, S., Hegselmann, S., Fujarski, M., Bickmann, L., Wild, B., Eils, R., & Varghese, J. (2025). Benchmark evaluation of DeepSeek large language models in clinical decision-making. *Nature Medicine*, 31, 2546–2549.
32. Goh, E., Gallo, R. J., Strong, E., Weng, Y., Kerman, H., Freed, J. A., ... & Rodman, A. (2025). GPT-4 assistance for improvement of physician performance on patient care tasks: a randomized controlled trial. *Nature Medicine*, 1–6.
33. Feng, C., Jumaah Al-Nussairi, A. K., Chyad, M. H., Sawaran Singh, N. S., Yu, J., & Farhadi, A. (2025). AI powered blockchain framework for predictive temperature control in smart homes using wireless sensor networks and time shifted analysis. *Scientific Reports*, *15*(1), 1–27.

Chapter 5

The large language models for public health surveillance and outbreak

Arezou Naghib, Farhad Soleimanian Gharehchopogh, Parisa Tavana, and Amir Fallahzadeh

5.1 INTRODUCTION

In today's world, where the speed of disease spread and its complexity is unprecedented, effective public health surveillance and timely detection of disease outbreaks are fundamental to curbing transmission, and mitigating public health burdens is more critical than ever [1]. Public health surveillance underpins our ability to detect and control infectious disease threats that operate as a continuous cycle of data collection, analysis, interpretation, and dissemination, all aimed at informing timely interventions and policy decisions [2]. Traditional surveillance pipelines rooted in clinical case reports from hospitals, laboratories, and health centers typically experience reporting delays of days to weeks, hampering rapid response efforts [2]. This was seen when confirmation of H1N1 cases in 2009 lagged behind community spread, and when initial COVID-19 responses were hindered by under-recognition of asymptomatic transmission [3]. Ferguson et al. [1] demonstrated that advancing detection by one generation time (roughly 4–7 days for many respiratory viruses) can reduce the final epidemic size by over 50% [1].

Researchers have begun integrating environmental and digital data streams with classical surveillance to overcome such delays. Wastewater-based epidemiology platforms, for example, detected severe acute respiratory syndrome coronavirus 2 (SARS-CoV-2) ribonucleic acid (RNA) in community sewage up to seven days before corresponding spikes in clinical admissions, providing an advanced warning that can guide preemptive interventions [4]. As pathogen transmission accelerates in speed and complexity-exemplified by global crises such as COVID-19-public health agencies must embrace agile, data-driven surveillance to spot outbreaks at inception and inform interventions [5, 6]. Furthermore, studies have shown that fusing digital-trace data-search-query volumes, social-media chatter, mobility logs, and smart thermometer readings can preempt official case counts by several days and boost predictive accuracy by over 20% [7]. The challenges in public health are the emergence of infectious diseases such as COVID-19 [8], the rise of non-communicable diseases (NCDs) such as

 DOI: 10.1201/9781003665083-5

heart disease and cancer, health inequities, challenges related to the collection, management, and analysis of data, ensuring data security and privacy, addressing biases, and the effective collaboration and communication among stakeholders [9].

Advances in natural language processing (NLP) have given rise to LLMs capable of parsing unstructured text at medical publications, clinical notes, news feeds, and social media streams to uncover early signals of emerging threats that elude legacy systems [10]. LLMs are promising tools for extracting main information from diverse free-text sources, including academic literature, electronic health records (EHRs), social media, and questionnaire responses [11]. Nonetheless, integrating LLMs into surveillance workflows presents challenges. Model performance hinges on access to representative, high-quality training data, and many public health datasets remain siloed or privacy-protected. Health data often remains siloed under strict confidentiality rules, constraining the volume, and diversity of training datasets for machine learning (ML) models [12]. Ethical dilemmas around using personal health posts for model training also demand rigorous governance. Moreover, the black-box nature of LLMs complicates interpretability, a critical requirement for policymakers who must trust algorithmic outputs before acting [12–14]. Such an integrated system could detect outbreaks earlier, accurately forecast their trajectories, and guide targeted public health responses in an increasingly interconnected world.

Table 5.1 summarizes the abbreviations used throughout this chapter. The rest of the chapter is structured as follows: Section 5.2 reviews health surveillance and outbreak management. Section 5.3 discusses the LLMs and their application in health surveillance and outbreaks. Section 5.4 discusses key capabilities and applications of LLMs relevant to public health. Section 5.5 considers adopting LLMs to public health needs. Section 5.6 reviews the articles and works on LLMs applications in health surveillance and outbreaks. Section 5.7 delves into the challenges and unresolved issues of deploying LLMs within the health surveillance and outbreak field. Finally, Section 5.8 concludes the chapter.

5.2 PUBLIC HEALTH SURVEILLANCE AND OUTBREAK MANAGEMENT

Public health surveillance is the bedrock of public health, playing a vital role in the early detection, control, and prevention of diseases. The ultimate goal of surveillance is to provide the necessary information for planning, developing, implementing, evaluating, and maintaining public health interventions. Surveillance systems are categorized into two main types: passive and active surveillance. In a passive surveillance method, healthcare and medical centers routinely to report public health authorities about incidents

Table 5.1 Chapter abbreviations

Abbreviation	*Definition*	*Abbreviation*	*Definition*
LLMs	Large language models	MLP	Multi-layer perceptron
NCDs	Non-communicable diseases	CNN	Convolutional neural networks
EHRs	Electronic health records	BiLSTM	Bidirectional long short-term memory
ML	Machine learning	BiGRU	Bidirectional gated recurrent units
NLP	Natural language processing	mBERT	multilingual bidirectional encoder representations from transformers
MCQs	Multiple choice questions	XLM-RoBERTa	Cross lingual-robustly optimized BERT pre-training approach
TF-IDF	Term frequency-inverse document frequency	mT5	Multilingual text-to-text transfer transformer
W2V	Word2Vec	WHO	World Health Organization
LR	Logistic regression	GDPR	European General Data Protection Regulation
MNB	Multinomial naive bayes	HIPAA	Health Insurance Portability and Accountability Act
SVM	Support vector machine	GPUs	Graphics processing units
DT	Decision tree	TPUs	Tensor processors
RF	Random forest	NLG	Natural language generation

of specific illnesses. This method is generally less costly and requires fewer personnel but may suffer from reporting delays and underreporting. With active surveillance, public health personnel actively seek out disease cases, for instance, by contacting healthcare providers, visiting homes, or conducting screening tests in communities. This method has high accuracy and quick detection, is more expensive, and needs more human resources [15].

Active surveillance is typically employed during suspected outbreaks or for specific diseases requiring early detection. Disease outbreak management is a multi-stage, dynamic process that requires rapid coordination and response from health authorities [15]. Active surveillance is typically employed during suspected outbreaks or for specific diseases requiring early detection. Disease outbreak management is a multi-stage, dynamic process that requires rapid coordination and response from health authorities. The key stages in this process include detection, investigation, control, and evaluation [16]. Modern public health surveillance relies on a wide array of data collected through traditional or non-traditional means. These data include clinical and laboratory reports, social media data, news and media reports, scientific articles, medical literature, and other non-traditional data [17–19]. Table 5.2 presents another classification of data sources in public health surveillance.

Table 5.2 Data sources in public health surveillance

Data type	*Description*	*Advantages*	*Limitations*
Social media data [23]	- Includes posts, comments, and user-generated text content from platforms like X, Facebook, and Instagram. - Used to identify disease symptoms, social reactions, and misinformation.	- Real-time access and high volume. - Broad geographical coverage. - Enables sentiment and behavioral analysis.	- Data noise and misinformation. - Demographic bias. - Privacy concerns.
Medical reports and clinical data [24]	- Structured data from EHRs, laboratory reports, and hospital records. - Includes diagnostic, treatment, and clinical outcome information.	- High accuracy and standardization. - Suitable for advanced analytics and outcome prediction. - Integrates well with epidemiological data.	- Restricted access due to privacy regulations. - Requires preprocessing for unstructured data. - High collection costs.
Epidemiological data [25]	- This includes demographic statistics, disease prevalence rates, and official reports from organizations such as the World Health Organization (WHO) and the CDC. - Data can be textual (reports) or numerical (statistics).	- High reliability. - Suitable for disease outbreak modeling and forecasting. - Global and regional coverage.	- Delays in data collection and publication. - Limited access to local data in some regions. - Complexity in analyzing textual data.

(Continued)

Table 5.2 (Continued)

Data type	*Description*	*Advantages*	*Limitations*
Biosensor and wearable data [26]	- Data collected from wearable devices.	- Real-time and personalized data. - Suitable for individual health monitoring. - Integrates with other data sources.	- High device costs. - Limited access in low-income regions. - Accuracy and standardization issues.
News and media reports [27]	News articles and media reports provide information on disease outbreaks, public health policies, or societal reactions.	- Broad and diverse coverage. - Useful for analyzing social and political trends. - Easy access.	- Potential media bias. - Incomplete or unstructured information. - Requires filtering to remove noise.
Online search data [23]	Data from user searches on engines reflect patterns related to disease symptoms or health concerns.	- Rapid and broad access. - Enables early trend detection. - Global coverage.	- Search behavior biases. - Privacy concerns. - Requires complex modeling for analysis.

5.3 LLMS

LLMs are a type of neural network-based language model. They're trained on massive amounts of unlabeled text data using a self-supervised learning method and contain billions of parameters [20]. LLMs demonstrated potential capability in various NLP tasks, including language summarization, translation, complex verbal patterns, text generation and synthesis, question answering, generating coherent and appropriate replies in a given context, sentiment analysis, etc. [21]. LLMs build on the transformer architecture. They employ self-attention mechanisms to model long-range dependencies in text, enabling nuanced understanding and fluent generation of natural language [10, 22]. LLMs can be leveraged in automated literature synthesis, early-warning signal detection, and dynamic scenario modeling in outbreak contexts. Moreover, LLMs facilitate real-time monitoring by parsing newswire and social-media text to flag atypical health-related discourse. During COVID-19, prototype systems built on LLMs tracked misinformation trends across multiple languages, enabling health authorities to deploy corrective messaging up to five days before official case surges [28]. In summary, LLMs grounded in the transformer paradigm offer unparalleled capacity to ingest and make sense of vast text streams, positioning them as essential components of next-generation, near-real-time public-health surveillance frameworks. LLMs can help medical educators,

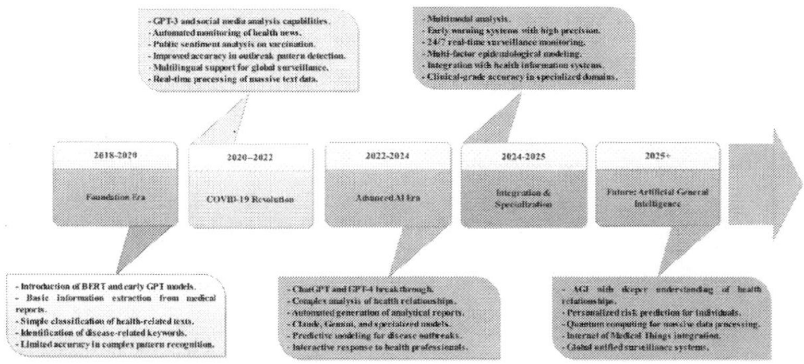

Figure 5.1 Evolution of LLMs in public health surveillance.

academics, healthcare professionals, and policymakers in providing a deeper understanding of infectious diseases, the COVID-19 pandemic, and vaccines related to COVID-19 [29]. Figure 5.1 shows the evolution of LLMs in public health surveillance. Also, Table 5.3 shows some of the LLMs in public health surveillance and outbreaks.

5.4 KEY CAPABILITIES AND APPLICATIONS OF LLMS RELEVANT TO PUBLIC HEALTH

LLMs can quickly analyze, summarize, generate textual information, and handle the massive and unstructured data in public health. These capabilities make LLMs highly pertinent for public health surveillance and outbreak management. LLMs are experts at understanding, interpreting, and generating human language and excel in NLP tasks [33]. They can spot patterns, key details, entities, and relationships in the text, giving insights into public health trends and events that humans find impossible to uncover alone [34]. This is particularly useful for populating structured databases from free-text clinical notes or surveillance reports, facilitating more systematic analysis of epidemiological data [35, 36]. LLMs can condense massive volumes of text data into concise and coherent summaries. In public health, this is invaluable for rapidly extracting key information from lengthy medical literature, clinical notes, public health reports, or news feeds during an outbreak [37, 38]. Given their training on vast multilingual datasets, many LLMs possess robust translation capabilities [39].

LLMs can translate health alerts, patient education materials, and research findings into multiple languages, enhancing accessibility and promoting equitable health information dissemination, particularly in diverse and underserved communities [39]. Also, LLMs can generate human-like text, which has myriad applications in public health communication, including drafting public health advisories, creating educational materials for various demographics, or even personalizing health messages [40].

Table 5.3 LLMs in the field of public health surveillance and outbreak

Model	*Features*	*Advantages*	*Disadvantages*	*Applications*
BERT [30]	- Bidirectional pre-training for deep contextual understanding. - Fine-tuning capability for specific domains like healthcare. - Entity extraction and relationship analysis.	- Strong contextual comprehension, ideal for medical report analysis. - Flexible for task-specific fine-tuning. - Robust performance in extracting insights from textual data.	- High computational resource requirements. - Complex training for small datasets. - Dependence on high-quality data.	- Analyzing medical reports to identify disease patterns. - Monitoring social media for public sentiment detection. - Extracting insights from scientific literature for emerging disease surveillance.
GPT-4	- Human-like text generation. - Multimodal data processing. - Broad contextual learning capabilities.	- High-quality and contextually relevant responses. - Suitable for automated reporting and query answering. - Handles diverse data sources effectively.	- High computational costs. - Requires extensive training data. - Potential biases in outputs.	- Predicting disease trends through textual data analysis. - Generating automated reports for public health authorities. - Real-time query response during health crises.
BioBERT [31]	- BERT variant fine-tuned for biomedical texts. - Processes scientific and medical literature. - High-accuracy medical entity extraction.	- High precision in biomedical text analysis. - Ideal for extracting epidemiological data. - Enhanced performance in health-specific tasks.	- Limited to biomedical data. - Requires fine-tuning for specific applications. - Computationally intensive.	- Monitoring scientific literature for emerging diseases. - Extracting epidemiological data from texts. - Supporting clinical decision-making systems.

(*Continued*)

Table 5.3 (Continued)

Model	*Features*	*Advantages*	*Disadvantages*	*Applications*
ChatGPT	- Conversational interface with natural language understanding - Code generation and data analysis capabilities. - Interactive user collaboration.	- User-friendly for non-technical users. - Supports disease transmission modeling. - Rapid response and analysis capabilities.	- Dependent on input quality. - Limited in handling complex data without customization. - Ethical concerns.	- Assisting in designing disease transmission models. - Analyzing epidemiological data for parameter estimation. - Educating and informing public health workers.
ClinicalBERT [32]	- BERT variant fine-tuned for clinical data. - Analyzes EHRs. - Contextual clinical information extraction.	- High accuracy in clinical data analysis. - Suitable for patient record surveillance. - Improves disease detection from textual data.	- Limited to clinical data. - Requires high-quality training data. - Integration challenges with existing systems.	- Monitoring EHR for early disease detection. - Analyzing hospital data for outbreak patterns. - Supporting automated diagnostics in emergencies.
LLaMA [26]	- Optimized for research purposes. - High efficiency in NLP. - Flexible for task-specific fine-tuning.	- High computational efficiency compared to peers. - Suitable for resource-constrained research. - Adaptable for health-related applications.	- Limited public access. - Requires fine-tuning for medical tasks. - Limited support for multimodal data.	- Analyzing textual data for disease surveillance. - Supporting epidemiological research. - Generating analytical reports for health policy.

LLMs offer distinct advantages over other ML methods used in the healthcare domain for years. These differences are from the architecture, scalability, and advanced NLP and generation capabilities of LLMs. Table 5.4 compares LLMs with other ML methods in the healthcare domain. Table 5.5 shows the applications of LLMs in public health surveillance.

Table 5.4 Comparison of LLMs vs. other ML methods in public health

Feature	*LLMs*	*Other ML methods*
Natural language understanding and generation [10]	- Understand nuances, ambiguities, and contextual subtleties of natural language. - Capable of summarizing, extracting information, and generating new text from unstructured medical data.	- Primarily relies on predefined patterns, fixed vocabularies, or manual feature engineering. - Less effective when facing linguistic variability and complex contexts.
Feature engineering [41]	- Ability to learn intrinsic representations (embeddings) and high-level features directly from data without requiring human expertise for feature extraction.	- Heavily dependent on manual feature engineering. - Needs domain expertise to extract and define relevant features from raw data. - Time consuming and costly.
Few-shot/ zero-shot learning [41]	- Performing new tasks with very few training examples (few-shot) or even no examples (zero-shot) due to training on vast datasets.	- Typically requires large volumes of labeled data for adequate performance. - Training for new tasks involves extensive data collection and re-labeling.
Scalability and flexibility	- Processing enormous amounts of textual data from diverse sources. - Adapting quickly to new patterns.	Often face challenges with the variety and high volume of unstructured data, potentially requiring frequent retraining or model reconstruction.
Complex reasoning and summarization	- Ability to identify complex patterns. - Summarizing scattered information - Performing text-based reasoning to understand trends and make predictions.	Generally, it struggles with complex reasoning and summarizing long, diverse texts, focusing more on specific classification or regression tasks.

(*Continued*)

Table 5.4 (Continued)

Feature	*LLMs*	*Other ML methods*
Model complexity and interpretability	- Often complex with low interpretability. - Difficult to understand how the model concludes.	Ranges from simple and highly interpretable models (e.g., linear regression) to more complex models with moderate interpretability (e.g., neural networks).
Computational resource needs	- Requiring significant computational power and energy for training and running large models	Generally, it requires fewer computational resources compared to LLMs.
Risk of bias and hallucinations [42]	- Risk of inheriting biases from training data and generating inaccurate information or hallucinations.	Risk of bias exists, but generally lower than LLMs, and "hallucinations" are less common.

Table 5.5 Applications of LLMs in public health surveillance

Section	*Application area*	*Specific use cases/Technical details*
Data Collection and processing from heterogeneous sources	Social media [7]	- Identifying unofficial symptoms and rumors. - Handling slang, informal language, and emerging terminologies.
	News and media reports	- Real-time monitoring and alerting.
	Scientific and research articles	- Accelerated knowledge discovery.
	Unofficial reports	- Qualitative data gathering.
	Clinical data	- Extraction of clinical concepts.
Early detection and outbreak alerting.	Identifying early signals.	- Semantic context understanding.
	Analyzing keyword and phrase trends.	- Deviation from baselines.
	Detecting geographical and temporal clusters.	- Spatiotemporal pattern recognition

(*Continued*)

Table 5.5 (Continued)

Section	*Application area*	*Specific use cases/Technical details*
Summarization and reporting	Automated summarization of public health reports.	- Concise information delivery.
	Generation of Analytical Reports.	- Tailored insights for decision-makers.
	Translation of information across languages.	- Multilingual health communication. - Facilitating international collaboration and equitable access to information.
Information classification and categorization	Classifying reports and texts.	- Automated categorization.
	Identifying risk factors and vulnerable populations.	- Pattern analysis for intervention.
Sentiment analysis and public understanding	Assessing public reaction.	- Gauging Public Acceptance.
	Identifying public concerns and misinformation.	- Infodemic management.

5.5 ADAPTING LLMS TO PUBLIC HEALTH NEEDS

Adapting LLMs for public health applications is a multi-step process that aims to increase accuracy, efficiency, and reliability in analyzing and extracting critical information from health data. These processes are data selection, preprocessing, pre-training and fine-tuning, and specialized training for specific tasks, and each process consists of sub-processes. LLMs are trained on large, general datasets by default. This general training gives the models a broad understanding of language. However, it requires additional tuning for specialized applications such as health data analysis. High-quality and relevant dataset selection is a crucial phase in adapting LLMs to public health needs. The data should have sufficient volume, be of high quality, and be directly applicable to public health issues. Health data is often heterogeneous and unstructured, and must be preprocessed before processing. Preprocessing steps include data cleaning, normalization/standardization of medical terms, and bias removal [31]. The data cleaning step has substeps, including removing noise, duplicate data, and irrelevant information. Normalization/standardization helps the model understand clinical concepts correctly and avoids ambiguity. Identify and mitigate potential biases in the data that could lead to unfair or inaccurate results. These biases can arise from under-representing specific groups, demographic differences, or even the way data is recorded. Although LLMs are pre-trained on general data, in some cases, it may be necessary to continue pre-training on a large corpus of general health data (e.g., PubMed articles, anonymized electronic health records). The pre-training phase enables the model to gain a deeper understanding of the language and concepts in the health domain, serving as a stronger starting point for fine-tuning. In this phase, the model is trained on task-specific health datasets to optimize its performance for specific tasks. These tasks can include information extraction, classification, and prediction. LLMs require particular approaches to health data analysis, including supervised learning, transfer learning, and multilingual learning.

5.6 RELATED WORKS AND CASE STUDIES

Kwok et al. [43] explored ChatGPT's role in developing infectious disease transmission models to enhance pandemic preparedness and democratize access to advanced modeling techniques for public health professionals. The authors used a case study approach, with the public health practitioner and ChatGPT collaborating to develop a mathematical transmission model. The article also involved verification and validation processes to ensure the accuracy, performance of the final model. The article found that ChatGPT can successfully develop a validated transmission model and provide estimates of key epidemiological parameters, such as the basic reproductive number (R0) and final epidemic size.

Espinosa et al. [44] investigated improving the performance of LLMs in domain-specific use cases with potential applications in public health and their varied performance across tasks and datasets. This article proposed an open-source model for intuitively and rapidly benchmarking LLMs for public health. Using a mix of high-performing open-source LLMs, the article found that prediction accuracy varied by task and dataset, with better results for objective information extraction. Importantly, it confirmed that smaller models sometimes outperformed larger ones, reinforcing the need for task-specific model selection. The findings indicated that the smaller models demonstrated competitive performance in particular situations (e.g., GPT-3.5 mini for vaccination stance or GPT-4o mini for disease tracking in WHO DONs). The research concluded that the open-source solution provides a structured, scalable, and user-friendly framework for LLM prediction and evaluation in public health. The article also acknowledged the exponential growth of new LLMs, underscoring the necessity for continuous benchmarking despite limitations like the technical expertise required for deployment and the lack of comprehensive usability assessment.

Jiang et al. [45] introduced the ALEX framework, a novel approach for improving social media data analysis in public health through balanced training and LLM-based explanation and correction. The article aimed to develop an effective text classification method for public health, specifically addressing challenges like data imbalance and limited input size. A core finding was that using LLMs for explanation and correction significantly boosts credibility and performance. Key aspects of the ALEX framework include a balanced training pipeline that involves data augmentation and weighted-loss fine-tuning. The authors judiciously used GPT-3.5 to verify specific BERT predictions, leading to improved F1 scores and accuracy, unlike direct, unconstrained integration that can decrease performance. The article also highlights the importance of prompt design and managing LLM hallucinations. The ALEX method's effectiveness was validated through extensive experiments across three SMM4H 2023 competition tasks, consistently demonstrating superior accuracy. The article acknowledged the inherent challenges of data imbalance and the potential for LLM hallucinations. Practically, this research has broad applications in enhancing the accuracy of public health text classification, including areas like COVID-19-related data and developing more effective strategies for handling imbalanced datasets.

Harris et al. [11] assessed the performance of LLMs across various public health tasks, utilizing a combination of six existing and seven newly annotated datasets. The evaluation involved eleven open-weight LLMs (ranging from 7 to 123 billion parameters) and three GPT-4 series models, primarily using zero-shot in-context learning, with some tasks also incorporating few-shot prompting. The research revealed a significant variation in LLM performance. While models excelled at simpler public health classification tasks (e.g., achieving over 80% micro-F1 on GI Illness Classification), they struggled with more complex ones, such as Contact Classification and BioDex Drugs Extraction, where scores dropped below 60% micro-F1. The article also highlighted that the latest open-weight models are becoming increasingly competitive with private models for public health applications. Llama-3.3-70B-Instruct emerged as the top performer, achieving the best results on eight of 16 tasks. The limitations of the article include the fact that some functions, such as Contact Classification and BioDex Drugs Extraction, are challenging for LLMs, and that further research is needed to investigate long-form natural language generation (NLG) tasks.

CareCall [46] is an LLM-driven chatbot that assists socially isolated individuals by making check-up phone calls and providing teleoperator oversight. The article, utilizing a qualitative approach with focus groups, interviews (34 participants from three stakeholder groups), and analysis of lived experiences, aimed to understand the benefits and associated challenges with the implementation of conversational AI in public health. CareCall demonstrated significant benefits, providing a holistic understanding of individuals through open-ended conversations and offloading public health workload. The article questioned the efficacy of using crowd workers for chatbot dialogue corpus creation, suggesting alternative approaches may be needed. The article concludes that LLM-driven chatbots hold the potential for scaling public health interventions through empathetic interactions and population monitoring. However, realizing this potential requires addressing personalization and emotional support challenges, particularly by improving long-term memory functions.

De Angelis et al. [47] discussed the emergence of LLMs, particularly ChatGPT. The objectives of the article were to highlight the potential risks and benefits of using LLMs in the context of public health and to develop shared guidelines and legislation that can influence a future where AI contributes positively to public health. The article reviewed the evolution of LLMs like ChatGPT, including the development of ChatGPT, and their applications in public health. The key findings of the article included the potential benefits of LLMs in supporting scientific research, such as suggesting research questions, generating summaries and recommendations of papers, generating hypotheses, writing scripts in multiple programming languages, and the risks associated with their use, including the spread of misinformation and the potential for AI-driven infodemic. However, the article also noted that LLMs can generate fake news articles, scientific abstracts, and papers, which can have serious consequences, particularly in health. The article proposed a detectable-by-design approach to mitigate the risks associated with LLMs.

Morita et al. [9] performed a comprehensive SWOT (Strengths, Weaknesses, Opportunities, and Threats) and PESTLE (Political, Economic, Social, Technological, Legal, and Environmental) analysis to examine the potential of ChatGPT in public health applications. Their objective was to identify the advantages, disadvantages, opportunities, threats (including misinterpretation, privacy concerns, and biases), and the external factors influencing ChatGPT's success in this domain. The article highlighted ChatGPT's potential for providing tailored health information and assistance, enhancing disease monitoring, and aiding in the identification of outbreaks. However, it also underscored significant challenges, including the risk of misinterpretation, privacy concerns, and biases in the data it's trained on. Through the PESTLE analysis, the authors emphasized how policymakers, healthcare institutions, and researchers can obtain crucial insights regarding the wider contextual elements that influence the application of ChatGPT. This understanding is vital for informed decision-making, anticipating challenges, and developing ethical standards and regulatory structures to enhance advantages while mitigating risks.

Meo et al. [29] investigated ChatGPT's understanding of public health, infectious diseases, the COVID-19 pandemic, and vaccines. The article aimed to evaluate the potential of ChatGPT in providing accurate information regarding public health, disease monitoring, early alerts, and identifying disease outbreaks. The methods used in the article include establishing a multiple choice questions (MCQs) bank, reviewing and confirming the questions, selecting 60 MCQs, and evaluating the knowledge level of ChatGPT on MCQs. The authors used a binomial test to calculate the *p*-value of ChatGPT's answers to the MCQs. The article used a standardized set of MCQs to evaluate knowledge of ChatGPT. The results showed ChatGPT's satisfactory performance across all three areas: public health, infectious diseases, and the COVID-19 pandemic, with 56.66%, 88.23%, and 92.30%, respectively (an overall score of 73.33%). The article acknowledged several limitations, including the small number of MCQs used for evaluation and the necessity for assessing ChatGPT in real-world and controlled environments. A key concern was ChatGPT's potential to generate incorrect answers. They could stem from outdated information, misinterpreting complex or lengthy questions, or formulas.

TepiSense [48] performs automatically real-time disease surveillance of epidemic-prone diseases using Twitter data. The proposed system has four modules: a preprocessor, feature extractor, classifier, and evaluator. TepiSense classified tweets related to diseases and further identified 'indication' tweets that highlight the presence of patients. TepiSense compares the performance of three feature extraction techniques (including term frequency-inverse document frequency (TF-IDF), Word2Vec (W2V), and TF-IDF+W2V), nine machine/deep learning models (including logistic regression (LR), multinomial naive bayes (MNB), support vector machine (SVM), decision tree (DT), random forest (RF), multi-layer perceptron (MLP), convolutional neural networks (CNN), bidirectional long short-term memory networks (BiLSTM), and bidirectional gated recurrent units (BiGRU)), and three LLMs (including multilingual bidirectional encoder representations from transformers (mBERT), cross lingual-robustly optimized BERT pre-training approach (XLM-RoBERTa), and multilingual text-to-text transfer transformer (mT5)). The article results showed that the mBERT model outperforms other models, achieving high F-measure values for topic and indication tweets classification.

Deiana et al. [49] evaluated the accuracy, clarity, and thoroughness of ChatGPT's replies concerning vaccination myths and misconceptions. The methods used in the article involve administering the WHO's 11 "myths and misconceptions" regarding vaccinations to both the free (GPT-3.5) and the paid (GPT-4.0) versions of ChatGPT, followed by a qualitative and quantitative assessment of the responses using established accuracy scales. The article involved two Raters who assessed the reactions of two versions of ChatGPT to 11 questions related to vaccination myths and misconceptions. The Raters assessed the reactions based on determinants such as scientific veracity, appropriateness of vocabulary, suitability of language, and logical arrangement. ChatGPT's responses were straightforward and had an accuracy rate of 85.4%, with the paid version (GPT-4.0) delivering better responses in terms of correctness, clarity, and thoroughness than the free version (GPT-3.5). The article also identified areas where both versions of ChatGPT provided inaccurate or misleading information. This article acknowledged several limitations, including the potential biases and limitations of the AI tool, the digital divide and accessibility issues related to the paid version of ChatGPT, the age of ChatGPT's training data, which dates back to 2021, and the potential for the Raters to have misunderstood the questions or the responses. It relied on a limited number of questions and Raters. The article also notes that the Raters were aware of the version from which the reactions originated, which could have affected their ratings.

Espinosa and Salathé [50] analyzed the LLMs's performance in understanding public health discourse and users' stances towards vaccination on social media. The authors used eight alternative methods to extract vaccination stances from tweets, including crowd annotators, a rule-based sentiment analysis tool, and six LLMs. The LLMs used were GPT-3.5, GPT-4, Mistral (7B), Mixtral (8x7B), Llama3 (8B), and Llama3 (70B). The article used a lexicon and rule-based sentiment analysis tool to compare it with the more sophisticated LLMs. The results showed that GPT-4, Llama3 (70B), and Mixtral (8x7B) demonstrated strong performance across various prompts, whereas GPT-3.5, Llama3 (8B), and Mistral (7B) exhibited greater variability and dependence on prompts. The article also found that LLMs outperformed crowdsourcing, especially in the less represented negative category. The article had several limitations, including using a limited number of tweets and the reliance on expert annotations as the gold standard.

5.7 CHALLENGES AND LIMITATIONS LLMS FOR PUBLIC HEALTH

LLMs have great potential to improve public health surveillance and disease outbreak management due to their advanced capabilities in NLP and textual data analysis. However, using this technology in the public health domain faces several challenges and limitations, including ethical and privacy issues, technical limitations, cultural/linguistic issues, and operational challenges. This section provides a comprehensive review of these challenges. Table 5.6 shows these challenges and suggests strategies for overcoming them.

5.7.1 Ethical and privacy issues

Health data often contain sensitive and personal information. Using LLMs to analyze these data requires compliance with strict privacy regulations, such as the European General Data Protection Regulation (GDPR) and the Health Insurance Portability and Accountability Act (HIPAA) in the United States. For example, extracting information from social media posts without explicit consent may lead to privacy violations [51]. Also, models trained on sensitive data may unintentionally reveal personal information in their outputs. LLMs may amplify biases present in the training data and

Table 5.6 Challenges of LLMs in public health surveillance and outbreak

Category	*Challenge*	*Proposed solutions*
Ethical and privacy issues	Compliance with privacy regulations	- Implement robust anonymization techniques before data processing. - Use federated learning to keep data localized and reduce sharing. - Develop clear consent protocols for social media data use.
	Unintentional disclosure of personal information	- Apply differential privacy during model training to minimize data leakage. - Regularly audit model outputs for sensitive information exposure. - Use synthetic data for training to reduce reliance on real patient data.
	Amplification of biases	- Diversify training datasets to include underrepresented communities. - Conduct bias audits and use fairness-aware algorithms. - Engage local stakeholders to validate model outputs for equity.
	Data ownership and consent ambiguities	- Establish transparent data governance frameworks. - Create standardized consent forms for multi-source data use. - Involve ethics boards to oversee data usage policies.
Technical limitations	Noisy and unstructured data	- Preprocess data with noise-filtering techniques. - Use domain-specific fine-tuning to improve the handling of unstructured data. - Integrate structured data to enhance accuracy.
	High computational costs	- Leverage cloud-based solutions with scalable pricing models. - Develop lightweight LLM architectures for low-resource settings. - Partner with tech companies to subsidize infrastructure costs.
	High energy consumption	- Optimize models for energy efficiency. - Use green computing initiatives, such as renewable energy-powered data centers. - Explore smaller and task-specific models to reduce energy use.

(*Continued*)

Table 5.6 (Continued)

Category	*Challenge*	*Proposed solutions*
Technical limitations	Opaque decision-making	- Implement explainable AI techniques to interpret outputs. - Develop hybrid models combining LLMs with rule-based systems. - Train policymakers on LLM limitations and interpretation.
	High latency in real-time analysis	- Use model distillation to create faster and smaller models. - Deploy edge computing for localized and low-latency processing. - Prioritize real-time data pipelines for surveillance tasks.
	Poor generalization to rare events	- Augment training data with simulated outbreak scenarios. - Use transfer learning from related domains to improve generalization. - Integrate expert knowledge to handle novel events.
Cultural and linguistic challenges	Limited multilingual performance	- Collect and incorporate multilingual health datasets for training. - Use transfer learning to adapt models to local languages. - Collaborate with local linguists to improve language models.
	Cultural misunderstandings	- Include cultural context in training data through local partnerships. - Develop culture-specific ontologies for health terms. - Validate outputs with local health experts to ensure relevance.
Operational limitations	Lack of infrastructure in resource-poor areas	- Deploy offline-capable and lightweight LLMs for low-resource settings. - Use mobile-based platforms for data collection and analysis. - Invest in local infrastructure development through global health partnerships.
	Potential for misuse or misinterpretation	- Provide training programs for public health officials on LLM use. - Establish clear guidelines for interpreting LLM outputs. - Implement safeguards to detect and prevent misuse.
	Need for interdisciplinary collaboration	- Form multidisciplinary task forces for LLM deployment. - Create platforms for knowledge sharing between AI and health professionals. - Fund joint research initiatives to align AI with public health goals.

lead to biased results in public health analyses. For example, if the educational data are collected primarily from English-speaking countries or areas with technological access, the model may perform poorly in analyzing data from underserved or non-English-speaking communities [12]. These biases can lead to inequities in health service delivery or policymaking. Also, determining who owns health data and obtaining informed consent for its use in LLM training or analysis is complex, especially when data are aggregated from multiple sources.

5.7.2 Technical limitations

Data used in public health surveillance, mainly social media data and news reports, are often unstructured and noisy. This noisy data reduces the accuracy of LLMs' analyses. Training and fine-tuning LLMs require advanced computational infrastructure, such as graphics processing units (GPUs) or tensor processors (TPUs), which are expensive. This can be a barrier to using LLMs in public health organizations in developing countries or with limited resources [52]. In addition, the high energy consumption of these models raises environmental concerns. LLMs are often described as "black boxes," meaning the decision-making process is opaque to users. This is a severe limitation in public health, where decisions must be justifiable and evidence-based [53]. For example, if an LLM predicts that an area is at risk of a disease outbreak, it is difficult to explain the reason for this prediction to policymakers. Public health surveillance often requires real-time or near-real-time analysis of data streams [54]. LLMs usually have high latency due to their computational complexity, which can delay critical outbreak detection [7]. Also, LLMs may struggle to accurately detect or predict rare or novel disease outbreaks because they rely on patterns in historical data [55].

5.7.3 Cultural and linguistic challenges

The efficacy of LLMs in global public health surveillance is significantly constrained by limited multilingual performance and a nuanced understanding of cultural differences. Many LLMs are trained primarily on English-language data, which can limit their performance in analyzing text data in other languages, especially in non-English-speaking countries. For example, analyzing social media posts in local languages in Africa or Asia has low accuracy due to a lack of multilingual training data [56]. Understanding cultural differences is critical in public health data analysis. For example, terms associated with disease symptoms or health behaviors may have different meanings in different cultures. Public health data analysis depends on interpreting human behavior, communication, and symptom descriptions. These are deeply embedded in cultural contexts. Terms associated with disease symptoms, health behaviors, or even common phrases expressing well-being or distress can carry vastly different meanings across cultures.

5.7.4 Operational limitations

The effective deployment of LLMs in public health surveillance is faced with operational limitations, particularly pronounced in resource-poor settings. In resource-poor areas, such as developing countries, may not be available the infrastructure necessary to deploy LLMs, including high-speed internet access or computing servers. The lack of this infrastructure creates a digital divide and limits the ability of local organizations to use LLMs [57]. Other challenges that LLMs face are the potential for misuse of the models or misinterpretation of the results. Public health officials may misapply LLM-derived insights or misinterpret sophisticated analytical results without adequate training and clear guidelines, which could result in poor decisions that have real adverse effects on population health. The challenge requires collaboration between AI experts, epidemiologists, data scientists, and policymakers. Such collaboration is vital to develop LLM solutions that are not only technologically sound but also contextually relevant, ethically robust, and operationally feasible for diverse global health environments.

5.8 CONCLUSION

Integrating LLMs into public health surveillance heralds a transformative shift in outbreak intelligence, leveraging their advanced NLP capabilities to analyze diverse data streams in near-real-time [58]. This makes it possible to obtain high-resolution epidemiological insights that significantly enhance the speed and precision of disease outbreak detection and response. But there are several vital challenges in public health, including critical ethical and privacy issues, inherent technical limitations, and cultural and linguistic barriers. Public health is an interdisciplinary domain that focuses on improving population health through evidence-based strategies and stands to benefit immensely from LLM-based chatbots. LLMs can serve as comprehensive and all-encompassing resources for disease information, health education, and pandemic preparedness. LLMs have the enormous potential to completely transform global health security by providing solutions that are quicker, more accurate, and inclusive. This chapter aimed to provide researchers with a comprehensive overview of the role, opportunities, and challenges associated with LLMs in public health surveillance and outbreaks, underscoring the imperative for robust ethics, stringent privacy safeguards, and rigorous validation practices to ensure their responsible and effective deployment in strengthening pandemic preparedness and advancing equitable public health outcomes worldwide. Our research showed that

LLMs significantly reduce outbreak detection times and enhance predictive accuracy by leveraging unstructured data sources. Yet, their widespread adoption is impeded by considerable ethical and infrastructural challenges. This necessitates robust interdisciplinary collaboration and culturally sensitive AI development to ensure equitable global public health outcomes.

REFERENCES

1. Ferguson, N.M., et al., Strategies for mitigating an influenza pandemic. *Nature*, 2006, 442(7101): p. 448–452.
2. Thacker, S.B. and R.L. Berkelman, Public health surveillance in the United States. *Epidemiologic Reviews*, 1988, 10(1): p. 164–190.
3. Heymann, D.L. and N. Shindo, COVID-19: what is next for public health? *The Lancet*, 2020, 395(10224): p. 542–545.
4. Li, X., et al., Wastewater-based epidemiology predicts COVID-19-induced weekly new hospital admissions in over 150 USA counties. *Nature Communications*, 2023, 14(1): p. 45–48.
5. Farhud, D.D. and S. Zokaei, Ethical issues of artificial intelligence in medicine and healthcare. *Iranian Journal of Public Health*, 2021, 50(11): p. i.
6. Gerke, S., T. Minssen, and G. Cohen, Ethical and legal challenges of artificial intelligence-driven healthcare, in *Artificial intelligence in healthcare*, 2020, Elsevier. p. 295–336.
7. Zhou, X., et al., PH-LLM: Public Health Large Language Models for Infoveillance. *medRxiv*, 2025: p. 2025.02.08.25321587.
8. Cruz, M.P., et al., COVID-19, a worldwide public health emergency. *Revista Clínica Española (English Edition)*, 2021, 221(1): p. 55–61.
9. Morita, P.P., et al., Applying ChatGPT in public health: a SWOT and PESTLE analysis. *Frontiers in Public Health*, 2023, 11: p. 1225861.
10. Vaswani, A., et al., Attention is all you need. *Advances in Neural Information Processing Systems*, 2017, 30, 5998.
11. Harris, J., et al., Evaluating large language models for public health classification and extraction tasks. *arXiv preprint arXiv:2405.14766*, 2024.
12. Obermeyer, Z., et al., Dissecting racial bias in an algorithm used to manage the health of populations. *Science*, 2019, 366(6464): p. 447–453.
13. Caruana, R., et al. Intelligible models for healthcare: Predicting pneumonia risk and hospital 30-day readmission. In *Proceedings of the 21th ACM SIGKDD International Conference on Knowledge Discovery and Data Mining*, 2015.
14. Lipton, Z.C., The mythos of model interpretability: In machine learning, the concept of interpretability is both important and slippery. *Queue*, 2018, 16(3): p. 31–57.
15. Mandl, K.D., et al., Implementing syndromic surveillance: a practical guide informed by the early experience. *Journal of the American Medical Informatics Association*, 2004, 11(2): p. 141–150.
16. Giesecke, J., *Modern infectious disease epidemiology*, 2017: CRC Press.

17. Chunara, R., J.R. Andrews, and J.S. Brownstein, Social and news media enable estimation of epidemiological patterns early in the 2010 Haitian cholera outbreak. *The American Journal of Tropical Medicine and Hygiene*, 2012, 86(1): p. 39.
18. Freifeld, C. and J. Browmstein, HealthMap: global disease alter map. *Journal of the American Medical Informatics Association*, 2008, 15(2): p. 150–157.
19. Roth, G.A., et al., Global, regional, and national age-sex-specific mortality for 282 causes of death in 195 countries and territories, 1980–2017: a systematic analysis for the Global Burden of Disease Study 2017. *The Lancet*, 2018, 392(10159): p. 1736–1788.
20. Shen, Y., et al., *ChatGPT and other large language models are double-edged swords*, 2023, Radiological Society of North America. p. e230163.
21. Raiaan, M.A.K., et al., A review on large language models: Architectures, applications, taxonomies, open issues and challenges. *IEEE Access*, 2024, 12: p. 26839–26874.
22. Rajkomar, A., J. Dean, and I. Kohane, Machine learning in medicine. *New England Journal of Medicine*, 2019, 380(14): p. 1347–1358.
23. Ginsberg, J., et al., Detecting influenza epidemics using search engine query data. *Nature*, 2009, 457(7232): p. 1012–1014.
24. Rajkomar, A., et al., Scalable and accurate deep learning with electronic health records. *NPJ Digital Medicine*, 2018, 1(1): p. 18.
25. Brownstein, J.S., et al., Combining participatory influenza surveillance with modeling and forecasting: Three alternative approaches. *JMIR Public Health and Surveillance*, 2017, 3(4): p. e7344.
26. Touvron, H., et al., Llama: Open and efficient foundation language models. *arXiv preprint arXiv:2302.13971*, 2023.
27. Leetaru, K. and P.A. Schrodt. Gdelt: Global data on events, location, and tone, 1979–2012. In *ISA annual convention*, 2013. Citeseer.
28. Cinelli, M., et al., The COVID-19 social media infodemic. *Scientific Reports*, 2020, 10(1): p. 16598.
29. Meo, S.A., et al., Medical knowledge of ChatGPT in public health, infectious diseases, COVID-19 pandemic, and vaccines: multiple choice questions examination based performance. *Frontiers in Public Health*, 2024, 12: p. 1360597.
30. Devlin, J., et al. Bert: Pre-training of deep bidirectional transformers for language understanding. In *Proceedings of the 2019 conference of the North American chapter of the association for computational linguistics: human language technologies, Volume 1 (long and short papers)*. 2019.
31. Lee, J., et al., BioBERT: a pre-trained biomedical language representation model for biomedical text mining. *Bioinformatics*, 2020, 36(4): p. 1234–1240.
32. Huang, K., J. Altosaar, and R. Ranganath, Clinicalbert: Modeling clinical notes and predicting hospital readmission. *arXiv preprint arXiv:1904.05342*, 2019.
33. Piya, F.L. and R. Beheshti, ConTextual: Improving Clinical Text Summarization in LLMs with Context-preserving Token Filtering and Knowledge Graphs. *arXiv preprint arXiv:2504.16394*, 2025.

34. Ntinopoulos, V., et al., Large language models for data extraction from unstructured and semi-structured electronic health records: a multiple model performance evaluation. *BMJ Health & Care Informatics*, 2025, 32(1): p. e101139.
35. Chen, D., et al., Large Language Model Applications for Health Information Extraction in Oncology: Scoping Review. *JMIR Cancer*, 2025, 11: p. e65984.
36. Zhan, Z., et al., RAMIE: retrieval-augmented multi-task information extraction with large language models on dietary supplements. *Journal of the American Medical Informatics Association*, 2025:,32(3), p. ocaf002.
37. Bednarczyk, L., et al., Scientific Evidence for Clinical Text Summarization Using Large Language Models: Scoping Review. *Journal of Medical Internet Research*, 2025, 27: p. e68998.
38. Aali, A., et al., A dataset and benchmark for hospital course summarization with adapted large language models. *Journal of the American Medical Informatics Association*, 2024: p. 470–479,. ocae312.
39. Malgaroli, M., et al., Large language models for the mental health community: framework for translating code to care, 2(1), 8. *The Lancet Digital Health*, 2025.
40. Hanna, J.J., et al., Assessing Racial and Ethnic Bias in Text Generation by Large Language Models for Health Care–Related Tasks: Cross-Sectional Study. *Journal of Medical Internet Research*, 2025, 27: p. e57257.
41. Brown, T., et al., Language models are few-shot learners. *Advances in Neural Information Processing Systems*, 2020, 33: p. 1877–1901.
42. Sallam, M. ChatGPT utility in healthcare education, research, and practice: systematic review on the promising perspectives and valid concerns. In *Healthcare*, 2023. MDPI.
43. Kwok, K.O., et al., Utilizing large language models in infectious disease transmission modelling for public health preparedness. *Computational and Structural Biotechnology Journal*, 2024, 23: p. 3254–3257.
44. Espinosa, L., et al., Open-source solution for evaluation and benchmarking of large language models for public health. *medRxiv*, 2025: p. 2025.03.20.25324040.
45. Jiang, Y., et al. Balanced and explainable social media analysis for public health with large language models. In *Australasian Database Conference*, 2023. Springer.
46. Jo, E., et al. Understanding the benefits and challenges of deploying conversational AI leveraging large language models for public health intervention. In *Proceedings of the 2023 CHI Conference on Human Factors in Computing Systems*, 2023.
47. De Angelis, L., et al., ChatGPT and the rise of large language models: the new AI-driven infodemic threat in public health. *Frontiers in Public Health*, 2023, 11: p. 1166120.
48. Tahir, B. and M.A. Mehmood, TepiSense: A Social Computing based Real-Time Epidemic Surveillance System using Artificial Intelligence. *IEEE Access*, 2025, 13, 23816-23832. .

49. Deiana, G., et al., Artificial intelligence and public health: evaluating ChatGPT responses to vaccination myths and misconceptions. *Vaccines*, 2023, 11(7): p. 1217.
50. Espinosa, L. and M. Salathé, Use of large language models as a scalable approach to understanding public health discourse. *PLOS Digital Health*, 2024, 3(10): p. e0000631.
51. Bender, E.M., et al. On the dangers of stochastic parrots: Can language models be too big?. In *Proceedings of the 2021 ACM Conference on Fairness, Accountability, and Transparency*, 2021.
52. Strubell, E., A. Ganesh, and A. McCallum. *Energy and policy considerations for modern deep learning research*. In *Proceedings of the AAAI Conference on Artificial Intelligence*, 2020.
53. Rudin, C., Stop explaining black box machine learning models for high stakes decisions and use interpretable models instead. *Nature Machine Intelligence*, 2019, 1(5): p. 206–215.
54. Yang, R., et al., Large language models in health care: Development, applications, and challenges. *Health Care Science*, 2023, 2(4): p. 255–263.
55. Tian, S., et al., Opportunities and challenges for ChatGPT and large language models in biomedicine and health. *Briefings in Bioinformatics*, 2024, 25(1): p. bbad493.
56. Conneau, A., et al., Unsupervised cross-lingual representation learning at scale. *arXiv preprint arXiv:1911.02116*, 2019.
57. Topol, E.J., High-performance medicine: the convergence of human and artificial intelligence. *Nature Medicine*, 2019, 25(1): p. 44–56.
58. Yang, H.F., et al., *Advancing real-time pandemic forecasting using large language models: A COVID-19 case study*, 2024, arXiv preprint arXiv:2404.06962..

Chapter 6

The role of large language models in delivering artificial intelligence-based psychological interventions and therapies

Arezou Naghib, Farhad Soleimanian Gharehchopogh, and Azadeh Zamanifar

6.1 INTRODUCTION

Artificial intelligence (AI) is one of the most significant scientific and technological advances of the 20th century. It has gradually entered various scientific fields and created significant developments in many disciplines [1]. One of these fields is psychology. The use of AI in psychology has contributed to a better understanding of human behavior and led to the creation of new tools for assessing, treating, and predicting psychological problems [2]. In recent years, remarkable advances in DL and NLP have led to the development of models that can process and produce human language at an unprecedented level [3]. LLMs such as ChatGPT (GPT-3, GPT-3.5, and GPT-4), LLaMA, Grok, PaLM, etc., relying on billions of parameters and extensive text data, have brought about profound developments in various sciences, especially psychology and mental health, as one of the most outstanding achievements of modern AI [4, 5]. By combining insights from LLMs with psycholinguistic tools like the Medical Research Council (MRC) psycholinguistic database and Linguistic Inquiry and Word Count (LIWC) dictionary, psychological profiling can help to improve understanding of the behaviors and motivations of individuals [6]. Figure 6.1 shows the history of the application of AI in psychology. Also, Table 6.1 presents LLMs in the field of psychology. The mental health systems in many countries face challenges such as a shortage of skilled human resources, high costs, and increased psychological burden due to socioeconomic and environmental factors.

These technologies, capable of near-human-level natural language processing and generation, offer a chance to develop novel solutions for intricate psychological problems. The use of LLMs as complementary tools in the psychological support process, especially in the stages of screening, early intervention, coping skills training, clinical education, psychological research, providing real-time support, digital psychotherapy, increasing the quality of care through data integration, and early diagnosis of mental illnesses, has attracted the attention of researchers and activists in the field of mental health [23]. Also, LLMs can tailor responses based on individual

 DOI: 10.1201/9781003665083-6

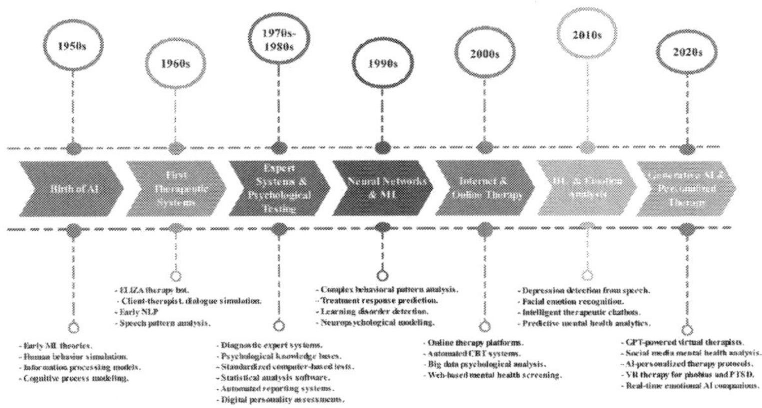

Figure 6.1 The history of the application of AI in psychology

needs, cultural contexts, or local languages and increase the effectiveness of interventions. LLMs enable researchers to engage in three key areas: measurement (e.g., probing psychological patterns in extensive text corpora), experimentation (through the rapid generation of stimuli and responses to refine factorial designs), and practice (by simulating authentic interactions to train therapists, counselors, teachers, or managers) [24, 25]. Of course, the emergence of AI in psychology cannot be considered a replacement for clinical interventions. AI-based technologies can serve as an auxiliary and supporting tool that plays a role in lower levels of interventions, including promoting psychological literacy, primary prevention, and reducing emotional burden.

Some AI-based digital platforms, such as Woebot [26], Wysa [27], and ViTalk [28], have provided users with mood monitoring, emotion regulation skills training, and simple cognitive-behavioral feedback. Preliminary studies also suggest that these tools can be effective in reducing mild to moderate symptoms of anxiety and depression. Globally, financial barriers, prohibitive costs, strained public services, or a shortage of qualified professionals severely limit access to mental healthcare services. Consequently, technological interventions have emerged to support care areas that some people cannot access. Their development and implementation are paramount for promoting sustainable good health, healthy lives, and well-being [12]. According to a report by the World Health Organization (WHO) in 2023, LLM-based tools could reduce the access gap to mental health services by 70% [29].

Along with the potential opportunities, using LLMs in mental health comes with significant conceptual, technical, and ethical challenges. Key concerns in this area include the trustworthiness of the model's generated content, the ability to understand psychological and individual differences,

Table 6.1 LLMs in the field of psychology

Model name	*Developer/ Country*	*Key features*	*Specific applications in psychology*
LLaMA [7]	Meta AI/USA	- Foundation models and chat-tuned versions. - Various model sizes available.	- Potential for narrative assessment - Fine-tuning for specific psychology tasks (e.g., question answering).
BERT [8]	Google Research/ USA	- Bidirectional encoder representations. - Pre-trained on massive text datasets. - Fine-tunable for NLP tasks.	- Sentiment analysis of text related to mental health. - Question answering in psychological contexts. - Potential for analyzing clinical notes.
Claude [9]	Anthropic/USA	- Advanced AI assistant focused on safety and accuracy. - High accuracy over long documents. - Low hallucination rates.	- Text generation for therapeutic content. - Summarizing research in psychology. - Potential for multilingual processing in diverse populations.
Gemini [10]	Google/USA	- Multimodal capabilities (text, image, audio, video). - Deep research capabilities. - Integration with various Google services.	- Development of mental health companion apps. - Potential for personalized therapy and well-being support. - Analysis of diverse data types in psychological research.

(Continued)

Table 6.1 (Continued)

Model name	*Developer/ Country*	*Key features*	*Specific applications in psychology*
Mistral [11, 12]	Mistral AI/France	- Open-source LLM. - Efficient and competitive performance. - Fine-tunable for NLP tasks.	- Text generation for psychological resources. - Summarization of psychological literature. - Building specialized psychology assistants through RAG.
ChatGPT [13, 14]	OpenAI/USA	- Transformer architecture with Reinforcement Learning from Human Feedback (RLHF). - Can remember conversation history and understand the context. - Supports multiple languages.	- Conversational AI for mental health support. - Psychoeducation about mental health conditions. - Potential for emotional support and empathetic responses.
PsycoLLM [15]	Stanford University/USA	- Specialized training in psychological datasets. - Focus on cognitive methods.	- Cognitive psychology research. - Modeling human thought processes.
Mental-FLAN-T5 [16]	Google Research/ USA	- Fine-tuned for diagnosis and interpretation of mental disorders. - Based on T5 architecture.	- Analyzing patient texts. - Classifying psychological symptoms.
Mental-Alpaca [17]	Mental Health Research Center/ USA	- Specialized version of Alpaca for mental health. - Trained on therapy protocols.	- Short-term interventions. - Monitoring treatment progress. - Providing therapy exercises.

(*Continued*)

Table 6.1 (Continued)

Model name	*Developer/ Country*	*Key features*	*Specific applications in psychology*
MentalBERT [18]	University of Cambridge/UK	- Specialized in detecting depression and anxiety from text.	- Initial screening, monitoring treatment progress. - Suicide risk assessment.
Replika [19]	Luka, Inc./USA	- Intelligent personal assistant with the ability to learn from user interactions. - Builds long-term relationships.	- Emotional companionship. - Educing loneliness. - Daily mental health support.
MoodKit [20, 21]	Thriveport LLC/ USA	- Based on CBT principles. - Self-help toolset.	- Improving mood. - Changing negative thought patterns. - Increasing resilience.
MindMate [22]	MindMate AI/ Canada	- Combines Eastern and Western approaches in psychology.	- Stress reduction, mental balance. - Combining mindfulness and CBT.

the risk of mistaking the model for a therapist, and privacy and data security issues. Furthermore, language models lack self-awareness, subjective experience, or clinical judgment. This chapter will examine the place of LLMs in psychological support from a comprehensive and analytical perspective. A historical overview of the use of technology in psychological services is provided. The structure and capabilities of LLMs and how they are used in mental health interventions are examined. Next, scientific and ethical opportunities and challenges related to this area are analyzed. Finally, suggestions for future directions in the intelligent and responsible integration of LLMs into psychological services are presented. This section dives into the LLMs, chatbots, and key capabilities of LLMs in psychology.

Table 6.2 summarizes the abbreviations used throughout this chapter. The rest of the chapter is structured as follows: Section 6.2 reviews the articles and works related to LLMs applications in psychology. Section 6.3 delves into the challenges and unresolved issues of deploying LLMs within the psychological field. Finally, Section 6.4 concludes the chapter.

Table 6.2 Chapter abbreviations

Abbreviation	*Definition*	*Abbreviation*	*Definition*
DL	Deep learning	RES	Rosenberg Self-Esteem Scale
NLP	Natural language processing	SCS	Self-Construal Scale
CBT	Cognitive behavioral therapy	ADHD	Attention-deficit/hyperactivity disorder
LLMs	Large language models	HCP	Human connectome project
AI	Artificial intelligence	KNN	K-nearest neighbors
LIWC	Linguistic Inquiry and Word Count	GT	Ground truth
MRC	Medical Research Council	MAE	Mean absolute error
RLHF	Reinforcement learning from human feedback	MP	Matching percentage
WHO	World Health Organization	MANAS	Mental assistance network for alleviating suffering
ML	Machine learning	KL	Kullback–Leibler
BFI	Big Five Inventory	JS	Jensen–Shannon
16PF	Sixteen Personality Factor Questionnaire	CS	Cosine Similarity

6.1.1 LLMs

LLMs are massive statistical models and DL-based AI algorithms designed to process, understand, and produce natural language [24]. These models are built on transformer architectures and use massive text datasets for training [4]. The transformer architecture was introduced in 2017 by Ashish [4]. It provides an attention mechanism that focuses on the relevant parts of the text [8]. LLMs are composed of multiple layers of neural networks that allow them to learn complex relationships between words, sentences, and concepts [30]. By using vast amounts of textual and linguistic data, these models gain the ability to learn linguistic patterns and implicit meanings, creating unique opportunities to analyze and generate large-scale language data [24]. LLMs have become a vital tool in psychological support due to their ability to simulate human conversations and understand emotions and feelings implicit in language. LLMs are used to query individuals' mental models of themselves and their environments (social and cognitive psychology), aid in evaluating intellectual abilities (intelligence assessment), infer personal differences in coping mechanisms (personality psychology), facilitate the reappraisal of stressful experiences (affective and clinical psychology), probe moral reasoning (moral psychology), analyze biases in decision-making (judgment and decision-making psychology), investigate the development of cognitive abilities across the lifespan (developmental psychology), explore the mental processes underlying novel thought (psychology of creativity), understand the multifaceted aspects of individual character (psychology of personality), and examine the mechanisms of knowledge acquisition and skill development (psychology of learning) [24, 25]. They can also help with counseling, digital cognitive-behavioral therapies, and even the prevention of mental health crises.

Comparing LLMs with traditional methods (such as face-to-face psychotherapy, manual data analysis, and classical training) demonstrates the advantages and limitations of this technology. Table 6.3 shows a comparison of LLMs with traditional methods. LLMs have advantages over conventional techniques in accessibility, speed, and scalability. For example, chatbots can serve millions of users simultaneously, while face-to-face psychotherapy is limited in time and space. Traditional methods have advantages in emotional understanding and managing complex cases. Manual data analysis, although time-consuming, can identify more subtle themes. LLMs perform better in research and education due to their speed and scalability [31]. However, in psychotherapy and early diagnosis, traditional methods still have advantages due to their ability to understand complex emotional and clinical contexts.

Table 6.3 Comparison of LLMs vs. traditional methods in psychology

Domain	*LLM method*	*Traditional method*	*LLM advantages*	*LLM limitations*
Psychotherapy	CBT-based chatbots	In-person therapy sessions	- High accessibility. - Lower cost. - Reduced stigma.	- Lack of deep emotional understanding. - Limitations in severe cases. - Ethical concerns.
Early detection	NLP-based text analysis (e.g., depression screening)	Clinical interviews	- High speed. - Rapid processing. - Handles large datasets. - Non-invasive.	- Data biases. - Lower accuracy for complex disorders. - Dependence on input data quality.
Cognitive assessment	Adaptive LLM-driven tests	Pen-and-paper or in-person tests	- Dynamic difficulty adjustment. - Advanced response pattern analysis.	- Fails to assess non-verbal cues (e.g., body language). - Validation challenges.
Psychology education	Virtual patient simulations	In-person workshops	- Scalability - Immediate feedback. - Personalized learning.	- Dependence on technology. - Limitations in real interaction.
Crisis support	AI-powered crisis chatbots (e.g., suicide prevention)	Phone hotlines	- Instant response. - User anonymity. - Wider geographic reach	- Risk of harmful responses. - No physical intervention capability.
Psychological research	Automated qualitative data analysis	Manual coding by researchers	- 80% faster analysis. - High accuracy for structured data.	- Requires human validation. - Interpretability issues. - Sensitive to textual errors.

6.1.2 Chatbots

A chatbot is a feature or the agent itself, enabling chat-based communication. Chatbots typically focus on communication through text or voice, and many can increasingly display images [32]. Early chatbots, such as ELIZA [33], PARRY [34], and ALICE [35], primarily relied on rule-based approaches [36]. These systems used simple parsing, keyword searching, and pattern-matching techniques to process user input and generate responses based on manually created rules [32]. Rule-based chatbots are effective for well-defined, domain-specific applications where the range of user queries is predictable, but they lack flexibility in handling novel or complex inputs [37]. The advent of LLMs has significantly revolutionized the field, leading to the rise of generative-based or AI chatbots [38]. These modern chatbots leverage Machine Learning (ML) and NLP techniques, with LLMs like GPT-3 and LaMDA at their core [39]. Trained on vast amounts of text and code, generative chatbots can understand the intent behind user input and generate novel, contextually relevant responses based on learned algorithms. Generative chatbots allow for a more human-like and flexible interaction than rule-based systems [40].

However, they also carry the risk of producing undesirable or inaccurate content. To leverage the strengths of both approaches, hybrid chatbots have emerged [36]. These systems combine rule-based components for handling specific, well-understood queries with generative models for more open-ended or complex interactions. This approach achieves a balance between accuracy, reliability, and flexibility. Chatbots can also be categorized based on their domain of application: Closed-domain chatbots and open-domain chatbots. Closed-domain chatbots are designed to operate within a specific area of knowledge or for a particular task [41]. Rule-based chatbots are often used in this context for customer support, FAQs, or specific information retrieval within a limited scope. Open-domain chatbots aim to engage in conversations on various topics, mimicking human-like dialogue [42]. Generative and hybrid chatbots are typically employed for this purpose, striving for natural and engaging interactions [42].

6.1.3 Key capabilities of LLMs in psychology

Using advanced statistical analysis and DL, LLMs can identify specific linguistic markers associated with mental states and recognize linguistic patterns in mental disorders. Research has shown that different mental disorders have distinct linguistic fingerprints [43]. By training on big data, LLMs can identify patterns relevant to early detection of depressive episodes, mood monitoring in bipolar disorders, anxiety, cognitive disorders, and assessment of emotional response to treatment with high accuracy. Studies have shown that LLM-based emotion analysis can predict meaningful mood changes with 75%–85% accuracy [44]. LLMs can analyze emotional content beyond the recognition of positive and negative emotions. Indeed, advanced LLMs can detect a wide range of complex emotions (shame, guilt, envy, and pride), track changes in the intensity and variety of emotions over time, and identify discrepancies between the expressed content and the underlying emotions. LLM-based CBT interventions can be 60%–70% as effective as traditional treatments, especially for mild to moderate disorders. LLMs can predict personality traits using psychological models such as the Big Five [45].

These analyses have applications in recruitment, career counseling, and psychological research. Empathy is a critical trait in therapy, and training programmers for therapists could reinforce this skill through interactive chat simulations, role-playing, and similar activities [46]. Empathy in LLMs is generated through complex algorithms that include detecting emotional states from text, matching responses to the tone and intensity of identified emotions, employing active listening techniques (reflection, summarization, and confirmation), and adapting to the user's communication style [47]. The fundamental difference between artificial empathy and human empathy is that LLMs do not have the actual subjective experience of emotions, and their empathy is an algorithmic simulation. However, research shows that even this artificial empathy can have a therapeutic effect, as it creates a feeling of being heard by the user.

Advanced LLMs are also capable of analyzing long-term trends in text data (such as social media posts, clinical notes, or questionnaire responses in early diagnosis of mental illnesses and analysis of behavioral patterns), which makes it possible to identify gradual changes in language style associated with worsening or improving the condition, detect cyclical patterns in mood disorders, predict the likelihood of relapse based on specific linguistic markers, and compare progress with standard treatment measures [48]. These models utilize NLP techniques such as topic modeling and sentiment analysis. Combining with behavioral data from sensors (sleep patterns, activity, and social interactions) can significantly increase the accuracy of these predictions. The authors in [49] showed that combining sentiment analysis and topic modeling increases recognition accuracy by up to 10%. Table 6.4 compares the key capabilities of LLMs in psychology in terms of scientific explanation, clinical applications, current limitations, and future potential. LLMs have significantly impacted psychology education and research, from simulating virtual clients to analyzing qualitative data and generating research hypotheses. LLMs prove effective for simulating virtual clients and analyzing qualitative data in psychology education and research. Qualitative and multilingual data analysis leads to increased accuracy, reduced analysis time, improved clinical skills, and facilitated cross-cultural and longitudinal study [50, 51].

Table 6.4 Key capabilities of LLMs in psychology

Key capability	*Scientific explanation*	*Clinical applications*	*Current limitations*	*Future potential*
Detecting language patterns related to mental disorders	Identifying specific linguistic markers	Assisting in the early detection of depression, anxiety, and cognitive disorders through the analysis of written text or speech transcripts.	- Varying accuracy across different languages. - Susceptibility to cultural differences in emotional expression.	Integration with other biomarkers to enhance diagnostic accuracy.
Analyzing emotional content	Extracting the intensity, variety, and emotional changes within text using sentiment analysis and emotion recognition technologies.	- Monitoring mood changes over time. - Identifying mood swings in bipolar disorder. - Evaluating treatment response.	- Difficulty detecting complex and multidimensional emotional states. - Challenges in understanding sarcasm and irony.	- Dynamic modeling of emotions and mood changes over time. - Predicting mental health crises.
Providing cognitive-behavioral interventions	Applying CBT principles, such as cognitive restructuring, identifying thinking errors, and behavioral techniques.	- Self-help for mild to moderate depression and anxiety. - Support between therapy sessions. - Reminder of exercises.	- Limitations in personalizing interventions. - Inability to react to non-verbal cues.	- Delivering adaptive interventions that change with patient progress. - Integration with augmented reality.

(*Continued*)

Table 6.4 (Continued)

Key capability	*Scientific explanation*	*Clinical applications*	*Current limitations*	*Future potential*
Facilitating empathy and active listening	- Creating a safe and non-judgmental conversational environment and responding with emotional reflection. - Summarizing and validating experiences.	- Reducing feelings of loneliness. - Creating a space for expressing difficult emotions and emotional support.	- Inability to achieve genuine empathy - limitations in understanding deep human needs.	- Creating deeper therapeutic relationships - increasing empathy capacity by learning from human psychotherapists.
Teaching psychological skills	Transferring practical knowledge about mindfulness skills, stress management, emotional regulation, and coping mechanisms.	Teaching breathing techniques, meditation, emotional self-awareness, and problem-solving skills.	- Challenges in monitoring the correct execution of techniques. - Difficulty in adapting instruction to different learning needs.	Providing fully personalized training programs based on individual learning styles and progress.
Monitoring and recording symptoms	- Analyzing long-term patterns in speech and writing - Identifying gradual changes in mental health.	- Recording and analyzing symptoms over time. - Early warning of relapse. - Assessing treatment effectiveness.	- Reliance on self-reporting. - Lack of access to biological indicators.	Integration with sensor and smartphone data for more comprehensive monitoring.

(*Continued*)

Table 6.4 (Continued)

Key capability	*Scientific explanation*	*Clinical applications*	*Current limitations*	*Future potential*
Adapting to Different Therapeutic Approaches	Adapting to various frameworks, including CBT, psychodynamic, humanistic, and systemic.	- Providing appropriate support for different therapeutic approaches. - Integrating various techniques.	- Lack of equal mastery across all approaches. - Challenges in integrating different theories.	Specialized models for each therapeutic approach with a deep understanding of theoretical foundations and specific techniques.
Summarizing specialized texts	Extracting and organizing key information from scientific psychology texts, treatment protocols, and patient files.	- Assisting professionals in updating knowledge. - Summarizing previous sessions. - Extracting information from files.	- Challenges in distinguishing critical from secondary information. - The need for human verification.	Clinical decision support systems based on up-to-date scientific evidence.
Facilitating cross-cultural communication	- Understanding and adapting to cultural differences in expressing psychological issues. - Adapting to different norms.	- Providing services to multicultural communities. - Reducing linguistic and cultural barriers to access mental health services.	- Differences in the depth of understanding of different cultures. - Challenges in translating specialized concepts between languages.	Dedicated models for specific cultures with a deep understanding of socio-cultural contexts.
Cognitive modeling	- Simulating human thinking processes. - Modeling cognitive structures and information processing.	- Helping to understand better cognitive processes in mental disorders. - Simulating maladaptive thinking patterns.	- Limitations in modeling the complexities of human cognition. - Oversimplification of models.	Developing more advanced computational models to understand cognitive disorders.

(Continued)

Table 6.4 (Continued)

Key capability	*Scientific explanation*	*Clinical applications*	*Current limitations*	*Future potential*
Supporting psychological research	- Analyzing large volumes of textual data. - Coding qualitative interviews. - Extracting hidden patterns.	- Accelerating the process of qualitative data analysis. - Identifying hidden relationships between variables. - Assisting in theory development.	- Need for human oversight. - Limitations in interpreting complex data.	- Revolutionizing psychological research methods. - Discovering new patterns in existing data.
Simulating Clinical Interviews	- Implementing standard interview protocols. - Asking appropriate follow-up questions. - Structuring the session.	- Training psychology students - Practicing interview skills. - Initial screening.	- Limitations in flexibility and adaptability to unexpected reactions. - Lack of complete contextual understanding.	Intelligent interviewers can recognize and respond to subtle communication cues.
Risk Assessment and Crisis Management	Identifying warning signs, including suicidal ideation, aggression, or harm to others.	- Triaging patients - Directing them to appropriate resources in a crisis. - Providing crisis intervention protocols.	- Limitations in accurately assessing risk without non-verbal information. - Legal and ethical challenges.	Advanced risk prediction systems combine various data sources.

6.2 RELATED WORK

This section analyzes existing articles on the role of LLMs in psychology and mental health. The reviewed articles are divided into two categories: review articles and research articles.

6.2.1 Review and survey article

Demszky et al. [24] explored the role of LLMs in psychology, such as educational technologies, virtual tutors, and coaching tools. The article discusses how LLMs function and the implications of this functionality for their applications within psychology. It also highlights the potential of LLMs for psychological measurement, experimentation, and practice, alongside identifying concerns and potential solutions regarding their use. The limitations of LLMs include their lack of cognitive capacities beyond language, their potential to reproduce biases present in the training data, and their reliance on high-quality annotated data for fine-tuning. Furthermore, the article highlights the need for technical expertise for the responsible use of LLMs, an area not typically covered in psychology methods training.

Hagendorff [25] investigated machine psychology and capabilities, limitations, and potential

applications of LLMs. The article outlined various fields of psychology and a set of crucial methods for conducting studies in machine psychology. According to the article, machine psychology can yield systematic insights into patterns of machine behavior and emergent reasoning abilities in LLMs that are not discernible through traditional benchmarks. Furthermore, it proposes treating LLMs as participants in psychology experiments, utilizing psychological test frameworks, and applying self-report and observational methods to examine their behavior and reasoning. The results showed that LLMs can exhibit human-like cognitive and social biases, such as moral disengagement and stereotyping. The methodologies employed in machine psychology involve treating LLMs as experimental subjects, using techniques like prompt design and completion, and evaluating their outputs through automated or manual means.

Almeida et al. [52] conducted a comparative study of four leading LLMs, including Gemini Pro, Claude 2.1, GPT-4, and Llama 2 Chat 70b, against human participants across eight survey-based experiments. According to their findings, GPT-4's responses were significantly more aligned with human responses than other models, achieving the highest correlation. Notably, even when LLM responses showed strong correlations with human data, systematic discrepancies persisted, including that these models sometimes tended to overemphasize effects seen in human data. Key differences emerged in reasoning about causation, intentionality, and moral judgments, with Gemini Pro and GPT-4 exhibiting a greater propensity to identify the cause of a protagonist who violated a norm, even in situations with unclear or multiple potential causes. The article's methodology involved generating 100 responses per LLM using a 3 (scenario) × 3 (deontic status) within-subjects design and replicating stimuli from the Many Labs 2 project. Data analysis combined experimental designs and statistical models, including hierarchical models, to account for scenario effects. The authors concluded that despite expert-level performance in various domains, fundamental differences exist between human and LLM responses, advocating for a granular approach to alignment research. The article acknowledges limitations such as the limited number of LLMs and studies, the potential for memorization due to the use of established stimuli, and the lack of systematic manipulation of the temperature parameter, also noting variability in valid output generation across models.

AlMakinah et al. [53] explored the potential and capabilities of AI-enabled chatbots (GPT v4, Mistral Large, and Llama V3.1) in providing mental health support, focusing on LLMs and their ability to deliver empathetic responses, and proposes a federated learning framework to address limitations such as trustworthiness, bias, and privacy challenges. The framework involves the participation of multiple edge nodes (hospitals and clinics) in the federated learning process. Each participating node will enlarge the final dataset and empower the ML model training process. The authors used cosine similarity analysis to compare the responses of LLMs to those of human therapists. They also employed a qualitative study to evaluate the emotional sensitivity and adaptive feedback of the LLMs' responses.

Pryss et al. [54] explored the potential of chatbots in medical and psychological treatment procedures, aiming to identify the challenges and opportunities of using chatbots and to propose a reference architecture for their implementation. The article identified five key issues in developing chatbot systems: the quality of the knowledge base, the need for a highly interdisciplinary team, the indispensability of an escalation service, the requirement for a mandatory rating system, and the need to evaluate input methods and languages. The article's limitations include its nature as a literature review, which lacks a direct and comprehensive evaluation of chatbot effectiveness in medical and psychological treatment, and its reliance on practical projects, which may restrict the generalizability of its findings.

6.2.2 Research article

Kjell et al. [3] explored how natural language responses and LLMs could be used to understand psychological constructs. The article employed various LLMs, including bidirectional encoder representations from transformers (BERT) and RoBERTa [55], to capture different psychological dimensions, and BERT and ELMo to analyze natural language responses. This article proposed five guiding principles for using AI: algorithmic discrimination protections, safe and effective systems, data privacy, notice and explanation, and the option to opt-out, coupled with human alternatives, consideration, and fallback mechanisms. The article has two objectives: enhancing the accuracy of language-based mental health assessments and exploring the potential of LLMs. Quantitatively, using the Diversity Index, the article found that natural language responses contain 4.8 times more self-information than rating scale responses. Key findings include the ability of LLMs to accurately predict mental health outcomes from natural language data and the potential of language-based assessments to move beyond standard rating scales for the evaluation of psychological constructs, including depression and suicide risk. Moreover, considering demographic factors like gender, age, and socio-economic status in language-based assessments can lead to more precise results. The limitations of this article include potential biases and risks associated with the need for further development and validation of these models. The researchers also acknowledged that information extracted from natural language responses might not always be relevant to the specific psychological construct examined.

Shen et al. [56] explored the potential of LLMs in conducting CBT, a widely used and effective psychological treatment. The article investigated whether LLMs could effectively replicate CBT techniques. The authors created a real-world CBT dataset from online video platforms and developed an automatic evaluation framework. This framework assessed LLMs on: emotion tendency (evaluating the emotional tone of the LLM's responses), structured dialogue pattern (analyzing the LLM's speaking style, topic consistency, and use of CBT techniques), and proactive inquiry ability (measuring the LLM's capacity to ask relevant and guiding questions). The authors evaluated four LLMs (ERNIE Bot, iFlytek Spark, ChatGPT, and Zhipai GLM) and explored the impact of integrating a CBT knowledge base to enhance the models' therapeutic capabilities. The results indicate that LLMs show promise in psychological counseling, particularly when combined with additional knowledge and technological tools. The article highlights the potential of LLMs to improve the accessibility and efficiency of mental health services.

Moell [57] comparatively evaluated the performance of GPT-4 and ChatGPT on 18 diverse psychological prompts encompassing depression, anxiety, and trauma. Blind evaluation by a clinical psychologist indicated GPT-4's superior capacity for generating clinically relevant and empathetic responses across all examined mental health domains. GPT-4 demonstrated proficiency in providing sympathetic and actionable advice, maintaining a nonjudgmental and validating tone, and exhibiting awareness of appropriate therapeutic strategies, achieving optimal scores for prompts concerning communication, attention-deficit/hyperactivity disorder (ADHD) management, and social skills enhancement. Conversely, ChatGPT's responses were frequently characterized as generalized, lacking in-depth analysis, and occasionally inconsistent with evidence-based practices. Both models exhibited overconfidence relative to human clinical judgment. The article concludes that GPT-4 demonstrates a greater understanding of appropriate clinical language and interventions and is more effective in generating clinically relevant and empathetic responses to psychological prompts than ChatGPT. Limitations include the automatic filtering of prompts related to self-harm, the use of a single evaluator, and the absence of data on user engagement and long-term effects. Future research should investigate the specific factors contributing to the observed performance differences and assess the generalizability of these findings across broader populations and mental health conditions.

Berrezueta-Guzman et al. [58] explored a new method for enhancing personalized and interactive ADHD therapy by integrating two advanced LLMs, including Claude-3 Opus and ChatGPT-4 Turbo, into a robotic assistant. The authors evaluated the performance of both models in a simulated therapeutic context, employing technical metrics (performance, responsiveness, integration ease) and clinical evaluations involving mock therapy sessions with therapists. ChatGPT-4 Turbo demonstrated superior responsiveness and performance, suggesting its suitability for real-time applications within therapy. In contrast, Claude-3 Opus demonstrated excellence in producing coherent and understandable text while prioritizing ethical considerations to ensure safe and engaging interactions. A customized ChatGPT model demonstrated strong emotional awareness and empathy and offered greater ease of integration and broader language support, whereas Claude-3 Opus was notable for creating a secure environment and respecting patient boundaries. However, the authors acknowledged limitations inherent in using LLMs in mental health, including concerns regarding data privacy, empathy, and successful user integration.

de Filippis and Al Foysal [39] used advanced NLP and ML algorithms to deliver immediate, user-centric care, and empathetic care. The authors examined the impact of three LLMs, including Woebot, Wysa, and Replika, on anxiety and depression scores. The methods used in the article involve a statistical analysis of the data collected from the six participants who engaged with the three chatbots. The study also employed bootstrapped sampling to provide insights into the effectiveness of the chatbots. The results showed these chatbots can significantly reduce symptoms of depression and anxiety, with Woebot displaying the most significant reduction in depression scores and Replika having a more pronounced effect on anxiety symptoms. The article has several limitations, including the relatively small sample size and the potential variability in user engagement.

Jiang and Yang [59] investigated the efficacy of AI-integrated applications, GymBuddy and Elomia, in reducing psychological symptoms in female middle school students experiencing psychological disorders, finding considerable improvements in somatic symptoms, anxiety and insomnia, social dysfunction, and severe depression. The authors used a quasi-experimental design, whereby participants were randomly allocated to either the intervention or the control group. Mental health outcomes were evaluated using standardized measures at baseline, midpoint, and endpoint, and the data were analyzed using mixed ANOVA. The results showed there are significant decreases in physical symptoms, anxiety, sleep disturbances, social impairment, and severe depression in students with psychological disorders who used AI-integrated applications. The article concludes that applications integrated with AI, such as GymBuddy and Elomia, can offer tailored support for people experiencing psychological disorders, and that digital solutions for mental health have significant potential in alleviating psychological distress. The article had several limitations, including the lack of complete randomization, a small sample size, a short-term follow-up period, reliance on self-report measures, and a quasi-experimental design. The article also focused on specific AI-driven applications, which may not represent other digital mental health tools.

Nazir et al. [60] used a customized data-to-text prompting method to prompt ChatGPT to impute missing values in biological and psychological datasets. The article showed that ChatGPT could effectively capture intricate patterns and dependencies in psychological and biological data through fine-tuning. The authors used the Human Connectome Project (HCP) dataset [61, 62]. The performance of ChatGPT was evaluated against conventional imputation techniques, including most frequent number-based imputation, mean-based imputation, and K-nearest neighbors (KNN). The results indicated that ChatGPT has a high Pearson correlation coefficient (*r*), with ground truth (GT) values, low mean absolute error (MAE) values, and high matching percentage (MP) values compared to other methods. The most frequent value imputation method showed lower correlations, ranging from 34.74% to 84.71%, which were inferior to ChatGPT. The proposed method may require high-volume data to train and fine-tune the ChatGPT model. The article does not discuss the potential biases in the data, which could impact the accuracy of the imputed values. In this article, ChatGPT's responses may be biased by its training data. Furthermore, more research is needed to evaluate its performance against other models, such as DL architectures.

Yonatan-Leus and Brukner [46] compared AI chatbot and human therapist responses to mental health inquiries on Reddit's "Ask a therapist" forum. The article investigated whether perceived empathy and the types of interventions differed between AI (GPT-4) and human therapists. The researchers coded and statistically analyzed responses using empathy scales focused on perspective-taking and empathic concern. The methods used in the article included coding and scoring responses by two coders, calculating inter-rater reliability, and statistical analysis of the differences between AI and human therapist responses. They found that AI scored higher in perceived perspective-taking and empathic concern and was more likely to offer supportive interventions. In contrast, human therapists were more prone to give advice and information, explore dysfunctional patterns, and ask clarifying questions. The article ensured high statistical power and inter-rater reliability. The article found that the expected power for the paired *t*-test was greater than 0.99 for a medium effect size ($d = 0.5$). However, the article's limitations included focusing on single interactions, not exploring therapist perspectives and reasons for formulating their interventions, using only one AI model (GPT-4), a limited sample size, using a blind research assistant, and not examining the experiences of those seeking help or the nuances of non-written communication.

Salah et al. [63] investigated how trust in ChatGPT, user perception, and stereotype perception of ChatGPT relate to psychological well-being and self-esteem, examining the moderating role of job anxiety. Based on survey data from 732 participants, which were analyzed using regression and SEM (SmartPLS), the results showed that stereotype perception significantly predicts self-esteem and user perception, and trust in ChatGPT has a positive direct impact. Furthermore, job-related anxiety moderated the connection between how users view ChatGPT and their psychological well-being, suggesting that seeing ChatGPT as impartial can enhance well-being through a sense of control. The article employed a cross-sectional design with online data collection and utilized the Rosenberg Self-Esteem Scale [64] and the Fornell–Larcker method [65] for validation. The article also used a two-stage analytical technique, which involves conducting a measurement model assessment to evaluate the reliability and validity of the data, followed by the evaluation of the structural model to test the hypothesized relationships between the variables. The results showed that the measurement model achieved satisfactory construct reliability and validity, and the structural model revealed significant relationships between the variables. The article had several limitations, including the cross-sectional design and use of a small sample size, which may affect the reliability and generalizability of the results. The article only examined the direct effects of stereotype perceptions, user perceptions, and trust in ChatGPT on self-esteem and psychological well-being; it did not consider other factors such as personality traits, social support, and coping strategies.

Tshimula et al. [6] explored how LLMs can be used in psychological profiling, emphasizing their capability to identify personality traits, values, and other noncognitive attributes. The authors also emphasized the importance of grasping social psychological theories to improve interactions with hacker groups and individuals, decode complex patterns of cybercriminal activity, leverage LLMs in cybersecurity to combat cybercrime, and examine textual data to identify the psychological characteristics of threat actors. The limitations of this article include the potential for misuse of LLMs, the need for further research, and the challenges of adapting human-centric ideas such as personality to AI systems.

Chou et al. [66] developed and evaluated a user-friendly chatbot intervention aimed at reducing psychological stress in older adults experiencing anxiety or depressive disorders amid the COVID-19 pandemic. The article found that the chatbot significantly decreased loneliness in adults aged 65 and older, as assessed by the University of California, Los Angeles Loneliness Scale (UCLA-LS). The chatbot, built using the LINE Official Account Manager, incorporated features like health diary data collection, hygiene education, and exercise videos. Participants engaged with the chatbot for a minimum of four weeks. The article employed a pre-post design, utilizing self-report questionnaires (UCLA-LS for loneliness, GDS for depression, and HADS-A for anxiety) to assess outcomes. Participant attitudes towards the chatbot were measured using a 7-point Likert scale. Statistical analysis was conducted with the assistance of Wei-Yang Chang and the Clinical Trial Center of Chang Gung Memorial Hospital. Results indicated a significant improvement in loneliness among adults aged 65 and older, with high chatbot utilization (over 82% daily engagement). Both age groups reported positive usability (mean scores of 6.33 and 6.05) and satisfaction (mean scores of 5.33 and 5.15). Limitations of the article included small sample size, restriction to literate mobile phone users with internet access, exclusion of individuals with severe physical or major neurocognitive illnesses, the absence of in-depth user interviews, and the potential influence of the pandemic context on the findings.

Blanco-Cuaresma [67] explored the application of LLMs for psychological assessments, specifically to identify suicidal risk levels, by analyzing text comments from 162 posts by 125 Reddit users on the "r/SuicideWatch" subreddit. This approach aimed to be privacy-focused and cost-effective. The article evaluated the performance of six open-source LLMs-OpenHermes, Orca 2, Starling, Dolphin, Mistral, and Zephyr-using a well-structured prompt with a single example. The article aimed to achieve two main goals: firstly, to identify key excerpts that reinforce a specific psychological evaluation of suicidal risk, and secondly, to condense the information to validate the assigned level of suicidal risk. The findings indicated that the LLMs were capable of generating text highlights and summaries that aligned with the pre-assigned suicidal risk levels. OpenHermes emerged as the best well-balanced model and excelled in summarization, while Dolphin and Zephyr demonstrated superior performance in the highlights subtask. The article had several limitations, including the lack of direct access to the gold-standard highlights and summaries, and the potential for biases within the LLMs.

Chen et al. [68] investigated the application of LLMs for enhanced identification and intervention of individuals at risk of suicide, particularly within vulnerable populations such as adolescents, by processing extended transcripts from psychological support hotlines. They proposed a straightforward LLM-based pipeline that summarizing approximately one hour of transcribed speech to extract crucial features for predicting suicidal behavior. This pipeline utilized a few-shot learning approach with LLMs, negating the need for additional training, and employed the Whisper2 model for transcription. A memory stream conditioning technique was used to synthesize the caller's emotional state and potential suicidal ideation. For the suicide prediction task, the article benchmarked five advanced DL models (LSTM, BiLSTM, GNNs, transformer, and Mamba) and integrated LLMs (ChatGLM-6B for summarization and GPT-4 for prediction). The proposed LLM-based pipeline achieved a notable F1 score of 76.47% on the test set, demonstrating a 27.82% improvement over manual scale ratings and a 7.08% increase compared to DL-based methods. The authors acknowledged limitations, including challenges in deploying larger LLMs within the hospital's experimental setting, data and privacy considerations, and the relatively limited size of the test set, which could affect the generalizability of the findings. Furthermore, they noted that the current model's real-time prediction efficiency requires improvement for immediate operator assistance.

Muqtadir et al. [69] introduced an ensemble retriever system designed to reduce hallucinations in LLMs used for mental health support. This system integrated knowledge graphs and vector stores to enhance the dependability and security of LLMs in mental health interventions. The ensemble retriever system included several components: a query processor, a vector store retriever, a knowledge graph store retriever, a fusion module, and a language model. The fusion module integrated results from the vector store and the knowledge graph store through processes, like preliminary filtering, re-ranking, weighted voting, decision fusion, entity context matching, and fact-checking. The article utilized open-source LLMs such as Google Gemma, Mistral, and Zypher to generate answers to user questions related to mental health. The system employed Cypher queries to retrieve data from the knowledge graph and uses natural language understanding to convert user queries into structured queries. Experimental results indicated that the ensemble retriever system effectively reduces hallucinations in LLMs, leading to a notable improvement in the precision and reliability of generated responses. The system outperformed the baseline LLMs and other single-retriever systems, increasing user confidence and satisfaction. The ensemble retriever system significantly improved accuracy and relevance compared to the baseline LLM system, with accuracy increasing from 78% to 92% and relevance scores improving from 70% to 88%. The ensemble retriever system also had drawbacks, including limitations in the knowledge graph's comprehensiveness and effectiveness, the introduction of noise in large datasets, and increased computational costs compared to single-retriever systems.

MENTALER [70] is a framework that enhances the capabilities of LLMs in providing mental health support by introducing a collaborative framework featuring analyzer, knowledge-collector, and strategy-planner roles. Its goal is to generate professional and human-like counseling texts to aid individuals experiencing psychological distress or tendencies toward self-harm and suicide. The article utilized the PsyQA dataset, an authoritative Chinese dialogue dataset focused on mental health support, covering nine broad topics and multiple subtopics encompassing various aspects of mental health. MENTALER outperformed other LLM-based methods in BLEU, F1, and D1 scores. MENTALER outperformed other LLM-based methods in BLEU, F1, and D1 scores. Also, MENTALER demonstrated superior performance in human evaluations, and evaluators preferred its generated texts over others regarding relevance, professionalism, and empathy. This framework may have limitations regarding its ability to handle complex mental health issues or its reliance on the quality of the training data.

Krabashini et al. [71] proposed a hybrid model, combining BERT and ensemble learning to enhance emotion detection accuracy and better manage interactions with users facing mental health challenges. The integration of BERT with ensemble learning techniques (Base Learner (BERT-based Classifier, Random Forest Classifier, and Naive Bayes Classifier) and Stacking Classifier) can significantly improve emotion detection in chatbots, particularly in mental health applications, by capturing nuanced emotional expressions and leveraging the strengths of multiple models. The model included several key phases: data preprocessing, feature extraction, and model training. The data preprocessing steps include tokenization, normalization, handling missing data, augmentation, padding, and truncation. The findings indicated that the hybrid model achieves an accuracy of approximately 85% on the test set, outperforming both the standalone BERT model and traditional classifiers, and demonstrates a 15% improvement in accuracy when classifying anxiety and depression-related emotions. The limitations of the article include the early plateau in validation accuracy during BERT training, suggesting the need for further exploration of hyperparameters, and the potential for improvement by expanding the dataset with more diverse emotional expressions.

The iCare chatbot [72] utilizes the DialoGPT architecture, a next-generation conversational AI specifically fine-tuned for dialogue generation. This chatbot employs a transformer-based architecture to capture extended contextual dependencies and attend to various input segments concurrently. For text data preprocessing, iCare incorporated NLP techniques, including tokenization, padding, and normalization. Furthermore, the article leveraged the Transformers library for text tokenization and the pre-trained DialoGPT model for training the iCare system. Designed to enhance accessible mental health support, iCare aims to detect emotional cues and respond empathetically by integrating AI and emotional intelligence, thereby addressing challenges in mental health treatment. The iCare model demonstrated relative equilibrium during training, evidenced by reduced validation loss and increased accuracy. The model also exhibited the capacity to generate empathetic and accurate responses to users, accompanied by a significant decrease in cross-entropy loss throughout training iterations. However, the chatbot's effectiveness relies on the quality and extent of the training data and its ability to adapt to diverse user inputs. As noted in the article, the capabilities of the iCare system are inherently limited by the scope of the available training data. Consequently, the model may encounter challenges in processing highly contextual and nuanced user inputs.

The Mental Assistance Network for Alleviating Suffering (MANAS) [73] is a mental health support program that utilizes AI techniques, personality analysis, emotion detection, and crisis intervention to provide personalized support, addressing gaps in existing systems by incorporating real-time emotion analysis and robust crisis detection protocols. Unlike existing chatbots, which rely on simple conversations and lack parameters for crisis intervention, MANAS uses the Big Five personality model and advanced NLP to provide personalized and empathetic responses tailored to the user's unique needs. The limitations of the article include the possible risks and challenges linked to the application of AI in mental health, such as data privacy concerns, the need for human intervention, and the limitations of AI responses.

ChatCounselor [74] is an LLM designed to provide mental health support, built on sincere dialogue between clients and licensed psychologists. The methods used in the article included data collecting, data processing (data cleaning, information extraction, and generating instruction data for instruction tuning), and counseling-specific instruction tuning involving 260 participants, each providing an average of 31 question-answer pairs. It leveraged GPT-4 as a dependable and effective referee for enabling automated assessment, as well as an extractor and filter for creating instruction pairs. It performed fine-tuning of the LLMs using the Psych8k dataset. The article uses closed-setting and open-setting question-and-answer benchmarks to assess the model's performance. The results showed that incorporating honest counseling conversations and expert insights in psychology, ChatCounselor surpassed current open-source models on the Counseling Bench and came close to matching ChatGPT's performance. The article finds that ChatCounselor exhibits exceptional performance compared to other LLMs, including LLaMA-7B, Alpaca-7B, ChatGLM-v27B, and Robins-v2-7 B. The article also finds that Vicuna-v1.3-7B approaches ChatCounselor's performance but still lags in applying specific strategies.

Lai et al. [75] introduced an AI-driven framework named Psy-LLM, which integrates pre-trained LLMs (PanGu [76] and Wen-Zhong [77]) with a dataset of professional psychology Q&A and psychological articles, to offer online consultation services, addressing the shortage of mental health professionals. The article revealed that the PanGu model exceeded the performance of the WenZhong model in language generation, achieving higher scores in human evaluations (Helpfulness, Fluency, Relevance, and Logic) and across various automatic evaluation metrics (perplexity, Distinct-n, and ROUGE-L). The authors also recognized several limitations of their models. The inherent constraints of autoregressive language models and the quality of the training data prevented the Psy-LLM framework from achieving human-level performance. Furthermore, while the generated responses demonstrated strength in psychological content, they occasionally lacked logical coherence. The article also highlighted the necessity of improved computing resources to optimize the platform's performance.

The RACLETTE [78] is a conversational system designed to detect, understand, and respond to emotional cues with human-like empathy. It addresses the need for empathetic AI in mental health support and the development of reliable assessment tools by fine-tuning an LLM to create effective conversational agents. The system utilizes a distinctive three-step framework and offers real-time updates to the individual's emotional profile, allowing for more accurate and compassionate responses. The article utilized three open-source datasets, including the Empathetic Dialogues dataset, the Reddit Mental Health dataset, and the DailyDialog dataset. This approach has demonstrated a 3% improvement in emotion classification accuracy when using accumulated emotion distributions. The article found that emotional embeddings reveal significant differences across Reddit communities, with similarities observed between those related to specific disorders. The emotional profile embeddings can be used to assess suicide risk, showing emotional proximity between suicide, depression, and borderline personality disorder. The RACLETTE system achieves a high recall of 0.95. The KL Divergence variant of RACLETTE demonstrates balanced performance across various metrics. The methodology involves fine-tuning the Mistral 7B model to extract emotional profiles from social media interactions, utilizing Top-K Sampling for diverse emotion generation, and aggregating predicted emotions through summation and normalization. Embeddings are compared using metrics such as Kullback–Leibler (KL) divergence, Cosine Similarity (CS), and Jensen–Shannon (JS) divergence. Limitations of the article include concerns about the quality and reliability of the emotional training data, potential data noise, the risk of misuse of AI as a clinical tool, and the necessity of implementing protections against damaging or biased outputs from the model.

Lee et al. [79] investigated how rapport and social presence with an AI therapy chatbot affect users' willingness to disclose personal information. This article aimed to ease the psychological burden of self-disclosure and encourage users to share their mental health challenges openly. The article used a completely automated text-driven system developed with Google Dialogflow, and participants were requested to fill out a series of preliminary questionnaires regarding their counseling/psychiatric experience. The results showed that social presence was a significant mediator between rapport and self-disclosure, and that fear of negative evaluation moderated the mediation effect of social presence. The article's limitations include its use of nonclinical samples, lack of long-term effect analysis of AI psychotherapy, and omission of the human-computer interaction aspect. Additionally, the findings on rapport and self-disclosure contradict previous studies, necessitating further research to clarify the relationships between rapport, social presence, and self-disclosure.

6.3 LIMITATIONS OF LLMS

Despite their advanced capabilities, LLMs also have limitations that must be considered in psychological applications. These limitations can be divided into eight categories: inherent limitations in understanding human experience, technical and algorithmic limitations, clinical and therapeutic limitations, cultural and linguistic limitations, ethical and legal limitations, research and evaluation limitations, therapeutic and neurobiological mechanisms, and operational and application limitations. An overview of each of these limitations follows. Table 6.5 shows these challenges and suggests strategies for overcoming them.

6.3.1 Inherent limitations in understanding human experience

Despite their ability to process and produce text in a human-like manner, LLMs lack phenomenological awareness, body-mind, emotions, a complete understanding of the subtleties of nonverbal communication, human lived experiences, and the complexities of interpersonal relationships, which can limit the quality of their interventions. LLMs don't have bodies or personal experiences. They cannot fully understand human emotions and psychological complexities and may not be able to provide accurate and tailored responses to the needs of the individual in some instances. They learn about emotions from text data but don't feel them. Their responses are based on patterns learned from vast datasets, not on personal experiences that shape identity, values, and beliefs. LLMs, unlike humans, lack an internal concept of the "other." They cannot infer the other person's intent, belief, or intention and respond solely based on statistical similarities. This limitation prevents a deep understanding of psychodynamic conflicts or the implicit meanings of human communication.

Table 6.5 Challenges of LLMs in psychology and proposed solutions

Challenges	*Suggested solutions*
• **Inherent Limitations in Understanding Human Experience** - Lack of phenomenological awareness, embodiment, or emotions - Inability to fully grasp nonverbal cues or psychodynamic conflicts	- Position LLMs as complementary tools for human therapists. - Develop multimodal models (text, voice, image) to approximate human interaction better. - Integrate with VR/AR for immersive, experiential therapy simulations. - Maintain and emphasize human connection. - Foster intelligent interaction between human therapists and AI systems for optimal outcomes.
• **Technical & Algorithmic Limitations** - Biases in training data (gender, race, and culture) - Hallucinations (false outputs) - Black-box decision-making	- Train models on curated, diverse datasets with psychological expertise. - Implement bias-detection algorithms and fairness audits. - Enhance explainability (e.g., transparency tools for clinicians). - Extensive research. - Develop clear ethical/legal standards. - Increase and prioritize transparency and interpretability. - Develop specialized and fine-tuned models. - Conduct Extensive and Multidisciplinary Research.
• **Clinical & Therapeutic Limitations** - Low accuracy for complex diagnoses (e.g., BPD, PTSD) - Inability to build the therapeutic alliance - Risk of patient over-reliance on AI	- Limit LLMs to triage/screening; defer diagnoses to humans. - Design crisis intervention protocols. - Train clinicians to evaluate AI suggestions critically. - Focus on a complementary and collaborative role for specialists. - Implement continuous monitoring and evaluation. - Develop specialized models for diagnosis/treatment.
• **Cultural & Linguistic Limitations** - Poor performance in low-resource languages - Misinterpretation of culture-specific expressions	- Develop multilingual models with local mental health data. - Collaborate with cultural experts to fine-tune responses. - Add modules to detect idioms/slang. - Develop culturally/linguistically tuned models. - Conduct cross-cultural multidisciplinary research. - Develop multimodal models.

(*Continued*)

Table 6.5 (Continued)

Challenges	*Suggested solutions*
• **Ethical & Legal Limitations** - Privacy/security risks with sensitive data - Lack of accountability for errors	- Establish legal frameworks for AI in mental healthcare. - Enforce data encryption and strict access controls. - Define liability standards for AI-generated advice. - Develop and enforce clear ethical and legal standards. - Educate on Limitations, risks, and proper use. - Increase transparency and auditability.
• **Research & Evaluation Challenges** - Reproducibility issues due to model updates - Lack of standardized benchmarks	- Conduct longitudinal studies with interdisciplinary teams. - Create open datasets for model validation. - Develop metrics beyond accuracy. - Conduct rigorous and methodological research. - Implement continuous monitoring and long-term evaluation. - Utilize LLMs in clinical research.
• **Neurobiological & Therapeutic Gaps** - Cannot facilitate emotional co-regulation or attachment - Limited understanding of mind-body connections	- Combine LLMs with biometric data (e.g., wearables) for holistic analysis. - Use AI to analyze neuroimaging data in research settings. - Complementary role for specialists. - Maintain and emphasize human connection. - Develop multimodal models. - Integrate with VR/AR for experiential learning.
• **Operational & Application Limitations** - Digital divide (limited access in low-income/rural areas) - Lack of clinician training in AI	- Invest in offline/low-cost AI tools for underserved regions. - Provide training programs for mental health professionals on AI integration. - Develop specialized and context-aware models. - Implement continuous monitoring and evaluation and quality assurance. - Integrate LLMs with other AI systems for digital therapy. - Increase transparency and collaboration to build trust.

6.3.2 Technical and algorithmic limitations

LLMs are trained on massive datasets. The performance of LLMs is highly influenced by the quality and quantity of their training data. These datasets may contain biases reflecting societal inequalities related to gender, race, culture, and other factors. Controlling for these biases is critical in the highly culturally dependent field of psychology, because this bias can manifest in their responses, leading to unfair, discriminatory, or culturally insensitive outputs in psychological applications. For example, if the training data contains gender biases, LLMs may unfairly attribute certain behaviors to certain genders [80, 81]. The phenomenon of "hallucination," or producing false and untrue information, is also a serious challenge. LLMs show overconfidence, even in ambiguous clinical cases where human experts acknowledge uncertainty. Relying solely on the responses produced by LLMs may result in the provision of inaccurate or inadequate information, especially in complex or critical cases. The complex nature of DL models makes it difficult to understand why an LLM produces a particular output. This lack of transparency, often called the "black box" problem, poses challenges for accountability, error detection, and building trust in psychological applications [48]. Clinicians must understand the reasoning behind an AI's suggestions, especially when dealing with sensitive mental health issues [82]. Also, LLMs are vulnerable to adversarial attacks, where subtly manipulated inputs can cause unexpected outputs. This vulnerability raises concerns about the potential malicious use or unintentional misguidance in psychological contexts.

6.3.3 Clinical and therapeutic limitations

LLMs have poor accuracy in diagnosing disorders with overlapping or complex symptoms, such as borderline personality disorder, bipolar disorder, and complex PTSD. Therefore, diagnosing complex disorders is one of the challenges for LLMs. In clinical settings, building a strong, trusting therapeutic alliance between therapist and client is a key factor in the effectiveness of psychotherapy. LLMs lack key capacities for building a therapeutic alliance, such as genuine mutual interaction, shared experience in the here and now, intuitive understanding of unspoken needs, and flexibility in the moment based on bodily reactions. Other concerns include the risk of clients becoming overly dependent on an AI system, without developing human coping skills, as well as the inability to manage severe psychological crises or make complex differential diagnoses. For a particular individual with unique and complex needs, standard and general advice from LLMs might not be appropriate. LLMs have serious limitations in crisis interventions, such as: inability to contact emergency services, limitations in assessing actual risk to self or others, inability to intervene in emergencies physically, and lack of access to one's support networks. LLMs may be unable to properly recognize and manage critical conditions such as suicidal ideation or psychosis, and delays in referral to human professionals can have serious consequences.

6.3.4 Cultural and linguistic limitations

LLMs are trained on data from diverse sources, but their understanding and application across different cultures and languages are still evolving. Psychological concepts and the expression of emotions can vary significantly across cultures. In Asian cultures, depression is often expressed with more physical symptoms and less overt sadness. In some indigenous cultures, specific psychological experiences can have different meanings, and some languages have different vocabulary for psychological states. Many current LLMs are trained primarily with English language input, which results in poorer performance in other languages and an incomplete understanding of cultural nuances. The performance of LLMs can be significantly lower for languages and dialects with less representation in their training data. This linguistic bias can limit the accessibility and effectiveness of AI-powered psychological tools for diverse populations. The nuances of language, including idioms, slang, and culturally specific communication styles, can be challenging for LLMs to interpret accurately, potentially leading to misunderstandings in therapeutic communication.

6.3.5 Ethical and legal limitations

Using LLMs in psychology raises several ethical and legal issues [83]. The privacy and security of sensitive patient data are a significant concern. Unlike human professionals, LLMs may store data for model improvement, are potentially vulnerable to security breaches, and have limited compliance with privacy standards and other regulations [84]. Ensuring users are fully aware of their interaction with an AI system, including its limitations and potential risks, necessitates obtaining informed consent. Liability and accountability for possible errors or harms resulting from the operation of LLMs (e.g., if they provide incorrect diagnoses or harmful advice) and a clear legal framework for compensation and hardship have not yet been clearly defined [83, 85]. The potential for misuse of these technologies, such as the generation of false information about mental health or impersonation of professionals, also needs to be considered. Also, unlike human professionals, LLMs are not subject to the oversight of professional associations, are not required to adhere to formal codes of ethics, and do not require periodic certification.

6.3.6 Research and evaluation limitations

Evaluating the effectiveness and safety of LLMs and demonstrating the validity and reliability of AI-powered psychological tools in psychological applications require rigorous research methodologies and careful consideration of potential biases and limitations. Methodological problems in LLM research in psychology include the lack of transparency in the underlying algorithms (black boxes), constant changes in the models, the reproducibility and generalizability of research results due to the dynamic nature of these models, their continuous updates, and the difficulty in standardizing the intervention for comparison with traditional treatments. Also, evaluating the long-term effects of AI tools on users' mental health beyond task-specific accuracy presents a significant challenge in designing comprehensive measures.

6.3.7 Therapeutic and neurobiological mechanisms

Many of the effects of psychotherapy are mediated by neurobiological changes that require human interaction. Therapeutic processes in human psychology often involve complex interpersonal interactions, shared emotional experiences, and neurobiological changes in the client's brain. LLMs cannot understand the underlying therapeutic and neurobiological mechanisms of psychological change, as they function at a computational level. LLMs lack an understanding of the neurobiological basis of mental disorders. They cannot participate in processes such as emotional co-regulation or developing secure attachment that are key to human therapy. Their understanding of the mind-body connection and the influence of biological factors on the psyche is also limited. Furthermore, human communication in treatment involves a significant non-verbal component, including cues like facial expressions, body language, and tone of voice, which are often crucial for understanding and empathy [86]. LLMs primarily process text and have limited capacity to interpret these essential cues.

6.3.8 Operational and application limitations

The practical implementation and integration of LLMs into existing mental health service delivery systems face several operational challenges, including the need for technical infrastructure, AI expertise to develop and maintain these systems, challenges related to collaboration between professionals and AI systems, lack of standard protocols for referral, limitations in information exchange with electronic health record systems, and training of users (both professionals and clients) to use them correctly [87]. The digital divide and the lack of equal access to LLM-based technology and services in low-income and rural areas, for older or disabled people, and technical limitations in developing countries can exacerbate inequalities in access to mental health services. Effectively scaling these solutions while preserving the quality and safety of services and simultaneously fostering acceptance and trust among users and professionals represents crucial interconnected operational challenges.

6.4 CONCLUSION AND FUTURE WORKS

The use of AI in psychology has made significant progress, from the early stages of computational modeling to advanced applications in psychological therapies. AI is becoming an increasingly important tool for analyzing human behavior, simulating cognitive processes, and addressing psychological problems. LLMs, with their unique capabilities in language processing and production, have significant potential to transform the field of psychological support. LLMs can provide potential opportunities such as increasing access and reducing costs, providing continuous and real-time support, personalizing interventions, screening and early detection, and providing a tool for training, empowering, and supporting human therapists. However, realizing this potential, there is a need to understand the scientific and ethical opportunities and challenges associated with this technology, conduct rigorous research, develop appropriate standards, and adopt a responsible and collaborative approach between professionals from different fields. This chapter reviewed LLMs, their key features, related works, and the challenges and limitations of using LLMs in psychology. Statistical results and empirical evidence indicate the high potential of LLMs in psychology. However, comparisons with traditional methods show that LLMs are more effective as a complement, not a substitute. Challenges such as data biases and a lack of emotional understanding require further research to optimize this technology.

REFERENCES

1. Russell, S.J. and P. Norvig, *Artificial intelligence: a modern approach*, 2016: Pearson.
2. Luxton, D.D., *Artificial intelligence in behavioral and mental health care*, 2015, American Society Assocation.
3. Kjell, O.N., K. Kjell, and H.A. Schwartz, Beyond rating scales: With targeted evaluation, large language models are poised for psychological assessment. *Psychiatry Research*, 2024, 333: p. 115667.
4. Ashish, V., Attention is all you need. *Advances in Neural Information Processing Systems*, 2017, 30: p. I.
5. Brown, T., et al., Language models are few-shot learners. *Advances in Neural Information Processing Systems*, 2020, 33: p. 1877–1901.
6. Tshimula, J.M., et al. Psychological Profiling in Cybersecurity: A Look at LLMs and Psycholinguistic Features. In *International Conference on Web Information Systems Engineering*, 2024. Springer.
7. Touvron, H., et al., Llama 2: Open foundation and fine-tuned chat models. *arXiv preprint arXiv:2307.09288*, 2023.

8. Devlin, J., et al. Bert: Pre-training of deep bidirectional transformers for language understanding. In *Proceedings of the 2019 Conference of the North American Chapter of the Association for Computational Linguistics: Human Language Technologies, Volume 1 (long and short papers)*, 2019.
9. Anthropic. *CLAUDE-2-100k (July 11 version) [Large language model]*. 2023; Available at: https://www.anthropic.com/index/claude-2 (Accessed March 2, 2024).
10. Perera, P., *Preparing to revolutionize education with the multi-model GenAI tool Google Gemini? A journey towards effective policy making*, 2023 CQ university.
11. Tsai, H.-C., Y.-F. Huang, and C.-W. Kuo, *Comparative analysis of automatic literature review using mistral large language model and human reviewers*, EUROPE PMC, 2024.
12. Bird, J.J., et al. Generative AI in Psychological Therapy: Perspectives on Computational Linguistics and Large Language Models in Written Behaviour Monitoring. In *Proceedings of the 17th International Conference on PErvasive Technologies Related to Assistive Environments*, 2024.
13. Liu, J., ChatGPT: Perspectives from human–computer interaction and psychology. *Frontiers in Artificial Intelligence*, 2024, 7: p. 1418869.
14. Uludag, K., Testing creativity of ChatGPT in psychology: Interview with ChatGPT. In *Chatbots and Mental Healthcare in Psychology and Psychiatry*, 2025, IGI Global Scientific Publishing. p. 181–192.
15. Hu, J., et al., Psycollm: Enhancing llm for psychological understanding and evaluation. *IEEE Transactions on Computational Social Systems*, 2024 12(2),539-551.
16. Chung, H.W., et al., Scaling instruction-finetuned language models. *Journal of Machine Learning Research*, 2024, 25(70): p. 1–53.
17. Taori, R., et al., *Stanford alpaca: An instruction-following llama model*, 2023, Stanford, CA, USA.
18. Ji, S., et al., Mentalbert: Publicly available pretrained language models for mental healthcare. *arXiv preprint arXiv:2110.15621*, 2021.
19. Possati, L.M., Psychoanalyzing artificial intelligence: The case of Replika. *AI & Society*, 2023, 38(4): p. 1725–1738.
20. Dhamane, B., et al. Machine Learning based Mood Disorder Detection System. In *2023 8th International Conference on Communication and Electronics Systems (ICCES)*, 2023. IEEE.
21. Jitanan, M., et al., The Development of "Friend from Heart" Application Based on Line System to Promote Well-Being of Undergraduate Students of Faculty of Education, Kasetsart University. *Higher Education Studies*, 2021, 11(2): p. 215–223.
22. McGoldrick, C., S. Crawford, and J.J. Evans, MindMate: A single case experimental design study of a reminder system for people with dementia. *Neuropsychological Rehabilitation*, 2021, 31(1): p. 18–38.
23. Pandey, H.M., Harnessing Large Language Models for Mental Health: Opportunities, Challenges, and Ethical Considerations. *arXiv preprint arXiv:2501.10370*, 2024.
24. Demszky, D., et al., Using large language models in psychology. *Nature Reviews Psychology*, 2023, 2(11): p. 688–701.

25. Hagendorff, T., Machine psychology: Investigating emergent capabilities and behavior in large language models using psychological methods. *arXiv preprint arXiv:2303.13988*, 2023.
26. Fitzpatrick, K.K., A. Darcy, and M. Vierhile, Delivering cognitive behavior therapy to young adults with symptoms of depression and anxiety using a fully automated conversational agent (Woebot): a randomized controlled trial. *JMIR Mental Health*, 2017, 4(2): p. e7785.
27. Inkster, B., S. Sarda, and V. Subramanian, An empathy-driven, conversational artificial intelligence agent (Wysa) for digital mental well-being: real-world data evaluation mixed-methods study. *JMIR mHealth and uHealth*, 2018, 6(11): p. e12106.
28. Daley, K., et al., Preliminary evaluation of the engagement and effectiveness of a mental health chatbot. *Frontiers in Digital Health*, 2020, 2: p. 576361.
29. *Mental Health Atlas 2023*, 2023, World Health Organization. .
30. Johnsen, M., *Large language models (LLMs)*, 2024: Maria Johnsen.
31. Raiaan, M.A.K., et al., A review on large language models: Architectures, applications, taxonomies, open issues and challenges. *IEEE Access*, 2024, 12: p. 26839–26874.
32. Kiuchi, K., K. Otsu, and Y. Hayashi, Psychological insights into the research and practice of embodied conversational agents, chatbots and social assistive robots: a systematic meta-review. *Behaviour & Information Technology*, 2024, 43(15): p. 3696–3736.
33. Weizenbaum, J., ELIZA—a computer program for the study of natural language communication between man and machine. *Communications of the ACM*, 1966, 9(1): p. 36–45.
34. Colby, K.M., PARRYing. *Behavioral and Brain Sciences*, 1981, 4(4): p. 550–560.
35. AbuShawar, B. and E. Atwell, ALICE chatbot: Trials and outputs. *Computación y sistemas*, 2015, 19(4): p. 625–632.
36. Lokman, A.S. and M.A. Ameedeen. Modern chatbot systems: A technical review. In *Proceedings of the Future Technologies Conference (FTC) 2018: Volume 2*, 2019. Springer.
37. Halvoník, D. and J. Kapusta, Large Language Models and Rule-Based Approaches in Domain-Specific Communication. *IEEE Access*, 2024, 12, 107046-107058. .
38. Chow, J.C., L. Sanders, and K. Li, Impact of ChatGPT on medical chatbots as a disruptive technology. *Frontiers in artificial Intelligence*, 2023, 6: p. 1166014.
39. de Filippis, R. and A. Al Foysal, Chatbots in psychology: Revolutionizing clinical support and mental health care. *Voice of the Publisher*, 2024, 10(3): p. 298–321.
40. Ilieva, G., et al., Effects of generative chatbots in higher education. *Information*, 2023, 14(9): p. 492.
41. Agarwal, R. and M. Wadhwa, Review of state-of-the-art design techniques for chatbots. *SN Computer Science*, 2020, 1(5): p. 246.
42. Adiwardana, D., et al., Towards a human-like open-domain chatbot. *arXiv preprint arXiv:2001.09977*, 2020.

43. Pennebaker, J.W., M.R. Mehl, and K.G. Niederhoffer, Psychological aspects of natural language use: Our words, our selves. *Annual Review of Psychology*, 2003, 54(1): p. 547–577.
44. Eichstaedt, J.C., et al., Facebook language predicts depression in medical records. *Proceedings of the National Academy of Sciences*, 2018, 115(44): p. 11203–11208.
45. Goldberg, L.R., The development of markers for the Big-Five factor structure. *Psychological Assessment*, 1992, 4(1): p. 26.
46. Yonatan-Leus, R. and H. Brukner, Comparing perceived empathy and intervention strategies of an AI chatbot and human psychotherapists in online mental health support. *Counselling and Psychotherapy Research*, 2025, 25(1): p. e12832.
47. Wu, Y., et al. LLM-Based Empathetic Response Through Psychologist-Agent Debate. In *Asia-Pacific Web (APWeb) and Web-Age Information Management (WAIM) Joint International Conference on Web and Big Data*, 2024. Springer.
48. Guo, Z., et al., Large language models for mental health applications: Systematic review. *JMIR Mental Health*, 2024, 11(1): p. e57400.
49. De Choudhury, M., et al. Predicting depression via social media. In *Proceedings of the International AAAI Conference on Web and Social Media*, 2013.
50. Shan, X., et al. Cross-Cultural Implications of Large Language Models: An Extended Comparative Analysis. In *International Conference on Human-Computer Interaction*, 2024. Springer.
51. Park, C. and H. Kim, Understanding LLM Development Through Longitudinal Study: Insights from the Open Ko-LLM Leaderboard. *arXiv preprint arXiv:2409.03257*, 2024.
52. Almeida, G.F., et al., Exploring the psychology of LLMs' moral and legal reasoning. *Artificial Intelligence*, 2024, 333: p. 104145.
53. AlMakinah, R., et al., Enhancing Mental Health Support through Human-AI Collaboration: Toward Secure and Empathetic AI-enabled chatbots. *arXiv preprint arXiv:2410.02783*, 2024.
54. Pryss, R., et al., Using Chatbots to support medical and psychological treatment procedures: challenges, opportunities, technologies, reference architecture. *Digital Phenotyping and Mobile Sensing: New Developments in Psychoinformatics*, 2019: p. 249–260.
55. Liu, Y., et al., Roberta: A robustly optimized bert pretraining approach. *arXiv preprint arXiv:1907.11692*, 2019.
56. Shen, H., et al. Are Large Language Models Possible to Conduct Cognitive Behavioral Therapy?. In *2024 IEEE International Conference on Bioinformatics and Biomedicine (BIBM)*, 2024. IEEE.
57. Moell, B., Comparing the efficacy of GPT-4 and Chat-GPT in mental health care: A blind assessment of large language models for psychological support. *arXiv preprint arXiv:2405.09300*, 2024.
58. Berrezueta-Guzman, S., et al. Exploring the efficacy of robotic assistants with ChatGPT and Claude in enhancing ADHD therapy: Innovating treatment paradigms. In *2024 International Conference on Intelligent Environments (IE)*, 2024. IEEE.

59. Jiang, J. and Y. Yang, GymBuddy and Elomia, AI-integrated applications, effects on the mental health of the students with psychological disorders. *BMC Psychology*, 2025, 13(1): p. 1–9.
60. Nazir, A., M.N. Cheeema, and Z. Wang, ChatGPT-based biological and psychological data imputation. *Meta-Radiology*, 2023, 1(3): p. 100034.
61. Van Essen, D.C., et al., The WU-Minn human connectome project: an overview. *Neuroimage*, 2013, 80: p. 62–79.
62. Van Essen, D.C., et al., The Human Connectome Project: a data acquisition perspective. *Neuroimage*, 2012, 62(4): p. 2222–2231.
63. Salah, M., et al., Chatting with ChatGPT: decoding the mind of Chatbot users and unveiling the intricate connections between user perception, trust and stereotype perception on self-esteem and psychological well-being. *Current Psychology*, 2024, 43(9): p. 7843–7858.
64. Gnambs, T., A. Scharl, and U. Schroeders, The structure of the Rosenberg self-esteem scale. *Zeitschrift für Psychologie*, 2018.
65. Fornell, C. and D.F. Larcker, *Structural equation models with unobservable variables and measurement error: Algebra and statistics*, 1981, Sage Publications: Los Angeles, CA.
66. Chou, Y.-H., et al., User-friendly Chatbot to mitigate the psychological stress of older adults during the COVID-19 pandemic: Development and usability study. *JMIR Formative Research*, 2024, 8: p. e49462.
67. Blanco-Cuaresma, S., Psychological Assessments with Large Language Models: A Privacy-Focused and Cost-Effective Approach. *arXiv preprint arXiv:2402.03435*, 2024.
68. Chen, Y., et al., Deep Learning and Large Language Models for Audio and Text Analysis in Predicting Suicidal Acts in Chinese Psychological Support Hotlines. *arXiv preprint arXiv:2409.06164*, 2024.
69. Muqtadir, A., et al., Mitigating Hallucinations Using Ensemble of Knowledge Graph and Vector Store in Large Language Models to Enhance Mental Health Support. *arXiv preprint arXiv:2410.10853*, 2024.
70. Gu, Z. and Q. Zhu. MENTALER: Toward Professional Mental Health Support with LLMs via Multi-Role Collaboration. In *2024 IEEE International Conference on Bioinformatics and Biomedicine (BIBM)*, 2024. IEEE.
71. Krabashini, N.P., et al. Enhancing Emotion Detection in Chatbots for Improved Mental Health Support: Addressing Limitations in Mental Disorders and Emotion Detection. In *2024 17th International Congress on Image and Signal Processing, BioMedical Engineering and Informatics (CISP-BMEI)*, 2024. IEEE.
72. Kaviyaraj, R., A. Gautam, and S. Vashistha. iCare: Harnessing AI and Emotional Intelligence to Revolutionize Accessible Mental Health Support. In *2024 International Conference on Emerging Research in Computational Science (ICERCS)*, 2024. IEEE.
73. Gayathri, S., M.S. Pradeep, and N.S.S.L.V. Prasad. MANAS: Integrating Advanced AI for Personalized Mental Health Support, Crisis Intervention, and Medical Insights. In *2025 3rd International Conference on Intelligent Data Communication Technologies and Internet of Things (IDCIoT)*, 2025. IEEE.

74. Liu, J.M., et al., Chatcounselor: A large language models for mental health support. *arXiv preprint arXiv:2309.15461*, 2023.
75. Lai, T., et al., Supporting the demand on mental health services with AI-based conversational large language models (LLMs). *BioMedInformatics*, 2023, 4(1): p. 8–33.
76. Zeng, W., et al., PanGu-α: Large-scale autoregressive pretrained Chinese language models with auto-parallel computation. *arXiv preprint arXiv:2104.12369*, 2021.
77. Zhang, J., et al., Fengshenbang 1.0: Being the foundation of chinese cognitive intelligence. *arXiv preprint arXiv:2209.02970*, 2022.
78. De Grandi, A., et al., The Emotional Spectrum of LLMs: Leveraging Empathy and Emotion-Based Markers for Mental Health Support. *arXiv preprint arXiv:2412.20068*, 2024.
79. Lee, J., D. Lee, and J.-g. Lee, Influence of rapport and social presence with an AI psychotherapy chatbot on users' self-disclosure. *International Journal of Human–Computer Interaction*, 2024, 40(7): p. 1620–1631.
80. Bender, E.M., et al. On the dangers of stochastic parrots: Can language models be too big?. In *Proceedings of the 2021 ACM Conference on Fairness, Accountability, and Transparency*, 2021.
81. Bolukbasi, T., et al., Man is to computer programmer as woman is to homemaker? debiasing word embeddings. *Advances in Neural Information Processing Systems*, 2016, 29, 4356-4364.
82. Rudin, C., Stop explaining black box machine learning models for high stakes decisions and use interpretable models instead. *Nature Machine Intelligence*, 2019, 1(5): p. 206–215.
83. Jobin, A., M. Ienca, and E. Vayena, The global landscape of AI ethics guidelines. *Nature Machine Intelligence*, 2019, 1(9): p. 389–399.
84. Williamson, S.M. and V. Prybutok, Balancing privacy and progress: a review of privacy challenges, systemic oversight, and patient perceptions in AI-driven healthcare. *Applied Sciences*, 2024, 14(2): p. 675.
85. Vayena, E., A. Blasimme, and I.G. Cohen, Machine learning in medicine: addressing ethical challenges. *PLoS Medicine*, 2018, 15(11): p. e1002689.
86. Molto, J., et al. An LLM-powered Socially Interactive Agent with Adaptive Facial Expressions for Conversing about Health. In *Companion Proceedings of the 26th International Conference on Multimodal Interaction*, 2024.
87. Khowaja, S.A., et al., Chatgpt needs spade (sustainability, privacy, digital divide, and ethics) evaluation: A review. *Cognitive Computation*, 2024, 16(5): p. 2528–2550.

Chapter 7

Explainable AI (XAI): Making LLM decisions transparent and trustworthy

Amirfarhad Farhadi, Azadeh Zamanifar, and Fouad Bahrpeyma

7.1 LARGE LANGUAGE MODELS

Large language models have contributed greatly to the field of artificial intelligence. This technology, which is built upon transformer models (a neural network architecture based on self-attention mechanism, composed of an encoder and a decoder, capable of capturing long-term dependencies efficiently—Figure 7.1), pushed the boundaries of natural language processing (NLP), providing vast applications of artificial intelligence in various areas, ranging from coding and translational healthcare to many other fields.

According to Reference [2]:

> "At their core, LLMs are designed to comprehend, learn, and generate coherent and contextually relevant language on an unparalleled scale. Historically, the development of Language Models (LMs) has been rooted in the quest to understand and replicate human language".

LLMs such as BERT, GPT-3, GPT-4, Llama and Claude, despite their applications in many areas, have some issues, which are regarding lack of transparency; that is, how they come to the results. When a number of human experts discuss a subject, in addition to sharing some level of common knowledge that they agree upon, they usually argue in order to prove or disprove their theories; this process is necessary for producing the soundest results, supported by evidence and rationality. This process matters most when LLMs are used in high-stakes applications in which wrong decisions may cause serious side effects.

The efforts that try to make LLMs more interpretable and clarify the internal processes of reasoning in artificial intelligence as a whole, especially deep neural networks, shape a body of knowledge called explainable AI. In the following section, we briefly introduce XAI, especially those aspects of that are more relevant to our topic.

DOI: 10.1201/9781003665083-7

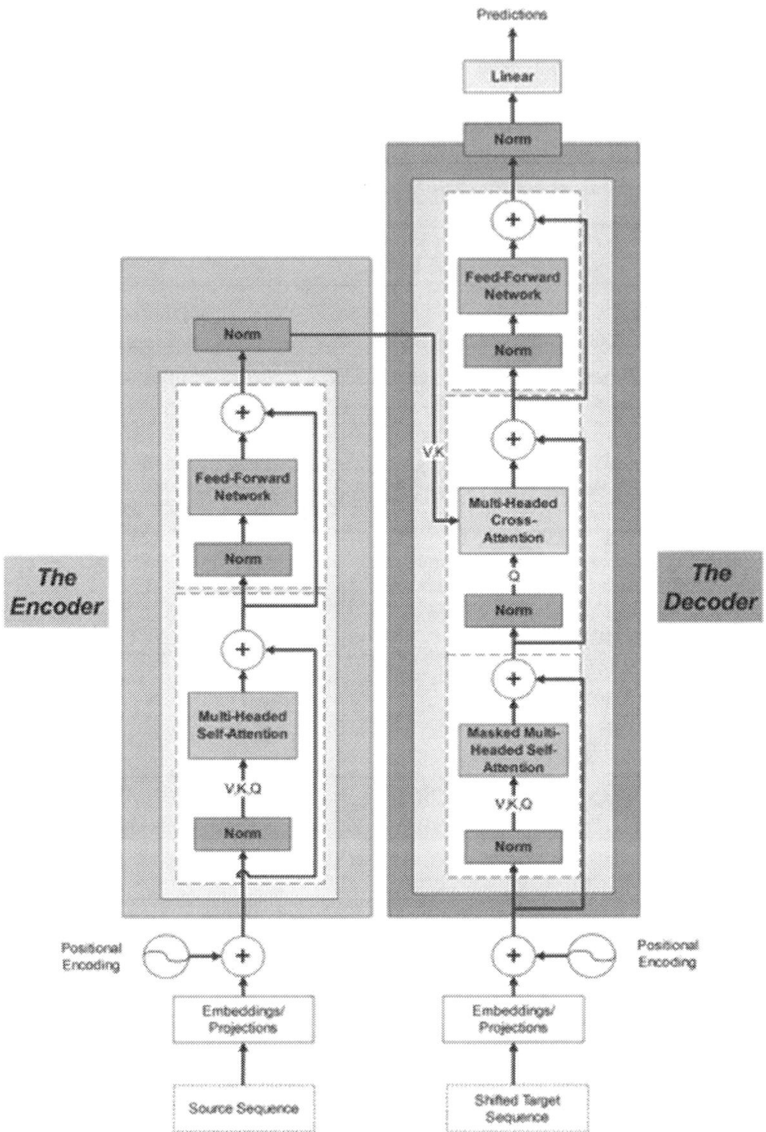

Figure 7.1 The transformer model architecture. Adapted from Reference [1].

7.2 EXPLAINABLE AI

Earlier AI systems were mainly logical and symbolic, making them more suitable to be explained by tracing and understanding the logical inferences they performed [3].

Recent rapid developments in AI, especially in the field of deep learning, resulted in complicated, opaque systems, making error detection, correction, and public trust challenging.

The explanation above justifies the importance of the field of explainable AI, or XAI for short. The following Figure 7.2 demonstrates the Google Trends Popularity Index regarding explainable artificial intelligence during the last 10 years (from 2015 to 2025).

As the trend shows, increasing attention is being directed toward improving interpretability and explainability (two main goals of XAI) of AI systems to shed some light on the black-box nature of these complicated systems, making them more trustworthy.

So far, we have used the terms interpretability and explainability almost interchangeably, but in fact they differ both in concept and approach. In order to make this distinction clearer, it seems necessary to define them in a rigorous mathematical way. There have been some efforts made to arrive at such definitions; but because we are not sure about their universality, we will not consider them and will take a more intuitive approach instead, which suffices our purpose.

The *"interpretability"* of an AI system may roughly be defined as "the ability to explain or to present in understandable terms to a human" or "the degree to which a human can understand the cause of a decision" [4].

"Explainability" on the other hand, is associated with the internal logic and mechanisms that are inside a machine learning (ML) system. In a more explainable system, it is easier for humans to understand the internal procedures that occur while the model is training or making decisions [4].

Therefore, interpretability does not necessarily mean one can comprehend the internals of an AI system; it is associated with the identification of the cause-and-effect relationships with system's inputs and outputs [4]. The following picture depicts the distinction between interpretability and explainability (Figure 7.3).

While the main purpose of this field of study is to help understand AI systems, there is also a legal aspect, too: some regulatory frameworks exist, such as the General Data Protection Regulation (2016/679, GDPR), which is a privacy and data protection regulation [5].

According to Art. 5 of GDPR, titled: *Principles relating to processing of personal data*: "Personal data shall be processed lawfully, fairly and in a

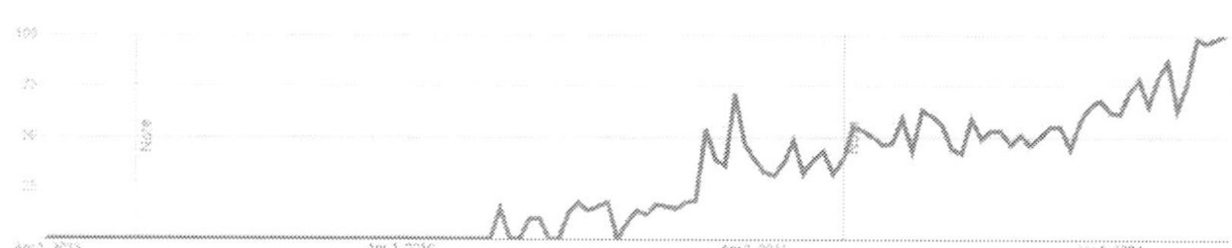

Figure 7.2 The Google Trends Popularity Index related to explainable artificial intelligence.

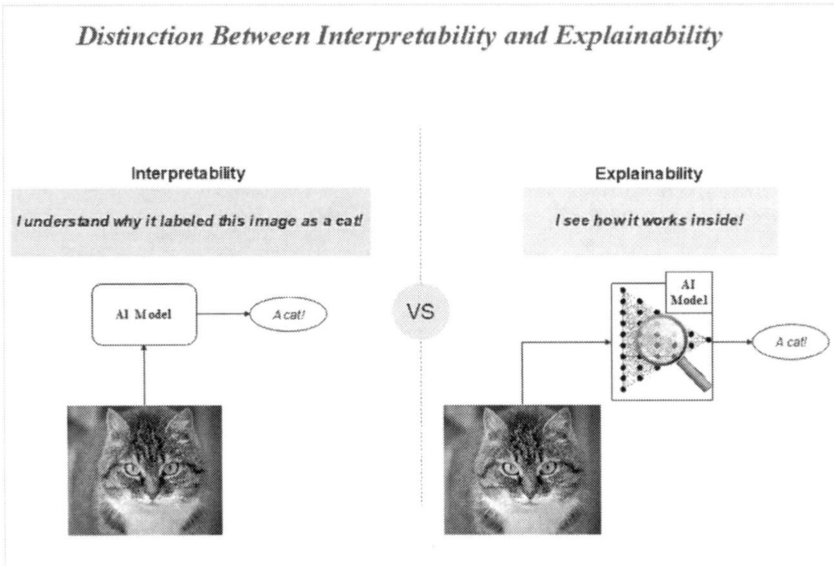

Figure 7.3 The distinction between interpretability and explainability.

transparent manner in relation to the data subject ('lawfulness, fairness and transparency')" (https://gdpr-info.eu/art-5-gdpr/) [5]. So, XAI is not a field of study to just fulfill one's sense of curiosity or only make AI systems more comprehendible, but XAI is also justifiable by legal concerns, too.

With the progress of XAI, researchers not only try to understand the existing AI systems, but they try to invent explainable and interpretable AI systems in the first place and leave those systems which are less transparent. Adopting this approach, while adhering to the three principles, namely, "lawfulness," "fairness," and "transparency," allows for what is called *responsible AI* [6].

So far, we have tried to discuss the nature of XAI. Now, we briefly discuss how we can make AI systems explainable, as well as how to make explainable AI systems. It is worth noting that before the birth of XAI, one of the most important aspects of designing AI systems was their predictive power. With the advancement of more complicated, nonlinear models (such as deep neural networks or DNNs), researchers tried to clarify these models, moving away from models that are less explainable, and instead try to design the models with explainability in mind from scratch. With further advancements in the field of XAI, we no longer need to give up the predictive power in favor of interpretability, and can take full advantage of powerful, nonlinear AI models in practical applications [6].

XAI techniques can be roughly classified into three main categories based on their approaches to interpretability, model dependency, and explanation mechanism (Figure 7.4); obviously the boundaries are not so clear.

1. **Intrinsically Interpretable Models (Self-explainable Models):** These methods are designed to be interpretable at their core, prioritizing transparency over predictive power. Regression, decision trees, and k-nearest neighbors (k-NNs) are some well-known examples of this category. Despite their explanatory power, they may exhibit less performance in more complicated tasks compared to methods from other categories [6]. These methods are referred to as "white-box" or "ante-hoc" models, too [7].
2. **Model-agnostic Methods:** These are post-hoc techniques that can virtually be applied to all machine learning models; they are universal and best suited to explain black-box models, such as deep neural networks. These methods aim to approximate or explain the behavior of the model or its prediction logic mathematically. Some techniques belonging to this category include partial dependence plots (PDPs), individual conditional expectation (ICE), accumulated local effects (ALE) plot, local interpretable model-agnostic explanations (LIME), SHapley Additive explanations (SHAP), Global Surrogate, and so on. These methods are widely used in our domain of interest, i.e., healthcare, due to their flexibility [6, 7].
3. **Example-based Explanations:** This category refers to some post hoc, model-agnostic methods utilizing examples as explanations for an AI model's output and probably are the most aligned methods with the process of learning in human beings, in which learning takes place by providing and investigating some examples.

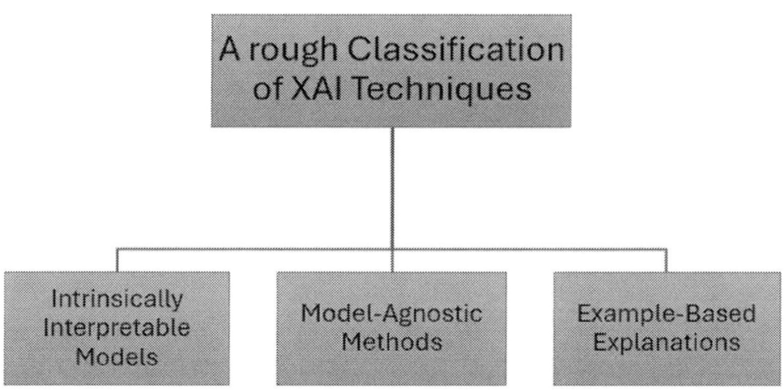

Figure 7.4 A rough classification of XAI techniques.

These examples can be drawn from data or can be generated, and generally fall under some categories, namely, similar examples (factuals), counterfactuals, and semi-factuals, representing the closest and the farthest samples respectively, which the model can make a similar or different output (prediction).

To mention some examples of the methods, we can name case-based explanations (CBE), which are based on the method of case-based reasoning (CBR), nearest unlike neighbors (NUN), and so on [8]. For example, [9] tries to explain the artificial neural networks (ANNs) using the case-based reasoning method. These techniques proved to be useful in domains that need clear, understandable explanations, such as medical diagnostics [6, 7].

As mentioned before, these are not the only categories, and some papers provide some other categorizations based on input and output format (such as numerical, textual, visual, ...), local methods (targeting a specific decision) vs. global methods (trying to clarify the system's behavior in general) and some other criteria [7, 8]. But for our purpose, this categorization suffices.

As it is obvious, the stated methods (categories) are general and each category can include several instances as special cases. Now, we should turn our attention to our model of interest, i.e., LLMs.

With LLMs, in which human-AI interaction is more obvious, significant efforts have been made to improve this interaction. LLMs show remarkable power in comprehending and generating human language, making it possible for people to ask their questions and receive their answers in their own language. As another step forward, it seems necessary to reduce the opacity accompanying LLMs in order to make it possible for people to track the steps LLMs take to arrive at the conclusions and intervene whenever necessary to correct errors and biases to avoid difficulties and get better results, which leads to mitigating risks usually associated with the applications of these kinds of systems [5].

As LLMs are a specific class of deep neural networks at their core, the points discussed in this section may generally be applied to them. But in the following section, we discuss the problems of interpretability and explainability in LLMs as a special case with more details, because LLMs are increasingly gaining attention as one of the widely used AI systems in healthcare.

7.3 EXPLAINABLE LLMS

In the previous sections, we discussed the concept and importance of explainability and interpretability in AI models in general and provided some examples. In this section, we investigate these issues in LLMs, especially when they are applied to healthcare systems or processes.

Given their widespread applications across domains and their ease of use through natural language interaction on the one hand, and their inherent complexity on the other hand, it becomes essential to develop and apply effective techniques to make LLMs more transparent and trustworthy. This is especially important when it comes to some critical tasks, such as clinical decision support and diagnostics, medical documentation and note taking, patient communication and education, biomedical literature analysis, drug discovery and development, and mental health support. Clearly, a full discussion of this topic is beyond this chapter's scope, thus what follows is just a brief overview of the subject, but before continuing our discussion on explainable AI, it seems necessary to mention some challenges regarding making AI systems explainable; as explaining LLMs can be challenging in certain ways, as presented hereafter:

i. **Model Complexity and Opacity:** LLMs have complicated and opaque (not transparent) architectures with billions of parameters [10]. No existing method provides a comprehensive, scalable explanation of LLMs' knowledge representation or reasoning pathways [10]. The operational principles of the transformer architecture—the foundation of modern LLMs—remain almost uncharacterized, with gaps in theoretical understanding of that by researchers [10]. This complexity makes model explanation really challenging.
ii. **Scale of Data and Training:** LLMs are trained on massive and diverse datasets [10]. Understanding what went into training phases may be challenging, if not impossible [10]. The extensive size of the system complicates the development and deployment of transparency approaches, constrained by computational resource limitations [11]. Checking for contamination in training data is hard due to the opacity and scale of datasets [10].
iii. **Unpredictable Capability:** LLMs may have complex and unforeseen capabilities that cannot be fully predicted beforehand, even by their creators, until their behavior on certain inputs is observed [10]. This makes defining basic details like input/output spaces or mappings tricky [10]. The extensive and incompletely defined space of capabilities stated in advance also contributes to making the process of evaluation challenging [10].
iv. **Faithfulness vs. Plausibility:** Explanations must be both plausible (sound and logical) and faithful (reflecting the true system's reasoning processes). LLMs act almost perfectly in terms of plausibility (because of training on human-generated data and applying RLHF). However, these explanations, seeming logical and sound, do not guarantee to reflect the truth and can be inconsistent, implausible, or misleading, resulting in unwanted side effects, security concerns, and lack of trust [12].

v. **Lack of Ground Truth and Evaluation Standards:** Evaluating the faithfulness of explanations is challenging because there is often no ground truth (factual and accurate data used as benchmarks) about the model's internal reasoning process [11]. There is currently no universally agreed-upon metric or formal technique for measuring faithfulness [12]. Currently existing evaluation metrics for explanations are often inconsistent [11]. For natural language explanations, standard statistical evaluations are lacking, and metrics for open-ended text have limitations [13].
vi. **Understanding for End-users:** While XAI tries to make models more comprehensible, end-users, particularly nonexperts, may find understanding the workings of the XAI methods themselves challenging [13]. Even exposing internals of a simple model can lead to information overload and confusion, making users less able to spot mistakes [10]. There is no consensus on what constitutes an objective, understandable explanation for every end-user [7]. This matter is largely subjective, depending on each user's mentality.
vii. **Model Dependency and Feature Interactions:** Some explanation methods, like SHAP and LIME, can be affected by the specific machine learning (ML) model used and the presence of collinearity among features [14]. LIME treats feature as independent and struggles with nonlinear dependencies [14]. SHAP can suffer from unrealistic data instances when features are correlated [14].
viii. **Applications Involving Multiple Components:** LLM-infused applications often involve multiple interacting models, tools, and external services [10]. Providing transparency requires explaining the entire system, not just the LLM in isolation. This issue contributes to adding even more complexity to make the system understandable [10].
ix. **Conflict Between Performance and Explainability:** Increasing explainability may come at the cost of a decrease in predictive power, especially in more complicated tasks. There are good examples of opaque AI models and architectures with great predictive power (e.g., deep neural networks). We should consider a trade-off between performance and explainability, depending on the application domain.
x. **Emerging Capabilities:** LLMs show new, unforeseen, surprising capabilities as their scale increases, whose origins are not fully understood [11]. Explaining these emerging capabilities is an open challenge to be addressed, especially for proprietary models [11].
xi. **Hallucination and Unreliable Behavior:** LLMs may suffer from the problem of hallucination, generating nonsensical or unfaithful responses, which creates significant compliance concerns and makes reliable explanation difficult [11]. Their behavior can be unreliable, such as producing nondeterministic output for the same input [10]. The issue of producing nondeterministic outputs from a unique input

may be attributed to the implementation of LLMs, in which some mechanisms are used to adjust the system's dependency on the stored data, which may result in different outputs from the same input.

xii. **Talent Scarcity:** Interpreting the outputs of LLMs in specialized fields like healthcare often requires deep expertise in both computer science and the domain itself—an interdisciplinary skill set that is relatively rare in practice.

xiii. **Defining Usefulness and Appropriateness:** What constitutes a useful notion of uncertainty for LLMs is unclear [10]. Different model capabilities and tasks may require different types of explanations [10]. The appropriateness of explanations depends heavily on the specific application context and stakeholder needs [12].

xiv. **Ethical and Safety Concerns:** Ethical concerns arise significantly from the model's lack of interpretability, making it challenging to analyze or constrain harms like misinformation, bias, and manipulation [11]. Auditing these models and ensuring alignment with human values requires XAI techniques [11].

Considering all the challenges mentioned above (and possibly those not mentioned), it's unlikely that we'll ever achieve complete transparency with LLMs. However, it's important that we keep working to make them as understandable and trustworthy as possible. In the following section, we briefly discuss some goals regarding making LLMs explainable.

Some goals of making LLMs explainable are as follows; we should note that the goal of explainability for LLMs is multifaceted:

- For end-users, by transparently revealing and clarifying the reasoning mechanisms behind AI-generated outputs, it helps users develop informed trust—clearing up what LLMs can do, where they might fail, and why [11]. This is of great importance because it allows users to adjust their expectations beforehand, mitigating the risks involved in utilizing these systems blindly.
- For researchers and developers, it provides insight for debugging, identifying biases, risks, and areas for performance improvement. It helps track model capabilities, compare different models, and develop more reliable, ethical, and safer models [11].
- It is particularly crucial in applications where decision-making transparency is of great importance, such as healthcare diagnostics, legal advice, and financial forecasting, in which any inappropriate decision may lead to irreversible, serious consequences [11].

In the following section, we discuss some methods and techniques to make LLMs more explainable. Due to the high level of interest in this topic and the wide range of ongoing efforts, it is not possible to provide a comprehensive list of such methods and techniques.

7.4 METHODS AND TECHNIQUES TO MAKE LLMS EXPLAINABLE

Methods and techniques to make LLMs more explainable draw from the broader field of Explainable Artificial Intelligence (XAI) and also include approaches tailored (designed) specifically for the characteristics and usage paradigms of LLMs. These techniques can be broadly categorized as follows:

1. **Intrinsic Explanations:** These approaches aim to expose and clarify the model's inner workings directly [10], which include:
   - **Interpretable Models/Architectures:** Using simpler models that are inherently understandable, such as rule-based models or linear regression, are traditional approaches. Generalized Additive Models (GAMs), linear combinations of simple models, are also described as inherently explainable [7]. Research is ongoing to develop models with more transparent internal structures [15].
   - **Analyses and Visualization:** Analyzing and visualizing aspects like neural activations or feature elimination can help make sense of internal structures. For Transformer models, leveraging attention weights has been explored to show input influence [15].
2. **Post Hoc Explanations:** These are generated *after* the model has made a prediction and are used to approximate its behavior. They are useful for complex or black-box models where internals are not accessible [10] or it is hard to understand the model's internals. This method includes:
   - **Global Explanations:** Provide an overview of the model's overall logic [10, 11]. Techniques include:
     - Neuron activation analysis.
     - Concept-based explanations [11].
     - Mechanistic Interpretability: Reverse-engineering the internal mechanisms and computational patterns within LLMs to understand how they process information [11].
     - Partial dependence plots (PDPs) and Permutation Feature Importance are general methods applicable to ML models.
   - **Local Explanations:** Provide the reasoning behind a particular model output [10]. Techniques include:
     - **Feature Attribution Scores:** Measure the importance of each input feature with respect to a specific output [10, 11]. Methods include gradient-based methods (like Integrated Gradients) and perturbation-based methods, which estimate importance by introducing noise. Attention weights themselves, or combined with other quantities, can indicate feature importance. Token importance is another form [12]. Contrastive explanations,

which extend input saliency methods like Gradient Norm, are also used [16].

- **Surrogate Models:** These involve training simpler, interpretable models (like linear models or decision trees) using the original model's inputs and outputs to locally approximate the complex model's behavior [10]. Local interpretable model-agnostic explanations (LIME) and SHapley Additive exPlanations (SHAP) are widely used examples, which approximate complex models with simpler ones [10, 13]. Adaptations using a classifier model built on top of the LLM allow for explaining the output using methods like SHAP, serving as a surrogate model. However, traditional SHAP and LIME can face significant limitations with LLMs due to complexity and nonlinearity [10, 11].
- **Counterfactual Explanations:** These show how a different output may be made by modifying the inputs [10, 12].
- **Example-based Explanations:** These involve use of examples, such as prototypes or influential training examples, to support reasoning [10]. Identifying influential examples is also important [11].
- **Natural Language Explanations (Rationalization):** This involves providing justifications for a model's output in natural language [10, 11]. These rationales are human-comprehensible and accessible, especially for nontechnical users [13]. Rationalization can involve extracting relevant parts of the input or generating new text [10]. These can be generated by separate models or by the LLM itself [12]. Rule-based explanations also fit in this category, providing human-readable justifications [7].

3. **Prompting-based Explanation Techniques:** These are tailored for LLMs used in a prompting paradigm [11]. These methods include:
   - **Chain-of-Thought (CoT) Explanations:** Providing intermediate reasoning steps in prompts to guide the model's generation and make the model explain its reasoning [12].
   - **Explaining In-context Learning (ICL):** Understanding how LLMs learn from limited examples provided in the prompt [11].
   - **Representation Engineering:** Explaining models using a top-down approach by analyzing and controlling internal representations of high-level concepts and functions [11].
   - **Uncertainty Quantification:** Developing methods to estimate the reliability of LLM predictions. This can involve consistency-based estimation (generating multiple responses), verbal expressions of confidence (using hedging language or stating confidence levels), or aggregating token-level uncertainty [10, 11].

- **Interpretable Prompting:** Crafting prompts to encourage LLMs to provide reasoning. Techniques include requesting structured representations (diagrams/flowcharts), step-by-step reasoning, incorporating XAI techniques in prompts, or asking for analogies and examples [11, 17].
- **Transparency and Documentation:** Methods and techniques providing information about the model and its training [10], documenting aspects like the training data sources, evaluation results, and limitations, which can help manage stakeholder expectations. Model reporting frameworks can be used, although characterizing the functional behavior of LLMs can be difficult. Transparently communicating evaluation details is also crucial [10].

4. **Tailoring Explanations:** Adapting explanations to the specific needs and technical understanding of different stakeholders (e.g., developers, compliance officers, end-users). Natural language explainers can translate technical outputs like feature attributions into human-understandable formats [10, 12].

Achieving explainability for LLMs often relies on techniques that require access to the model's internal workings. Appropriate explanation methods vary depending on application, audience needs, and desired presentation style (rules, numbers, text, or images) and other criteria discussed before.

Having discussed some general strategies for making LLMs more explainable, we now focus on their application in healthcare, where the notion of explainability is highly critical.

7.5 EXPLAINABLE LLMS USED IN HEALTHCARE

The use of AI in healthcare and medicine experienced some stages, from the early rule-based systems to the modern LLMs, based on transformer architecture, such as GPT-4 [18].

Generally, LLM applications in healthcare and medicine can be categorized as follows (Figure 7.5) [18]:

1. **LLMs for Patients:** includes health education, patient care, virtual medical assistants, and so on [18].
2. **LLMs for Doctors:** includes medical diagnosis, clinical decision support, medical literature analysis, and so on [18].
3. **LLMs for Materials/Research:** includes drug discovery, automated medical report synthesis, radiology and imaging, and so on [18].

We can consider the topic of "LLMs for healthcare" as the intersection of these three categories.

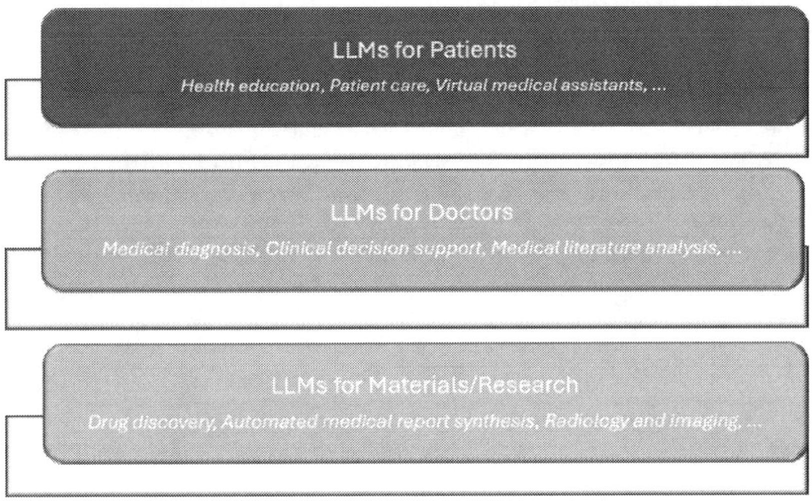

Figure 7.5 LLM applications in healthcare.

It should be noted that, in spite of categorization of application domains, as the domains are relevant, we can use methods from Transfer Learning, especially Domain Adaption, in which the goal is to transfer knowledge from a source domain (where you have labeled data) to a target domain (where you usually have little or no labeled data), despite differences in the data distributions between the two domains, in order to utilize pre-trained models of high performance and precision in new domains [19]. Additionally, despite the apparent differences between some application domains, it seems interesting to try making some successful models applicable for healthcare by means of methods from transfer learning. For example, it is worth investigating the application of some models developed for solving optimization problems in multi-objective, complicated, nonlinear domains such as supply chain management (SCM), where LLMs may fail to provide a satisfactory solution, to optimize some procedures targeting the performance of healthcare delivery to patients [20, 21], or some techniques developed for quick prediction of the next states in dynamic environments [22], in order to take provisional actions, leading to making critical and urgent tasks, such as treatment, more agile .

Let's examine some of the more interesting, challenging use cases in more detail; obviously a detailed treatment of all possible use cases would exceed the scope of this chapter.

Medical Diagnosis: Data analysis, clinical research, and professional guidelines play a critical role in various diagnostic procedures and clinical predictions [18, 23]. Large language models (LLMs) show promise in supporting medical diagnosis by analyzing patient symptoms, medical records, and other relevant data, assisting in the accurate identification of diseases or conditions [24]. LLMs can also contribute to broader healthcare tasks, including clinical decision support, clinical trial recruitment, data management, research facilitation, and patient education [23, 25]. Supporting this perspective, recent studies have introduced methods employing transformer-based models—such as BERT, RoBERTa, and DistilBERT—to predict COVID-19 diagnoses based on textual reports of sudden changes in chemosensory perception [18, 26]. Other research has explored the application of LLMs for diagnosing conditions like Alzheimer's disease [18, 27] and dementia [18, 28]. Additionally, a growing body of literature advocates for the integration of LLM-based chatbots to support similar diagnostic and clinical objectives [18].

Clinical Decision Support: The field of clinical decision support systems (CDSS) has historically evolved from rule-based engines, probabilistic modeling, and expert systems. However, with the recent developments in transformer-based neural architectures, particularly large language models (LLMs), there has been a significant shift toward more contextual, adaptive, and scalable decision-making tools. LLMs, such as GPT-4, Med-PaLM, and DeepSeek, are now being evaluated not just as passive assistants but as active collaborators in diagnostic reasoning, treatment planning, and health system optimization.

LLMs are increasingly becoming valuable tools for assisting healthcare professionals in clinical decision-making. By processing large volumes of medical data, these models can offer evidence-based recommendations that support more accurate diagnoses, informed treatment choices, and improved patient outcomes. The integration of artificial intelligence with clinical expertise presents significant potential to enhance healthcare delivery. Recent studies have highlighted the promise of LLMs in clinical decision support, particularly in specialized fields such as radiology [18, 29], oncology [18, 30], dermatology, and so on.

Here, we mention some recent publications (all from 2025) that explore the multifaceted roles of LLMs in CDSS, highlighting methodological innovations, ethical challenges, and implementation considerations.

7.5.1 Evaluating accuracy in dose computation

In high-risk contexts, such as anesthesiology, the precision of dose calculation is nondebatable. Suppan et al. (2025) benchmarked the performance of three famous LLMs—ChatGPT, Claude, and Med-PaLM—in determining the maximum tolerable doses of local anesthetics. The study's design involved simulated clinical scenarios where the models had to calculate doses based on patient weight, drug type, and concentration. Med-PaLM turned out to be the most reliable model, but significant variability was noted among the responses generated by the other two LLMs. Notably, Claude tended to be more conservative (acted more cautiously), often underestimating dosages, while ChatGPT occasionally exceeded safe ranges, which could be dangerous in clinical practice. The authors discussed rigorous domain fine-tuning and post-hoc model auditing before clinical deployment [31].

This study strongly suggests that LLMs cannot be treated as infallible sources of clinical truth. Instead, their recommendations must be integrated into clinician-led workflows that include redundancy and verification protocols; because any fault may lead to serious irreversible side effects. It seems there is a long way ahead to make use of LLMs in this scenario safely, without the need for expert supervision.

7.5.2 Natural language to evidence-driven recommendations

A main difficulty in evidence-based medicine is the amount of time needed for literature reviews and synthesis. To address this difficulty, Li et al. [32] developed *Quicker*, an LLM-augmented pipeline that translates clinician-posed natural language questions into structured recommendations. The model parses the question, retrieves high-quality studies, incorporates findings, and ranks them by relevance and methodological rigor. Unlike static knowledge bases, Quicker offers dynamic updates, ensuring that decisions are anchored in the latest evidence.

Notably, the study tested the system in real-time emergency care situations, where time-to-decision is of great importance. Physicians reported significant reductions in cognitive load and decision latency, indicating the system's practicality [32]. This work indicates a move toward real-time literature triage as a core functionality of LLM-integrated CDSS.

7.5.3 Information rationalization and trust in LLMs

Trust in AI systems is unpredictable not just in terms of correctness but also interpretability and justification. To address this important issue, Tan et al. [33] investigated how LLMs could be utilized to assess the quality and factual integrity of online health information. Their approach combined classification tasks with rationale generation, in which the model had to explain why a given health paper was classified as trustworthy or not trustworthy.

They found that users—both clinicians and patients—usually show considerably more trust in model outputs when accompanied by transparent justifications. Interestingly, the study also revealed that users retained information longer when presented with rationale-rich outputs. This finding supports a growing literature suggesting that LLMs can serve as cognitive frameworks, not just information providers [33].

7.5.4 Improving health equity through algorithmic standardization

Health inequalities remain a constant challenge across global and national healthcare systems. Jain et al. [34] explored whether LLMs could act as equalizers in care delivery by standardizing clinical decision-making protocols in under-resourced hospitals. Their study highlighted how LLMs reduced diagnostic and treatment variability among less-experienced junior residents, who often lacked specialty support, making high-quality medicine more accessible and also, reducing related risks.

However, the study revealed that LLMs can inherit biases from their training data. Thus, models trained mainly on English-language and Western data might preserve systemic inequalities, making them inappropriate to be used globally [34].

7.5.5 Behavioral health insights from clinical reports

Unstructured clinical notes are a rich but underutilized valuable resource for behavioral health monitoring. Harel-Canada et al. [35] used LLMs to mine these informative notes for indicators of substance use, particularly in patients with overlapping mental health conditions. Their LLM-based system significantly outperformed baseline NLP models in sensitivity and specificity, uncovering latent risk profiles that could prompt early intervention when necessary.

This study demonstrates how LLMs can be deployed in longitudinal patient monitoring, where early flags from free text reports may precede formal diagnosis. However, the authors caution against over-reliance on this method, as false positives may lead to stigmatization or unnecessary surveillance [35].

7.5.6 Phenotypic clustering in critical care

Precision medicine increasingly relies on data-driven phenotyping. Nagori et al. [36] explored this in pediatric sepsis, applying LLMs to cluster patients based on lab values, vitals, and treatment responses. Compared to k-means and hierarchical clustering, the LLM-based approach provided more clinically meaningful subtypes—distinguished by severity, organ dysfunction patterns, and response to treatment.

The study represents a methodological leap by integrating context-aware embeddings with clinical time-series data, bridging the gap between textual and numerical inputs. The authors predict future intensive care unit (ICU) dashboards where LLMs continuously provide patients with dedicated and more effective care pathways [36].

7.5.7 Agentic architectures for autonomous care planning

While most CDSS frameworks rely on reactive querying, Sapkota et al. [37] propose a shift toward agentic LLMs—systems capable of setting subgoals, assigning tasks, and learning from feedback. Their taxonomy differentiates passive "assistive LLMs" from proactive "agentic LLMs" with semi-autonomous reasoning abilities.

Though still experimental, such models could manage multi-step workflows like discharge planning, chronic care management, or multidisciplinary case coordination. The ethical implications of these systems are serious: How do we assign accountability in systems that not only assist but *make important, technical decisions*? [37].

7.5.8 Multilingual LLMs and global health

The healthcare landscape is linguistically diverse, yet most medical AI systems remain English-centric. Zhou et al. [38] evaluated *DeepSeek-R1*, a multilingual LLM fine-tuned for clinical applications such as clinical decision support, patient engagement, and medical education in Mandarin, Spanish, and Arabic. The model demonstrated high semantic retention across languages, even in zero-shot tasks.

This development is critical for global telemedicine platforms, nongovernmental organizations (NGOs), and international humanitarian missions. LLMs like DeepSeek can enable cross-cultural diagnostics and medical decision support, enabling more fair care regardless of language limitations and barriers [38].

7.5.9 LLMs as diagnostic benchmarks

In one of the most rigorous comparisons to date, Xu et al. [39] evaluated LLM performance in predicting immunotherapy response for hepatocellular carcinoma patients. When blinded to ground-truth outcomes, LLMs matched expert oncologists in 78% of cases, with particularly strong performance in cases with structured electronic health record (EHR) input.

The study highlights LLMs' role not just as powerful tools but also as diagnostic benchmarks—entities against which human decision-making can be assessed and calibrated. Such benchmarking could help identify practice variation and support continuing medical education [39].

Together, these studies outline a way toward *LLM-integrated clinical intelligence systems*, combining statistical precision with linguistic refinement. The central theme is not replacement but augmentation—LLMs as intelligent collaborators that expand clinicians' cognitive capacity, not replace their judgment. However, realizing this vision needs careful investigation of legal, ethical, and epistemological aspects.

The following years will probably see the rise of *hybrid intelligence systems*, where human control, LLM reasoning, and real-time data unite to optimize care significantly.

It should be noted that, despite their promise, LLMs remain unregulated in most domains. Teles et al. [40] conducted a comprehensive literature review describing some risks, including hallucinated outputs, adversarial prompt exploitation, privacy breaches, and nondeterminism. They recommend for an AI-specific regulatory framework modeled after pharmacovigilance (drug safety) protocols—requiring rigorous phase-wise testing, side-effect reporting, and explainability audits.

Additionally, the authors advise academic journals and conferences to require model documentation checklists similar to CONSORT (Consolidated Standards of Reporting Trials—an evidence-based, standardized guideline designed to improve the transparency and quality of reporting for randomized controlled trials) for clinical trials, improving transparency and reproducibility in LLM-based medical studies [40].

Medical Literature Analysis: One of the most interesting capabilities of LLMs among many, is their ability to extract valuable, structured information from tons of unstructured clinical texts, such as procedure reports and clinical letters. LLMs do this by extracting some certain entities, including symptoms, diagnoses, and treatments. For example, LLM-AIx pipeline extracts symptoms and laterality of pulmonary embolism from clinical letters [41].

Another application of LLMs in this area is the summarization of medical literature, enabling health professionals to get familiar with the most recent and relevant information efficiently and in a short amount of time, making the process of knowledge discovery much faster. For example [42], highlights the use of LLMs such as GPT-3, T5, and PEGASUS for summarizing medical literature. These models achieve a precision of 65% in named entity recognition (NER) tasks, demonstrating their effectiveness in extracting important entities from summaries. The resulting entity-annotated summaries provide concise representations of medical literature, making information extraction and knowledge discovery much easier [42].

To name another application of LLMs in this area, we can mention literature-based discovery and hypothesis generation (LBD) in which unseen relationships are discovered based on biomedical literature, which is of great importance to treat diseases [43]. For example [43], describes an LLM-based framework that integrates semantic enhancement tools, continuous learning, and domain-specific fine-tuning to analyze vast amounts of text and identify complex patterns. This approach has been validated through empirical studies on the effects of garlic on blood pressure and nutritional supplements on health outcomes, demonstrating its effectiveness in generating testable hypotheses [43].

Drug Discovery: Integrating large language models (LLMs) into drug discovery and design is a promising approach, offering new methodologies and improving existing processes.

LLMs proved their potential in understanding disease mechanisms, facilitate drug design, and optimize clinical trials, making it possible to generate new drug molecules and predict drug-target interactions (DTIs), resulting in more optimized drugs [44, 45]. For example, DrugLLM is an LLM for drug design, capable of generating new molecules with desired properties based on few examples [44].

This activity, which traditionally requires a decade and billions of dollars, benefits greatly from the computational power of LLMs. These techniques not just outperform the traditional techniques, but LLM-powered techniques and related transformer-based methods frequently deliver stronger performance than traditional computational techniques in predicting molecular interactions and assessing aspects of drug efficacy [46].

As models such as BioGPT and ChemGPT are fine-tuned with domain-specific corpora, their outputs are increasingly relevant for early-phase drug development.

LLMs (such as BERT, GPT-3, GPT-4, and so on) use attention mechanisms to process large amounts of text and encode contextual information across long sequences. In drug discovery, these models are further specialized via domain-specific training using corpora like PubMed, DrugBank, and ChEMBL. BioBERT, for instance, has demonstrated strong performance in biomedical named entity recognition (NER) and relation extraction, crucial for identifying chemical-protein interactions [47]. Among all, the BioBERT is of greater importance because the newer models (e.g., PubMedGPT, BioGPT, BioMedLM) often benchmark themselves against it, because it was the first large-scale, domain-specific adaptation of BERT to biomedical text.

Some more advanced variants, such as BioMistral and Med-PaLM, are optimized to understand and generate pharmacological content.

Also, integrations with graph neural networks (GNNs) and vision transformers allow LLMs to process not only text but also chemical graphs and molecular imaging data, improving the richness of drug modeling [48].

In this section, we briefly mention some methodologies and applications of LLMs in drug discovery and related topics pipeline as follow.

7.5.10 Federated learning for privacy-preserving drug design

Federated Learning (FL—a type of machine learning approach where multiple devices or organizations collaboratively train a shared model while keeping their data local—that is, without sharing raw data for the purpose of confidentiality concerns) is as a promising approach in drug design, particularly when combined with LLMs. Traditional supervised learning approaches face challenges when dealing with healthcare data, which is often unstructured and subject to strict regulations. This makes it difficult to access sensitive personal information necessary for effective analysis. FL allows distributed training across edge devices, preserving data privacy by not requiring direct access to sensitive information. This method is useful in healthcare, where data privacy is of great importance. For instance, FL can train models on decentralized datasets, such as electronic health records (EHRs) or clinical trial data, without compromising patient confidentiality. Integrating FL with LLMs enhances the ability to process unstructured healthcare data, making it a powerful tool for predicting adverse drug reactions (ADRs) and other drug-related events [49].

It is worth noting that in addition to FL methods, and in order to provide data to advance research and education, the synthetic data generation (SDG) method, in which data are generated by GenAI (generative AI) models, can provide similar fabricated data to be used in different situations without compromising patient confidentiality [50]. The applications of GenAI models are not limited to just synthetic data generation, and can include various healthcare domains, such as medical imaging, pandemic prediction, clinical administration support, professional education, and patient engagement [51]. GenAI has the potential to revolutionize the healthcare sector by processing extensive data, predicting needs, formulating solutions, and fundamentally altering healthcare delivery [52]. Considering the potentials of LLM and GenAI models, integrating both in a unified framework should be investigated actively as this approach seems very promising.

7.5.11 Model distillation for efficient biomedical knowledge extraction

Model distillation has become a key methodology in LLM-driven drug design, particularly for biomedical knowledge extraction. This trend is driven by the need to reduce computational costs while maintaining high performance. Model distillation has emerged as a key strategy in this regard, allowing researchers to create smaller, task-specific models that retain much of the performance of their larger counterparts [53].

By distilling large models like GPT-3.5 into smaller, task-specific models such as PubMedBERT, researchers have achieved significant improvements in performance. This approach not only reduces computational costs but also enhances model interpretability. For example, a distilled PubMedBERT model outperformed its teacher model, GPT-3.5, by over 6 absolute points in F1 score for adverse drug event (ADE) extraction tasks. The distilled model is over 1,000 times smaller than its teacher model (GPT-3.5), consequently, it is much more agile. Additionally, it surpassed GPT-4 by over 5 absolute points in the same metric. This highlights the efficiency and effectiveness of the distillation process. This methodology has been successfully applied to other biomedical tasks, such as gene-disease association extraction and protected health information identification [53].

7.5.12. Few-shot learning for adverse drug event extraction

Few-shot learning, meaning that the model can perform well on new tasks with only a few examples provided at the time of use [54], has proven to be an effective methodology in LLM-driven drug design, particularly for tasks like ADE extraction. By exploiting in-context examples, models can achieve high performance with minimal labeled data. For instance, a system based on generalized linear models (GLMs), a pre-trained LLM, used a two-step prompting strategy to extract ADEs from text data. The first step involved extracting potential ADEs, while the second step filtered out false positives using a tailored prompt. This approach achieved excellent recall rates, significantly outperforming other participants in the social media mining for health (SMM4H) shared task [55].

7.5.13 Transformer models for ADR classification

Transformer models have become an essential tool for LLM-driven drug design, particularly for tasks like ADR classification. Models such as BERT, DistilBERT, BioBERT, and RoBERTa have been widely used to classify texts into ADR and non-ADR categories. Among these, RoBERTa has shown superior performance, outperforming other models in ADR classification tasks. The success of transformer models in this domain can be attributed to their ability to capture contextual relationships in text data, making them highly effective for identifying adverse events in clinical texts [56].

7.5.14 Drug safety monitoring

The adoption of LLMs in pharmacovigilance (the science and activities relating to the detection, assessment, understanding, and prevention of adverse effects or any other medicine-related problem) has been gaining attention, particularly for tasks like literature screening and ADR prediction. LLMs have shown promising results in automating literature screening, achieving high reproducibility and sensitivity. The ability of LLMs in natural language processing (NLP) has become a key trend in drug design; NLP technologies underpinning LLMs, by providing a comprehensive toolkit for processing unstructured healthcare data, enabling the prediction of ADR outcomes and the extraction of biomedical knowledge. For example, NLP techniques have been used to process unstructured ADR data, enabling LLMs to predict ADR outcomes effectively. This integration has also facilitated the development of automated systems for pharmacovigilance, enhancing the efficiency and accuracy of drug safety monitoring [53].

For instance, models like GPT-3.5 and GPT-4 have been used to categorize medical publications as relevant or irrelevant for safety signal reviews, achieving a reproducibility of 93% and sensitivity of 97%. This trend underscores the transformative potential of LLMs in drug safety monitoring and pharmacovigilance [57].

Despite the numerous advantages of LLMs in drug design, data privacy and security remain significant concerns. The use of sensitive healthcare data in training LLMs raises ethical and legal issues, particularly in the context of data privacy regulations like GDPR. While federated learning offers a privacy-preserving approach to model training, there are still challenges in ensuring the security of distributed datasets. Addressing these concerns is crucial for the widespread adoption of LLMs in drug design [49].

Other important issues are bias and fairness in LLM-driven drug design. LLMs can inherit biases present in the training data, leading to unfair or discriminatory predictions. For example, models trained on datasets with imbalanced representation of certain patient groups may perform poorly on underrepresented groups. Addressing these biases is essential to ensure that LLMs are fair and equitable in their predictions [56].

Finally, the generalizability of LLMs across different datasets and domains remains a challenge. While LLMs have shown impressive performance in specific tasks, their ability to generalize to new datasets and domains is often limited. For example, models trained on one dataset may not perform well on another dataset with different characteristics. This limitation underscores the need for further research into the generalizability of LLMs in drug design [53, 57].

7.6 DRUG REPURPOSING VIA LITERATURE MINING

Drug repurposing refers to the process of identifying new therapeutic uses for existing drugs; it happened to find novel, unforeseen use-cases for some drugs totally different from the main purpose(s) assumed at the time of discovery. This approach proved to be cost-effective and time-efficient in drug discovery.

The integration of transformer models and large language models (LLMs) enable us to predict unforeseen drug-disease associations, drug-target interactions, and the identification of new therapeutic potentials for approved drugs. What follows is an exploration of some of the methodologies, techniques, and successful examples of drug repurposing using LLMs.

Some techniques addressing the problem of drug repurposing are:

7.6.1 Multi-source prompt frameworks

The application of multi-source prompts has been proved to be functional in improving the performance of LLMs in drug repurposing. For example, DrugReAlign uses target summaries and drug-target interaction data as multi-source prompts to enhance the predictive accuracy of LLMs. This framework was rigorously validated using molecular docking and drug-target interaction (DTI) datasets. The results indicate that the framework is both efficient and reliable in predicting potential new uses for existing drugs, showcasing its practical applicability in drug discovery. This approach ensures that the model can utilize diverse data sources to make more accurate predictions supported by evidence [58].

7.6.2 Message-passing transformer networks

Message-passing transformer networks (MPTN) have been proposed to improve the extraction of semantic information from biomedical data. These networks integrate transformer modules into message-passing mechanisms to update entity embeddings and predict new drug-disease associations. The study revealed that MPTN outperformed existing knowledge graph embedding (KGE) learning methods in predicting new therapeutic pathways for drugs. This indicates that the integration of message-passing mechanisms with transformer architecture enhances the model's ability to capture complex relationships in biomedical data [59].

To state a successful instance of drug repurposing using LLMs, we can mention DRTerHGAT, a ternary heterogeneous graph attention network, has demonstrated promising results in identifying drugs for Alzheimer's disease by integrating protein features and graph convolutional networks [60].

LLMs for Patients: Large Language Models may serve patients as well in different scenarios. LLMs have demonstrated the ability to generate high-quality patient educational materials (PEMs) that are both accurate and understandable. Studies have shown that models such as ChatGPT 4.0 and Gemini 1.0 Pro can produce consistent responses on drug information, therapeutic goals, administration, side effects, and interactions. However, they may lack guidance on specific details like expiration dates and medication disposal, highlighting the need for oversight by healthcare professionals [61].

For instance, a cross-sectional study evaluating ChatGPT 4.0 and Gemini 1.0 Pro found that detailed prompts yielded comprehensible outputs for the average adult. ChatGPT 4.0 achieved higher understandability and readability scores compared to Gemini 1.0 Pro, particularly when using detailed prompts [61].

One of the most significant applications of LLMs in patient education is their ability to simplify complex medical information into more readable formats. Online PEMs often exceed the recommended sixth-grade reading level, making them inaccessible to many patients. LLMs such as ChatGPT, Gemini, and Claude have been shown to optimize the readability of these materials without compromising accuracy [62].

A cross-sectional study demonstrated that LLMs significantly improved the readability of PEMs from organizations like the American Heart Association (AHA), American Cancer Society (ACS), and American Stroke Association (ASA). For example, ChatGPT improved readability from a 10.1-grade level to 7.6, while Gemini reduced it to 6.6-grade level [62].

LLMs also can make clinical notes more accessible to patients by simplifying complex medical jargon and providing context. A mixed-methods study using GPT-4 to augment clinical notes found that patients who received augmented notes showed a significant increase in their understanding of follow-up actions and self-reported confidence [63].

Additionally, LLMs can extract information from clinical notes and present it in a more patient-friendly format. For example, the NoteAid EHR Interaction Pipeline uses LLMs to explain EHR content and answer patient questions, demonstrating the potential of LLMs in patient education [64].

In surgical contexts, LLMs have been used to provide patients with clear and accurate information about their conditions and treatments. A study evaluating LLMs like ChatGPT and Google Bard for patient education on lumbar disc herniation found that the models provided satisfactory responses; exactly stated, out of the responses, 27.2% were excellent, 43.9% satisfactory with minimal clarification, 18.3% satisfactory with moderate clarification, and 10.6% unsatisfactory. But it is highlighted that human oversight and continuous improvements are necessary; there is still a significant portion that may require improvement and the occasional inaccuracies noted in the responses show the importance of rigorous oversight, especially with the introduction of regulations like the new EU AI Act [65].

Another study focusing on bariatric surgery found that LLMs like GPT-4 could simplify responses to FAQs, achieving readability levels as low as the sixth grade. This highlights the potential of LLMs to make complex surgical information more accessible to patients [66].

LLMs can also generate tailored educational content for disadvantaged populations, including those with limited health literacy or language barriers. A study evaluating GPT-3.5 Turbo, GPT-4, and GPT-4 Turbo found that these models could produce high-quality, tailored content for cancer survivors and their caregivers, with translations into Spanish and Chinese achieving high accuracy rates (88.9% for Spanish and 81.1% for Chinese) [67].

This application is particularly important for addressing health inequities, as it ensures that patients from diverse backgrounds can access understandable and relevant health information.

LLMs can also facilitate clinical communication by generating responses to patient questions and concerns. A study evaluating the performance of fine-tuned LLMs for generating responses to patient messages found that models like CLAIR-Long provided increased patient educational content and received positive evaluations for responsiveness, empathy, and accuracy [68].

Additionally, LLMs have been used to enhance doctor-patient communication in specific clinical contexts, such as prostate cancer management. A study comparing LLMs like ChatGPT 3.5, Gemini, and Co-Pilot to the official Romanian Patient's Guide found that LLMs provided more accurate and user-friendly information, highlighting their potential to enhance shared decision-making [69].

Beyond patient education, LLMs have been integrated into medical education to enhance clinical reasoning and training. For example, a virtual patient platform combining social robots with LLMs was tested in a pilot study with medical students, who preferred the platform for its authenticity and learning effectiveness [70]. This application demonstrates the versatility of LLMs in both patient and medical education, offering interactive and realistic simulations for training purposes.

Some challenges regarding the application of LLMs for patients are accuracy and reliability, the need for human oversight, and some ethical and regulatory considerations.

As LLMs continue to make progress, their application in patient education will enhance health literacy, improve patient outcomes, and reduce disparities in healthcare access. However, it seems the effective usage requires some knowledge on prompt engineering, which cannot be expected from a nonexpert patient needing help and guidance in a short amount of time. The models developed for this purpose should thus target these people, their demands, and situations.

There is also another important issue to be addressed: many people tend to use LLMs for almost any kind of question these days, especially those regarding healthcare and medications; as the accuracy of any AI model is limited and may be affected by multiple factors, extra attention should be paid to the correctness of the answers (outputs) because any inappropriate answer may lead to serious consequences, affecting lives. Maybe it would be better to make some limitations on the questions that can be asked from these systems, or the answers by these systems should be controlled seriously.

Finally, as stated several times before, due to the sensitivity of AI models to input data leading to biases or even worth fraudulent activities, it is highly important to utilize some techniques for fraud detection in order to maintain the trustworthiness of these systems, including LLMs. Some researchers proposed such techniques to overcome this issue; for example, health insurance bidirectional encoder representations from transformers

(HI-BERT), which is based on BERT with some adjustments made to vocabulary, is proposed to get more accurate results compared to the basic BERT with security in mind [71].

7.7 CONCLUSIONS

The inherent complexity of LLMs—these incredibly powerful, universal AI models—probably prevents us from achieving full transparency (at least at the near future). Despite various ongoing efforts, their understandability and trustworthiness require further improvements. Achieving explainability requires insight into the model's internal processes and a tailored approach that considers the application's context, stakeholder requirements, and desired output. In spite of numerous challenges, the critical need for trustworthy AI, especially in life-critical fields such as healthcare, highlights XAI's crucial role in clarifying the strengths and weaknesses of these amazing models. As their application in healthcare seems promising, until reaching a nearly full explainability for these models, any application in such critical domains must be supervised and controlled by human experts to mitigate the accompanied risks.

REFERENCES

1. Vaswani, A., et al., Attention Is All You Need. *arXiv*, 2023.
2. Matarazzo, A. and R. Torlone, A Survey on Large Language Models with some Insights on their Capabilities and Limitations. *arXiv*, 2025.
3. Gunning, D. and D.W. Aha, DARPA's Explainable Artificial Intelligence Program. *AI MAGAZINE - Association for the Advancement of Artificial Intelligence*, 2019, 40(2), 44.
4. Linardatos, P., V. Papastefanopoulos, and S. Kotsiantis, Explainable AI: A Review of Machine Learning Interpretability Methods. *Entropy*, 2020.,23(1), 18
5. Martins, T., et al., Explainable Artificial Intelligence (XAI): A Systematic Literature Review on Taxonomies and Applications in Finance. *IEEE Access*, 2024, 12, 618-629.
6. Samek, W., et al., Explaining Deep Neural Networks and Beyond: A Review of Methods and Applications. *Proceedings of the IEEE*, 2021, 109,247-278.
7. Vilone, G. and L. Longo, Classification of Explainable Artificial Intelligence Methods through Their Output Formats. *Machine Learning & Knowledge Extraction*, 2021, 3, 615-661.
8. Poch´e, A., L. Hervier, and M.-C. Bakkay, Natural Example-Based Explainability: a Survey. *arXiv*, 2023.
9. Keane, M.T. and E.M. Kenny, How Case-Based Reasoning Explains Neural Networks: A Theoretical Analysis of XAI Using Post-Hoc Explanationby-Example from a Survey of ANN-CBR Twin-Systems. *arXiv*, 2019.

10. Vaughan, Q.V.L.a.J.W., AI Transparency in the Age of LLMs: A HumanCentered Research Roadmap. *Harvard Data Science Review*, 2024.
11. Zhao, H., et al., Explainability for Large Language Models: A Survey. *arXiv*, 2023.
12. Agarwal, C., S.H. Tanneru, and H. Tanneru, Faithfulness vs. Plausibility: On the (Un)Reliability of Explanations from Large Language Models. *arXiv*, 2024.
13. Gurrapu, S., et al., Rationalization for Explainable NLP: A Survey. *arXiv*, 2023.
14. Salih, A.M., et al., A Perspective on Explainable Artificial Intelligence Methods: SHAP and LIME. *arXiv*, 2024.
15. González-Arencibia, M., et al., Explainable Artificial Intelligence as an Ethical Principle. *Ingeniería*, 2024, 29.
16. Yin, K. and G. Neubig, Interpreting Language Models with Contrastive Explanations, in *Proceedings ofthe 2022 Conference on Empirical Methods in Natural Language Processing*, 2022, p. 184–198.
17. Sonsoles López-Pernas, Y.S., Eduardo Oliveira, Mohammed Saqr, LLMs for Explainable Artificial Intelligence: Automating Natural Language Explanations of Predictive Analytics Models, in *Advanced Learning Analytics Methods: AI, Precision and Complexity*, 2025, Springer. https://lamethods.org/book2/chapters/ch11-llmsxai/ch11-llmsxai.html.
18. Al Nazi, Z. and W. Peng, Large Language Models in Healthcare and Medical Domain: A Review. *arXiv*, 2024.
19. Safarpour Motealegh Mahalegi, H., et al., Generative Adversarial Networks for Heterogeneous Unsupervised Domain Adaptation Detection, in *IEEE 28th International Conference on Intelligent Engineering Systems (INES)*, 2024, IEEE. p. 235–244.
20. Farhadi, A., et al., Leveraging Blockchain and ANFIS for Optimal Supply Chain Management. *arXiv*, 2024.
21. Zeng, Y., et al., Integrating type-2 fuzzy logic controllers with digital twin and neural networks for advanced hydropower system management. *Scientific Reports*, 2025, 15(1),5140.
22. Jahanmanesh, P., A. Farhadi, and A. Zamanifar, Mobility management with AI. *IEEE Access*, 2025, 13: p. 83022–83060.
23. Chen, Z., M.M. Balan, and K. Brown, Language Models Are Few-shot Learners for Prognostic Prediction. *arXiv*, 2023.
24. Chen, X., et al., Enhancing diagnostic capability with multi-agents conversational large language models. *npj Digital Medicine*, 2025, 8(159).
25. Vivian Weiwen Xue, P.L.a.W.C.C., The potential impact ofChatGPT in clinical and translational medicine. *Clinical and Translational Medicine*, 2023, 13(3), 1206.
26. Li, H., et al., Text-based predictions of COVID-19 diagnosis from self-reported chemosensory descriptions. *Communications Medicine*, 2023, 3(1), 104.
27. Ban, Y., et al., Diagnosis ofAlzheimer's disease using hypergraph p-Laplacian regularized multi-task feature learning. *Journal of Biomedical Informatics*, 2023, 140, pp.104326-104326.

28. Agbavor, F. and H. Liang, Predicting dementia from spontaneous speech using large language models. *PLOS Digital Health*, 2022, 1(12), e0000168.
29. Wang, S., et al., Interactive computer-aided diagnosis on medical image using large language models. *arXiv*, 2023.
30. Sorin, V., et al., Large language models for oncological applications. *Journal of Cancer Research and Clinical Oncology*, 2023: , 149(11)p. 1–4.
31. Suppan, M., et al., Performance of 3 conversational AI models for computing maximum safe doses of local anesthetics. *JMIR AI*, 2025, 4, e66796.
32. Li, D., et al., From Questions to Clinical Recommendations: Large Language Models Driving Evidence-Based Clinical Decision Making. *arXiv*, 2025.
33. Tan, D., et al., Identification of Online Health Information Using Large Pretrained Language Models: Mixed Methods Study. *Journal of Medical Internet Research*, 2025, 27 pe70733, .
34. Jain, B., R. Doshi, and S. Nundy, Leveraging Artificial Intelligence to Advance Health Equity in America's Safety Net. *The Journal of General Internal Medicine*, 2025, 1-4.
35. Harel-Canada, F., A. Salimian, and B. Moghanian, Enhancing Substance Use Detection in Clinical Notes with Large Language Models. *Research Square*, 2025, rs3.
36. Nagori, A., et al., Contextual Phenotyping of Pediatric Sepsis Cohort Using Large Language Models. *arXiv*, 2025.
37. Sapkota, R., K.I. Roumeliotis, and M. Karkee, AI Agents vs. Agentic AI: A Conceptual Taxonomy, Applications and Challenges. *arXiv*, 2025.
38. Zhou, J., et al., Large Language Models for Transforming Healthcare: A Perspective on DeepSeek-R1. *MedComm – Future Medicine*, 2025., 4(2), e70021.
39. Xu, J., et al., Predicting Immunotherapy Response in Unresectable Hepatocellular Carcinoma: A Comparative Study of Large Language Models and Human Experts. *Journal of Medical Systems*, 2025, 49, 64.
40. Teles, A., et al., Large Language Models for Medical Applications. *Frontiers in Medicine*, 2025, 12, 1625293.
41. Wiest, I.C., et al., LLM-AIx: An open source pipeline for Information Extraction from unstructured medical text based on privacy preserving Large Language Models. *medRxiv*, 2024.
42. Sasikala, D., R. Sudarshan, and S. Sivasathya, Harnessing LLMs for Medical Insights:NER Extraction from Summarized Medical Text. In *2024 15th International Conference on Computing Communication and Networking Technologies (ICCCNT)*, 2024.
43. Taleb, I., A.N. Navaz, and M.A. Serhani, Leveraging Large Language Models for Enhancing Literature-Based Discovery. *Big Data and Cognitive Computing*, 2024, 81: p. 14.
44. Liu, X., et al., DrugLLM: Open Large Language Model for Few-shot Molecule Generation. *arXiv*, 2024.
45. Bhattacharya, D., et al., Large Language Models as Molecular Design Engines. *ChemRxiv*, 2024.
46. Kalakoti, Y., S. Yadav, and D. Sundar, TransDTI: Transformer-Based Language Models for Estimating DTIs and Building a Drug Recommendation Workflow. *ACS Omega*, 2022, 7, 2706-2717.

47. Lee, J., et al., BioBERT: a pre-trained biomedical language representation model for biomedical text mining. *Bioinformatics*, 2020, 36(4), 1234-1240.
48. Yadalam, P.K., et al., Analyzing and exploring Graph Attention Networks and protein-based language models for predicting Porhyromonas gingivalis resistant efflux protein sequences. *Dental and Medical Problems*, 2025, 62(2), 265-273.
49. Guo, D. and K.-K.R. Choo, Applications of Federated Large Language Model for Adverse Drug Reactions Prediction: A Scoping Review. *Journal of Medical Internet Research*, 2024, 12.
50. Farhadi, A. and A. Taheri, Application of GenAI in Synthetic Data Generation in the Healthcare System, in *Application of Generative AI in Healthcare Systems*, 2025, Springer Nature. p. 67–89.
51. Rashidieranjbar, F., A. Farhadi, and A. Zamanifar, Revolutionizing Healthcare with Generative Artificial Intelligence Technologies, in *Generative Artificial Intelligence (AI) Approaches for Industrial Applications*, 2025, Springer Nature Switzerland. p. 189–221.
52. Safarpour Motealegh Mahalegi, H., et al., Application of Generative AI in Resource Optimization in Healthcare Systems, in *Application of Generative AI in Healthcare Systems*, 2025, Springer Nature. p. 175–195.
53. Gu, Y., et al., Distilling Large Language Models for Biomedical Knowledge Extraction: A Case Study on Adverse Drug Events. *arXiv*, 2023.
54. Brown, T.B., Mann, B., Ryder, N., Subbiah, M., Kaplan, J., Dhariwal, P., Neelakantan, A., Shyam, P., Sastry, G., Askell, A., Agarwal, S., Herbert-Voss, A., Krueger, G., Henighan, T., Child, R., Ramesh, A., Ziegler, D. M., Wu, J., Winter, Language Models are Few-Shot Learners, in *34th Conference on Neural Information Processing Systems (NeurIPS 2020)*, 2020: Vancouver, Canada. p. 1877–1901.
55. Ke, Y., et al., Extraction and Normalization of Adverse Drug Events with a Large Language Model, in *Proceedings of the 9th Social Media Mining for Health Applications*, 2024. p. 48–54.
56. Keerthana, P.P., et al., The Detection of Adverse Drug Reactions in Clinical Text Data Using Transformer Models, in *2023 Fourth International Conference on Smart Technologies in Computing, Electrical and Electronics (ICSTCEE)*, 2023: Bengaluru, India.
57. Li, D., et al., Assessing the performance of large language models in literature screening for pharmacovigilance: a comparative study. *Frontiers in Drug Safety and Regulation*, 2024, 4: p. 1379260.
58. Wei, J., et al., DrugReAlign: a multisource prompt framework for drug repurposing based on large language models. *BMC Biology*, 2024, 22(1), 226.
59. Liu, Y., et al., MPTN: A message-passing transformer network for drug repurposing from knowledge graph. *Computers in Biology and Medicine*, 2024, 168, 107800
60. He, H., et al., DRTerHGAT: A drug repurposing method based on the ternary heterogeneous graph attention network. *Journal of Molecular Graphics and Modelling*, 2024, 130, 108783.
61. Sridharan, K. and G. Sivaramakrishnan, Investigating the capabilities of advanced large language models in generating patient instructions and patient educational material. *European Journal of Hospital Pharmacy*, 2024.

62. Will, J., et al., Leveraging Large Language Models to Improve Readability of Online Patient Education Materials: Cross-sectional Study. *Journal of Medical Internet Research*, 2024, 36(9), 1115-1122.
63. Mannhardt, N., et al., Impact of Large Language Model Assistance on Patients Reading Clinical Notes: A Mixed-Methods Study. *arXiv*, 2024.
64. Zhang, X., Z. Yao, and H. Yu, EHR Interaction Between Patients and AI Note Aid EHR Interaction. *arXiv preprint arXiv:2312.17475*, 2023.
65. Lang, S., et al., Are large language models valid tools for patient information on lumbar disc herniation? The spine surgeons' perspective. *Brain and Spine*, 2024, 4.
66. Srinivasan, N., et al., Large language models and bariatric surgery patient education: a comparative readability analysis of GPT-3.5, GPT-4, Bard, and online institutional resources. *Surgical Endoscopy*, 2024: 11, p. 2522–2532.
67. Liu, D., et al., Evaluation of Large Language Models in Tailoring Educational Content for Cancer Survivors and Their Caregivers: Quality Analysis. *JMIR Cancer*, 2025, 11, e67914.
68. Liu, S., et al., Leveraging Large Language Models for Generating Responses to Patient Messages. *medRxiv*, 2023.
69. Geantă, M., et al., The Potential Impact of Large Language Models on Doctor–Patient Communication: A Case Study in Prostate Cancer. *Healthcare*, 2024, 12(15), 1548.
70. Borg, A., I. Parodis, and G. Skantze, Creating Virtual Patients using Robots and Large Language Models: A Preliminary Study with Medical Students, in *HRI '24: Companion of the 2024 ACM/IEEE International Conference on Human-Robot Interaction*, 2024. p. 273–277.
71. Najafi Lataran, P., et al., Developing a BERT-Enhanced Blockchain Model for HealthInsurance Fraud Detection. *Journal of Information Systems Research and Practice*, 2024, 2(3): p. 56–61.

Chapter 8

Ethical implications for LLMs

Mohammad Saleh and Azadeh Tabatabaei

8.1 INTRODUCTION

Large language models, such as GPT-4o [1], Gemini 2.5 [2], Qwen2.5VL [3], and Google's MedLM [4], are artificial intelligence tools trained on vast text datasets to generate human-like responses. In medicine and healthcare, LLMs support tasks like medical transcription, answering patient queries, diagnostic support, and clinical decision-making [5, 6]. Their ability to process unstructured data makes them valuable for improving efficiency and access to care. LLMs in public health offer opportunities for health campaigns, outbreak monitoring, and enhancing health literacy, particularly in resource-poor countries where access to health information is limited. LLMs can provide affordable health information, which may help address gaps in mental health treatment. However, there are significant concerns. LLMs can be misused to disseminate *misinformation* on a large scale, potentially leading to AI-driven infodemics that overwhelm and mislead the public. This could also result in a flood of low-quality content in scientific literature. Additionally, the commercial nature of LLMs raises issues regarding the concentration of power, lack of transparency, and accessibility for marginalized communities. The high costs of development and the use of biased training data—primarily sourced from wealthy, English-speaking regions—can further exacerbate health disparities.

LLMs and their variants, such as multi-modal large language models (MM-LLMs) and large vision language models (LVLMs), have seen significant progress recently [7]. They can generate entirely fabricated yet remarkably authentic health articles [8]. Addressing misinformation created by LLMs can be more challenging than combating infodemics caused by human-written content [9] for several reasons. First, unsuspecting users who may lack a deep understanding of clinical contexts and medical research often find it difficult to differentiate between LLM-generated false health content and genuine medical information. If they depend on LLMs for health advice, it can lead to misunderstandings and potentially harmful outcomes. Second, malicious actors can manipulate LLMs to create plausibly accurate yet incorrect medical content, promoting alternative

DOI: 10.1201/9781003665083-8

healthcare treatments or debunked theories for profit-making. This threatens the credibility of legitimate health information and poses significant risks to public health [10].

8.2 ETHICAL PRINCIPLES IN HEALTHCARE

AI *ethics* refer to the moral principles and practical guidelines that ensure the responsible development and use of artificial intelligence. It prioritizes human values, safety, security, and environmental sustainability, thereby aligning AI systems with societal benefits. As shown in Figure 8.1, understanding core ethical principles in healthcare—*beneficence*, *non-maleficence*, *autonomy*, and *justice* [11]—is crucial before examining the key ethical challenges of LLMs in this domain. These principles guide healthcare professionals to prioritize patient well-being and uphold high standards of care.

Beneficence. The ethical obligation to act for the benefit of others is a core ethical principle in healthcare, mandating that healthcare providers act in the patient's best interest. LLMs can enhance outcomes by providing accurate, evidence-based insights that support clinical decisions. A critical aspect of this principle is ensuring that these systems are designed to prioritize patient welfare through rigorous validation and clinical trials. As we integrate LLMs into decision-making processes, it is essential to endorse this core ethical commitment, ensuring that these technologies assist rather than hinder clinician judgment and patient health. Based on the beneficence

Beneficence	**Nonmaleficence**
LLMs rapidly produce discharge summaries from progress notes, nursing notes, lab data, and examination reports, freeing up clinician time.	Do not rely on it for critical consent or high-risk procedures. Prioritize documentation and verification to protect clinicians from litigation.
Justice	**Autonomy**
Reducing the strain on clinicians' time allows more patients to access care, although manual summary editing can be time-consuming.	Ensure patient awareness of the utilization of LLMs and secure documented consent for the sharing of potentially sensitive conversational data.

Figure 8.1 Key ethical principles in healthcare.

principle, LLMs boost patient outcomes via streamlined admin [12], better clinical decisions, and improved treatment advice, enhancing care [13].

Non-maleficence. The ethical principle requiring professionals to avoid causing harm—physical, psychological, or social—to patients. It demands a cautious approach to treatment and intervention, emphasizing careful consideration of potential risks and benefits. Careful selection of training datasets is essential for responsible data handling, balancing LLM potential with patient privacy and ethical standards [4].

Autonomy. It involves recognizing and supporting individuals' rights to make informed decisions about their healthcare [14]. Table 8.1 outlines autonomy challenges and their solutions. Healthcare professionals must obtain informed consent before any treatment or intervention, providing patients with comprehensive information regarding risks, benefits, and alternatives to empower informed decisions [15]. When LLMs offer insights and recommendations, patients must be made aware of how these systems operate and the data they utilize. Lack of informed consent can undermine autonomy and trust. Ethical guidelines stress the importance of transparent communication about LLM involvement. Transparency in communication fosters informed consent, allowing patients to understand the role of AI in their care [16].

Justice. This principle ensures equitable access to resources, addressing disparities through fair allocation and policies, such as free prescriptions for low-income individuals, thus striving for an effective and equitable system that meets diverse needs [20]. Furthermore, the principle of justice mandates fairness in the distribution of benefits and burdens in healthcare. The potential for bias in AI algorithms poses a significant risk to equitable healthcare delivery. For instance, if the training data reflect systemic inequalities, the resulting agentic systems may perpetuate these biases, thus disproportionately affecting vulnerable populations. To combat this, developers must strive to create diverse and representative training datasets while employing robust validation methodologies to mitigate bias. LLMs have the potential to address disparities in healthcare access, especially in low-resource settings [21], by enhancing the capabilities of healthcare

Table 8.1 Autonomy challenges and solutions

Challenge	*Description*	*Solution*	*Study*
Opaque AI	Patients unaware of AI's role in care.	Disclose AI use and obtain consent.	[17]
Data Control	Patients lack authority over data use.	Implement patient-controlled data frameworks.	[18]
Over-Reliance	Clinicians defer to AI, reducing patient input.	Negotiate clinicians to prioritize patient preferences.	[19]

providers and improving patient education. However, deploying LLMs in healthcare presents key ethical and practical challenges that require resolution to ensure equitable and just outcomes.

Comparative Ethics Frameworks in AI Ethics. Beyond clinical principles such as beneficence and autonomy, the ethical evaluation of LLMs in healthcare benefits from broader philosophical perspectives, particularly utilitarianism and deontology [22]. A utilitarian approach evaluates AI systems based on outcomes, aiming to maximize the overall well-being. From this perspective, deploying LLMs is ethically justifiable if they improve diagnostic accuracy, reduce costs, or expand access to care, regardless of how these benefits are distributed [23]. In contrast, deontological ethics emphasizes duties and rights, suggesting that the use of LLMs must respect patient autonomy, informed consent, and dignity regardless of outcomes [24]. For instance, even if AI recommendations optimize treatment at scale, deontological reasoning would question their use if patients are unaware of AI involvement or lack meaningful choice. These frameworks can lead to different ethical conclusions, underscoring the importance of integrating both consequentialist outcomes and rights-based safeguards in designing and regulating LLM-driven healthcare systems [20].

8.3 KEY ETHICAL CHALLENGES

The ethical landscape of LLMs in healthcare is multifaceted, encompassing issues of *fairness*, *transparency*, *privacy*, and *accountability*. Research highlights concerns such as LLMs reproducing biases from training data, which can lead to unequal treatment of marginalized groups, and generating "*hallucinations*"—plausible but incorrect outputs [25].

Privacy, Data Security, and Information Ethics. LLMs require extensive amounts of patient data, which raises critical ethical questions, especially regarding sensitive information like genetic or mental health data. Safeguarding this sensitive patient information is essential for the ethical use of LLMs in healthcare. To function effectively, LLMs often need access to large datasets, including electronic health records (EHRs) that contain personally identifiable information (PHI). In the United States, the Health Insurance Portability and *Accountability* Act (HIPAA) and, in Europe, the General Data Protection Regulation (GDPR) mandate strict protections for PHI, requiring secure handling of this data [26]. Risks include data breaches, the re-identification of anonymized data, and unauthorized use of patient information. For example, research highlights that even de-identified data can be re-identified with minimal spatiotemporal data points, necessitating advanced cybersecurity measures such as differential privacy and air-gapped systems for high-risk data.

Protecting patient data requires a careful balance of these competing interests, which calls for robust security measures and may necessitate limiting the scope of data used for training LLMs. This includes managing trade-offs between model performance and patient data privacy [27]. In 2025, the European Union ruled against an LLM that was trained on psychotherapy transcripts obtained without consent, citing violations of information ethics. This ruling underscores the concerns surrounding AI in healthcare, particularly ethical considerations related to data privacy, trust, and accountability. This emphasizes the importance of obtaining informed consent and adhering to ethical and legal standards when developing and deploying LLMs, especially those that handle sensitive patient data. This aligns with broader trends focusing on responsible AI development, aimed at building user trust.

Information ethics addresses the moral principles surrounding data collection, storage, use, and dissemination of data. In healthcare, where patient data are highly sensitive, AI introduces challenges such as privacy breaches, biased outputs, and opaque decision-making. Ethical frameworks, including autonomy, beneficence, non-maleficence, and justice, guide the responsible integration of LLMs into the healthcare system. Figure 8.2 illustrates the responsible AI Framework's emphasis on critical ethical concerns, such as transparency and fairness.

Information ethics in healthcare [20] are essential for balancing societal benefits, patient rights, and data utility. It involves the moral assessment of information-related activities and their effects on human values. The integration of information technology in healthcare has the potential to improve patient care and societal well-being; however, it also raises ethical concerns regarding patient rights and the use of data. Information ethics examines how to maximize data utility, such as in health research, while

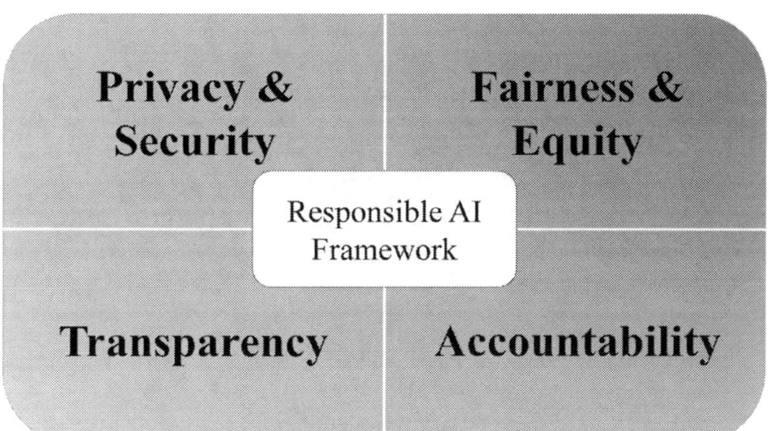

Figure 8.2 Responsible AI framework

protecting patient rights and ensuring responsible data management. It is important to note that in today's digital health ecosystems, patients often lack awareness and control over the collection, use, and sharing of their protected health information (PHI). This process involves various regulations and providers of healthcare services. Patients may utilize electronic services without fully understanding the privacy features, levels of trust, or ethical implications [28]. Figure 8.3 illustrates an ideal information ethics framework that balances societal benefits, data utility, and patient rights.

Bias, Fairness, and Health Equity. Training data that reflects historical inequities can perpetuate disparities, such as the underdiagnosis of diseases in marginalized groups. One potential solution is diversifying training datasets and implementing fairness-aware algorithms [29]. Electronic Health Records (EHRs), a main source of data, may contain systemic biases, including the underdiagnosis of conditions in minority groups, which LLMs can further amplify. Studies reveal that LLMs such as GPT-4 [30] displayed racial bias and gender biases, which could lead to unequal treatment [31, 32]. Such biases worsen health disparities, particularly for marginalized communities. Mitigating bias requires diverse, representative training data and continuous fairness monitoring.

LLM biases conflict with healthcare ethics principles like non-maleficence, and justice [13]. LLMs risk widening digital divides if access is limited to well-funded institutions or high-income regions. Research notes that training data often originates from English-speaking, high-income countries, underrepresenting global perspectives [33]. Ensuring affordability and accessibility is vital for equitable healthcare delivery.

In healthcare systems, it is desirable to consider implementing bias auditing by conducting pre- and post-deployment assessments using fairness metrics, such as demographic parity [34] and equal accuracy across diverse

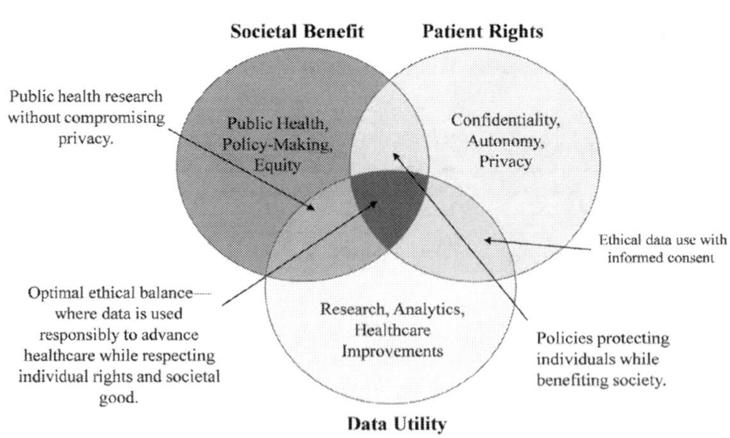

Figure 8.3 Information ethics framework.

populations. It is also essential to ensure that our training data accurately represents diverse demographics and clinical scenarios; resampling or adversarial de-biasing can mitigate bias [35]. Furthermore, involving patients, ethicists, and marginalized communities in development can help identify oversights.

Recent advancements also explore technical strategies to unveil latent biases in medical AI systems. For example, researchers propose a counterfactual analysis framework utilizing conditional latent diffusion models to identify hidden biases in medical imaging tasks [99]. This method facilitates robust hypothesis testing across patient subgroups and conditions, providing a scalable approach to ensure fairness in high-stakes diagnostic models. Integrating such tools into LLM development pipelines could enhance fairness-aware AI governance and uphold ethical imperatives such as justice and non-maleficence.

Transparency and Explainability. System transparency and *explainability* are related concepts [36]. Transparency reveals how an AI system works, while explainability clarifies the reasoning behind its decisions. Transparency provides the foundation for understanding the specific insights offered by explainability. It ensures AI decisions are understandable, fostering trust. *Explainable AI (XAI)* techniques, such as saliency maps, clarify how AI systems process data, but complex models like deep neural networks resist simple explanations. LLMs are often described as "black boxes" due to their complex architectures, undermining clinician trust and patient understanding. This opacity is problematic in healthcare, where explainability is critical for trust and accountability. Research emphasizes the need for interpretable AI to allow clinicians to verify LLM outputs [15]. Techniques like retrieval-augmented generation are proposed to enhance transparency. Explainability techniques, though valuable, are often impractical for real-time applications due to computational constraints [37].

Accuracy and Reliability. LLMs demonstrate promising accuracy in clinical contexts, with studies showing their responses can rival those of specialist endodontists [38]. This suggests potential utility as a low-cost decision-support tool for clinicians. However, their probabilistic nature introduces critical risks:

1. **Hallucinations and Inconsistencies**
   LLMs may generate plausible but factually incorrect information ("hallucinations") [39, 40], such as recommending discontinued drugs or underestimating risks for specific demographics. Repeated queries on the same topic often yield inconsistent answers, undermining reliability [10, 41].
2. **Unsubstantiated Claims**
   Even when citing sources, LLMs frequently provide contradictory or unsupported information. State-of-the-art models produce ~30%

unsubstantiated statements, with nearly half of the responses lacking full credibility [42].

3. **Jailbreaking Vulnerabilities**
   Bypassing safety protocols ("*jailbreaking*") can expose protected health information (PHI) or enable fraudulent medical advice [43]. For example, adversarial prompts have tricked clinical LLMs into revealing anonymized records, risking insurance fraud or phishing attacks [44].

Mitigation Strategies

- *Data Curation*: Exclude low-quality or biased sources from training datasets.
- *Model Retraining*: Teach LLMs to recognize and block jailbreaking prompts by linking them to prohibited outcomes.
- *Red-teaming*: Mandate adversarial testing ("red team" audits) for healthcare LLMs to preempt exploits.

Without these safeguards, inaccuracies or breaches could erode trust in AI tools, leaving developers, institutions, and regulators vulnerable to liability.

LLM-Driven Care. Patient autonomy—the right to make informed, voluntary decisions about one's care—is a cornerstone of medical ethics. However, the integration of LLMs into healthcare introduces complex challenges. While LLMs can enhance clinical decision-making, their recommendations may unintentionally compromise autonomy if individuals are unaware of their AI-driven origins [45]. Studies emphasize the need for explicit informed consent, requiring clinicians to disclose the use of LLMs and offer alternatives—especially during early implementation phases [25].

Data Privacy, Ownership, and Autonomy. In this context, the incorporation of LLMs raises significant questions about data governance. Processing sensitive patient information carries the risk of privacy breaches, which can erode trust and compromise autonomy. *Regulatory* frameworks, such as the General Data Protection Regulation (GDPR), affirm patients' rights to access, correct, or delete their data, yet ambiguities surrounding consent protocols remain [46]. For instance, in mental healthcare, clinicians have expressed concerns about LLMs accessing deeply personal information, which could disproportionately affect therapeutic relationships. Initiatives like the Collaborative Healthcare Data Ownership (CHDO) framework advocate for shared governance—where patients retain control over their data while researchers access anonymized datasets [47]. This model helps reconcile the competing interests of patients, providers, and developers. Beyond compliance, proactive education for patients regarding their data rights and implementing robust security measures are crucial for safeguarding autonomy [16].

Ethical data usage also extends to the training practices of LLMs. Utilizing unlicensed or copyrighted data poses legal risks and undermines transparency. Solutions such as watermarking outputs and employing blockchain-based tracking for provenance aim to address intellectual property concerns while ensuring accountability [26].

Human-centered Limitations: Dialogue and Empathy. A significant risk associated with LLMs is their potential to diminish clinician-patient dialogue. Studies indicate that patients presented with LLM-generated treatment plans are less likely to question these recommendations, which can indicate reduced agency [48]. However, when designed to augment—rather than replace—clinicians, LLMs have been found to enhance shared decision-making in fields such as oncology, highlighting the importance of human-AI collaboration.

Moreover, LLMs inherently lack empathy, which is a crucial aspect of patient care. Unlike clinicians, they cannot interpret emotional cues or provide compassionate support, risking a decline in trust within sensitive specialties like psychiatry or pediatrics. This limitation underscores the need for clear boundaries: LLMs should be utilized as tools to enhance the human elements of care, not replicate them.

Achieving a balance between autonomy and LLM-driven care requires transparency, stringent data governance, and human oversight. By prioritizing patient education, equitable data frameworks, and empathetic clinician engagement, healthcare systems can leverage the potential of AI while maintaining ethical standards [49–51].

Accountability and Responsibility in LLMs for Healthcare. Accountability and responsibility are crucial for the ethical use of large language models (LLMs) in healthcare, especially given their potential to produce incorrect, biased, or harmful outputs. Accountability is defined as the obligation of an individual or organization (such as a developer, clinician, or institution) to provide justification for their actions to a relevant audience (like regulatory bodies or patients) based on ethical and legal standards. In contrast, responsibility refers to the moral duty to act ethically, which is guided by an individual's internal judgment instead of external oversight. While accountability focuses on external justifications, responsibility is grounded in an internal moral compass. Both elements are essential for ensuring that AI systems are trustworthy. Table 8.2 outlines key accountability issues and provides solutions for addressing them.

Challenges in Assigning Accountability and Responsibility. The unclear decision-making processes of LLMs hinder accountability. Clinicians, ultimately responsible for patient care, often lack insight into an LLM's internal workings. Simultaneously, developers cannot completely predict how their models will function in actual clinical environments. This uncertainty leads to a "many hands" issue, where accountability is spread among various stakeholders—developers, clinicians, healthcare organizations, and

Table 8.2 Accountability of LLMs

Accountability issue	*Description*	*Proposed solution*	*Study*
Hallucinations	LLMs generate fabricated or incorrect information.	Using retrieval-augmented generation (RAG).	[57]
Lack of Transparency	Opaque training data sources obscure bias origins.	Disclose dataset details for scrutiny.	[58]
Inconsistent Outputs	Probabilistic nature leads to varying responses.	Implement continuous monitoring and quality checks.	[59]

even patients. For example, if an LLM produces a misdiagnosis or an unfair treatment suggestion, establishing liability becomes a contentious matter:

- *Developers* must ensure model accuracy, transparency, and fairness in training data.
- *Clinicians* are responsible for critically validating LLM outputs against clinical expertise.
- *Institutions* must enforce governance policies to mitigate risks.

To tackle these challenges, researchers and practitioners have proposed solutions for enhancing accountability:

1. Transparency in Training Data: Disclosing dataset sources, quality, and limitations to enable bias detection [26].
2. Shared Accountability Models: Distributing liability among developers, clinicians, and institutions through contractual and regulatory frameworks.
3. Dynamic Safety Assurance: Continuous monitoring, failure-mode analysis, and post-deployment updates to adapt to emergent risks [52].
4. Regulatory Oversight: Adopting frameworks like the FDA's Total Product *Lifecycle* approach to evaluate LLMs across development, validation, and deployment phases [53].

Case Study: Bias and Shared Responsibility. A notable example from clinician discussions involves an LLM recommending suboptimal treatment for minority patients due to biased training data [16]. This incident underscores the *shared responsibility* of:

- *Developers* to curate representative datasets and audit models for disparities.
- *Clinicians* are to recognize and override flawed recommendations.
- *Institutions* should adopt equity-focused governance strategies.

Strong accountability systems built on transparency, shared responsibility, and adaptable regulations are essential to ensure that LLMs improve healthcare quality rather than detract from it. By defining roles and encouraging collaboration among stakeholders, the healthcare sector can reduce risks while effectively leveraging the potential of LLMs.

Environmental Impact of LLMs. The production and use of LLMs have considerable environmental repercussions, mainly due to the high energy demands of training extensive neural networks. Research indicates that training a single cutting-edge LLM can release over 500 metric tons of CO_2, which is akin to the lifetime carbon footprint of five gasoline-fueled vehicles [54]. In healthcare, where ethical resource distribution is crucial, such energy consumption raises serious sustainability issues. Detractors point out that the high computational needs can burden energy supplies, potentially siphoning power away from hospitals or worsening environmental disparities, thereby contravening the principle of non-maleficence. For example, training one LLM can utilize more electricity than 100 US households do in a year [54], highlighting ethical dilemmas in areas with limited resources.

Emerging frameworks, like those in Recent Advances in LLMs for Healthcare, advocate for "*green AI*" practices, including:

- Efficient model architectures (e.g., sparse training, quantization).
- Renewable energy-powered data centers.
- Carbon offset programs for unavoidable emissions.

Ethically, prioritizing sustainability aligns with healthcare's obligation to "first, do no harm," ensuring AI advancements do not come at the expense of public or planetary health.

Interoperability and Standards. LLMs must seamlessly integrate with existing healthcare IT systems (e.g., EHRs, clinical decision-support tools) to avoid errors that jeopardize patient safety. Poor *interoperability*—such as misaligned data formats or incompatible APIs—can lead to misinterpreted diagnoses or treatment delays, violating non-maleficence and beneficence [55]. For example, an LLM generating recommendations in a non-standardized format might be misread by a hospital's system, leading to incorrect drug dosages.

Adherence to interoperability standards (e.g., HL7 FHIR, DICOM) ensures equitable access and reduces bias by enabling consistent performance across diverse healthcare settings [56]. Ethical imperatives include:

- Regulatory compliance: Mandating *alignment* with frameworks like the EU's AI Act or HIPAA.
- Open standards adoption: Preventing vendor lock-in that could marginalize underfunded clinics.

By prioritizing interoperability, developers uphold justice and accessibility, ensuring LLMs benefit all populations equally.

8.4 FURTHER CONSIDERATIONS

Aligning LLMs with Human Values. Alignment of LLMs with medical ethics and human values (e.g., beneficence, justice) is critical for safe healthcare integration. Techniques like Reinforcement Learning from Human Feedback (RLHF [60]) fine-tune LLMs to reflect stakeholder preferences, as demonstrated by Med-PaLM's 19% improvement in medical question-answering accuracy [61].

However, alignment remains challenging due to LLMs' complexity and healthcare's diversity. For instance, LLMs struggle to generalize to non-English-speaking populations, limiting ethical applicability, and biased training data can perpetuate disparities—e.g., a cost-prioritizing algorithm systematically underestimated Black patients' needs [62].

To address these issues, synthetic data generation and AI feedback mechanisms [53]. are proposed to improve alignment while preserving privacy. For example, LLMs trained on biased datasets have recommended treatments favouring privileged groups, underscoring the urgency of fairness-focused alignment [16]. Clinicians advocate for diverse training data and stakeholder collaboration to mitigate such risks [16].

Operationalizing Alignment: Stakeholders should adopt frameworks prioritizing:

- *Quality Control:* Regular validation of LLM outputs.
- *Privacy and Security:* Robust data protection (e.g., HIPAA-compliant encryption).
- *Explainable AI (XAI):* Interpretable decision-making for clinicians/patients.
- *Bias Mitigation:* Strategies like adversarial de-biasing and fairness audits.
- *Shared Liability:* Proportional accountability for developers, clinicians, and institutions.
- *Regulatory Modernization:* Updated liability laws (e.g., FDA's 2023 guidance) and IP safeguards.

Technical advancements (e.g., knowledge graphs for clinical reasoning) and regulatory collaboration are essential to ensure LLMs benefit healthcare equitably.

Ethical Challenges in LLM Autonomy. As LLMs progress toward greater autonomy, their societal impact grows while transparency diminishes, necessitating robust ethical oversight and alignment with human values [63–66]. Debates about whether LLMs are mere tools or potential moral agents hinge on competing ethical frameworks [55, 67]. Some argue LLMs lack genuine moral understanding, operating solely on statistical patterns in training data [20, 68], while others speculate about future LLMs as non-human moral agents, challenging anthropocentric ethics [69]. In healthcare, these debates are urgent. Granting LLMs autonomy in tasks like diagnosis or treatment planning raises questions about accountability: if an LLM errs, who is liable—the developer, clinician, or system itself? Current LLMs lack the accuracy and reliability required for such accountability [70, 71]. Furthermore, comparative studies show humans outperform LLMs in complex healthcare tasks requiring empathy and contextual judgment [72–74], underscoring the irreplaceable role of clinicians.

These limitations reinforce the need for LLMs to remain assistive or semi-autonomous in the near term, with human oversight ensuring ethical deployment.

The agency of LLMs in healthcare encompasses a range of roles, from purely assistive to semi-autonomous, with full autonomy remaining elusive owing to ethical and safety constraints. LLMs, such as Med-PaLM 2, developed by Google, are primarily assistive, supporting clinicians by answering medical questions, generating medical reports, and aiding clinical reasoning [61]. For instance, Med-PaLM 2 enhances electronic health record (EHR) management and diagnostic support but requires clinician validation, indicating limited autonomy [75]. Despite Med-PaLM 2's expert performance on USMLE-style questions, its integration into clinical workflows remains assistive owing to the potential for errors and biases [61].

While preliminary studies of multi-agent LLMs show promise for semi-autonomous healthcare coordination, rigorous clinical validation is required [33]. Complete autonomy remains unlikely in the near term because of LLM limitations (e.g., misinformation, bias, and lack of empathy) and regulatory obstacles (e.g., FDA guidelines for adaptive AI requiring human oversight) [76].

Global Health Equity and Federated Learning. Federated learning (FL) trains AI models on decentralized data, preserving privacy by maintaining local patient information. This aligns with regulations such as the GDPR and HIPAA and enables hospitals to collaborate without sharing sensitive EHRs [77]. Federated learning promotes global health equity by enabling collaborative model development across institutions, particularly benefiting low-resource settings facing data scarcity and privacy challenges (Figure 8.4). [78].

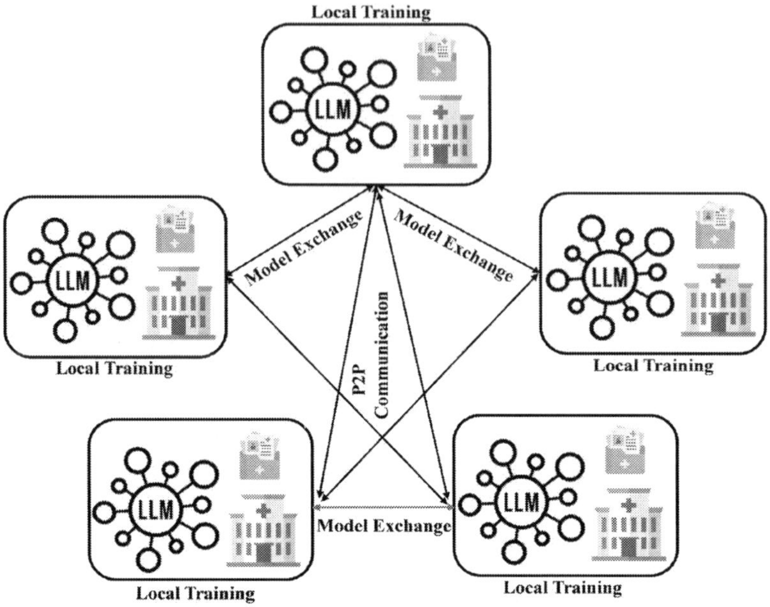

Figure 8.4 The architecture of a decentralized federated learning.

For example, FL has improved brain tumor segmentation across heterogeneous datasets [79], although challenges such as data heterogeneity and model drift persist [80].

Crucially, FL mitigates biases in LLMs trained predominantly on high-income country data, which often underperform in global health contexts (e.g., misdiagnosing tropical diseases) [79, 81]. By enabling localized model adaptation, FL democratizes access to AI while maintaining privacy.

Toward Equitable and Accountable LLMs in Healthcare. Existing frameworks like HIPAA and GDPR mandate data security and transparency but lag behind LLM advancements, necessitating updates to address AI-specific risks (e.g., algorithmic bias, hallucinations) [82]. The WHO's 2024 guidance on AI ethics provides 40+ recommendations, including protecting autonomy, ensuring equity, and enforcing accountability [83]. For example, it urges governments to:

- Invest in ethical public AI infrastructure.
- Mandate post-deployment audits for high-risk LLMs.

The EU AI Act [84] and FDA's 2023 guidelines for AI/ML-based software [76] adopt risk-based approaches, requiring rigorous validation and continuous monitoring. Developers must prioritize accuracy and stakeholder engagement, particularly for healthcare LLMs where errors can harm patients [85]. Harmonizing these frameworks is critical to prevent fragmented policies and ensure global AI safety.

Ethical Problems and Solutions in LLM Implementation. LLMs are increasingly used in healthcare for diagnosis support, patient education, and clinical decision-making. For instance, they can generate clear, tailored educational content, improving patient understanding and reducing clinician time spent on routine explanations [86]. LLMs also aid diagnostic processes by synthesizing data and suggesting diagnoses, improving efficiency and potentially reducing errors [81]. However, ethical concerns exist, as LLM recommendations may reflect training data biases, leading to disparities or inaccurate advice for underrepresented groups. Concerns about misinformation and lack of transparency in output generation can also undermine trust and accountability.

To address these issues, developers and researchers have implemented several strategies. Some research focuses on using a wider variety of data to train the AI to include broader demographic and clinical variations, mitigating biases, and improving generalizability [86]. Transparency measures, such as explainable AI frameworks, are also being integrated to allow clinicians to understand and validate LLM suggestions before applying them in practice. These efforts collectively aim to harness the benefits of LLMs—enhanced efficiency and personalized care—while maintaining ethical standards through continuous monitoring, inclusive data practices, and promoting interpretability in AI-driven healthcare tools.

Understanding Patient Perspectives on LLMs in Healthcare. Patient acceptance and trust are critical determinants in the successful integration of AI technologies in healthcare. Recent studies consistently highlight that while patients recognize the potential benefits of AI—such as improved diagnostic accuracy and personalized treatment—significant concerns persist regarding data privacy, transparency, and the perceived loss of human oversight [87]. For instance, research suggested that patients often worry about how their sensitive health information is collected, stored, and used, emphasizing the need for stringent data protection measures [88]. Additionally, patients express a strong preference for AI systems that operate under human supervision, ensuring that final clinical decisions involve healthcare professionals who can contextualize AI outputs with empathy and ethical judgment [89]. This underscores that trust is not solely dependent on the technology's accuracy but also on preserving the human element of care.

Incorporating patient feedback is important for the ethical implementation of AI in healthcare, as it ensures alignment with patient values and expectations. Engaging patients early and continuously in the design, implementation, and evaluation phases allows developers and clinicians to address concerns about autonomy, transparency, and fairness [90]. Such

Table 8.3 Trust-building strategies for LLM usage adoption

Strategy	*Description*	*Impact*	*Study*
Explainability	Use XAI to clarify AI decisions.	Increases clinician confidence.	[95]
Transparency	Document training data and methods.	Builds accountability.	[96]
Education	Train clinicians on AI capabilities.	Reduces skepticism.	[97]
Integration	Embed AI in clinical workflows.	Enhances usability.	[98]

participatory approaches foster greater trust and acceptance by making AI tools more responsive to diverse patient needs and cultural contexts. Moreover, patient-centered frameworks help mitigate risks of bias and reinforce accountability mechanisms, promoting equitable access to AI benefits [91]. Ultimately, embedding patient voices in AI governance supports the creation of technologies that advance medical outcomes and uphold ethical standards grounded in respect for patients' rights and dignity.

Building Clinician Trust. While LLM-generated responses are often preferred for their clarity, relying on unaudited AI can result in misdiagnoses and potentially harmful treatments. This highlights the importance of trustworthiness in LLMs [36, 92, 93]. Key factors that contribute to this trust include explainability, transparency, reliability, integration into workflows, and education [94]. Research indicates that clinicians are more likely to trust AI when its reasoning is clear and it is seamlessly integrated into electronic health records (EHRs). Involving clinicians in the development of AI systems and providing training on the limitations of AI can further enhance this trust. Table 8.3 summarizes strategies for increasing clinician confidence in LLMs and ensuring their trustworthy integration into healthcare workflows.

Efforts to benchmark LLMs' clinical competence also play an important role in cultivating clinician trust. For instance, MedQA-CS is a framework based on Objective Structured Clinical Examinations (OSCEs) to evaluate LLMs in realistic clinical tasks such as symptom analysis and patient education [100]. MedQA-CS emphasizes contextual understanding and communication skills, unlike traditional multiple-choice tests, which are vital for patient safety and clinician collaboration. Incorporating such structured evaluations could help developers align LLM capabilities with practical clinical workflows and trust-building metrics.

8.5 CONCLUSION

The medical community must take decisive action to address critical issues of privacy, bias, accuracy, and transparency to ensure the ethical use of LLMs in healthcare settings. By committing to robust guidelines, involving all relevant stakeholders, and adopting best practices, such as informed consent and alignment techniques, we can safeguard patient welfare, advance equity, and ensure accountability. Standardized protocols and comprehensive legal frameworks are vital, and continuous research involving clinicians, patients, and regulators is essential for navigating these ethical complexities and promoting the safe, effective, and equitable integration of LLMs into healthcare. Future research should focus on LLMs' long-term effects of LLMs on care quality, culturally sensitive AI alignment, and scalable ethical oversight. Multi-stakeholder collaboration is crucial for navigating AI innovations and ensuring equitable healthcare.

REFERENCES

1. A. Hurst, A. Lerer, A. P. Goucher, A. Perelman, A. Ramesh, A. Clark, A. Welihinda, A. Hayes, A. Radford, et al., "GPT-4o System Card," *arXiv preprint arXiv:2410.21276*, Oct. 25, 2024. https://doi.org/10.48550/arXiv.2410.21276
2. K. Kavukcuoglu, "Gemini 2.5: Our most intelligent AI model," Google DeepMind Blog. Available at: https://blog.google/technology/google-deepmind/gemini-model-thinking-updates-march-2025/ [Accessed May 20, 2025].
3. S. Bai, et al., "Qwen2.5-VL Technical Report," *arXiv preprint arXiv:2502.13923*, Feb. 19, 2025 . https://doi.org/10.48550/arXiv.2502.13923
4. K. Singhal, et al., "Toward expert-level medical question answering with large language models," *Nature Medicine*, 2025. Available at: https://www.nature.com/articles/s41591-024-03423-7 [Accessed May 12, 2025].
5. L. G. McCoy, et al., "Understanding and training for the impact of large language models and artificial intelligence in healthcare practice: a narrative review," *BMC Medical Education*, 2025. Available at: https://bmcmededuc.biomedcentral.com/articles/10.1186/s12909-024-06048-z [Accessed May 13, 2025].
6. A. J. Thirunavukarasu, et al., "Large language models in medicine," *Nature Medicine*, 2025. Available at: https://www.nature.com/articles/s41591-023-02448-8 [Accessed May 20, 2025].

7. D. Zhang, et al., "MM-LLMs: Recent Advances in MultiModal Large Language Models," in L.-W. Ku, A. Martins, and V. Srikumar (Eds.), *Findings of the Association for Computational Linguistics: ACL 2024*. Bangkok, Thailand: Association for Computational Linguistics, Aug. 2024, pp. 12401–12430. https://doi.org/10.18653/v1/2024.findings-acl.738
8. D. Wang and S. Zhang, "Large language models in medical and healthcare fields: applications, advances, and challenges," *Artificial Intelligence Review*, 57(11), 299, 2024. https://doi.org/10.1007/s10462-024-10921-0
9. L. De Angelis, et al., "ChatGPT and the rise of large language models: the new AI-driven infodemic threat in public health," *Frontiers in Public Health*, 11, 1166120, 2023. https://doi.org/10.3389/fpubh.2023.1166120
10. C. Chen and K. Shu, "Combating misinformation in the age of LLMs: Opportunities and challenges," *AI Magazine*, 45(3), 354–368, 2024. https://doi.org/10.1002/aaai.12188
11. B. Varkey, "Principles of Clinical Ethics and Their Application to Practice | Medical Principles and Practice | Karger Publishers." Available at: https://karger.com/mpp/article/30/1/17/204816/Principles-of-Clinical-Ethics-and-Their [Accessed May 12, 2025].
12. H. Saraç, İ. T. Ulusoy, J. Alpay, H. Ödemiş, and M. Söğüt, "Evaluating the Potential Role of AI Chatbots in Designing Personalized Exercise Programs for Weight Management," *International Journal of Human–Computer Interaction*, Feb. 2025. 1-8, Available at: https://www.tandfonline.com/doi/abs/10.1080/10447318.2025.2462752 [Accessed May 20, 2025].
13. L. Zhui, L. Fenghe, W. Xuehu, F. Qining, and R. Wei, "Ethical Considerations and Fundamental Principles of Large Language Models in Medical Education: Viewpoint," *Journal of Medical Internet Research*, 26(1), e60083, Aug. 2024. https://doi.org/10.2196/60083
14. D. S. Bitterman, H. J. W. L. Aerts, and R. H. Mak, "Approaching autonomy in medical artificial intelligence," The Lancet Digital Health, 2020. Available at: https://www.thelancet.com/journals/landig/article/PIIS2589-7500(20)30187-4/fulltext [Accessed May 20, 2025].
15. S. M. Pressman, et al., "AI and Ethics: A Systematic Review of the Ethical Considerations of Large Language Model Use in Surgery Research," *Healthcare*, 12(8), 825, 2025. Available at: https://www.mdpi.com/2227-9032/12/8/825 [Accessed May 12, 2025].
16. T. Mirzaei, L. Amini, and P. Esmaeilzadeh, "Clinician voices on ethics of LLM integration in healthcare: a thematic analysis of ethical concerns and implications," *BMC Medical Informatics and Decision Making*, 24(1), 250, Sep. 2024. https://doi.org/10.1186/s12911-024-02656-3
17. I. G. Cohen, "Informed Consent and Medical Artificial Intelligence: What to Tell the Patient," *Georgetown Law Journal*, 108, 1425–1457, 2019. Available at: https://dx.doi.org/10.2139/ssrn.3529576 [Accessed May 20, 2025].
18. M. C. Compagnucci, et al., AI in eHealth: Human Autonomy, Data Governance and Privacy in Healthcare. Cambridge University Press, 2022. Available at: https://doi.org/10.1017/9781108921923 [Accessed May 20, 2025].

19. D. Kim, N. Vegt, V. Visch, and M. B.-D. Vos. "How Much Decision Power Should (A)I Have?: Investigating Patients' Preferences Towards AI Autonomy in Healthcare Decision Making," in *Proceedings of the 2024 CHI Conference on Human Factors in Computing Systems*. 2025. https://dl.acm.org/doi/full/10.1145/3613904.3642883 [Accessed May 20, 2025].
20. L. Floridi, *The Ethics of Information*. Oxford University Press, 2013. Available at: https://doi.org/10.1093/acprof:oso/9780199641321.001.0001 [Accessed May 20, 2025].
21. X. Zhao, S. M. Sriwarnasinghe, J. Tang, S. Wang, H. Wang, and S. Morikawa, "Collaborative Participatory Research with LLM Agents in South Asia: An Empirically-Grounded Methodological Initiative and Agenda from Field Evidence in Sri Lanka," *arXiv preprint arXiv:2411.08294*, Nov. 13, 2024. https://doi.org/10.48550/arXiv.2411.08294
22. T. L. Beauchamp and J. F. Childress, *Principles of Biomedical Ethics*. Oxford University Press, 2019. Available at: https://global.oup.com/ushe/product/principles-of-biomedical-ethics-9780190640873 [Accessed May 24, 2025].
23. P. Boddington, *Towards a Code of Ethics for Artificial Intelligence*. Springer, 2017. Available at: https://link.springer.com/book/10.1007/978-3-319-60648-4 [Accessed May 24, 2025].
24. P. Tseng and Y. Wang, "Deontological or Utilitarian? An Eternal Ethical Dilemma in Outbreak," *PubMed Central*. Available at: https://pmc.ncbi.nlm.nih.gov/articles/PMC8391290/ [Accessed May 24, 2025].
25. R. C. Armitage, "Implications of Large Language Models for Clinical Practice: Ethical Analysis Through the Principlism Framework," *Journal of Evaluation in Clinical Practice*, 31(1), e14250, Feb. 2025. https://doi.org/10.1111/jep.14250
26. J. C. L. Ong, *et al.*, "Ethical and regulatory challenges of large language models in medicine," *The Lancet Digital Health*, 6(6), e428–e432, Jun. 2024. https://doi.org/10.1016/s2589-7500(24)00061-x
27. T. Carvalho, N. Moniz, P. Faria, and L. Antunes, "Towards a data privacy-predictive performance trade-off," *Expert Systems With Applications*, 223, 119785, Aug. 2023. https://doi.org/10.1016/j.eswa.2023.119785
28. P. Ruotsalainen and B. Blobel, "Health Information Systems in the Digital Health Ecosystem—Problems and Solutions for Ethics, Trust and Privacy." Available at: https://www.mdpi.com/1660-4601/17/9/3006 [Accessed May 18, 2025].
29. M. Hort, Z. Chen, J. M. Zhang, M. Harman, and F. Sarro, "Bias Mitigation for Machine Learning Classifiers: A Comprehensive Survey," *ACM Journal on Responsible Computing*, 1(2), 11:1–11:52, Jun. 2024. https://doi.org/10.1145/3631326
30. de J. Achiam, *et al.*, "GPT-4 Technical Report," *arXiv preprint arXiv:2303.08774*, Mar. 04, 2024. https://doi.org/10.48550/arXiv.2303.08774
31. J. Haltaufderheide, and R. Ranisch, "The ethics of ChatGPT in medicine and healthcare: a systematic review on Large Language Models (LLMs)," *npj Digital Medicine*, .,7(1), 183 Available at: https://www.nature.com/articles/s41746-024-01157-x [Accessed May 12, 2025].

32. T. Zack, *et al.*, "Assessing the potential of GPT-4 to perpetuate racial and gender biases in health care: a model evaluation study," *The Lancet Digital Health*, 6(1), e12–e22, Jan. 2024. https://doi.org/10.1016/S2589-7500(23)00225-X
33. H. Li, J. T. Moon, S. Purkayastha, L. A. Celi, H. Trivedi, and J. W. Gichoya, "Ethics of large language models in medicine and medical research," *The Lancet Digital Health*, 5(6), e333–e335, Jun. 2023. https://doi.org/10.1016/s2589-7500(23)00083-3
34. L. Rosenblatt and R. T. Witter, "Counterfactual Fairness Is Basically Demographic Parity," *Proceedings of the AAAI Conference on Artificial Intelligence*, 37(12), Art. no. 12, Jun. 2023. https://doi.org/10.1609/aaai.v37i12.26691
35. S. V. Chinta, *et al.*, "AI-Driven Healthcare: A Review on Ensuring Fairness and Mitigating Bias," *arXiv preprint arXiv:2407.19655*, May 03, 2025, . https://doi.org/10.48550/arXiv.2407.19655
36. M. Saleh and A. Tabatabaei, "Building Trustworthy Multimodal AI: A Review of Fairness, Transparency, and Ethics in Vision-Language Tasks," *International Journal of Web Research*, 8(2), 11–24, Apr. 2025. https://doi.org/10.22133/ijwr.2025.503147.1264
37. O. Akinrinola *et al.*, "Navigating and reviewing ethical dilemmas in AI development: Strategies for transparency, fairness, and accountability," *GSC Advanced Research and Reviews*, 18(3), Art. no. 3, 2024. https://doi.org/10.30574/gscarr.2024.18.3.0088
38. N. D. Portilla, M. Garcia-Font, V. Nagendrababu, P. V. Abbott, J. A. G. Sanchez, and F. Abella, "Accuracy and Consistency of Gemini Responses Regarding the Management of Traumatized Permanent Teeth," *Dental Traumatology*, 41(2), 171–177, 2025. https://doi.org/10.1111/edt.13004
39. L. Huang, *et al.*, "A Survey on Hallucination in Large Language Models: Principles, Taxonomy, Challenges, and Open Questions," *ACM Transactions on Information Systems*, 43(2), 1–55, Jan. 2025. https://doi.org/10.1145/3703155
40. H. Liu, *et al.*, "A Survey on Hallucination in Large Vision-Language Models," *arXiv preprint arXiv:2402.00253*, May 06, 2024. https://doi.org/10.48550/arXiv.2402.00253
41. I. J. Borges do Nascimento, *et al.*, "Infodemics and health misinformation: a systematic review of reviews," *Bulletin of the World Health Organization*, 100(9), 544–561, Sep. 2022. https://doi.org/10.2471/blt.21.287654
42. K. Wu, *et al.*, "An automated framework for assessing how well LLMs cite relevant medical references," *Nature Communications*, 16(1), 3615, Apr. 2025. https://doi.org/10.1038/s41467-025-58551-6
43. R. Hamid, and S. Brohi, "A Review of Large Language Models in Healthcare: Taxonomy, Threats, Vulnerabilities, and Framework." . Available at: https://www.mdpi.com/2504-2289/8/11/161 [Accessed May 18, 2025].
44. G. Mondillo, *et al.*, "Jailbreaking large language models: navigating the crossroads of innovation, ethics, and health risks," *Journal of Medical Artificial Intelligence*, 8, Mar. 2025. https://doi.org/10.21037/jmai-24-170

45. E. Topol, "Deep Medicine: How Artificial Intelligence Can Make Healthcare Human Again:: 9781541644632: Amazon.com: Books." . Available at: https://www.amazon.com/Deep-Medicine-Artificial-Intelligence-Healthcare/dp/1541644638 [Accessed May 19, 2025].
46. European Parliament and Council of the European Union, General Data Protection Regulation (GDPR) – Legal Text. Available at: https://gdpr-info.eu/ [Accessed May 20, 2025].
47. S. Liu and L. R. Guo, "Data Ownership in the AI-Powered Integrative Health Care Landscape," *JMIR Medical Informatics*, 12, e57754, 2024. https://doi.org/10.2196/57754.
48. S. Johri, *et al.*, "An evaluation framework for clinical use of large language models in patient interaction tasks," *Nature Medicine*, 31(1), 77–86, Jan. 2025. https://doi.org/10.1038/s41591-024-03328-5
49. K. He, et al., "A Survey of Large Language Models for Healthcare: from Data, Technology, and Applications to Accountability and Ethics," *arXiv preprint arXiv:2310.05694*, Oct. 2023. Available at: https://arxiv.org/abs/2310.05694 [Accessed May 19, 2025].
50. G. Shteynberg, et al., "Does it matter if empathic AI has no empathy?," *Nature Machine Intelligence*, 6(5), 496–497, May 2024. Available at: https://doi.org/10.1038/s42256-024-00841-7 [Accessed May 20, 2025].
51. J. Huang, et al., "Apathetic or Empathetic? Evaluating LLMs' Emotional Alignments with Humans," *Advances in Neural Information Processing Systems*, 37, 97053–97087, Dec. 2024. Available at: https://doi.org/10.48550/arXiv.2308.03656 [Accessed May 20, 2025].
52. F. Lareyre and J. Raffort, "Ethical Concerns Regarding the Use of Large Language Models in Healthcare," *EJVES Vascular Forum*, 61(1), pp-1 Oct. 2023. https://doi.org/10.1016/j.ejvsvf.2023.10.003
53. K. Ding, et al., "Aligning Large Language Models with Healthcare Stakeholders: A Pathway to Trustworthy AI Integration," *arXiv preprint arXiv:2505.02848*, May 2025. Available at: https://arxiv.org/abs/2505.02848 [Accessed May 19, 2025].
54. E. Strubell, A. Ganesh, and A. McCallum, "Energy and Policy Considerations for Deep Learning in NLP," *arXiv preprint arXiv:1906.02243v1*. Available at: https://arxiv.org/abs/1906.02243v1. [Accessed May 24, 2025].
55. E. M. Bender, T. Gebru, A. McMillan-Major, and S. Shmitchell, "On the Dangers of Stochastic Parrots: Can Language Models Be Too Big?" in *Proceedings of the 2021 ACM Conference on Fairness, Accountability, and Transparency*, in FAccT'21. New York, NY, USA: Association for Computing Machinery, Mar. 2021, pp. 610–623. https://doi.org/10.1145/3442188.3445922
56. Health Level Seven International, "Overview - FHIR v5.0.0," HL7.org .. Available at: https://www.hl7.org/fhir/overview.html [Accessed May 24, 2025].
57. A. Li, R. Shrestha, T. Jegatheeswaran, H. O. Chan, C. Hong, and R. Joshi, "Mitigating Hallucinations in Large Language Models: A Comparative Study of RAG-enhanced vs. Human-Generated Medical Templates," *medRxiv*, Sep. 28, 2024. https://doi.org/10.1101/2024.09.27.24314506.

58. E. M. Smith, M. Hall, M. Kambadur, E. Presani, and A. Williams, "'I'm sorry to hear that': Finding New Biases in Language Models with a Holistic Descriptor Dataset," *arXiv preprint arXiv:2205.09209*, Oct. 27, 2022. https://doi.org/10.48550/arXiv.2205.09209
59. S. Behore, L. Dumont, and J. Venkataraman, "Enhancing Reliability in Large Language Models: Self-Detection of Hallucinations With Spontaneous Self-Checks,". Available at: https://www.authorea.com/doi/full/10.22541/au.172591474.45065639?commit=5c3caaa663d1123b079882ae7501d480e3831a68 [Accessed May 20, 2025].
60. L. Ouyang, *et al.*, "Training language models to follow instructions with human feedback," *Advances in Neural Information Processing Systems*, 35, 27730–27744, 2022. https://doi.org/10.48550/arXiv.2203.02155
61. K. Singhal, *et al.*, "Large language models encode clinical knowledge," *Nature*, 620(7972), 172–180, Aug. 2023. https://doi.org/10.1038/s41586-023-06291-2
62. Z. Obermeyer, B. Powers, C. Vogeli, and S. Mullainathan, "Dissecting racial bias in an algorithm used to manage the health of populations," *Science*, 366(6464), 447–453, Oct. 2019. https://doi.org/10.1126/science.aax2342
63. "Plurals: A System for Guiding LLMs via Simulated Social Ensembles | Proceedings of the 2025 CHI Conference on Human Factors in Computing Systems," *ACM Conferences*. Available at: https://dl.acm.org/doi/10.1145/3706598.3713675 [Accessed May 19, 2025].
64. J. Qiu, K. Lam, G. Li, A. Acharya, T. Wong, A. Darzi, W. Yuan and E. J. Topol, "LLM-based agentic systems in medicine and healthcare," *Nature Machine Intelligence*, 6, 1418–1420, 2024. https://doi.org/10.1038/s42256-024-00944-1
65. Z. Xi, *et al.*, "The rise and potential of large language model based agents: a survey," *Science China Information Sciences*, 68(2), 121101, Jan. 2025. https://doi.org/10.1007/s11432-024-4222-0
66. T. Schick, *et al.*, "Toolformer: language models can teach themselves to use tools," in *Proceedings of the 37th International Conference on Neural Information Processing Systems*, in NIPS '23. Red Hook, NY, USA: Curran Associates Inc., Dec. 2023, pp. 68539–68551. https://dl.acm.org/doi/10.5555/3666122.3669119
67. P. Butlin, *et al.*, "Consciousness in Artificial Intelligence: Insights from the Science of Consciousness," *arXiv preprint arXiv:2308.08708*, Aug. 22, 2023. https://doi.org/10.48550/arXiv.2308.08708
68. A. Ferrario, M. Loi, and E. Viganò, "In AI We Trust Incrementally: a Multi-layer Model of Trust to Analyze Human-Artificial Intelligence Interactions," *Philosophy & Technology*, 33(3), 523–539, Sep. 2020. https://doi.org/10.1007/s13347-019-00378-3.
69. R. Long *et al.*, "Taking AI Welfare Seriously," *arXiv preprint arXiv:2411.00986*, Nov. 04, 2024. https://doi.org/10.48550/arXiv.2411.00986
70. J. Browning, "Personhood and Ai: Why Large Language Models Don?T Understand Us," *AI & Society*, 39(5), 2499–2506, 2023. https://doi.org/10.1007/s00146-023-01724-y

71. P. Rahmanzadehgervi, L. Bolton, M. R. Taesiri, and A. T. Nguyen, "Vision language models are blind," *presented at the Proceedings of the Asian Conference on Computer Vision*, 2024, pp. 18–34. Available at: https://openaccess.thecvf.com/content/ACCV2024/html/Rahmanzadehgervi_Vision_language_models_are_blind_ACCV_2024_paper.html [Accessed May 20, 2025].
72. M. Huang, X. Zhang, C. Soto, and J. Evans, "Designing LLM-Agents with Personalities: A Psychometric Approach," *arXiv preprint arXiv:2410.19238*, Oct. 25, 2024. https://doi.org/10.48550/arXiv.2410.19238
73. "Do Large Language Models Understand Medical Codes." Available at: https://arxiv.org/html/2403.10822v2 [Accessed May 22, 2025].
74. Z. Ye, M. Sun, H. Gao, C. Yu, and Y. Shi, "MOAT: Evaluating LMMs for Capability Integration and Instruction Grounding," *arXiv preprint arXiv:2503.0934*, Mar. 12, 2025. https://doi.org/10.48550/arXiv.2503.09348
75. T. Tu, *et al.*, "Towards Generalist Biomedical AI," *NEJM AI*, 1(3), AIoa2300138, Feb. 2024. http://dx.doi.org/10.1056/AIoa2300138
76. C. for D. and R. Health, "Artificial Intelligence and Machine Learning in Software as a Medical Device," *FDA*, Mar. 2025. Available at : https://www.fda.gov/medical-devices/software-medical-device-samd/artificial-intelligence-and-machine-learning-software-medical-device [Accessed May 22, 2025].
77. T. Wang, *et al.*, "Analyzing the Impact of Personalization on Fairness in Federated Learning for Healthcare," *Journal of Healthcare Informatics Research*. Available at: https://link.springer.com/article/10.1007/s41666-024-00164-7 [Accessed May 19, 2025].
78. A. Holzinger, *et al.*, "Human-in-the-Loop Integration with Domain-Knowledge Graphs for Explainable Federated Deep Learning," SpringerLink Available at: https://link.springer.com/chapter/10.1007/978-3-031-40837-3_4 [Accessed May 19, 2025].
79. N. Rieke, *et al.*, "The future of digital health with federated learning," *npj Digital Medicine*. Available at: https://www.nature.com/articles/s41746-020-00323-1 [Accessed May 23, 2025].
80. H. B. McMahan, E. Moore, D. Ramage, S. Hampson, and B. A. y Arcas, "Communication-Efficient Learning of Deep Networks from Decentralized Data," *arXiv preprint arXiv:1602.05629*, Jan. 26, 2023. https://doi.org/10.48550/arXiv.1602.05629
81. P. Rajpurkar, E. Chen, O. Banerjee, and E. J. Topol, "AI in health and medicine," *Nature Medicine*, 28(1), 31–38, Jan. 2022. https://doi.org/10.1038/s41591-021-01614-0
82. S. Adams, "The Ethical Implications of Using Large Language Models in HealthTech," Hire Remote Developers | Build Teams in 24 Hours - Gaper.io. Available at: https://gaper.io/ethical-implications-llm-in-healthtech/ [Accessed May 12, 2025].
83. "Ethics and governance of artificial intelligence for health: Guidance on large multi-modal models." Available at: https://www.who.int/publications/i/item/9789240084759 [Accessed May 23, 2025].

84. "Regulation - EU - 2024/1689 - EN - EUR-Lex. Available at: https://eur-lex.europa.eu/legal-content/EN/TXT/?uri=OJ%3AL_202401689 [Accessed May 20, 2025].
85. W. J. Waldock, J. Zhang, A. Guni, A. Nabeel, A. Darzi, and H. Ashrafian, "The Accuracy and Capability of Artificial Intelligence Solutions in Health Care Examinations and Certificates: Systematic Review and Meta-Analysis," *Journal of Medical Internet Research*, 26(1), e56532, Nov. 2024. https://doi.org/10.2196/56532
86. S. Aydin *et al.*, "Large language models in patient education: a scoping review of applications in medicine - PubMed." Available at: https://pubmed.ncbi.nlm.nih.gov/39534227/ [Accessed May 23, 2025].
87. S. Moy, *et al.*, "Patient Perspectives on the Use of Artificial Intelligence in Health Care: A Scoping Review - PMC." Available at: https://pmc.ncbi.nlm.nih.gov/articles/PMC11000703/ [Accessed May 23, 2025].
88. C. Longoni, *et al,* "Resistance to Medical Artificial Intelligence," *Journal of Consumer Research. 46(4), 629-650,* Available at: https://academic.oup.com/jcr/article-abstract/46/4/629/5485292?redirectedFrom=fulltext [Accessed May 23, 2025].
89. P. M. Doraiswamy, C. Blease, and K. Bodner, "Artificial intelligence and the future of psychiatry: Insights from a global physician survey," *Artificial Intelligence in Medicine*, 102, 101753, Jan. 2020. https://doi.org/10.1016/j.artmed.2019.101753
90. B. Mittelstadt, "Principles alone cannot guarantee ethical AI," *Nature Machine Intelligence*, 1(11), 501–507, Nov. 2019. https://doi.org/10.1038/s42256-019-0114-4
91. M. J. Rigby, *et al.*, "Ethical Dimensions of Using Artificial Intelligence in Health Care," *Journal of Ethics* . Available at: https://journalofethics.ama-assn.org/article/ethical-dimensions-using-artificial-intelligence-health-care/2019-02 [Accessed May 23, 2025].
92. V. Shrivastava, P. Liang, and A. Kumar, "Llamas Know What GPTs Don't Show: Surrogate Models for Confidence Estimation," *arXiv preprint arXiv:2311.08877*, Nov. 15, 2023. https://doi.org/10.48550/arXiv.2311.08877.
93. P. Xia, *et al.*, "CARES: A Comprehensive Benchmark of Trustworthiness in Medical Vision Language Models," *Advances in Neural Information Processing Systems*, 37, 140334–140365, 2024. https://doi.org/10.48550/arXiv.2406.06007
94. H. Andersson, A. Svensson, C. Frank, A. Rantala, M. Holmberg, and A. Bremer, "Ethics education to support ethical competence learning in healthcare: an integrative systematic review," *BMC Medical Ethics*, 23(1), 29, Mar. 2022. https://doi.org/10.1186/s12910-022-00766-z
95. O. Wysocki, *et al.*, "Assessing the communication gap between AI models and healthcare professionals: Explainability, utility and trust in AI-driven clinical decision-making," *Artificial Intelligence*, 316, 103839, Mar. 2023. https://doi.org/10.1016/j.artint.2022.103839

96. A. Kiseleva, D. Kotzinos, and P. De Hert, "Transparency of AI in Healthcare as a Multilayered System of Accountabilities: Between Legal Requirements and Technical Limitations," *Frontiers in Artificial Intelligence*, 5, May 2022, p 879603 ,https://doi.org/10.3389/frai.2022.879603
97. C. Elendu *et al.*, "Ethical implications of AI and robotics in healthcare: A review," *Medicine (Baltimore)*, 102(50), e36671, Dec. 2023. https://doi.org/10.1097/md.0000000000036671
98. S. M. Varnosfaderani, and Forouzanfar, "The Role of AI in Hospitals and Clinics: Transforming Healthcare in the 21st Century," *Bioengineering*, 11(4), 337, 2024. https://doi.org/10.3390/bioengineering11040337 [Accessed May 20, 2025].
99. H. Ma, F. Quinzan, T. Willem, and S. Bauer, "AI Alignment in Medical Imaging: Unveiling Hidden Biases Through Counterfactual Analysis," *arXiv preprint arXiv:2504.19621*, Apr. 2025. https://doi.org/10.48550/arXiv.2504.19621
100. Z. Yao, M. Jiang, L. Zuo, et al., "MedQA-CS: Benchmarking Large Language Models Clinical Skills Using an AI-SCE Framework," *arXiv preprint arXiv:2410.01553*, Oct. 2024. https://doi.org/10.48550/arXiv.2410.01553

Chapter 9

Limitations of large language models in healthcare systems

Farshid Babapour Mofrad and Midya Yousefzamani

9.1 INTRODUCTION

A large language model (LLM) is a state-of-the-art artificial intelligence system that has been "trained" on huge textual source collections consisting of billions of words originating from a variety of sources, including articles in peer-reviewed academic journals, books, and online content. Although there is a great deal of variability in terms of the exact architecture of LLMs, they typically consist of neural networks built on deep learning, one of the most powerful and successful methodologies developed thus far. LLMs can learn representations that capture and encode the complex associative and semantic relationships between words found in the text they have been trained on Reference [1, 2]. The capacity of these models to develop detailed, fluent and relevant text in response to user inputs in natural language content has positioned them as potentially transformative across a range of fields, including healthcare [3]. Consider examples such as ChatGPT from OpenAI, Med-PaLM from Google, and BioGPT from Microsoft, all of which have key accomplishments in biomedical and clinical applications, such as generating patient education materials, answering medical inquiries, and performing with proficiency similar to human professionals (in observational studies in non-laboratory settings) on standardized assessments including the United States Medical Licensing Examination (USMLE) [4–6]. Their conversational interface and capacity for contextual understanding mark a significant departure from traditional natural language processing systems, prompting strong interest from clinicians, researchers, and developers alike [7].

In recent years, unprecedented advancements in the field of artificial intelligence have sparked an unparalleled enthusiasm for large language models (LLMs) to become part of healthcare systems in meaningful ways [8]. Prevailing LLMs have recently shifted from general and generalized purpose capacities applied through the lens of natural language processing. They are moving into more tuned scenarios to meet the immense demands of clinical settings [9, 10]. This transition has primarily been propelled by two factors: the increasingly sophisticated capabilities of these models, and

 DOI: 10.1201/9781003665083-9

the drive to develop novel, scalable, efficient, and context-aware tools to fit contemporary medical needs [11–13]. In practice, LLMs have found their way into many varied health care settings, where they are designed to support clinical reasoning, improve decision-making, and improve administrative workflows [4, 14, 15]. A current and prevalent use case is the analysis of unstructured medically derived data, specifically, physicians' notes and radiology reports [5, 16]. In these instances, LLMs protocolize the processes of documenting and summation of clinically related information [17]. LLMs also provide improved patient communication through a dialog system that responds to medical inquiries, manual scheduling of medical visits, or completion of a protocol for triaging associated with various symptoms, thereby enhancing accessibility and engagement [18, 19].

To address deficiencies of general-purpose LLMs, specifically relevancy to and differentiation in the medical profession, many generalized models have been comprised from general or incremental fine-tuning of biomedically driven corpora [20]. Some LLM variants include Bio BERT [11], SCIBERT [21], PubMedBERT [12], and ClinicalBERT [22], which have demonstrated improved performance on information extraction tasks specific to the biological and health biomedical domains and clinical NLP implementation plans [23]. Most recently, two large-scale models, GatorTron, and instruction-tuned models, have performed higher-order clinical reasoning on complex medical benchmarking tasks such as Med-PaLM 2 [24]. However, open-source conversational agents trained in real-world medical conversations, such as ChatDoctor and Baize-Healthcare, have not yet demonstrated consistent reliability in patient-facing applications [19, 25]. These systems can support multi-turn conversations and context-specific recommendations, moving conversational AI closer to functional implementation in clinical workflows. While LLMs will continue to develop, their use in healthcare to provide diagnostic assistance and support patient engagement creates new possibilities. However, the effective implementation of such applications requires not only technical capabilities but also alignment with clinical needs and regulatory and ethical considerations [8, 26]. Although these developments are promising, the potential and use of LLMs in clinical settings pose critical limitations and challenges. Issues related to clinical accuracy, questions of bias, interpretability, regulatory compliance, and patient safety remain important concerns. It is critical to evaluate generative AI not only based on its potential and capabilities, but its limitations as the health sector moves towards the use of generative AI tools to assist with the delivery of patient care [4, 7]. This chapter characterizes the current and anticipated applications of large language models (LLMs) in healthcare. The range of clinical uses of LLMs has been contextualized, including decision support, documentation, communication with patients, and for the advancement of research. After noting the potential of LLMs to create transformative opportunities in caring for patients, the chapter then discusses several limitations. The limitations include technical limitations such as hallucinations, limited real-time reasoning, and absent multimodal integration, along with practical limitations such as trust, interpretability, and bias, especially where existing health inequities and disparities may be exacerbated by LLMs using biased training data. The ethical and legal risks associated with LLMs have been elaborated on, including potential privacy of patient data, informed consent, liability, and the use of generative texts. They point to the barriers to implementation posed by the "black box" nature of the data, without validated clinical outcomes. The chapter then reviews other challenges, including security risks and human-AI collaboration challenges, including prompt injection and model inversion. The authors conclude with their suggestions for mitigation, including some way to develop explainable, clinically aligned, privacy-preserving LLMs in healthcare to promote responsible, equitable, and evidence-based implementation of LLMs in the care of patients now, and in the future.

9.2 OVERVIEW OF LLM APPLICATIONS IN HEALTHCARE

The diverse uses of large language models (LLMs) have characterized across many components of health care and articulate potential uses, advantages, and challenges of the technology. LLMs are extremely valuable tools to support practitioners in managing vast amounts of unstructured data such as clinical notes, electronic health records, medical literature, as well as reports resulting from the medical imaging process. Applications ranging from clinical decision support to patient communications, pharmacy disciplines, medical documentation, and drug discovery are changing how to think about and engage in health systems, and how a new set of technologies are only scratching the surface of their potential. While LLMs are promising, the implementation of LLMs into healthcare, there are still limitations in the technology, mostly to do with data integrity, interpretability of the model, and lastly, the need for a human role in any new paradigm of work. In this section, the applications will be elaborated on and examined with greater attention to their implications, the current state of research, and the challenges associated with their implementation.

9.2.1 Clinical decision support

Extensive evidence demonstrates that large language models (LLMs) are promising clinical decision support tools that can analyze large amounts of unstructured patient data, help create differential diagnoses, and suggest possible treatments [4, 14]. LLMs are being deployed for clinical decision-making due to their informed ability to look up and summarize evidence-based data buried in electronic health records, imaging reports, and biomedical literature [24, 27]. Initial studies, focused on high-stakes areas (e.g., radiology, oncology, dermatology), suggest that LLMs may be useful to clinicians, improving diagnostic performance through increasing the efficiency of comparison and judgment, resulting in improved accuracy [28–30]. Nonetheless, and in spite of their strong performance on standardized tests such as medical licensing exams, recent study findings demonstrate significant limitations in using language models to assist clinical decision-making in practice [31].

Nevertheless, despite their successful performance on objective assessments of knowledge and skills, such as medical licensure examinations, current outcomes demonstrate a marked insufficiency in real-world medical settings. Limitations highlighted included problems with generating complex patient clinical presentations, difficulty integrating and synthesizing laboratory test results, non-adherence to clinical practice guidelines, and the models being sensitive to the response structure and format of the input data [32, 33]. These limitations raise concerns about the safety and reliability of using LLMs for independent clinical decision-making [34]. Moreover, other potential concerns surround the inconsistency of behavior recommending a diagnostic test and limited robustness with treatment planning for patients with serious or complex manifestations. Although the deficiencies identified in performance necessitate human oversight and clinical assessment, LLMs have great potential to assist healthcare providers. It should also be noted that the current models lack the needed clinical reasoning, accuracy and timeliness to operate fully autonomously in situ within mission critical healthcare domains [33].

9.2.2 Patient communication

Large language models (LLMs) are rapidly creating potential breakthroughs in patient communications, particularly through the use of chatbots and virtual health assistants [35]. LLMs are interacting with the patient in a real-time, conversational dialog to provide general medical information, help to triage symptoms, organize referrals, facilitate videoconferencing or in-person appointments, and provide reminders for medications or follow-up care [19]. ChatDoctor and Baize-Healthcare, which integrated LLMs pre-trained on real-world medical dialog and structured Q&A data, such as MedQuAD, indicate that LLMs may be more accurate and influenced by their training than LLMs are to successfully provide useful responses for multi-turn conversations, such as those using ChatGPT [19, 25]. It has already seen examples of patients unwinding if they used ChatGPT informally as a second opinion or initial characterization of symptoms [35]. The potential for LLMs in this realm is their reduction of clinician workloads, improvement in patient engagement, and ultimately, improvement in access to care [19, 35]. At the same time, LLMs and other technologies need to be deployed slowly to avoid risks, such as inaccurate results, diminishing the clinician-patient empathetic engagement, and patient misunderstanding of the provided advice [35]. It is also essential that patients are assured that the features integrated into chatbot-generated output are clinically relevant, consistent with vetted evidence-based clinical guidelines, especially when interacting with patients where significant ethical and patient safety factors exist [19, 33].

9.2.3 Medical documentation and summarization

It is very difficult to effectively document or summarize medical information in the healthcare profession due to the enormous amount of data clinicians need to document and summarize (e.g., radiology reports, patient progress notes, and communication between physicians and patients) [36]. Medical data is often very complex and time-consuming to document. The burden can result in substantial work-related stress for healthcare professionals and lessen their focus on patient care [37, 38]. The recent development of large language models (LLMs), such as GPT-4, has provided possibilities for workloads that may help alleviate some of this burden because LLMs clearly have a useful role in summarizing medical texts and letters [36]. There is a growing body of research indicating LLMs perform well at summarizing medical texts. For example, in a study, a paper has been summarized, and then it compares each of the summaries to LLMs using the same text [36]. The study found that outputs from LLMs were at least as accurate (or more) than those produced by medical experts in terms of correctness, completeness, and conciseness [36]. Therefore, the research suggests that LLMs trained properly or fine-tuned could not only achieve the same level as but could outperform medical experts when summarizing medical texts. LLMs have been relatively strong at summarizing most medical texts, including radiology reports and progress notes, especially when data from previous learning strategies that included task/context metacognitive learning strategies and fine-tuning the model showed antecedent data that established the domain terminology to build upon and help summarize [36]. Despite the high potential LLMs offer in allowing for very high-quality medical documentation to be created quickly, limitations in their use in medical documentation still exist. A major concern is their potential to generate inaccurate or misleading information, which may result in significant medical errors. While LLMs demonstrate competency in many responsibilities, they generally are unable to extract most of the relevant information from different sources or misinterpret important information [39]. The research identified that, while LLMs can summarize information well, it was still possible that LLMs generated factual inaccuracies or did not consider all key medical information. Thus, while LLMs can potentially be valuable, the summaries created through their use should be assessed by medical experts before implementation as documentation [36]. To enhance the use of LLMs in the process of medical documentation, models need to be combined with human expertise and fine-tuning within the application of the models [39]. This combined framework would enable LLMs to adequately capture the nuances in clinical text while providing a summary that is accurate and clinically relevant [36]. LLMs hold remarkable promises to lessen the burden of documentation in healthcare but should be used as an adjunct to human decision-making, rather than a complete replacement [39]. Future research efforts should encompass the advancement of model accuracy, with the reduction of misinformation and more rigorous fine-tuning and recalibrating to allow safe integration in clinical workflows [36].

9.2.4 Biomedical research and literature mining

The potential use of LLMs to quickly process enormous amounts of unstructured clinical and research literature can be valuable to clinicians and researchers to maintain credibility as scientific knowledge is evolving, and LLMs can also support in identifying emerging trends, or simply to read through dozens or hundreds of articles to synthesize the key findings of published studies, and subsequently distill useful clinical information from reports, systematic reviews, and clinical trials to provide practitioners with evidence-based practice that might lead to more efficient decision-making [6, 40]. One of the great benefits of LLMs is in carrying out an automated literature review. LLMs can locate relevant articles, distill the key findings from within these articles, and compile a structured overview of the state of science, which usually takes weeks for a skilled research assistant to complete, into a summary just like that [35]. In addition to these useful applications, there are also serious limitations. Texts in the biomedical domain often rely on dense and technical language that domain trained LLMs can misunderstand and potentially misrepresent, as supporting the nuances in phrasing that constitutes much biomedical literature can be difficult even for sophisticated LLMs and could lead to partial or incorrect interpretations [41]. LLMs cannot independently validate the accuracy of information and, when trained on healthcare data, they can reproduce existing biases in the result [42]. To further reiterate, while LLMs may provide improved comprehension and relevance in a controlled research environment, they will struggle to keep pace with real-world clinical data due partly to the differences in format, context, and specificity, but mostly due to being limited by the scope of what was in their training data. Furthermore, since LLMs are trained on historical data, it is likely they will lag behind the most current medical developments, as the old data used to train the LLMs did not necessarily account for developments that could have occurred after the model was trained [3, 41].

9.2.5 Drug discovery and diagnostics

The utilization of large language models (LLMs) is revolutionizing the field of drug discovery by allowing for the generation of faster and more data-driven methodologies [41]. LLMs can feasibly assess numerous biomedical data sets to find potential targets for drug intervention, identify links between disease-related pathways, and proceed with drug development in its preliminary stages. In particular, the LLMs can also predict drug-drug interactions by scanning chemical and molecular data sets for correlating activity, thereby facilitating the reduction of adverse effects in utilization, namely in chronic users who utilize various medications [6, 40]. Furthermore, LLMs can also be applied to drug repositioning efforts. The goal of drug repositioning efforts is to find new applications for previously developed drugs, which can reduce the time and cost of drug evaluation [40, 41]. If LLMs are trained on patient-centered data, it is possible they can additionally support an improved personalized treatment strategy by determining an individual's potential response to a specific medication. However, important limitations exist. LLMs rely heavily on the training data, which is often incomplete, biased, and unstructured. As a result, the prediction to real-world context may be full of inaccuracies and misrepresentations [42, 43]. While LLMs appear competent for novel conditions in a theory-generated and validated setting, their black box nature of LLMs diminishes researcher or clinician trust in the output [43]. In this way, explainable AI (EX-AI) can also play an important role here. Finally, LLMs have significant potential in drug discovery, but limitations remain that need to be addressed for proper use and benefit in healthcare [44]. On the other hand, large language models (LLMs) are increasingly being considered in diagnostic settings in which they help clinicians analyze patient symptoms, medical history, and clinical notes to generate differential diagnoses. There is compelling evidence that, when fine-tuned, LLMs can achieve diagnostic performance approaching that of experienced radiologists for even challenging imaging tasks regarding progressive bone metastasis or detecting brain tumors, and other diagnosis. LLMs are beneficial to clinicians because they can rapidly process radiological reports and also improve diagnostic accuracy. While the LLMs may have demonstrated effectiveness for some types of diagnostic decision-making, definitive clinical validation must still be established prior to mass implementation into standard diagnostic workflow [45, 46].

Figure 9.1 provides a detailed summary of LLM applications in healthcare, including their advantages and disadvantages. The figure presented identifies LLM as a tool to enhance diagnostic accuracy, documentation

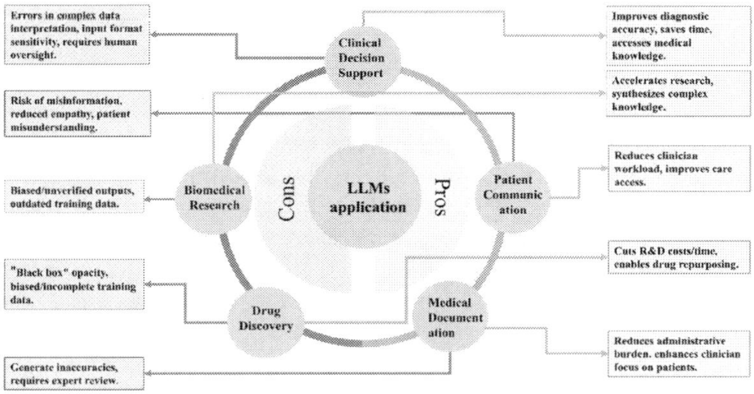

Figure 9.1 Benefits and challenges of LLM applications in healthcare domains.

processes, support patient interaction, facilitate biomedical research, and assist in drug discovery processes.

9.3 TECHNICAL LIMITATIONS OF LLMS

LLMs have performed well in many areas, but their technical limitations still pose challenges, especially when used in complex and high-stakes fields like healthcare [47]. This section will provide more elaboration on these limitations related to data dependency, model transparency, reasoning abilities, and language context. Situational examples will be given to inform LLM limitations regarding task-specific failures, imaginative failures, or adversarial failures, recognizing the depth and dynamic nature of a real-world environment. Several inherent limitations and challenges that can hinder LLMs' performance and reliability will be discussed in the following subsections.

9.3.1 Training data requirements

In order to appropriately learn patterns within language and respond appropriately, large language models (LLMs) require large pre-training datasets [48]. The textual data used to train LLMs usually consists of a wide variety of health-related documents, such as clinical notes, medical records, biomedical scholarly articles, healthcare guidelines, and resources to educate patients [49]. However, huge amounts of data involved can raise multiple issues regarding quality as well as size. Due to the copious amounts of data used to train these models, it becomes virtually impossible to manually review the entire contents of a dataset for quality assurance, and subsequently, issues like duplication and biased data exist [48, 49]. Duplicates in the dataset can bias the model by overstating some patterns, negatively affect the output accuracy, and overall quality of the model [50]. Additionally, because LLMs are based on massive, generalized datasets, there can be issues regarding privacy and data leakages using this data. For example, dataset contents may inadvertently contain sensitive or personally identifiable information (PII) such as telephone numbers, email addresses, or other sensitive related information [49]. This raises ethical issues surrounding privacy, specifically regarding revealing personal information of individuals [48]. Issues like these support the need for careful data curation and anonymization efforts at the data preparation stage to effectively reduce or eliminate sensitive and identifiable information in training datasets [50]. In addition, the potential overlap of training and test data is a considerable issue. The size of datasets used for training makes it difficult to ensure no overlap between the training data and the input provided during the test phase, which could result in the model reporting incorrect evaluation metrics of performance, or in some instances not able to generalize learning to new data, as the model might simply memorize data in the training set. In a brief summary, the performance reported by a model on the test data might not reflect its performance on unseen inputs in a real-world setting. Leveraging transfer of learning and synthetic data, alongside rigorous anonymization and deduplication processes, can improve training data quality. Looking ahead, federated learning frameworks may enable secure, decentralized access to diverse datasets while preserving patient privacy and data integrity [48, 50].

9.3.2 Tokenization problems

Natural language understanding in large language models (LLMs) implemented in health contexts begins with tokenization, taking as input text and dividing it into smaller pieces of text known as tokens. Tokens can consist of an entire word, subwords, or even individual characters. These tokens enable the model to take clinical narratives, patient notes, and biomedical literature [51]. However, the process of tokenization also has limitations that decrease model accuracy and fairness in medical contexts. Medical terminology frequently has complex and compound terms, or commonly, abbreviations that medical professionals use to shorten phrases or medication names. So, those abbreviations may get tokenized in different ways. If the content of clinical tokens gets tokenized differently, this can affect the clinical tokens, and the model may generate irrelevant or unsafe responses when used in patient physiology, diagnosis, treatment design, or even documentation scenarios [52]. For example, the inherent differences in token boundaries when working with multilingual clinical data or patients who input their responses using languages with unique writing formats could disrupt the model's ability to interpret a patient's symptom or translate specific terminology correctly, or follow clinical prompts as intended [52]. Overall, addressing these tokenization issues could lead to more consistent, fair, and precise interpretation of user prompt inquiries for an LLM, especially across a multilingual user demographic. Developing domain-specific and multilingual-aware tokenizers can mitigate tokenization inconsistencies in clinical language. In the long term, establishing unified biomedical vocabulary standards will support fairer and more accurate LLM interpretation across diverse healthcare populations [53].

9.3.3 Computational cost

The pre-training of large language models (LLMs) requires enormous computation resources that come with both financial and environmental costs [54]. The large size of these models necessitates larger datasets and has more complex architectures, further increasing the computational cost [54]. Larger versions of LLMs dramatically increases the needed both in hardware and financial costs, limiting their accessibility, especially to smaller research institutions and companies [48]. To remedy these problems, approaches like "Computer Optimal Training" were proposed to reduce training costs relative to the size of the dataset and model [48]. Although these methods have helped mitigate some computational costs of training and operating LLMs, the demands of online and offline (pre-training) of LLMs remains an impediment to their popularity, especially in resource-limited settings. Therefore, efficient training of AI models is key to improving accessibility and sustainability of AI methods [54]. Optimized training algorithms and hardware-efficient design can help reduce computational burden. In the future, Green AI initiatives aim to promote sustainable scaling and make LLM training more accessible in low-resource settings [55].

9.3.4 Fine-tuning challenges

Fine-tuning large language models (LLMs) to particular tasks requires substantial computational resources, especially in memory, processing power, and storage [56]. Depending on the size of the model, resource usage can be staggering, as storing the models' parameters and gradients (e.g., during back-propagation) will use a significant fraction of resources available to the LLM, and create difficulty for small institutions, or organizations that do not have direct access to LLMs when only required resource access [54]. Fine-tuning using task-specific data can improve accuracy in LLMs for specific applications [57]. Because LLMs require significantly large computational resources, techniques like parameter-efficient Fine-tuning are used as a mechanism to mitigate some of the capacity constraints, so only some of the parameters of the model are adjusted, rather than the total parameters of the model being retrained [57]. While these strategies permit providing services with reduced computational resources, the overall fine-tuning resource demand is substantial, which effectively stops access to LLMs with fine-tuning to only well-funded organizations. These points need for additional mechanisms, or improvement mechanisms to optimize fine-tuning specifically. Techniques like few-shot learning and parameter-efficient fine-tuning reduce resource demands, while future efforts should focus on developing automated fine-tuning pipelines to improve accessibility for smaller institutions [58, 59].

9.3.5 Inference latency

A major hurdle for large language models (LLMs) is high inference latency, mostly due to the model footprint and the lack of model parallelism, which means slower output generation processing times. When LLMs are very large and complex, their computation load increases, and the response time can suffer from delays, which is an impediment to real-time applications [60]. There are many techniques to help optimize performance that can assist in improving response time, including efficient attention, which processes data input more rapidly, pruning to reduce the model's unnecessary parameters, and quantization to reduce the precision of computation for reducing footprint [60, 61]. These strategies are too important to achieve better overall efficiency in actual applications. Techniques such as pruning, quantization, and efficient attention mechanisms can reduce inference latency, while future improvements are expected through hardware–software co-design to optimize real-time LLM deployment [55].

9.3.6 Limited context length

LLMs have limitations based on their context length, which is the number of tokens or words, they can remember while processing information at once [62]. Based on these limitations, LLMs are not very effective in interpreting and analyzing long sequences of text. For example, when LLMs interpret a long document or conversation, they could quite easily lose track of initial pieces of information to the extent that their overall understanding of context becomes reduced [62]. The effect undermines semantic analysis and significantly hampers the accuracy of generated responses, specifically because they may misinterpret or neglect key points of early mentioned information. Furthermore, positional embedding schemas and efficient attention methods have been created to help LLMs focus on their context. However, context length is an inherent limitation when attempting to retain and make use of a larger quantity of information, especially when the tasks are more complex [62, 63]. Hierarchical attention and optimized positional embedding can help LLMs better manage context within current limits, while future research should explore modular and memory-augmented models to support dynamic and extended contextual understanding [53].

9.3.7 Knowledge updating and refinement

Retraining LLMs is a very costly and inefficient endeavor due to requiring vast data and infrastructure to achieve. The cost of ongoing retraining is impossible for most organizations, especially those without resources. Various proposals, such as model editing and web plugins, potentially address this limitation. What mentioned above could allow for continuous and manageable way to update knowledge by allowing the model to adjust behavior through means other than full retraining. There are significant limitations on the generalizability of these approaches, thus all models or model architectures can't adapt to the real world. For this reason, maintaining and updating LLMs in this way, so that they remain functionally current over time, is a major obstacle to their longevity. Model editing and plugin-based updates offer a practical alternative to full retraining, while future efforts should focus on integrating real-time knowledge bases to maintain up-to-date model behavior efficiently [64].

9.3.8 Cost barriers

The training and execution of large language models (LLMs) such as GPT-4 and Gemini Ultra, carry significant computational and monetary burdens. The costs of building high-performance GPUs, acquiring large-scale datasets (typically in petabytes), and energy usage, inevitably lead to operational and infrastructure costs in the million-dollar range [65]. While new technologies can have radical implications across settings, including healthcare, the economic costs have kept them from being adopted more widely. Potential benefits of LLMs in medical settings could include support in clinical decision-making, time-savings in administrative duties, and enhanced provision of personalized care. Yet many small clinics, hospitals, and even some well-endowed institutions do not adopt these technologies because they remain unaffordable. Cost-saving methods, such as low-rank approximations or smaller models, help marginally, but do not address the very real scarcity of an organization's resources [51]. One way to reduce LLM costs in healthcare is through model fine-tuning on smaller, pre-trained models on domain-specific data, which is then projected to reduce the computational requirements while delivering similar performance [11].

9.3.9 Foundation model risks

Foundation models—the underlying architecture for many machine learning applications—raise significant concerns, specifically around bias, privacy, and hallucination. LLMs, which have been trained on large data sets sourced from the internet, have been found to absorb any bias the training data held. The inclusion of bias can demonstrate some of society's injustices to the extent that the responses might differ pertaining to race, gender, socioeconomic status, and other demographics. Consequently, those who implement these models—policymakers—must engage in deliberation about whether the responses produced by LLMs might inadvertently produce a form of bias and reinforce these pre-existing biases. This can have harmful effects, particularly in any sensitive applications, such as hiring, healthcare, or law enforcement [40]. Hallucination, or the generation of nonsensical or untrue content, is a significant risk associated with LLMs in addition to bias [41]. Hallucinations occur when the model generates content that sounds plausible, but is ultimately incorrect or misleading based on factual information because the LLM lacks knowledge or sufficient context in the immediate content to have a clear answer [66]. For example, an LLM may fabricate answers when encountering a question or scenario that is beyond their training data or understanding. This presents a particularly dangerous situation in high-stakes areas where meaningful accuracy and trustworthiness are crucial [67]. As the LLM field continues to grow, addressing these risks through bias-mitigation techniques, fact-checking, and other forms of transparency will hopefully support the possibility of utilizing these models in a safe and effective manner [68]. The application of bias-mitigation strategies such as bias education, one-shot, and few-shot bias demonstrations leads to improvements in performance within medical applications in LLMs [69]. Systematic bias-mitigation and integrated fact-checking can reduce harmful outputs today, while the longer-term goal is to build decentralized LLM ecosystems that diversify training data and governance, further safeguarding against bias, privacy loss, and hallucinations [55].

In summary Table 9.1, have discussed a few important technical limitations of LLMs. This is not to say that LLMs do not show remarkable capabilities, these challenges, including reliance on data, high computational costs, context ceilings, and bias/hallucination risks, are still substantial limitations to overcome in a healthcare setting, particularly for single-patient applications. Future approaches to mitigating these challenges may include improving existing constraints by federated learning and energy efficient architectures.

9.4 ETHICAL AND LEGAL CHALLENGES

Large language models (LLMs) in healthcare raise glaring ethical and legal issues, including the risk of presenting sensitive medical information to the patient without suitable emotional support [43]. A growing ability

Table 9.1 Key technical limitations of LLMs in healthcare: challenges, solutions, and future directions

Categories	*Challenges*	*Solutions*	*Future directions*
Training Data Requirements	Data quality; duplication; privacy concerns; and memorization issues.	Leverage transfer learning and synthetic data.	Federated learning to pool decentralized data.
Tokenization Challenges	Abbreviations and multilingual data cause tokenization errors.	Develop domain-specific tokenizers.	Unified biomedical vocabulary standards.
Computational Costs	High resource and energy demand limit accessibility.	Optimized training algorithms; hardware-efficient design.	Green AI initiatives for sustainable scaling.
Fine-Tuning Challenges	Resource-intensive fine-tuning limits small-scale access.	Few-shot learning and human-in-the-loop validation.	Automated fine-tuning pipelines.
Inference Latency	Slow output generation in real-time settings.	Model pruning, quantization, and efficient attention.	Hardware-software co-design for latency reduction.
Limited Context Length	Inability to handle long documents or retain early context.	Hierarchical attention mechanisms.	Modular models for dynamic context handling.
Knowledge Updating	Lack of efficient methods to update models without full retraining.	Model editing and plugin-based knowledge updates.	Integration with real-time knowledge bases.
Cost Barriers	High cost in computation and hardware for training and deployment.	Open-source models and cloud-based APIs.	Public-private partnerships for equitable access.
Foundation Model Risks	Bias, hallucinations, and lack of factual grounding.	Bias mitigation, fact-checking, and transparency tools.	Decentralized LLM ecosystems.

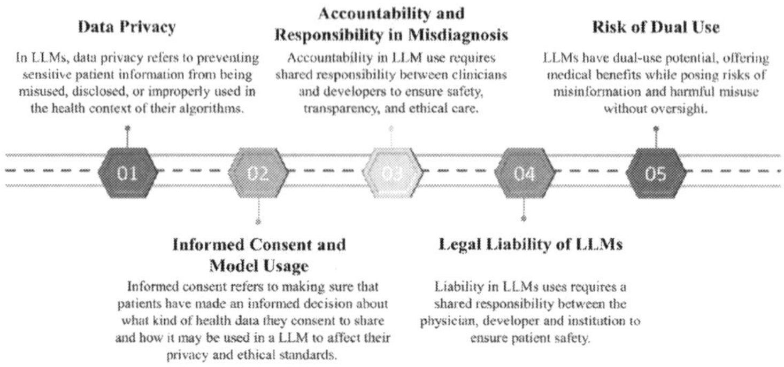

Figure 9.2 Key ethical and legal considerations in implementing LLMs in healthcare.

to distinguish human (or human-authored) from machine (or machine-authored) content with a potential for misinformation or malpractice and a potential for oversight in ensuring accuracy and ethical responsibility [70 –72]. Also critical is ensuring responsible use of patient data, otherwise the patient autonomy will be compromised, and biased (or inaccurate) medical decisions will be made [73]. Finally, the evolution of LLMs as a field will bring ethical and legal issues such as data privacy, informed consent, and AI-assisted diagnosis accountability to the forefront of healthcare systems, and these issues must be addressed responsibly before LLMs are implemented into healthcare systems for patient diagnosis and treatment. An overview of some potential ethical and legal issues is represented in Figure 9.2.

9.4.1 Data privacy

Data privacy poses an important ethical dilemma in using LLMs for healthcare. For LLM's, the risk of data privacy abuse is heightened because they are often trained on large datasets containing sensitive, identifiable personal health data [74]. Using patient data for training in LLMs without proper informed consent both violates patient autonomy and undermines patient data protection. These regulations are strict and emphasize clear disclosures, honest handling of patient data, security of that data, and explicit consent for use of identifiable personal health data [44, 75]. Moreover, healthcare data is a valuable target for hackers, thus the risk of privacy and data breaches is always high, even when other privacy protections such as security measures are established. Thus, when LLMs store or transmit a patient's personal identifiable information, they may create vulnerabilities to more identifiable patient information, despite the security measures in place [76, 77]. LLMs become more vulnerable when their training data lacks diversity. This can lead to biased results, especially for marginalized or underrepresented groups. Misdiagnoses or poor-quality care may occur when LLMs are relied upon, especially if the model's predictions are biased due to the training data used [42, 78]. To work through the dilemmas above, a priority is that patient data is always only used if absolutely necessary, and always with explicit consent. As long as LLMs can meet the demands of data privacy and are transparent as to how they reach their conclusions about that training data and incidentally about ethics from patient care, LLMs should accept and assume standard data privacy protocols [73]. Establishing a regulatory oversight engagement will improve patient privacy and protection for the patient population as well as reduce bias and safeguard against ethical dilemmas related to LLMs and the use of data in patient care [79].

9.4.2 Informed consent and model usage

Informed consent is a key element when using patient data to develop LLMs, particularly within the medical sector [80]. This is because patients must be sufficiently informed about the use of their personal health information, including how the patient data will be used, the scope of its use, and any risks associated with its use to develop LLMs [81]. Informed consent is not simply about getting permission; it requires a clear understanding of how personal health information will be used. Healthcare providers must ensure that patients can accurately understand how their data is used in developing LLMs, and what implications this may have on their care [82, 83]. Where appropriate consent processes are lacking, ethical harms may include violations of patient autonomy and a breakdown of trust in the healthcare system [84]. Additionally, failure to appropriately consider consent can violate legal obligations, such as the US Health Insurance Portability and Accountability Act (HIPAA) or European Union General Data Protection Regulation (EU GDPR), which protect the rights of patients and protect their information [79, 85]. Therefore, healthcare organizations need to ensure that they have the right consent and have made competent arrangements for consent to be adequately communicated, to ensure that patient privacy has not been violated [43, 86, 87].

9.4.3 Accountability and responsibility in misdiagnosis

With the medical use of LLMs, responsibility and accountability will become even more important, especially if a misdiagnosis happens. Misdiagnoses raise challenging ethical issues regarding who is responsible: the clinician who automatically relies on the LLM, the developers of the LLM who trained the model on biased data, or the institution that endorsed the use of the LLM when it had known limitations [13, 33, 84]. To ensure ethical and safe occur, it is recommended that the various stakeholders, including healthcare professionals, healthcare institutions, and AI developers, create accountability frameworks. This will include pre-trial evaluation of artificial intelligence (AI) solutions before they are used in clinical practice, full transparency of how AI tools are developed, and continual audits of the AI in clinical practice. A shared sense of responsibility ensures high levels of care delivery and accountability to patient safety [74, 79, 84].

9.4.4 Legal liability of LLMs in healthcare decision-making

The use of large language models (LLMs) in healthcare is promising but complicated in relation to the law. If harm was caused by the diagnosis or treatment aided by an LLM, questions of liability arise and who is liable. There may be liability on the part of the clinicians who relied on the model, the developers who built it, or both. Clinicians have a duty, which cannot be delegated, for independent clinical judgment [73, 84]. Clinicians must critically evaluate LLM suggestions based on existing standards of care and particulars on how the suggestions fit into the needs of the patients. Practicing under the basis of an LLM does not excuse clinicians from liability if the recommendation conflicts with accepted guidelines or standards of care [79, 86]. LLM developers also hold responsibility. They must clearly communicate the model's capabilities, limitations, and known risks. Without transparency and communication, the act of meaningful informed judgment cannot be set, and physicians have no parameters to use or not use the systems [79, 84]. Healthcare institutions engage in liability as well. They should set up governance such as training providers how to properly use LLMs; monitoring and evaluating the LLM model; addressing issues surrounding liability where an LLM fails to provide care; and providing clinician education [79, 86]. These areas of governance help PCPs to deploy LLMs and avoid violation of their ethical duties and promote safety. Ultimately, the future of LLMs has many opportunities, but will be successful only if clinicians, LLM developers, and regulators are working together, they share liability, and responsibility is understood. Only when agreement is shared on these issues can LLMs benefit patient care in a legitimate, responsible, and predictive way [74, 79, 84].

9.4.5 Risk of dual use

The "dual use" concept highlights that technologies like large language models (LLMs) can be applied for both beneficial and harmful purposes. In the field of healthcare, the uses of LLMs can bring tremendous benefits, help with healthcare research, support clinical decisions, and improve patient outcomes; or if used wrongly or combined with misinformation, LLMs can create harm by generating false outputs [13, 41, 43]. To mitigate these risks, ethical and regulatory safeguards are essential. These safeguards should encompass transparency regarding the training data, articulating the limitations and safeguards for each model, and overseeing the interaction the LLMs have with decision-makers in the healthcare field and the public [74, 84]. An equally important safeguard will be user education that provides them with the skills to effectively judge the quality of the health information they come across. With effective supervision, accountability, and public education, LLMs will have the opportunity to make a meaningful contribution to trustworthy medical knowledge, and help reduce misuse of LLMs [41, 74, 79, 84].

9.5 SOCIO-TECHNICAL BARRIERS IN ADOPTING LLMS IN HEALTHCARE

Large language models (LLMs) genuinely possess transformative potential for healthcare; however, serious ethical and social issues must be addressed simultaneously (Refer to Table 9.2). Concerns such as algorithmic bias, healthcare inequities, privacy breaches, misinformation, and overreliance on automation may lead to serious and unintended consequences, and should be managed carefully [43, 74]. The responsible use of LLMs is vital and entails transparency, accountability, and collaboration among clinicians, developers, and policymakers. Without considered attention to these challenges, LLMs could exacerbate existing inequities and harm trust within our healthcare systems [84].

9.5.1 Bias in large language models in healthcare

The prospective biases within large language models (LLMs) generate major issues regarding potential usage in healthcare, where the challenges of fairness, accuracy, and equity matter [43]. Of course, developing and deploying LLMs requires training data of considerable size, which is often biased by race, gender, socioeconomic status, or even disease prevalence. This bias can be embedded into models, and continue downstream into bias in the delivery of care [43, 74]. For example, one study on skin cancer identified that models trained with a majority of patients with lighter skin performed poorly diagnosing conditions on patients with darker skin, thus created deleterious diagnostic errors for that population [42]. Similar findings have shown that LLMs may struggle to identify medical conditions in underrepresented groups, reinforcing inequities in clinical outcomes [42, 43]. Bias in LLMs goes beyond clinical errors—it can also manifest through perpetuating social stereotypes or producing convincing yet incorrect

Table 9.2 Summaries of socio-technical barriers in adopting LLMs in healthcare

Areas of concern	*Challenges*	*Implications*	*Recommendations*
Bias in LLMs	Bias from training data leads to unfair outcomes, especially for underrepresented groups. LLMs may perpetuate stereotypes or misdiagnose certain populations.	Reduced diagnostic reliability and increased risk of harm for minority populations; erosion of fairness and trust in AI tools.	Diversify training datasets, conduct regular audits, and involve ethicists and clinicians in model evaluation.
Health Equity	LLMs may favor well-represented populations in training data, worsening digital and care disparities for marginalized groups.	Decreased access and poorer outcomes for underserved communities; increased digital divide in healthcare.	Ensure inclusive datasets, audit model outputs, and train clinicians to recognize and mitigate biased responses.
Adoption Barriers	Technical complexity, data security concerns, and lack of regulatory frameworks hinder safe and equitable integration of LLMs into healthcare systems.	Mistrust of AI, risks to patient privacy, and potential for misinformation without clinical oversight or accountability.	Develop regulatory protocols, ensure transparency, protect data privacy, and foster collaboration among stakeholders.

medical information [13, 41]. Because LLMs learn from a mix of reliable and unreliable sources, they may generate plausible but inaccurate content that misleads users and influences poor clinical decisions [13]. Addressing these issues requires multi-level interventions. This includes using more diverse and representative training data, integrating bias detection mechanisms, and conducting regular audits [42, 74]. Ethics oversight should not involve the data scientists alone, but also the clinicians and ethicists who can provide valuable context and judgment. Making LLMs equitable is not just a technical hurdle—it is an ethical obligation [74, 84]. For these models to be used in healthcare or public-facing contexts, expectations and best practices should be clear in how models will be developed and used. Only then will LLMs legitimately support the goal of health equity and operating at the intersection of AI and care which allows for all patients experience the benefit of AI augmenting their care [43, 74].

9.5.2 Health equity and large language models

The application of large language models (LLMs) in health care has great potential, but it also raises questions related to health equity [74]. LLMs are built off enormous corpuses of text which may contain the biases of ethnicity, gender, socioeconomic status and prevalence of disease. Systemic inequalities in healthcare could be exacerbated through model biases creating biased recommendations in care [43]. The model tends to perform better for groups that are well-represented in its training data, and worse for those who are not. It could lead to generating inappropriate or poorly recommended care designations for underrepresented demographic groups, such as dark-skinned people or ethnic minorities [42, 74]. Notably, the deployment of LLMs into the health care system may further exacerbate digital health disparities. Marginalized participants who may face barriers to traditional healthcare may be more likely to use AI tools, which can yield inaccurate and biased information [74, 84]. This may entrench mistrust in health care systems and perpetuate disenfranchisement. Going forward, health care systems should be committed to equity when deploying LLMs [43]. Organizations can work towards equity by utilizing equitable representation in training datasets, clearly identifying and auditing bias, and preparing clinicians to recognize and mitigate bias in LLM outputs. LLMs can effectively address care gaps and improve patient access in a manner that better meets patient needs when equity is prioritized leading to more equitable health outcomes [74].

9.5.3 Barriers to LLMs adoption in healthcare

Using large language models (LLMs) in healthcare is not without major hurdles. There are technical hurdles to overcome and limits to the uptake of LLMs, especially due to high infrastructure costs for implementations in low-resource settings [33]. Other hurdles can be considered concerns under legal, ethical, and evidence-based lenses, including data ownership, data privacy, or institutional control, which can be challenged if closed-source vendor models are implemented; in this case, the potential for loss of control and data breaches is elevated [74, 84]. Related to operational readiness, LLMs introduce ethical and regulatory concerns related to biases from the training data (including challenges from a lack of transparency) and accountability in AI-assisted decisions [79, 84]. Without appropriate safeguards, the use of LLMs in healthcare risks reinforcing disparities based on race, sex, or socioeconomic factors [42]. Importantly, there is a lack of homogeneous standards or processes that classify their safety and effectiveness in clinical environments as well [81]. A successful system implementation will be dependent upon the collaboration of clinicians, developers, administrators, and regulators to develop legal, ethical, and evidence-based standards [73, 86]. New and changed processes, which require adequate training and the ability to communicate with developers adequately, will also be necessary for organizational buy-in by clinicians, as LLMs are not a support for, but are a competing interest to, clinical judgment [35, 86].

9.6 TECHNICAL AND REGULATORY CHALLENGES IN LLMS IN HEALTHCARE

Large language models (LLMs) have great potential for knowledge generation in healthcare, but their real-world implementation faces significant barriers. There are limitations of the models, challenges with interpretability, as well as concerns around privacy and regulation [40]. For LLMs to be securely embedded into clinical workflows, we must find ways to establish transparency, validate the models, and enrich them with the necessary databases, ensuring participants have enough protection around privacy and to overcome adversarial threats. Without thoughtful oversight, LLMs risk producing unreliable outputs, exposing systems to breaches, and compromising patient trust and safety [40, 75]. The following subsections examine the most pressing technical and regulatory challenges essential to the ethical and safe deployment of LLMs in medicine [79]. These challenges are summarized in Figure 9.3, which provides an overview of the key technical and regulatory concerns discussed in this section.

9.6.1 Black box

The "black box" nature of large language models (LLMs) remains a major barrier to clinical adoption since LLMs can produce fluent, high-confidence outputs without explanations[40, 44]. To address this, both technical and regulatory developments have been proposed. Domain-specific LLMs such

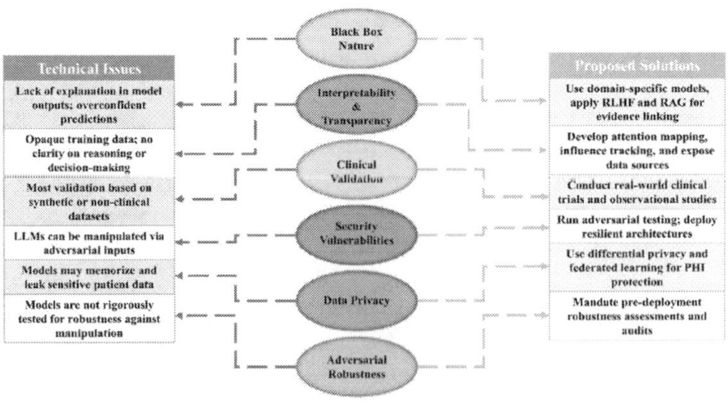

Figure 9.3 Key technical and regulatory barriers to LLM implementation in healthcare.

as ClinicalBERT, GatorTron, and Med-PaLM have been shown to be more effective at clinical tasks. Methods such as reinforcement learning with human feedback (RLHF) and retrieval-augmented generation (RAG) have been used for improving the accuracy and validity of responses by connecting them to trustworthy sources of information [4, 40, 41]. Interpretability has been addressed partially using attention mapping and influence tracing, which aim to reveal reasoning patterns relevant to the clinical context [44]. There are still regulatory loopholes since evaluation frameworks are not standardized and lack real-world validation methods [86]. Regulatory sandboxes have been proposed to enable safe testing of LLMs with actual clinical data. Domain-specific explain ability criteria, fairness audits, and equity benchmarks have also been proposed [73, 74]. Rigorous validation, including clinical trials or observational studies, should come before the implementation of novel methods. Ethical and effective use requires the involvement of physicians, data experts, ethicists, and patients. By removing technical uncertainty and legal ambiguity, LLMs can evolve from experimental technology into trusted systems supporting clinical decision-making [73, 79, 86].

9.6.2 Interpretability, transparency, and clinical validation of LLMs in healthcare

In order for large language models (LLMs) to be considered safe and effective in clinical practice, it is important that they offer interpretability, transparency of data sources, and validation [44]. Even if an LLM has a high degree of linguistic fluency, it is important to remember that they are still, at their core, statistically predicting the next word in a sequence of words, and therefore they do not offer true clinical reasoning, making it difficult for clinicians to understand how the model arrived at any of its conclusions or statements [3, 13]. A significant and important part of this problem is the transparency surrounding the materials the LLM was trained on and the decision-making processes used in providing outputs [79]. Determining whether model recommendations may be safe or fair, are grounded in the most up-to-date medical evidence, or simply apply clinically necessary population generalizations, is impossible without access to training datasets or insight into how an LLM generates an output [41, 79]. As such, this work would appear to have enormous implications for clinician trust and adoption of healthcare applications. Most literature demonstrating the clinically valid capabilities of LLMs bases the LLM experience upon controlled or synthetic data, and more importantly, no real-world validation has resulted from those real clinical experiences [86]. As a response to the above concerns, experts in the field recommend that large language models be evaluated in real-world populations and disease contexts through structured clinical trials and observational studies [73, 86]. Experts also recommend integrating other medical evaluations found in attention visualizations and evidence citations, to increase human oversight of any modelling work. Without such precautions being in place, the ethical and practical application of LLMs in medicine is questionable. Therefore, staying committed to robustly validating clinical use and other safety measurements will be critical for any ethical integration into clinical care [41, 70].

9.6.3 Security, data privacy, and adversarial vulnerabilities of LLMs in healthcare

As large language models (LLMs) are being explored for clinical use, grave concerns have been expressed regarding their security, data privacy, and vulnerability to adversarial attacks. This represents a significant challenge to safe use in healthcare contexts, where patient confidentiality is critical and system reliability is paramount [76]. Security vulnerabilities are built into the architecture of LLMs, confounding their use under adversarial prompts or inputs. These inputs can range from negligent to highly intentional manipulation to produce biased, harmful, or factually incorrect outputs from models, even when specific mitigation strategies have been developed [64, 66]. Compounding this issue, many models will typically provide responses based upon user prompts, even when the prompt could elicit factually incorrect or ethically inappropriate outputs. Data privacy is also a significant concern. Because LLMs are trained on large and opaque datasets, there is a risk that personally identifiable health information could be memorized and exposed by the model if proper safeguards are not in place [76, 77]. In healthcare contexts, which are even more troubling because of data privacy regulations requiring protection for sensitive data. In terms of risk reduction, domain-aware, privacy-preserving architectures have been proposed, using differential privacy or federated-learning schemes to help mitigate exposure of PHI while training [75]. It should be mandated that adversarial robustness testing be conducted prior to deploying models in clinical settings to ensure robustness to input manipulations [73, 76]. Finally, transparent documentation on data sources and risk audits should be established to mitigate unwanted data breaches and use AI responsibly. Without these foundational risks being addressed, LLMs cannot be safely or ethically integrated into healthcare systems [44, 73].

9.7 CONCLUSION

The incorporation of LLMs in healthcare, however, presents near-revolutionary opportunities, such as improving clinical decision support, decreasing documentation burden, enhancing patient communication, and potentially, supporting the drug discovery process [41, 43]. What is most salient about LLMs is their ability to engage and utilize large amounts of unstructured data to generate coherent responses replicating a human response, which inspires possible improvements in efficiency and access. These opportunities come with limitations involving technical, social, ethical, and regulatory challenges [43]. Specialized, domain-specific models, explain ability technology, and reinforcement learning from human feedback have demonstrated substantial improvements, but more work is needed to guarantee clinical robustness and safety [4]. There is, without doubt, ethical issues related to privacy, fairness, misinformation, and accountability. When LLMs do not use diverse or high-quality data, they could exacerbate existing health inequalities. Moreover, the lack of regulatory frameworks around liability complicates the safe and responsible use of LLMs in health contexts [43, 84]. The prospect of dual use–dissemination of health-related misinformation–indicates further considerations for the implementation of LLMs that necessitate oversight and governance of LLMs in health-related contexts. Future work should first center on thorough clinical validation using structured clinical trials and post-deployment monitoring [41, 74, 86]. Creating standardized evaluation processes, transparency, and implementing interpretability are all essential to the success of an LLM. Engaging interdisciplinary teams comprising clinicians, data scientists, ethicists, and policy makers to create thoughtful, ethical, and useful integration is also critically important [73]. Establishing standardized evaluation methods, being transparent, and implementing interpretability into LLM is paramount. Also critical will be the engagement of interdisciplinary teams, comprised of clinicians, data scientists, ethicists, and policymakers, to develop meaningful, ethical, and effective integration [44, 73]. In conclusion, the proper use of LLMs in health care will necessitate an alignment of innovation with human values, equity, and safety. With continued research, regulation, and involvement of stakeholders, LLMs can be developed from experimental mechanisms to trustworthy infrastructure for today's healthcare delivery systems.

REFERENCES

1. Esteva A, Robicquet A, Ramsundar B, et al. A guide to deep learning in healthcare. *Nature Medicine*. 2019;25(1):24–29.
2. Brown T, Mann B, Ryder N, et al. Language models are few-shot learners. *Advances in Neural Information Processing Systems*. 2020;33:1877–1901.
3. Harrer S. Attention is not all you need: the complicated case of ethically using large language models in healthcare and medicine. *EBioMedicine*. 2023;90, 104512,.
4. Singhal K, Azizi S, Tu T, et al. Large language models encode clinical knowledge. *Nature*. 2023;620(7972):172–180.

5. Kung TH, Cheatham M, Medenilla A, et al. Performance of ChatGPT on USMLE: potential for AI-assisted medical education using large language models. *PLoS Digital Health*. 2023;2(2):e0000198.
6. Luo R, Sun L, Xia Y, et al. BioGPT: generative pre-trained transformer for biomedical text generation and mining. *Briefings in Bioinformatics*. 2022;23(6):bbac409.
7. Bommasani R, Hudson DA, Adeli E, et al. On the opportunities and risks of foundation models. *arXiv preprint arXiv:210807258*, 2021.
8. Zhavoronkov A. Caution with AI-generated content in biomedicine. *Nature Medicine*. 2023;29(3):532.
9. He Y, Zhu Z, Zhang Y, et al. Infusing disease knowledge into BERT for health question answering, medical inference and disease name recognition. *arXiv preprint arXiv:201003746*, 2020.
10. Li C, Zhang Y, Weng Y, et al. Natural language processing applications for computer-aided diagnosis in oncology. *Diagnostics*. 2023;13(2):286.
11. Lee J, Yoon W, Kim S, et al. BioBERT: a pre-trained biomedical language representation model for biomedical text mining. *Bioinformatics*. 2020;36(4):1234–1240.
12. Gu Y, Tinn R, Cheng H, et al. Domain-specific language model pretraining for biomedical natural language processing. *ACM Transactions on Computing for Healthcare (HEALTH)*. 2021;3(1):1–23.
13. Shen Y, Heacock L, Elias J, et al. *ChatGPT and other large language models are double-edged swords*. Radiological Society of North America; 2023. p. e230163.
14. Voelker R. The promise and pitfalls of AI in the complex world of diagnosis, treatment, and disease management. *JAMA*. 2023;330(15):1416–1419.
15. Ayers JW, Poliak A, Dredze M, et al. Comparing physician and artificial intelligence chatbot responses to patient questions posted to a public social media forum. *JAMA Internal Medicine*. 2023;183(6):589–596.
16. Gilson A, Safranek CW, Huang T, et al. How does ChatGPT perform on the United States Medical Licensing Examination (USMLE)? The implications of large language models for medical education and knowledge assessment. *JMIR Medical Education*. 2023;9(1):e45312.
17. Ali SR, Dobbs TD, Hutchings HA, Whitaker IS. Using ChatGPT to write patient clinic letters. *The Lancet Digital Health*. 2023;5(4):e179–e181.
18. Garcia MB. Using AI tools in writing peer review reports: should academic journals embrace the use of ChatGPT? *Annals of Biomedical Engineering*. 2024;52(2):139–140.
19. Li Y, Li Z, Zhang K, et al. Chatdoctor: A medical chat model fine-tuned on a large language model meta-ai (llama) using medical domain knowledge. *Cureus*. 2023;15(6),14070.
20. Lei L, Liu D. A new medical academic word list: A corpus-based study with enhanced methodology. *Journal of English for Academic Purposes*. 2016;22:42–53.
21. Beltagy I, Lo K, Cohan A. SciBERT: A pretrained language model for scientific text. *arXiv preprint arXiv:190310676*, 2019.
22. Alsentzer E, Murphy JR, Boag W, et al. Publicly available clinical BERT embeddings. *arXiv preprint arXiv:190403323*, 2019.

23. Johnson AE, Pollard TJ, Shen L, et al. MIMIC-III, a freely accessible critical care database. *Scientific Data*. 2016;3(1):1–9.
24. Yang X, Chen A, PourNejatian N, et al. A large language model for electronic health records. *NPJ Digital Medicine*. 2022;5(1):194.
25. Xu C, Guo D, Duan N, McAuley J. Baize: An open-source chat model with parameter-efficient tuning on self-chat data. *arXiv preprint arXiv:230401196*, 2023.
26. Thirunavukarasu AJ, Hassan R, Mahmood S, et al. Trialling a large language model (ChatGPT) in general practice with the applied knowledge test: observational study demonstrating opportunities and limitations in primary care. *JMIR Medical Education*. 2023;9(1):e46599.
27. Zhou Z, Wang X, Li X, Liao L. Is ChatGPT an evidence-based doctor? *European Urology*. 2023;84(3):355–356.
28. Wang S, Zhao Z, Ouyang X, et al. Chatcad: Interactive computer-aided diagnosis on medical image using large language models. *arXiv preprint arXiv:230207257*, 2023.
29. Sorin V, Barash Y, Konen E, Klang E. Large language models for oncological applications. *Journal of Cancer Research and Clinical Oncology*. 2023;149(11):9505–9508.
30. Matin RN, Linos E, Rajan N. *Leveraging large language models in dermatology*. Oxford University Press US; 2023. p. 253–254.
31. Jin D, Pan E, Oufattole N, et al. What disease does this patient have? a large-scale open domain question answering dataset from medical exams. *Applied Sciences*. 2021;11(14):6421.
32. Rao A, Pang M, Kim J, et al. Assessing the utility of ChatGPT throughout the entire clinical workflow. *MedRxiv*. 2023:2023.02. 21.23285886.
33. Hager P, Jungmann F, Holland R, et al. Evaluation and mitigation of the limitations of large language models in clinical decision-making. *Nature Medicine*. 2024;30(9):2613–2622.
34. Goodman RS, Patrinely JR, Stone CA, et al. Accuracy and reliability of chatbot responses to physician questions. *JAMA Network Open*. 2023;6(10):e2336483.
35. Sallam M, editor ChatGPT utility in healthcare education, research, and practice: systematic review on the promising perspectives and valid concerns. *Healthcare*; 2023: MDPI.
36. Van Veen D, Van Uden C, Blankemeier L, et al. Adapted large language models can outperform medical experts in clinical text summarization. *Nature Medicine*. 2024;30(4):1134–1142.
37. Arndt BG, Beasley JW, Watkinson MD, et al. Tethered to the EHR: primary care physician workload assessment using EHR event log data and time-motion observations. *The Annals of Family Medicine*. 2017;15(5):419–426.
38. Robinson KE, Kersey JA. Novel electronic health record (EHR) education intervention in large healthcare organization improves quality, efficiency, time, and impact on burnout. *Medicine*. 2018;97(38):e12319.
39. Tang L, Sun Z, Idnay B, et al. Evaluating large language models on medical evidence summarization. *NPJ Digital Medicine*. 2023;6(1):158.
40. Nazi ZA, Peng W, editors. Large language models in healthcare and medical domain: A review. *Informatics*; 2024: MDPI.

41. Tian S, Jin Q, Yeganova L, et al. Opportunities and challenges for ChatGPT and large language models in biomedicine and health. *Briefings in Bioinformatics*. 2024;25(1):bbad493.
42. Yang Y, Liu X, Jin Q, et al. Unmasking and quantifying racial bias of large language models in medical report generation. *Communications Medicine*. 2024;4(1):176.
43. Omiye JA, Gui H, Rezaei SJ, et al. Large language models in medicine: the potentials and pitfalls: a narrative review. *Annals of Internal Medicine*. 2024;177(2):210–220.
44. Mökander J, Schuett J, Kirk HR, Floridi L. Auditing large language models: a three-layered approach. *AI and Ethics*. 2024;4(4):1085–1115.
45. Kanzawa J, Yasaka K, Fujita N, et al. Automated classification of brain MRI reports using fine-tuned large language models. *Neuroradiology*. 2024:, 66(12)1–7.
46. Kanemaru N, Yasaka K, Fujita N, et al. The fine-tuned large language model for extracting the progressive bone metastasis from unstructured radiology reports. *Journal of Imaging Informatics in Medicine*. 2025;38(2):865–872.
47. Sun Z. A short survey of viewing large language models in legal aspect. *arXiv preprint arXiv:230309136*, 2023.
48. Kaplan J, McCandlish S, Henighan T, et al. Scaling laws for neural language models. *arXiv preprint arXiv:200108361*, 2020.
49. Kaddour J. The minipile challenge for data-efficient language models. *arXiv preprint arXiv:230408442*, 2023.
50. Kaddour J, Harris J, Mozes M, et al. Challenges and applications of large language models. *arXiv preprint arXiv:230710169*, 2023.
51. Sennrich R, Haddow B, Birch A. Neural machine translation of rare words with subword units. *arXiv preprint arXiv:150807909*, 2015.
52. Fujii T, Shibata K, Yamaguchi A, et al. How do different tokenizers perform on downstream tasks in scriptio continua languages?: A case study in Japanese. *arXiv preprint arXiv:230609572*, 2023.
53. Amodei D, Olah C, Steinhardt J, et al. Concrete problems in AI safety. *arXiv preprint arXiv:160606565*, 2016.
54. Schwartz R, Dodge J, Smith NA, Etzioni O. Green AI. *Communications of the ACM*. 2020;63(12):54–63.
55. Finlayson SG, Subbaswamy A, Singh K, et al. The clinician and dataset shift in artificial intelligence. *New England Journal of Medicine*. 2021;385(3):283–286.
56. Devlin J, Chang M-W Lee K, Toutanova K, editors. Bert: Pre-training of deep bidirectional transformers for language understanding. *Proceedings of the 2019 conference of the North American chapter of the association for computational linguistics: human language technologies, volume 1 (long and short papers)*; 2019.
57. Li XL, Liang P. Prefix-tuning: Optimizing continuous prompts for generation. *arXiv preprint arXiv:210100190*, 2021.
58. Antunes RS, André da Costa C, Küderle A, et al. Federated learning for healthcare: Systematic review and architecture proposal. *ACM Transactions on Intelligent Systems and Technology (TIST)*. 2022;13(4):1–23.

59. Li R, Fu D, Shi C, et al. Efficient LLMs Training and Inference: An Introduction. *IEEE Access*. 13, 32944-32970, 2024.
60. Pagliardini M, Paliotta D, Jaggi M, Fleuret F. Faster causal attention over large sequences through sparse flash attention. *arXiv preprint arXiv:230601160*, 2023.
61. Yao Z, Yazdani Aminabadi R, Zhang M, et al. Zeroquant: Efficient and affordable post-training quantization for large-scale transformers. *Advances in Neural Information Processing Systems*. 2022;35:27168–27183.
62. Chen S, Wong S, Chen L, Tian Y. Extending context window of large language models via positional interpolation. *arXiv preprint arXiv:230615595*, 2023.
63. Li R, Su J, Duan C, Zheng S. Linear attention mechanism: An efficient attention for semantic segmentation. *arXiv preprint arXiv:200714902*, 2020.
64. Yao Y, Wang P, Tian B, et al. Editing large language models: Problems, methods, and opportunities. *arXiv preprint arXiv:230513172*, 2023.
65. Schick T, Schütze H. It's not just size that matters: Small language models are also few-shot learners. *arXiv preprint arXiv:200907118*, 2020.
66. Rawte V, Sheth A, Das A. A survey of hallucination in large foundation models. *arXiv preprint arXiv:230905922*, 2023.
67. McCoy RT, Pavlick E, Linzen T. Right for the wrong reasons: Diagnosing syntactic heuristics in natural language inference. *arXiv preprint arXiv:190201007*, 2019.
68. Raza S, Raval A, Chatrath V. Mbias: Mitigating bias in large language models while retaining context. *arXiv preprint arXiv:240511290*, 2024.
69. Schmidgall S, Harris C, Essien I, et al. Evaluation and mitigation of cognitive biases in medical language models. *npj Digital Medicine*. 2024;7(1):295.
70. Floridi L. The ethics of artificial intelligence: Principles, challenges, and opportunities. 2023.
71. Pal A, Umapathi LK, Sankarasubbu M. Med-halt: Medical domain hallucination test for large language models. *arXiv preprint arXiv:230715343*, 2023.
72. Liao W, Liu Z, Dai H, et al. Differentiating ChatGPT-generated and human-written medical texts: quantitative study. *JMIR Medical Education*. 2023;9(1):e48904.
73. Williams M, Karim W, Gelman J, Raza M. Ethical data acquisition for LLMs and AI algorithms in healthcare. *npj Digital Medicine*. 2024;7(1):377.
74. Organization WH. *Ethics and governance of artificial intelligence for health: large multi-modal models. WHO guidance*. World Health Organization; 2024.
75. De Maio C, Fenza G, Furno D, et al. Privacy-Preserving Healthcare Data Interactions: A Multi-Agent Approach Using LLMs. *Journal of Communications Software and Systems*. 2025;21(1):13–22.
76. Miranda M, Ruzzetti ES, Santilli A, et al. Preserving privacy in large language models: A survey on current threats and solutions. *arXiv preprint arXiv:240805212*, 2024.
77. Marks M, Haupt CE. AI chatbots, health privacy, and challenges to HIPAA compliance. *JAMA*. 2023;330(4):309–310.

78. Omar M, Sorin V, Agbareia R, et al. Evaluating and addressing demographic disparities in medical large language models: a systematic review. *International Journal for Equity in Health*. 2025;24(1):57.
79. Meskó B, Topol EJ. The imperative for regulatory oversight of large language models (or generative AI) in healthcare. *NPJ Digital Medicine*. 2023;6(1):120.
80. Protection FD. General data protection regulation (GDPR). *Intersoft Consulting*, Accessed in October. 2018;24(1).
81. Tilala MH, Chenchala PK, Choppadandi A, et al. Ethical considerations in the use of artificial intelligence and machine learning in health care: a comprehensive review. *Cureus*. 2024;16(6), e62443-e62443.
82. Oye E, Faith H. *Ethical Considerations in AI Healthcare Solutions*. 2025.
83. Arellano L, Alcubilla P, Leguízamo L. Ethical considerations in informed consent. In *Ethics-Scientific Research, Ethical Issues, Artificial Intelligence and Education*: IntechOpen; 2023.
84. Ong JCL, Chang SY-H, William W, et al. Ethical and regulatory challenges of large language models in medicine. *The Lancet Digital Health*. 2024;6(6):e428–e432.
85. Momani A. Implications of Artificial Intelligence on Health Data Privacy and Confidentiality. *arXiv preprint arXiv:2501.01639*, 2025.
86. Mennella C, Maniscalco U, De Pietro G, Esposito M. Ethical and regulatory challenges of AI technologies in healthcare: A narrative review. *Heliyon*. 2024;10(4), e26297-e26297.
87. Feretzakis G, Vagena E, Kalodanis K, et al. GDPR and Large Language Models: Technical and Legal Obstacles. *Future Internet*. 2025;17(4):151.

Chapter 10

Future trends and innovations in healthcare systems using LLMs

Kiana Pilevar Abrisham and Khalil Alipour

10.1 INTRODUCTION

Artificial intelligence (AI) has seen remarkable strides over the past few years, with large language models (LLMs) emerging as one of their most impactful innovations—especially within the healthcare field [1, 2]. Built on transformer-based neural architectures, these models have evolved from advanced text generators into versatile tools that interpret complex medical language and work across varied data types—such as images, clinical signals, and structured health records [3, 4].

Healthcare is a natural fit for LLMs due to its vast and often fragmented landscape of information [5–7]. Clinicians must frequently make time-sensitive decisions while navigating large volumes of diverse data—from electronic health records (EHRs) and clinical notes to real-time monitoring outputs and ever-expanding medical literature [8, 9]. LLMs help manage this complexity by synthesizing information from multiple sources and prioritizing the most relevant insights for each clinical context. They extract relevant details, generate concise summaries, and adapt language to fit different communication needs—supporting decisions, drafting clinical notes, clarifying treatment options, or guiding conversations with patients in a more accessible and patient-friendly way [10–13].

Some LLMs are already demonstrating advanced performance in specialized medical tasks. Fine-tuned models like BioBERT [14] and ClinicalBERT [15] have been designed to work with medical text, while others such as BioGPT and Med-PaLM have excelled in standardized evaluations like the USMLE, pointing to their growing potential in clinical workflows [16, 17]. One illustrative use case is shown in Figure 10.1, where wearable devices and LLM-based analytics are combined to offer real-time, personalized health monitoring.

Beyond direct patient care, LLMs are also playing a role in how healthcare systems communicate and operate. They're being used to simplify technical terms for patients, automate documentation tasks like billing or reporting, and even act as digital assistants during clinical encounters [18]. In research, they help make sense of large volumes of literature and

DOI: 10.1201/9781003665083-10

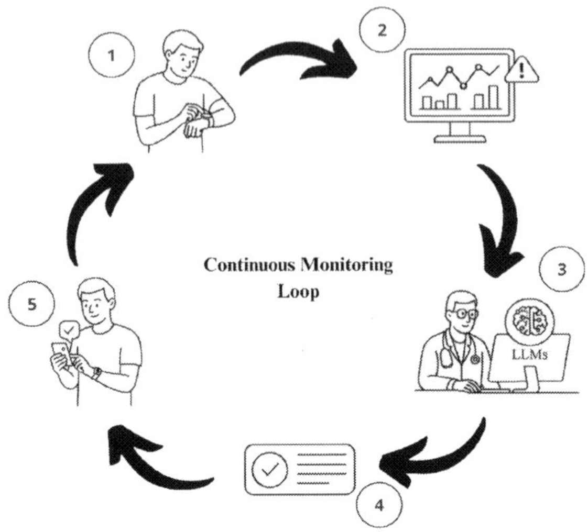

Figure 10.1 Continuous monitoring loop integrating LLM-based signal analysis, wearable devices, and feedback mechanisms in real-time clinical environments.

integrate data from different biomedical sources, accelerating discovery and collaboration [19, 20].

As LLMs continue to evolve, their connection to other technologies—such as federated learning, edge-AI, and multimodal interfaces—is enabling new forms of real-time, personalized, and scalable health interventions. They are not just improving existing processes but changing how healthcare itself is imagined and delivered [21].

In the sections ahead, this chapter examines the many ways LLMs are reshaping healthcare—from diagnostic support and patient education to scientific innovation and global coordination. These developments suggest a future of care that is not only more intelligent but also more equitable, responsive, and attuned to the needs of those it serves.

10.2 EMERGING TRENDS AND INNOVATIONS IN HEALTHCARE USING LLMS

LLMs are quickly moving from research labs into everyday healthcare—playing an active role in how care is delivered, studied, taught, and managed. They're helping address some of the most common challenges in the field, like scattered data, decision overload, communication barriers, and time-consuming workflows. As illustrated in Figure 10.2, ten key areas already show how these models can make a meaningful impact across the

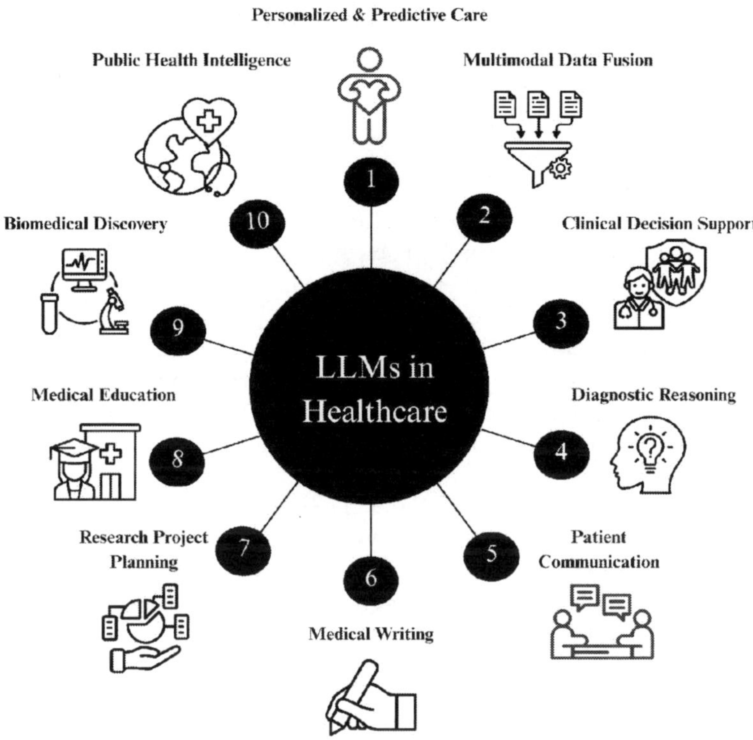

Figure 10.2 Ten emerging domains where LLMs are transforming healthcare, including clinical, research, educational, and operational applications.

healthcare landscape. The following subsections take a closer look at each of these domains.

10.2.1 Advancing personalized and predictive healthcare

Personalized and predictive medicine has come a long way in recent years, and LLMs are starting to contribute in practical ways. What makes them useful is how they can pull together many kinds of patient information, including test results, clinical notes, genetic data, and daily routines [22, 23]. Looking at this information all at once helps clinicians get a clearer understanding of what's going on with a patient and how their condition may be changing. That, in turn, can support better decisions and more tailored care.

A good example of this is the development of digital twins—virtual versions of patients that change in real time as new data becomes available.

These digital simulations give clinicians a safe way to explore how different treatments might work before making any actual decisions [24, 25].

LLMs also show promise in pharmacogenomics. By looking at a patient's genes alongside their medical history, the model can suggest which medications are more likely to be effective—and which ones may lead to side effects. This kind of insight helps doctors make safer and more personalized drug choices [26].

When used with wearable devices, LLMs can pick up early warning signs in a person's vital signs or physical state. This helps clinicians detect problems early and intervene before complications develop [27].

In critical care settings like the ICU or during surgery, these models can act as real-time assistants. They constantly monitor patient data, flag concerning patterns, and recommend changes to treatment as needed [28]. Since they're designed to learn from experience, they also improve with use—making them even more helpful in situations where conditions can change rapidly [29].

By pulling together insights from a person's genes, lifestyle, and health data, LLMs are helping medicine move toward care that is more personalized and responsive. The ability to provide timely, well-informed guidance helps doctors make safer, more thoughtful choices—tailored to what each patient actually needs.

10.2.2 Multimodal data fusion and clinical intelligence

Medical data today comes in many forms—imaging results, lab values, sensor data, clinical notes—but these are often kept in separate systems. This separation can make it harder to develop a full picture of a patient's condition. Multimodal LLMs aim to address this challenge by analyzing information from multiple sources simultaneously, allowing clinicians to better interpret complex cases [30].

In clinical practice, these models could interpret MRI scans, match findings with EHR narratives, incorporate genetic data, and generate a unified diagnostic summary. This layered approach supports more accurate diagnoses and better treatment decisions [31]. For example, in remote monitoring, an LLM might detect early signs of deterioration by linking biosignal changes with behavior and medication patterns—making early intervention possible [32].

In telemedicine, this becomes even more relevant. LLMs can assess spoken symptoms, images, and patient surveys in real time to guide triage or treatment. This is especially valuable in underserved settings where specialists may not be available [33].

Beyond the individual level, multimodal LLMs can enhance hospital-wide decision-making. They help track clinical patterns across departments, improve care coordination, and support smarter use of resources. By analyzing population-level data across different systems, they help institutions respond more quickly to emerging needs [34].

What sets these models apart is their flexibility—they can draw from diverse formats and specialties, linking fragmented data to offer clearer insights. With better data integration, clinical teams can reach decisions more confidently and act with greater precision.

10.2.3 Real-time clinical decision support and optimization

In today's fast-paced healthcare environments, clinicians often face information overload and time pressure. LLMs are emerging as powerful allies in real-time clinical decision support (CDS), acting as intelligent copilots that interpret complex inputs and deliver actionable recommendations across diverse settings—from outpatient clinics to emergency departments and intensive care units [35].

Within EHR systems, LLMs can automatically summarize patient histories, detect inconsistencies, and extract overlooked clinical clues. They also assist in suggesting appropriate diagnostic tests or treatments by referencing the latest medical evidence. This reduces cognitive burden and enhances efficiency—especially during high-stakes consultations where speed and accuracy are critical [36].

In acute care scenarios—such as intensive care units (ICUs) or EDs—LLMs support real-time clinical decision-making by continuously synthesizing incoming information like vital signs, lab values, and clinician notes. Rather than simply integrating data, they prioritize actionable findings, highlight urgent patterns, and deliver context-aware recommendations that guide rapid interventions in critical situations [28].

Importantly, many LLMs are designed with adaptive learning capabilities. They evolve with each interaction, refining their recommendations as they encounter new patient patterns, rare conditions, or institutional practices. This feedback mechanism allows the system to improve over time, keeping it aligned with changing clinical demands.

Recent evaluations show that LLMs perform well in specialized fields such as oncology [37], genetics [38], and general biomedicine [39]. When combined with biomedical knowledge graphs, their outputs become even more contextually grounded and reliable [40, 41].

Beyond diagnosis and treatment, LLMs also play a critical role in workflow optimization. They can automatically generate discharge summaries, progress notes, and billing records—enhancing documentation accuracy and significantly reducing the administrative load on clinicians [42–44].

Overall, LLM-powered decision support systems represent a major shift in clinical practice. While these systems can speed up routine tasks, their real value may lie in how they adapt care to the needs of each individual. Over time, they could also help clinicians catch diagnoses more accurately, ease some of the daily workload, and possibly improve patient outcomes—though that will depend on how they're integrated into practice.

10.2.4 Augmented clinical reasoning and diagnostic support

LLMs are increasingly proving valuable as cognitive collaborators in clinical reasoning. Their ability to recognize patterns, generate hypotheses, and synthesize complex inputs allows them to support physicians through the often uncertain and multifaceted diagnostic process. By rapidly analyzing patient-reported symptoms, free-text clinical notes, lab results, and longitudinal histories, LLMs help generate differential diagnoses, guide investigations, and prioritize next steps [45].

Across a wide range of specialties—from internal medicine and gastroenterology to dermatology and dentistry—LLMs are being used to interpret ambiguous symptom presentations and map them to guideline-based protocols or published literature [46]. When given free-text entries such as a patient's chief complaint, these models can extract key features, propose likely conditions, and recommend additional questions or tests to refine the diagnostic pathway. Many systems now provide accompanying rationale or cite evidence, enhancing transparency and encouraging clinician-patient collaboration [47].

LLMs are particularly impactful in time-constrained or resource-limited settings, where they help mitigate diagnostic delays, reduce cognitive biases, and offer decision support in the absence of specialist input. Their reliability and speed can make a significant difference in triage situations or in clinics with limited resources [48].

Additionally, LLMs serve as literature-aware diagnostic assistants, capable of surfacing rare case reports or relevant research that may otherwise be overlooked. They can help clinicians identify atypical conditions, catch inconsistencies in documentation, or propose confirmatory steps aligned with best practices [49].

As these models keep learning—especially from a wider range of clinical data like images, signals, and structured records—they're becoming better at picking up on the details that matter most in diagnosis. The goal isn't to replace human judgment but to support it. By offering consistent, evidence-informed suggestions, LLMs can help reduce guesswork, bring more clarity to complex decisions, and give both clinicians and patients a little more confidence in the care being delivered.

10.2.5 Enhancing patient communication and care in nursing and allied health

Good care starts with clear communication—but in reality, that's not always easy. Medical conversations often involve terms or instructions that feel confusing, especially for someone who isn't used to healthcare settings. If things aren't explained clearly, patients can walk away uncertain about what they just heard. This can make it more difficult to follow through with the care they need.

That's where new tools like ChatGPT are starting to make a difference. These language models can rephrase clinical content in simpler terms and adjust their tone depending on who they're addressing [50, 51]. How health information is explained often depends on who's receiving it. A child might need just the basics, while a caregiver may want more detailed guidance. The same goes for instructions about medication—some patients need step-by-step directions, while others are already familiar with the routine. Being able to adjust the message like this helps ensure everyone involved understands the key information [52].

In mental health contexts, many individuals turn to these tools to explore symptoms or ask questions in private before seeking professional help. The ability to get information anonymously and at any time makes it easier for some to take the first step [53, 54]. The always-available format and non-judgmental tone can make these interactions feel safer and less intimidating [55, 56]. Some users also find comfort in the empathetic tone these systems can provide, especially during times of illness or emotional distress [57].

Nurses and allied health professionals often spend the most time with patients, and communication is a big part of their daily work. LLMs can help by organizing patient data from EHRs, past notes, or wearable devices, making it easier to create or update care plans [58]. They can also assist with administrative tasks, like generating progress reports or handoff notes, which gives healthcare staff more time to focus on direct care [59].

In everyday care, these models can also help patients manage routine tasks such as remembering to take medication, staying hydrated, or tracking symptoms. Because they can use past data to guide these suggestions, the support often feels timely and specific rather than generic.

In remote or underserved areas, where healthcare access can be limited, LLMs provide basic support by helping patients check their health status, understand their condition, or decide whether to seek care [33, 60]. While they don't replace clinical judgment, they offer a useful first step—especially when delays in care could make a difference.

All in all, LLMs are changing the way patients interact with healthcare information. When patients can actually follow the conversation, they tend to feel more included in their care. That sense of involvement can go a long way—it builds trust and helps everyone work together more effectively. In many cases, that kind of partnership can make a lasting difference in health outcomes.

10.2.6 Elevating biomedical writing and scientific communication

Language models are reshaping how biomedical professionals draft, revise, and communicate knowledge—whether for research, teaching, or patient care. Tools like GPT-4, BioGPT, and ClinicalBERT give researchers, clinicians, and students new ways to work more efficiently when producing scientific or clinical texts [61].

These models can help with drafting papers, editing for clarity and tone, or restructuring content—especially when time or writing support is limited. For biomedical researchers, LLMs assist in composing literature reviews, abstracts, introductions, and grant proposals, helping authors synthesize complex information and present it in formats ready for submission [62]. In clinical settings, they support the creation of discharge summaries, referral letters, patient instructions, and insurance documentation, easing administrative burdens so providers can spend more time on direct patient care [63, 64].

One of the key strengths of LLMs is their ability to support clear and accurate scientific writing. They're especially helpful for multilingual researchers, assisting with translation, grammar refinement, and adapting content to meet journal or conference requirements [65]. More broadly, these tools act as writing assistants across educational and publishing contexts—rewording unclear passages, identifying gaps in logic, summarizing lengthy sections, or tailoring text to specific submission templates. This allows authors to spend less time on language mechanics and more on the content itself [66].

LLMs not only improve language but also help explain complex biomedical topics—such as statistical methods, disease mechanisms, or clinical protocols—in a way that fits the audience, whether it's a journal editor, a research collaborator, or the general public. This ability to tailor explanations enhances both the clarity and impact of scientific writing and helps bridge gaps between disciplines [67].

As LLMs help improve how biomedical content is written and presented, they're becoming more useful across the entire research and publication workflow. Their impact isn't limited to individual authors—these tools are also being used in team-based writing, interdisciplinary projects, and global collaborations. Looking ahead, they could also find a place in peer review, research oversight, or even mentoring early-career researchers.

10.2.7 Streamlining research design and project management

LLMs are increasingly supporting the full scope of medical research—not just writing, but also planning, execution, and day-to-day project management. These models are particularly helpful when researchers need to organize messy or fragmented information and link ideas across different fields. They can offer tailored suggestions that support more collaborative and efficient work among clinicians, scientists, and project leads.

At the beginning of a project, researchers often turn to prior studies to refine their direction and identify promising research questions. LLMs can speed up this process by scanning large volumes of academic literature and surfacing key trends, ongoing debates, and areas that remain underexplored. This helps research teams shape more focused objectives and avoid redundant or outdated approaches [68].

As planning moves forward, these models can also assist with drafting study protocols and outlining methodological details. They may suggest appropriate controls, statistical techniques, or outcome measures that align with established practices. Sometimes, LLMs are also used to prepare participant materials—such as consent forms or ethics submissions—helping ensure both clarity and regulatory alignment [69].

Once the project is underway, LLMs can assist with managing data and logistics. They help label datasets using standardized terms, check that metadata is complete, or trace how data has been collected and processed. In collaborative environments, they're often used to draft emails, meeting notes, and shared progress updates. Research teams have also begun using them to adapt older grant materials, prepare budget breakdowns, and forecast potential delays. In many cases, these tools provide an added layer of insight for managing complex research workflows [70].

By handling routine documentation and repetitive tasks, LLMs allow researchers to focus more on experimental design and analysis. This coordination support is already proving useful in large-scale or multi-institutional studies, where aligning contributors and managing details can be particularly demanding. As these models continue to evolve, they may help establish workflows that are easier to manage and more responsive to the needs of modern research.

10.2.8 Intelligent medical education and competency assessment

As healthcare education evolves to keep pace with modern clinical demands, LLMs are becoming powerful tools in both structured instruction and lifelong learning. Building on their role in research and communication, these models are now helping students, educators, and institutions improve how medical knowledge is taught, practiced, and assessed [71–73].

A major advantage of LLMs in education is their ability to support personalized learning experiences. They can generate realistic case scenarios, clinical vignettes, and role-play interactions tailored to the learner's knowledge level, interests, and goals. Interactive quizzes—ranging from multiple choice and fill-in-the-blank to open-ended reasoning—can be aligned with course objectives and include instant feedback that helps learners reflect and adjust [74, 75]. This flexibility allows the learning process to adapt to different cognitive styles, levels of preparation, and cultural contexts—supporting broader engagement and accessibility [76].

LLMs are also being used to improve exam preparation and performance evaluation. They can create large sets of practice questions mapped to licensing standards or institutional requirements and explain both correct and incorrect answers in detail [77]. For instructors, these tools support automated grading for objective questions and even help evaluate written responses, making it easier to manage large cohorts without compromising fairness or consistency [78, 79]. With fewer administrative tasks, educators have more time to focus on mentoring and curriculum design.

Recent developments also show that LLMs are improving in clinical accuracy. For example, GPT-4 reached 76.4% on surgical board-style questions, a notable increase from GPT-3.5's 46.8%, showing progress in handling advanced reasoning tasks [80]. When embedded in chat-based tutors or voice-guided simulators, they can offer interactive training that mirrors real-time clinical decision-making—complete with time pressure and diagnostic uncertainty [81].

Outside of formal education, LLMs support ongoing professional growth. They allow clinicians to revisit important topics, explore unfamiliar conditions, and practice complex decisions on demand. In areas with limited access to continuing education or up-to-date resources, these tools help reduce barriers by providing timely, relevant medical information [82].

The way medical knowledge is delivered—and just as importantly, how learning gaps are identified—is beginning to shift with the integration of LLMs. Their growing presence in education is opening the door to more flexible, scalable, and personalized learning environments that can better support the ongoing development of clinical expertise in a rapidly evolving healthcare landscape.

10.2.9 Biomedical research and scientific discovery

LLMs are becoming valuable allies in biomedical research, changing how scientists generate hypotheses, interpret results, and move discoveries closer to clinical application [83]. While early use focused on literature search and summarization, these models now support a wide range of analytical tasks across areas like drug development, genomics, and systems biology [84].

In early-stage drug research, LLMs are being used to explore how compounds might interact, assess potential toxicity, and inform predictions about how drugs behave in the body. This can reduce the reliance on costly lab work during the initial screening process and speed up decision-making about which candidates to test further [85].

In genomics, researchers use LLMs to annotate new genes, connect genetic variants with disease traits, and analyze regulatory networks. By drawing from both published studies and genomic databases, these models help identify relationships that are difficult to spot through manual review alone. This has particular value in understanding rare diseases, inherited syndromes, and complex conditions like cancer or autoimmune disorders [86].

Although predicting protein structures is still best handled by models like AlphaFold, LLMs contribute by retrieving background knowledge, summarizing functional roles, and interpreting interaction partners or clinical relevance. They provide a layer of context that complements structural predictions with biological meaning and translational potential [87].

LLMs are also being used to make connections that might otherwise be missed between different areas of science. For instance, a model trained on pharmacological data and clinical case reports might suggest new uses for existing drugs. Similarly, by combining environmental research with clinical outcomes, they can help researchers explore how exposures contribute to long-term health risks. This ability to cross disciplines gives researchers a new way to look at complicated medical problems [88].

By supporting faster knowledge access, deeper context, and broader connections, LLMs are reshaping how biomedical science is done. Their growing role could shorten discovery cycles, support more collaborative science, and contribute to a more integrated and responsive research ecosystem.

10.2.10 Public health surveillance and global coordination

LLMs are becoming increasingly useful in modern public health systems, where they support real-time monitoring, early outbreak detection, and accessible communication on a global scale [89]. Their capacity to process diverse data sources—including clinical records, emergency room (ER) logs, and informal online content like news and social media—makes them well-suited for identifying population-level health risks early [90, 91].

By continuously analyzing these signals, LLMs can detect patterns that may point to emerging infections, environmental threats, or mental health trends. These insights can help public health officials respond faster—whether by reallocating resources, introducing containment efforts, or sharing localized guidance with the public [92]. In this role, they support more proactive surveillance and better-informed risk management.

In public health communication, LLMs also help translate and tailor information for people who speak different languages or come from diverse backgrounds. They can translate campaign content into different languages, simplify complex terms, and tailor messages for specific groups based on culture or risk profile. Whether accessed through websites, mobile apps, or chat-based systems, LLMs can improve how messages are received and understood—helping promote vaccination, clarify public health measures, and push back against misinformation with context-aware responses [93].

Beyond messaging, LLMs contribute to secure and scalable global analytics through integration with federated learning. This method allows model training across distributed health institutions while keeping patient data private and local. It enables collaboration across regions with varying populations and health challenges, without violating data protection laws [94].

LLMs are also being paired with explainable AI (XAI) techniques to make their outputs more transparent. For instance, if a model prioritizes vaccine access for certain groups or flags areas at risk of system overload, it can explain why. This added layer of reasoning helps build trust with policymakers and health professionals, supporting clearer and more accountable decisions [95].

Together, these capabilities—ranging from language support to secure learning and explainable predictions—highlight how LLMs are helping modernize and connect public health efforts across borders. While not a replacement for established methods, LLMs are gradually becoming part of how public health systems coordinate, communicate, and detect emerging issues—particularly in the face of challenges like pandemics and climate-related health risks.

10.3 TRANSFORMATIVE STUDIES IN BIOMEDICAL SIGNAL ANALYSIS: OPPORTUNITIES FOR LLM INTEGRATION

Deep learning is starting to play a more active role in how clinicians and researchers work with biomedical signals. Instead of analyzing these measurements in isolation, newer models can connect the dots across biosignal data—captured from wearables and other non-invasive devices—and relate them to broader health patterns. This shift has opened the door to new ways of supporting diagnosis, tracking changes over time, and responding to individual needs more quickly. Using data already collected in routine care, these tools can speed up diagnosis and make it more accessible.

With this progress, researchers are beginning to explore how LLMs might complement and extend these systems. Unlike conventional signal-processing tools, LLMs can bring in contextual understanding—linking signal-derived outputs with information from electronic health records, behavioral patterns, environmental factors, and clinician notes. This broader perspective allows for more personalized insights and may improve the way these predictions are interpreted and acted upon.

This section reviews recent studies in signal-based diagnosis that highlight how deep learning has evolved in this space. It also looks at how LLMs might be used to build on existing signal-based systems—helping tailor insights more closely to the individual and making outputs easier to interpret. When integrated thoughtfully, they could help bridge the gap between raw sensor data and practical clinical decisions. Figure 10.3 gives a visual overview of this concept, showing where LLMs may fit into different signal-driven use cases.

10.3.1 Real-time stress detection using edge-AI

Rostami et al. [96] developed a real-time stress detection system using photoplethysmography (PPG) signals and a long short-term memory (LSTM) deep learning model, deployed on a Raspberry Pi—a low-power, cost-effective embedded device. The system was designed to process physiological data locally, eliminating the need for cloud services or external pre-processing. With over 91% accuracy in distinguishing between stress and non-stress states, the model shows promise for affordable, everyday mental health support.

Integrating an LLM—either via a connected platform or a lightweight, device-optimized variant—could make the system more responsive and context-aware. Rather than simply detecting stress, the system could incorporate additional information such as recent sleep patterns, calendar activity,

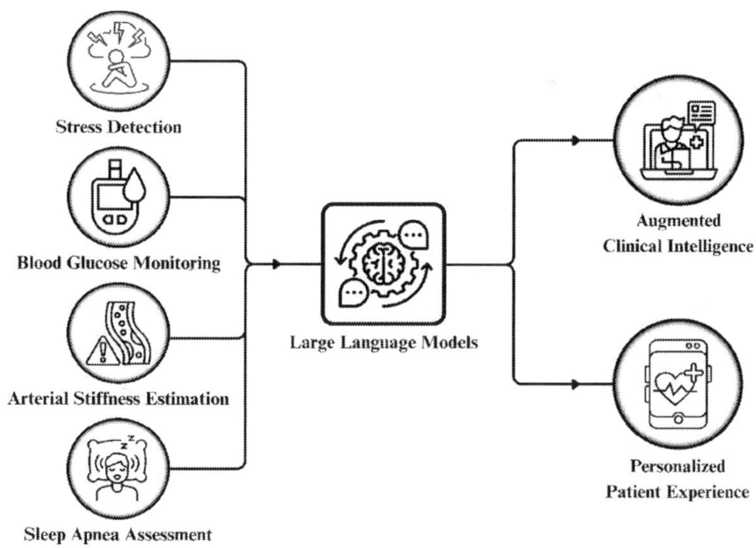

Figure 10.3 Conceptual illustration of how LLMs could be integrated with deep learning-based biomedical signal analysis to augment clinical intelligence and personalize patient care across multiple diagnostic domains.

or user-reported mood to better interpret each episode. This deeper context would allow the system to offer personalized, situation-specific support—for example, coping strategies, lifestyle suggestions, or timely alerts.

In work or academic settings, such integration could evolve into intelligent mental health assistants that not only detect stress but also engage users through natural, empathetic conversation. These assistants could provide mindfulness prompts, cognitive-behavioral strategies, or reminders to take breaks based on individual stress patterns—encouraging proactive mental health care. As LLMs continue to improve in multimodal understanding, their combination with biosignal-driven edge-AI offers a promising path toward accessible, private, and personalized emotional well-being tools.

10.3.2 Blood glucose monitoring using PPG and deep learning

Zeynali et al. [97] proposed a non-invasive method for estimating blood glucose levels using only PPG signals, removing the need for finger-prick tests or continuous glucose monitors. Their approach used a hybrid deep learning architecture that combined convolutional neural networks (CNN), LSTM units, and an attention mechanism. The model analyzed 15-second segments of raw PPG data and outperformed traditional feature-based methods in regression tasks. The attention layer helped the system focus on the parts of the waveform most relevant to glucose changes, allowing it to maintain low root-mean-square error (RMSE) values even in conditions that mimic real-time use.

Adding an LLM to this type of system could make glucose tracking more personalized and practical for daily use. An LLM might relate estimated glucose trends to recent meals, physical activity, or medication habits—helping users better understand how their choices affect their glucose levels and what they can do in response. It could offer suggestions in plain language, such as dietary tips, reminders to hydrate or exercise, or early alerts about patterns that suggest hypo- or hyperglycemia. This kind of timely guidance could help users avoid fatigue, confusion, or more serious complications.

In clinical care, LLMs could summarize longer-term glucose data, link it to behavior logs, and highlight concerning trends for a healthcare provider to review. These summaries would make it easier to share meaningful updates between patients and care teams, promoting shared decision-making and reducing the need for invasive monitoring. As these systems advance, they may offer a new way to manage chronic conditions by combining signal interpretation with real-time, conversational feedback.

10.3.3 Arterial stiffness assessment using PPG spectrograms

Abrisham et al. [98] developed a deep learning framework to estimate carotid-femoral pulse wave velocity (cf-PWV)—a widely accepted marker of arterial stiffness—using spectrograms generated from PPG signals. The model, based on a CNN-BiLSTM-Attention architecture, was trained on data from six different age groups and showed strong agreement with reference cf-PWV values. It performed consistently across the age groups, suggesting robustness within healthy populations and sensitivity to age-related variation.

A key part of this method was the transformation of raw PPG waveforms into time-frequency spectrograms, enabling the network to capture signal patterns in both timing and frequency. The use of attention mechanisms helped the model focus on waveform segments that carried the most information about vascular stiffness—such as inflection points, changes in pulsatility, and harmonic structure—improving interpretability and diagnostic reliability.

Pairing this type of vascular aging model with an LLM could enhance its clinical relevance. LLMs could integrate cf-PWV estimates with additional context—such as lifestyle factors, medication use, comorbidities, or family history—to generate personalized vascular health summaries. These might include tailored risk scores, preventive care suggestions, and tools for tracking changes in vascular health over time.

In routine care—such as general practice or remote consultations—advanced equipment for measuring arterial stiffness isn't always available. In such cases, a system combining deep learning with an LLM could support providers by offering suggestions on whether to refer a patient, adjust treatment, or explain risks in clearer terms. For patients, the system could offer gentle nudges—like staying physically active, eating a bit healthier, or finding ways to unwind. Over time, it might also help them keep an eye on their vascular health in a simple way, flagging changes that are worth checking before they become more serious.

10.3.4 Pediatric sleep apnea estimation from SpO_2 signals

Mortazavi et al. [99] developed a deep learning model to estimate sleep apnea severity in children using overnight peripheral oxygen saturation (SpO_2) recordings. Their framework combined ResNet, CNN, and BiGRU-Attention components to detect apnea-hypopnea patterns and classify severity levels. Trained on a well-balanced dataset with clearly labeled categories, the model achieved over 92% accuracy in identifying moderate-to-severe cases versus mild or normal ones. This approach offers a promising alternative to traditional polysomnography, which remains costly and difficult to access for routine pediatric screening.

The model's architecture used CNN layers to extract spatial features, ResNet blocks for deeper representation learning, and BiGRU-Attention layers to model temporal dynamics and highlight signal segments most relevant to apnea events. Together, these components enabled the system to capture both the timing and frequency of oxygen desaturation episodes associated with sleep-disordered breathing.

With LLM integration, such systems could go beyond prediction to provide more personalized and context-aware insights. An LLM could examine multi-night patterns, relate apnea severity to medical history, developmental milestones, or medications, and generate clear summaries of sleep health. These reports might explain potential impacts—such as effects on cognition, behavior, or physical growth—and suggest next steps based on established pediatric sleep guidelines.

Caregivers could receive easy-to-understand updates that clarify when and why clinical follow-up is needed, while healthcare providers might benefit from automatically generated documentation aligned with clinical standards. These tools could also support families between appointments by answering common questions, offering small adjustments to bedtime routines, or helping monitor ongoing symptoms. In this way, they may expand the reach of pediatric sleep care—particularly in settings where specialist access is limited.

10.3.5 Toward intelligent, patient-centric biosignal systems

The examples in this section highlight a clear shift: biosignal analysis is evolving beyond standalone prediction models. Researchers are now building systems that combine signal interpretation with broader context and communication—often with the help of LLMs. While deep learning uncovers important patterns in physiological data, LLMs make those insights easier to understand, personalize, and use in real time.

Looking ahead, this combined approach opens the door to several possibilities:

- **Bringing Data Together**: Connecting sensor readings, medical history, and behavioral data into one system to support clearer, more meaningful decisions.
- **Timely, Personalized Guidance**: Offering on-device prompts and tips tailored to daily routines and individual health trends.
- **Private, Collaborative Learning**: Improving systems through decentralized updates without sharing sensitive data.

- **Clearer Explanations**: Helping both clinicians and patients make sense of predictions through straightforward, supportive language.
- **Reducing Paperwork**: Auto-generating care summaries, follow-up steps, and documentation for clinical or insurance use.
- **Supportive Conversations**: Providing simple, motivating, and informative interactions to help people stay engaged with their care.

Altogether, these advances suggest a future where digital tools not only detect what's happening in the body—they also help explain and act on it. This shift supports more connected, personalized care in both clinical and everyday settings.

10.4 CONCLUSION

LLMs are reshaping the future of healthcare in ways that go far beyond their early roles in language processing. What began as tools for generating and understanding text has evolved into a powerful class of systems that are transforming how knowledge moves through the healthcare ecosystem. From diagnostics and clinical support to research, patient communication, education, and public health planning, LLMs are becoming active contributors to modern care.

This chapter has explored how LLMs function not just as tools, but as intelligent collaborators. They help make sense of complex data, connect insights across sources, and deliver information in ways that are easier for clinicians and patients to understand. Whether summarizing years of medical records, connecting biosignal trends with everyday habits, or putting technical findings into plain language, LLMs are helping make complex information easier to understand and use in real-world care.

Their integration into healthcare systems paves the way for more proactive, connected, and patient-centered care. LLMs make it possible to monitor health continuously, tailor recommendations in real time, and guide clinical decisions at the moment they're needed. In combination with tools like virtual patient modeling, collaborative training methods, and smart triage systems, they are helping build systems that adapt more effectively to individual needs and real-time conditions.

A standout benefit of these models lies in how they simplify and personalize health communication. They help make health information easier to understand by putting medical terms into everyday language and adjusting how things are explained based on each person's background or comfort level. This flexibility also makes it easier to connect across different languages or cultural perspectives, so more people can feel included and informed. In the research world, LLMs support discovery by making it easier to explore new areas, connect concepts from different fields, and notice patterns that may not be obvious at first glance.

Their potential grows even further when paired with newer technologies—like health-tracking wearables, genomic analysis platforms, or edge-based AI systems. These combinations allow for deeper understanding by blending different types of information—such as notes, sensor data, or scans—into insights that can support faster, more informed decisions.

As these tools become more capable, LLMs may play increasingly active roles: helping guide discussions between patients and providers, supporting clinical judgment, strengthening education for healthcare teams, or informing broader decisions at the system level. By learning through continued use, they can evolve alongside the needs of individuals and institutions.

More broadly, this is not just about new technologies being added to healthcare—it points to a deeper transformation. The focus is shifting toward care that is more personalized, inclusive, and mindful of individual experiences, where digital systems are designed to support people with both intelligence and compassion.

REFERENCES

1. J. W. Ayers *et al.*, "Comparing physician and artificial intelligence chatbot responses to patient questions posted to a public social media forum," *JAMA Internal Medicine*, vol. 183, no. 6, pp. 589–596, 2023.
2. R. Li, A. Kumar, and J. H. Chen, "How chatbots and large language model artificial intelligence systems will reshape modern medicine: fountain of creativity or pandora's box?," *JAMA Internal Medicine*, vol. 183, no. 6, pp. 596–597, 2023.
3. T. Minssen, E. Vayena, and I. G. Cohen, "The challenges for regulating medical use of ChatGPT and other large language models," *JAMA*, vol. 330, no. 4, pp. 315–316, 2023.
4. Z. Kanjee, B. Crowe, and A. Rodman, "Accuracy of a generative artificial intelligence model in a complex diagnostic challenge," *JAMA*, vol. 330, no. 1, pp. 78–80, 2023.
5. K. He *et al.*, "A survey of large language models for healthcare: from data, technology, and applications to accountability and ethics," *Information Fusion,118*, p. 102963, 2025.
6. Y. Wang, Y. Zhao, and L. Petzold, "Are large language models ready for healthcare? a comparative study on clinical language understanding," in *Machine Learning for Healthcare Conference*, 2023: PMLR, pp. 804–823.
7. P. Yu, H. Xu, X. Hu, and C. Deng, "Leveraging generative AI and large language models: a comprehensive roadmap for healthcare integration," in *Healthcare*, 2023, vol. 11, no. 20: MDPI, p. 2776.

8. W. Peng, L. Feng, G. Zhao, and F. Liu, "Learning optimal k-space acquisition and reconstruction using physics-informed neural networks," in *Proceedings of the IEEE/CVF Conference on Computer Vision and Pattern Recognition*, 2022, pp. 20794–20803.
9. W. Peng, E. Adeli, T. Bosschieter, S. H. Park, Q. Zhao, and K. M. Pohl, "Generating realistic brain mris via a conditional diffusion probabilistic model," in *International Conference on Medical Image Computing and Computer-Assisted Intervention*, 2023: Springer, pp. 14–24.
10. R. Voelker, "The promise and pitfalls of AI in the complex world of diagnosis, treatment, and disease management," *Jama*, vol. 330, no. 15, pp. 1416–1419, 2023.
11. K. Singhal *et al.*, "Large language models encode clinical knowledge," *Nature*, vol. 620, no. 7972, pp. 172–180, 2023.
12. A. Abd-Alrazaq *et al.*, "Large language models in medical education: opportunities, challenges, and future directions," *JMIR Medical Education*, vol. 9, no. 1, p. e48291, 2023.
13. M. Mehrabanian and Y. Zariat, "ChatGPT passes anatomy exam," *British Dental Journal*, vol. 235, no. 5, pp. 295–295, 2023.
14. J. Lee *et al.*, "BioBERT: a pre-trained biomedical language representation model for biomedical text mining," *Bioinformatics*, vol. 36, no. 4, pp. 1234–1240, 2020.
15. K. Huang, J. Altosaar, and R. Ranganath, "Clinicalbert: Modeling clinical notes and predicting hospital readmission," *arXiv preprint arXiv:1904.05342*, 2019.
16. T. H. Kung *et al.*, "Performance of ChatGPT on USMLE: potential for AI-assisted medical education using large language models," *PLoS Digital Health*, vol. 2, no. 2, p. e0000198, 2023.
17. R. Luo *et al.*, "BioGPT: generative pre-trained transformer for biomedical text generation and mining," *Briefings in bioinformatics*, vol. 23, no. 6, p. bbac409, 2022.
18. P. P. Ray, "Broadening the horizon: a call for extensive exploration of ChatGPT's potential in obstetrics and gynecology," *American Journal of Obstetrics & Gynecology*, vol. 229, no. 6, p. 706, 2023.
19. J. G. Kovoor, A. K. Gupta, and S. Bacchi, "ChatGPT: effective writing is succinct," *BMJ*, vol. 381, 1125, 2023.
20. H. Askr, E. Elgeldawi, H. Aboul Ella, Y. A. Elshaier, M. M. Gomaa, and A. E. Hassanien, "Deep learning in drug discovery: an integrative review and future challenges," *Artificial Intelligence Review*, vol. 56, no. 7, pp. 5975–6037, 2023.
21. A. J. Thirunavukarasu, D. S. J. Ting, K. Elangovan, L. Gutierrez, T. F. Tan, and D. S. W. Ting, "Large language models in medicine," *Nature medicine*, vol. 29, no. 8, pp. 1930–1940, 2023.
22. I. A. Bernstein *et al.*, "Comparison of ophthalmologist and large language model chatbot responses to online patient eye care questions," *JAMA network open*, vol. 6, no. 8, p. e2330320, 2023.
23. M. Javaid, A. Haleem, and R. P. Singh, "ChatGPT for healthcare services: An emerging stage for an innovative perspective," *BenchCouncil Transactions on Benchmarks, Standards and Evaluations*, vol. 3, no. 1, p. 100105, 2023.

24. M. Agrawal, S. Hegselmann, H. Lang, Y. Kim, and D. Sontag, "Large language models are few-shot clinical information extractors," *arXiv preprint arXiv:2205.12689*, 2022.
25. A. Pan, D. Musheyev, D. Bockelman, S. Loeb, and A. E. Kabarriti, "Assessment of artificial intelligence chatbot responses to top searched queries about cancer," *JAMA Oncology*, vol. 9, no. 10, pp. 1437–1440, 2023.
26. J. Pan, "Large language model for molecular chemistry," *Nature Computational Science*, vol. 3, no. 1, p. 5, 2023.
27. Y. Kim, X. Xu, D. McDuff, C. Breazeal, and H. W. Park, "Health-llm: Large language models for health prediction via wearable sensor data," *arXiv preprint arXiv:2401.06866*, 2024.
28. J. Liang *et al.*, "Online training of large language models: Learn while chatting," *arXiv preprint arXiv:2403.04790*, 2024.
29. S. R. Ali, T. D. Dobbs, H. A. Hutchings, and I. S. Whitaker, "Using ChatGPT to write patient clinic letters," *The Lancet Digital Health*, vol. 5, no. 4, pp. e179–e181, 2023.
30. R. Kiros, R. Salakhutdinov, and R. Zemel, "Multimodal neural language models," in *International Conference on Machine Learning*, 2014: PMLR, pp. 595–603.
31. D. Driess *et al.*, "Palm-e: An embodied multimodal language model," Proceedings of the 40th International Conference on Machine Learning (ICML), 2023.
32. T. Zhang *et al.*, "Flexible electronics for cardiovascular healthcare monitoring," *The innovation*, vol. 4, no. 5, 2023.
33. E. Eisenstein, C. Kopacek, S. Cavalcante, A. Neves, G. Fraga, and L. Messina, "Telemedicine: a bridge over knowledge gaps in healthcare," *Current Pediatrics Reports*, vol. 1, pp. 1–6, 2020.
34. P. Zhang and M. N. Kamel Boulos, "Generative AI in medicine and healthcare: promises, opportunities and challenges," *Future Internet*, vol. 15, no. 9, p. 286, 2023.
35. A. Cooper and A. Rodman, "AI and medical education-a 21st-century Pandora's box," *The New England Journal of Medicine*, vol. 389, no. 5, pp. 385–387, 2023.
36. K. Jeblick *et al.*, "ChatGPT makes medicine easy to swallow: an exploratory case study on simplified radiology reports," *European Radiology*, vol. 34, no. 5, pp. 2817–2825, 2024.
37. J. Holmes *et al.*, "Evaluating large language models on a highly-specialized topic, radiation oncology physics," *Frontiers in Oncology*, vol. 13, p. 1219326, 2023.
38. D. Duong and B. D. Solomon, "Analysis of large-language model versus human performance for genetics questions," *European Journal of Human Genetics*, vol. 32, no. 4, pp. 466–468, 2024.
39. I. Jahan, M. T. R. Laskar, C. Peng, and J. Huang, "Evaluation of ChatGPT on biomedical tasks: A zero-shot comparison with fine-tuned generative transformers," *arXiv preprint arXiv:2306.04504*, 2023.

40. A. Gilson *et al.*, "How does ChatGPT perform on the United States Medical Licensing Examination (USMLE)? The implications of large language models for medical education and knowledge assessment," *JMIR Medical Education,* vol. 9, no. 1, p. e45312, 2023.
41. P. Sharma *et al.*, "Performance of ChatGPT on USMLE: Unlocking the potential of large language models for AI-assisted medical education," *arXiv preprint arXiv:2307.00112,* 2023.
42. N. Clynch and J. Kellett, "Medical documentation: part of the solution, or part of the problem? A narrative review of the literature on the time spent on and value of medical documentation," *International Journal of Medical Informatics,* vol. 84, no. 4, pp. 221–228, 2015.
43. T. Henry, "Do you spend more time on administrative tasks than your peers," *American Medical Association,* 2018.
44. Y. Shen *et al.*, "*ChatGPT and other large language models are double-edged swords,*" Radiological Society of North America, 2023, vol. 307, p. e230163.
45. R. Dias and A. Torkamani, "Artificial intelligence in clinical and genomic diagnostics," *Genome Medicine,* vol. 11, no. 1, p. 70, 2019.
46. S. A. Alowais *et al.*, "Revolutionizing healthcare: the role of artificial intelligence in clinical practice," *BMC medical education,* vol. 23, no. 1, p. 689, 2023.
47. C. Han *et al.*, "Evaluation of GPT-4 for 10-year cardiovascular risk prediction: insights from the UK Biobank and KoGES data," *iScience,* vol. 27, no. 2, 2024.
48. Z. Nazi and W. Peng, "Large language models in healthcare and medical domain: A review," *Informatics*, vol. 11, p. 57, 2024.
49. M. Benary *et al.*, "Leveraging large language models for decision support in personalized oncology," *JAMA Network Open,* vol. 6, no. 11, p. e2343689, 2023.
50. J. Nguyen and C. A. Pepping, "The application of ChatGPT in healthcare progress notes: a commentary from a clinical and research perspective," *Clinical and Translational Medicine,* vol. 13, no. 7, p. e1324, 2023.
51. T. Zhang and T. Feng, "Application and technology of an open source AI large language model in the medical field," *Radiology Science,* vol. 2, no. 01, pp. 96–104, 2023.
52. J. A. Omiye, J. C. Lester, S. Spichak, V. Rotemberg, and R. Daneshjou, "Large language models propagate race-based medicine," *NPJ Digital Medicine,* vol. 6, no. 1, p. 195, 2023.
53. T. Lai *et al.*, "Scaling up Global Mental Health Psychological Services with AI-based Large Language Models. arXiv 2023," *arXiv preprint arXiv:2307.11991.*
54. D. Bill and T. Eriksson, "*Fine-tuning a LLM using reinforcement learning from human feedback for a therapy chatbot application,*" KTH Royal Institute of Technology, 2023.
55. M. Balas and E. B. Ing, "Conversational AI models for ophthalmic diagnosis: comparison of ChatGPT and the Isabel pro differential diagnosis generator," *JFO Open Ophthalmology,* vol. 1, p. 100005, 2023.

56. M. Bilal, Y. Jamil, D. Rana, and H. H. Shah, "Enhancing awareness and self-diagnosis of obstructive sleep apnea using AI-powered Chatbots: the role of ChatGPT in revolutionizing healthcare," *Annals of Biomedical Engineering*, vol. 52, no. 2, pp. 136–138, 2024.
57. V. Sorin *et al.*, "Large Language Models and Empathy: Systematic Review," *Journal of Medical Internet Research*, vol. 26, p. e52597, 2024.
58. A. Spinewine, P. Evrard, and C. Hughes, "Interventions to optimize medication use in nursing homes: a narrative review," *European Geriatric Medicine*, vol. 12, pp. 551–567, 2021.
59. X. Meng *et al.*, "The application of large language models in medicine: A scoping review," *Iscience*, vol. 27, no. 5, 2024.
60. J. Chervenak, H. Lieman, M. Blanco-Breindel, and S. Jindal, "The promise and peril of using a large language model to obtain clinical information: ChatGPT performs strongly as a fertility counseling tool with limitations," *Fertility and Sterility*, vol. 120, no. 3, pp. 575–583, 2023.
61.]. C. Peng *et al.*, "A study of generative large language model for medical research and healthcare," *NPJ Digital Medicine*, vol. 6, no. 1, p. 210, 2023.
62. H. Decker *et al.*, "Large language model-based chatbot vs surgeon-generated informed consent documentation for common procedures," *JAMA Network Open*, vol. 6, no. 10, pp. e2336997, 2023.
63. J. Wang, Y. Huang, C. Chen, Z. Liu, S. Wang, and Q. Wang, "Software testing with large language models: Survey, landscape, and vision," *IEEE Transactions on Software Engineering*, 2024, 50(4), 911.
64. Y. Gu, J. Cao, Y. Guo, S. Qian, and W. Guan, "Plan, generate and match: Scientific workflow recommendation with large language models," in *International Conference on Service-Oriented Computing*, 2023: Springer, pp. 86–102.
65. S. Lappin, "Assessing the strengths and weaknesses of large language models," *Journal of Logic, Language and Information*, vol. 33, no. 1, pp. 9–20, 2024.
66. M. Sallam, "The utility of ChatGPT as an example of large language models in healthcare education, research and practice: Systematic review on the future perspectives and potential limitations," *MedRxiv*, p. 2023.02. 19.23286155, 2023.
67. A. Arora and A. Arora, "The promise of large language models in health care," *The Lancet*, vol. 401, no. 10377, p. 641, 2023.
68. A. Dunn *et al.*, "Structured information extraction from complex scientific text with fine-tuned large language models," *arXiv preprint arXiv:2212.05238*, 2022.
69. J. Yang *et al.*, "Harnessing the power of llms in practice: A survey on chatgpt and beyond," *ACM Transactions on Knowledge Discovery from Data*, vol. 18, no. 6, pp. 1-32, 2024.
70. C. Arighi, S. Brenner, and Z. Lu, "Large language models (LLMs) and ChatGPT for biomedicine," in *Pacific Symposium on Biocomputing 2024*, 2023: World Scientific, pp. 641–644.
71. Q. Lyu *et al.*, "Translating radiology reports into plain language using chatgpt and gpt-4 with prompt learning: Promising results, limitations, and potential," *arXiv preprint arXiv:2303.09038*, 2023.

72. J. R. Benoit, "ChatGPT for clinical vignette generation, revision, and evaluation," *MedRxiv,* p. 2023.02. 04.23285478, 2023.
73. A. H. Kumar, "Analysis of ChatGPT tool to assess the potential of its utility for academic writing in biomedical domain," *Biology, Engineering, Medicine and Science Reports,* vol. 9, no. 1, pp. 24–30, 2023.
74. M. Cascella, J. Montomoli, V. Bellini, and E. Bignami, "Evaluating the feasibility of ChatGPT in healthcare: an analysis of multiple clinical and research scenarios," *Journal of medical systems,* vol. 47, no. 1, p. 33, 2023.
75. K. Lower, I. Seth, B. Lim, and N. Seth, "ChatGPT-4: transforming medical education and addressing clinical exposure challenges in the post-pandemic era," *Indian Journal of Orthopaedics,* vol. 57, no. 9, pp. 1527–1544, 2023.
76. W. Dai *et al.*, "Can large language models provide feedback to students? A case study on ChatGPT," in *2023 IEEE international conference on advanced learning technologies (ICALT)*, 2023: IEEE, pp. 323–325.
77. Y. Zhuang, Y. Yu, K. Wang, H. Sun, and C. Zhang, "Toolqa: A dataset for llm question answering with external tools," *Advances in Neural Information Processing Systems,* vol. 36, pp. 50117–50143, 2023.
78. J. Robinson, C. M. Rytting, and D. Wingate, "Leveraging large language models for multiple choice question answering," *arXiv preprint arXiv:2210.12353,* 2022.
79. A. Extance, "ChatGPT has entered the classroom: how LLMs could transform education," *Nature,* vol. 623, no. 7987, pp. 474–477, 2023.
80. N. Oh, G.-S. Choi, and W. Y. Lee, "ChatGPT goes to the operating room: evaluating GPT-4 performance and its potential in surgical education and training in the era of large language models," *Annals of Surgical Treatment and Research,* vol. 104, no. 5, pp. 269–273, 2023.
81. S. Pahune and N. Rewatkar, "Large language models and generative AI's expanding role in healthcare," *ResearchGate*, 2024., 11(3), 57
82. R. A. Khan, M. Jawaid, A. R. Khan, and M. Sajjad, "ChatGPT-Reshaping medical education and clinical management," *Pakistan Journal of Medical Sciences,* vol. 39, no. 2, p. 605, 2023.
83. R. Qureshi, D. Shaughnessy, K. A. Gill, K. A. Robinson, T. Li, and E. Agai, "Are ChatGPT and large language models "the answer" to bringing us closer to systematic review automation?," *Systematic Reviews,* vol. 12, no. 1, p. 72, 2023.
84. Q. Chen *et al.*, "Large language models in biomedical natural language processing: benchmarks, baselines, and recommendations," *arXiv preprint arXiv:2305.16326*, 2023.
85. H. Atas Guvenilir and T. Doğan, "How to approach machine learning-based prediction of drug/compound–target interactions," *Journal of Cheminformatics,* vol. 15, no. 1, p. 16, 2023.
86. M. Toufiq *et al.*, "Harnessing large language models (LLMs) for candidate gene prioritization and selection," *Journal of translational medicine,* vol. 21, no. 1, p. 728, 2023.
87. T. Hegedűs, M. Geisler, G. L. Lukács, and B. Farkas, "Ins and outs of AlphaFold2 transmembrane protein structure predictions," *Cellular and Molecular Life Sciences,* vol. 79, no. 1, p. 73, 2022.

88. S. Thapa and S. Adhikari, "ChatGPT, bard, and large language models for biomedical research: opportunities and pitfalls," *Annals of biomedical engineering*, vol. 51, no. 12, pp. 2647–2651, 2023.
89. A. E. Aiello, A. Renson, and P. Zivich, "Social media-and internet-based disease surveillance for public health," *Annual review of public health*, vol. 41, p. 101, 2020.
90. A. E. Wilson, C. U. Lehmann, S. N. Saleh, J. Hanna, and R. J. Medford, "Social media: a new tool for outbreak surveillance," *Antimicrobial Stewardship & Healthcare Epidemiology*, vol. 1, no. 1, p. e50, 2021.
91. K.-H. Chang, "*Natural language processing: Recent development and applications*," MDPI, 2023, vol. 13, p. 11395.
92. M. B. Garcia, "Using AI tools in writing peer review reports: should academic journals embrace the use of ChatGPT?," *Annals of Biomedical Engineering*, vol. 52, no. 2, pp. 139–140, 2024.
93. N. J. Volpe and R. G. Mirza, "Chatbots, artificial intelligence, and the future of scientific reporting," *JAMA Ophthalmology*, vol. 141, no. 9, pp. 824–825, 2023.
94. T. Che *et al.*, "Federated learning of large language models with parameter-efficient prompt tuning and adaptive optimization," *arXiv preprint arXiv:2310.15080*, 2023.
95. H. Zhao *et al.*, "Explainability for large language models: A survey," *ACM Transactions on Intelligent Systems and Technology*, vol. 15, no. 2, pp. 1–38, 2024.
96. A. Rostami, K. Motaman, B. Tarvirdizadeh, K. Alipour, and M. Ghamari, "LSTM-based real-time stress detection using PPG signals on raspberry Pi," *IET Wireless Sensor Systems*, vol. 14, no. 6, pp. 333–347, 2024.
97. M. Zeynali, K. Alipour, B. Tarvirdizadeh, and M. Ghamari, "Non-invasive blood glucose monitoring using PPG signals with various deep learning models and implementation using TinyML," *Scientific Reports*, vol. 15, no. 1, p. 581, 2025.
98. K. P. Abrisham, K. Alipour, B. Tarvirdizadeh, and M. Ghamari, "Advancing PPG-based cf-PWV estimation with an integrated CNN-BiLSTM-Attention model," *Signal, Image and Video Processing*, vol. 18, no. 12, pp. 8621–8633, 2024.
99. E. Mortazavi, B. Tarvirdizadeh, K. Alipour, and M. Ghamari, "Deep learning approaches for assessing pediatric sleep apnea severity through SpO2 signals," *Scientific Reports*, vol. 14, no. 1, p. 22696, 2024.

Index

Made in the USA
Las Vegas, NV
19 May 2026

ec57c00e-58a9-4c9f-af54-36401d2dd147R02